Territory of Desire

Territory of Desire

Representing the Valley of Kashmir

Ananya Jahanara Kabir

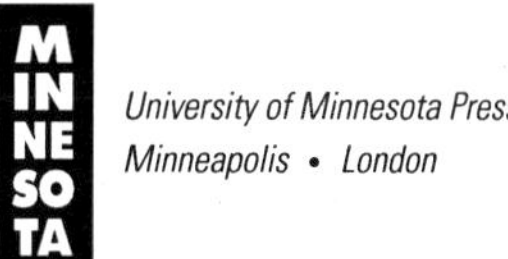

University of Minnesota Press
Minneapolis • London

Excerpts from the poems "Watsun" and "Jalwa te zubur" are reprinted courtesy of Rahman Rahi. Excerpts of the poem "I Failed to Know" are reprinted courtesy of Naseem Shifaie. Excerpts of the poems "Mahavipada" and "Hangul" are reprinted courtesy of Agnishekhar.

Excerpts from the poems "The Blessed Word: A Prologue," "Farewell," "I See Kashmir from New Delhi at Midnight," "The Last Saffron," "I Dream I Am the Only Passenger on Flight 423 to Srinagara," "A Pastoral," "The Country without a Post Office," and "A History of Paisley" are from *The Country without a Post Office* by Agha Shahid Ali; copyright 1997 by Agha Shahid Ali. Excerpts from the poems "I Dream I Am at the Ghat of the Only World" and "Lenox Hill" are from *Rooms Are Never Finished* by Agha Shahid Ali; copyright 2002. All are reprinted by permission of W. W. Norton and Company, Inc.

"Postcard from Kashmir," by Agha Shahid Ali, is from *The Half-Inch Himalayas* (Middletown, Conn.: Wesleyan University Press, 1987); copyright 1987 by Agha Shahid Ali. Reprinted by permission of Wesleyan University Press.

Portions of chapter 1 were published previously as "Nipped in the Bud? Pleasures and Politics in the 1960s 'Kashmir Films,'" *South Asian Popular Culture* 3 (2005): 83–100. Reprinted with permission from Taylor and Francis. http://www.informaworld.com.

Published by the University of Minnesota Press
111 Third Avenue South, Suite 290
Minneapolis, MN 55401-2520
http://www.upress.umn.edu

Library of Congress Cataloging-in-Publication Data

Kabir, Ananya Jahanara, 1970–
Territory of desire : representing the Valley of Kashmir/Ananya Jahanara Kabir.
p. cm.
Includes bibliographical references and index.
ISBN 978-0-8166-5356-0 (hc : alk. paper)—ISBN 978-0-8166-5357-7 (pb : alk. paper)
1. Kashmir, Vale of (India)—Symbolic representation. 2. Art and social conflict—India—Kashmir, Vale of. 3. Desire in art. I. Title.
DS485.K246K33 2009
954'.6—dc22 2008038196

Printed in the United States of America on acid-free paper

The University of Minnesota is an equal-opportunity educator and employer.

18 17 16 15 14 13 12 11 10 09 10 9 8 7 6 5 4 3 2 1

To my friends from and in Kashmir

tumhaare chashm-e-karam ho to kaam ho jaaye
adaa se dekh lo—qissa tamaam ho jaaye

Your benevolent gaze would render this work complete
Glance but once with desire—the story would be complete

and to

Ayaz Muhamed Ali and Lara Portia Kabir Jennings

ostro chander bashona bholatey oruno onuragey
udilo robi—neerob keno kobi

O Poet, why forlorn? As the moon's
desires fade, a new sun is born.

Contents

Acknowledgments

I would like to acknowledge, first, Mrinal Dasgupta, Khairanara Kabir, and Zuglul Kabir, who put aside legitimate concerns about my safety to support my convictions. Certain people have exerted a talismanic influence. Naila Kabeer, Khushi Kabir, and Leila Kabir Fernandes gave me the courage I solicited to embark on the new path. Emma Alexander-Mudaliar, Urvashi Butalia, Huma Dar, Antara Dev Sen, Shireen Huq, Ayesha Jalal, Ato Quayson, Girish Shahane, Samira Sheikh, and Inder Tikku all triggered the most fortuitous connections, both intellectual and interpersonal. Nilima Sheikh is at the heart of the book. Sugata Bose generously encouraged its emergence, and Joya Chatterji its completion. Emma Rothschild and Amartya Sen have been intellectual guardians and role models extraordinaire. To them all, boundless thanks.

From August 2003 onward I have enjoyed the hospitality of Abdul Rahman and Zooni Ratta of the HB Holiday Inn, Srinagar. Javed and Abroo Ratta have been friends whose love I cannot ever repay; Uwais Ratta called shikaras and kept the Kashmiri chai going. Together, they gave me a Srinagar home. Agha Ashraf Ali is a beacon of modernity in the darkness of a conflict zone; fortunate are those who experience his beautiful home and garden, his splendid soirées, and his joie de vivre. Irfan Hasan smoothed my research path with level-headed sanity. The acuity and cynicism of my first Kashmiri interlocutors, Gowhar Fazili and Idrees Kanth, cleared many a naïve mist. The Fazilis' hospitality introduced me to Kashmiri domesticity. Gowhar, your will to live has been my most valuable lesson from Kashmir. Others who most generously gave me time in Srinagar are Afzal Abdullah, Farida Abdullah, Nusrat Andrabi, Hameeda Bano, Shakeel Bakshi, Abir Bazaz, Ifat Hamid, Muzamil Jaleel, Qulub Hussain, Jagdish Mehta, Farooq Nazki, Mohammed Shafi Lone, Abdal Mahjoor, Atif Mahjoor and Nayeema Ahmad, Yasin Malik, Bashir Manzar, Neerja Mattoo, Ghulam Majrooh, Shabbir Mirza, Parvez Imroz, Khurram Parvez, Rahman Rahi, Naseem Shifaie, Jyoti Singh, Shujah Sultan, and G. M. Var. Masood Hussain's charm, friendship, and art are precious gifts. In Jammu, Bimla Raina, Pandit Agnishekhar, and Sanjana Kaul shared difficult memories, while Rajendar and Neelam Tiku offered incredible hospitality and spiritual succor. Thank you all for trusting me enough to let me into your world.

This book was officially born with my move to the School of English, University of Leeds. It is a real pleasure to thank the flexible and inspiring Postcolonial team: Samuel Durrant, Graham Huggan, my "mentor" John McLeod, Stuart Murray, and Brendon Nicholls. Fiona Douglas, David Fairer, Vivien Jones, Edward Larrissy, and David Lindley gave valuable support and advice at different moments. John Whale, Anthea Fraser Gupta, and Robert Jones made the house rock after 5 P.M. The machine's smooth functioning owes to its administrative staff; in particular, Sue Baker and Pam Rhodes aided my research through efficiency and good humor. I cherish and benefited from Shirley Chew's affection and guidance, Alfred Hiatt's intellectual companionship, and Jay Prosser's uniquely cerebral intuition. Three cohorts of M.A. students in "Representing Kashmir" made me think harder. Richard Brock, the manuscript's first reader; Jayshree Kewalramani, who keeps me pedagogically accountable; Varun Zaiwalla, who led me to unexpected sources; Erik Peeters, heroic compiler of the bibliography; and my Ph.D. students Nukhbah Langah and Cathy Lean, who put up with my travels and saved me from last-minute scrapes, all assisted and challenged me in different ways—a heartfelt thank you.

Research for this book was funded by the British Academy through a British Academy South Asian Society Research Grant (2003) and two Small Research Grants (2004 and 2005). Writing during 2006 was facilitated by a semester-long study leave awarded by the School of English, University of Leeds, and a second semester of leave funded by the Arts and Humanities Research Council, United Kingdom. I am extremely grateful to these institutions. I am deeply and proudly indebted to the Centre for History and Economics, Kings College, Cambridge, which since 2002 has enabled me to continue thinking of Cambridge as home. Crucially, I thank the Centre's Foundations of Democracy program, directed by Amartya Sen, for a travel grant in 2005; Emma Rothschild, for her sustained interest in my projects; and Inga Huld Markan and William O'Reilly, who make things happen.

For help with primary resources, I thank: in Delhi, Rahaab Allana and the Alkazi Collection of Photography, Sushobha Barve, Sheba Chacchi, Ashok Jaitly, Jaya Jaitly, Hemant Mehta and Sanjeev Saith, M. K. Raina, and Inder Tiku; in Bombay, Cawas Bharucha, Madhusree Dutta and the staff at Majlis, Beena Sarkar Ellias, Shireen Gandhy of Chemould Gallery, Simeen Oshidar, and Hansa Thapliyal; in London, Stéphanie Roy of the Alkazi Collection of Photography and Ainslee Cameron at the

British Library. A special thanks to the brilliantly informed staff at Bahri and Sons Bookshop, Delhi, for helping me locate excellent secondary material. *Territory of Desire* has gained much from invitations to speak at Sarai (Delhi), SOAS, the universities of Winnipeg and Manitoba, the Centre for History and Economics seminar at Cambridge, the Commonwealth and Postcolonial Seminar at the University of Stirling, the Centre for the Study of the Social Sciences, Kolkata, and the South Asia Seminar, Leeds, and I thank their respective facilitators Abir Bazaz, Subir Sen, Emma Rothschild, Emma Alexander-Mudaliar, Rosinka Chaudhuri, James Proctor, and William Gould.

Others who have combined friendship and scholarship are Emma Alexander-Mudaliar and Samira Sheikh, historians who buttress my literary flights of fancy; Shomikho Raha, for most stimulating conversations about the Indian State (and for photocopy rescue); Ato Quayson, whose energy, vision, and advice always clarify the larger picture; Girish Shahane, my guide through contemporary Indian art; Kaushik Bhaumik, my Virgil in Filmistan; and Deanne Williams and Alfred Hiatt for witty and elegant prose. I remain very grateful to Jason Weidemann and Adam Brunner of the University of Minnesota Press, and Rukun Advani and Anuradha Roy of Permanent Black, for so expertly and patiently aiding the production process. Special thanks to Chitralekha Zutshi, the unanonymous reader, for enthusiastic support and robust critique. I completed the final revisions with you as imagined ideal reader in mind.

The "Veeraswamy Gang" is my UK support system. For food, friendship, and fun, I specifically thank: in London, Srabanti Huda, Naila Kabeer, and Saira Kabir and Paul Jennings; in Bedford, Yasmin Mahmood; in Cambridge, Andreas Bücker, Gaurav Raina, Montu Saxena and Prajakti Kalra, and Shailaja and Stephen Fennell; in Leeds, Marta Bolognani; in Toronto, Deanne Williams and Terry Goldie, Niloufer Pasha and Soven Ghosh, and Rashida Bharmal and Jeff McMaster. Nargis Islam, Indrani Ghosh, and Deanne Williams share the prize for deterritorialized phone therapy. Gavin Salam, Aude Malapert de Bazentin and Gérard Cohen, and the staff of Lutetia on the Isle St Louis ensured a perfect three months in Paris, during which this book was finished. I also thank my in-laws, the Dasguptas and the Acharyas, for being wonderfully intelligent company in Delhi; Lalita Dasgupta of Amber Tours, who organized my travel; Deepak Dasgupta, who fueled my research, literally and metaphorically; Gilgamesh Kabir and Megan Davis-Kabir, and Girish Shahane and Jabeen

Merchant for Bombay entertainment; my extended family in Calcutta, who recharged my batteries; my cousins Deep Chaim Kabir and Paroma Sinha, who entertained and organized. An increasing, younger "family" demands a refocusing on less abstract things; to those whose growing up I experience at reasonably close quarters, I dedicate this book. And for keeping me fit, keeping me laughing, and keeping me company, an ardent thank you to Mrinal.

Introduction

The Valley and the Nation

I wrote you a letter in such ember-hot words
That, reading them, you may have yourself been illuminated
But you did not deign to meet me halfway—
Even the Zabarvan hills feel the pain of that rejection.

—Rahman Rahi

Each night put Kashmir in your dreams

—Agha Shahid Ali

Territory of Desire is about Indian desire for the Valley of Kashmir, and Kashmiri responses to that desire. Bereft of mineral wealth, locked within inhospitable terrain, but professed by all to be a singularly beautiful place, the Valley has, in the course of the twentieth century, emerged as a bone of contention for three nationalisms, Indian, Pakistani, and aspirant Kashmiri.[1] The entangled trajectories of these nationalisms have led the Valley, and the wider region of Jammu and Kashmir of which it is part, through a turbulent and tragic history. It is my contention that this history is not merely to be viewed through the lens of high politics, international relations, and research into official archives. For such research often presupposes that which is the starting point of this book: *why* and *how* has the Valley come to be so intensely desired? To re-inscribe desire into the geopolitical claims that (to use phrases in common circulation through India and Pakistan) "Kashmir is an integral part of India" or, in Pakistan's view, that Kashmir is its "jugular vein" and its "unfinished business," is to ask further questions about collective desire. Turning to the words of the Kashmiri poets I borrow for my epigraphs: who has the right to "dream" of the Valley? Who has the capacity—not the same thing as right—to demand that another should dream of Kashmir? Who is the lover who asks in vain to be met halfway, and what political shape does the pain of rejection take?[2]

A Tale of Two Cities

"Identity, Alienation, Amity": this was the title of an art exhibition that ran through September 2005 at Bombay's rather plush Tao Art Gallery. Twenty-four, mostly well-established, artists, working on the theme of "Kashmir," contributed their works to this exhibition, which was curated by Bina Sarkar Ellias, the editor of *International Gallerie,* a biannual Indian magazine for "arts and ideas." *Gallerie* had already established a liberal, humanitarian approach to this subject when, the previous year, it had devoted an entire issue to "Kashmir."[3] This beautifully presented volume had showcased, through large, high-quality color photographs, the suffering of Kashmiris juxtaposed against the fabled natural beauty of the Valley; there were also rather moving essays by Kashmiri intellectuals about the detrimental impact of longstanding conflict on Kashmiri culture. A number of these photographs reappeared in a special section of the exhibition that was spread out over three floors and a separate atrium, and that displayed paintings as well as some complex installations. While the artworks were priced in keeping with the spiraling value of contemporary Indian art, 10 percent of the profits were committed to established charities in Kashmir.[4]

Neither Ellias, nor the owner of Tao, nor the majority of the twenty-four artists on display, is from Kashmir. However, the presence of a few Kashmiri artists enabled this exhibition to offer at least two distinct sets of artistic responses to the same national problem and to the attendant issues of "identity," "alienation," and "amity."[5] The choice and sequence of words in the title suggested that while "identity" and "alienation" are part of the political problem, in an underlying "amity" between Kashmiri and non-Kashmiri a solution, or perhaps compromise, might be sought. This belief clearly animated the events of the opening night. Sitting on the atrium floor with wine glasses in hand, the "art crowd" of Bombay saw the (Kashmiri) classical musician Pandit Shiv Kumar Sharma inaugurate the exhibition by lighting a lamp. They heard the beautiful (Kashmiri) wife of the manager of Jammu and Kashmir Bank—major sponsors of the exhibition—praise the venture. Finally, all settled down to listen to two members of the Bombay intelligentsia read out from two Kashmiri poets: the fourteenth-century Sufi Lal Ded and the contemporary late Agha Shahid Ali. Lal Ded's highly wrought and abstract Kashmiri was rendered in English translation. Ali, having written in English, posed no such problems of communication.[6]

What cultural politics undergird such benign and well-meant occasions? Rather than elaborate on them right now, I shall hope that, by the end of this book, the reader to whom they might now appear opaque will return to the above account with a more knowing eye. It will be useful instead to foreground here certain key aspects of this inquiry. As part of the audience, I caught the eye of a young Kashmiri writer, living in Bombay, whom I had first met the previous year in Srinagar, capital of Jammu and Kashmir. The discrepancy between the two settings in which we encountered each other hit me hard—all the more because I had flown in from Srinagar that very morning. In Srinagar, moreover, I had been invited to the opening of another art exhibition at the Jammu and Kashmir Academy, celebrating the career of a senior Kashmiri artist, M.A. Mahboob.[7] This far more modest affair in a temporarily cleared room of the Academy nevertheless radiated immense excitement because of the promise, announced by a state minister at the ceremony, that finally Srinagar would have its first dedicated gallery for art exhibitions. Barely separated by a week, these two events nevertheless belonged to different time-worlds.

The two opening nights I witnessed were marked by (rephrasing Arjun Appadurai) "disjuncture and difference in the national economy."[8] Whereas one event was symbolic of India's "maximum city,"[9] celebrated in literature, film, and fashion for its collision of postcolonial chaos and postmodern excess, the other embodied Srinagar as cosmopolitanism denied. With the tourist economy having dwindled to nothingness for fifteen years during the height of the conflict, the departure of different groups of Kashmiris from the Valley under various forms of pressure, the choking of daily life thanks to the long-standing presence of the Indian army, and the demands made on public space by reactive pro-Kashmiri and pro-Islamic groups, Srinagar today is socially and culturally repressed. Emblazoned with arrested modernity, psychosocial violence, and urban decay, its deeply depressing ambience mocks the long tradition, both Kashmiri and non-Kashmiri, of celebrating the natural beauty of the Valley in which it nestles. The difference of tone, scale, and mood evident in the two exhibitions, then, must be returned to an awareness that "the postcolony is made up of not one 'public space' but of several, each having its own logic, yet liable to be entangled with other logics when operating in certain contexts."[10]

This observation by Achille Mbembe, although aimed at the African postcolony, takes us to the heart of my inquiry. The relationship between postcolonial India and the Kashmir Valley has been one of profound inequality, which is stamped *materially* on discrepantly modern public spaces. I will return later to my understanding of materiality and its effects. First, let us pause at the variously entangled public spaces that Mbembe outlines: if such "entanglement" means that "the postcolonial subject has to learn to bargain in this conceptual marketplace,"[11] then some collective identities within India have learned to bargain successfully with what Mbembe calls the *commandement.*[12] Kashmiris, however, have not been one of them. Why? This question, too, is one of this book's driving forces. Within "that model of domination that we call democracy," and within the complex, yet generally acknowledged as successful, federal shape it has assumed in India, why has the state of Jammu and Kashmir not been able to fight its corner through the ballot box?[13] Political commentators attribute the Kashmiri demand for *aazadi* (freedom) to the failure of Indian democracy in Jammu and Kashmir.[14] I seek to broaden analysis of that failure by rethinking what constitutes and fashions "political representation."[15] The key issues within this exercise are the categories signaled in the book's title—"territory," "desire," and "representation" itself—and it is to an explication of these categories that I will now turn.

First, however, I want to clarify this book's focus on three overarching issues: the immense symbolic capital the Valley's topography has accrued since its indirect incorporation within the British Empire in 1846; the inheritance of this capital by postcolonial India, within which the Valley has been politically embedded since 1947; and the capacity of "texts," broadly defined, to recreate individuals as citizens, united through shared objects of desire. I thereby examine the roots of Indian desire for the Kashmir Valley, as well as foreground Kashmiri modes of self-representation emergent especially since the onset of armed resistance to India in 1989. Representation and self-representation, hegemony and resistance, are, I argue, founded on the perpetuation of collective desire for the Valley. By illustrating the links between colonialism, modernity, and postcolonial violence, by connecting the conflict to intranational power struggles, and by restoring the creative intellectual's democratic importance, I seek to elucidate the deep causes of this specific geopolitical conflict. But I also insist that Jammu and Kashmir now represents a long-term conflict zone, the ethical dimensions of which complicate considerably postcolonial theories of identity formation, nationalism, and, indeed, resistance. Moreover, borrowing as I do from a variety of commentators on a range of postcolonial conflict zones, this inquiry into a particular "land and its lure"[16] is offered to all those probing the nexus between power, territory, violence, and desire within the nation-state.

Within any conflict, an early casualty is transparency of terminology. It is thus also necessary at the outset to clarify my own practices of nomenclature. My argument distinguishes the "Kashmir Valley," or "the Valley," a discrete geographic, ethnolinguistic region, from the federal administrative unit (state) within India called "Jammu and Kashmir." This latter term derives from the erstwhile princely state of Jammu and Kashmir, a British colonial creation that lasted from 1846 to 1947 as one of the components of princely India. Since the undivided boundaries of princely Jammu and Kashmir continue to furnish the vision of an independent Kashmir, I also use "Jammu and Kashmir" for that vision, with context-driven specifications. For that section of princely Jammu and Kashmir now under Pakistani jurisdiction, I use the official Pakistani title of Azad ("Free") Kashmir. When I simply use "Kashmir," I move away from inter- and intranational entities toward an imaginary, imaginative construct the history of which I shall uncover here. This "Kashmir," a symbolic, metonymic extension of the geographical Valley, converts it to the fantasy of "paradise on earth," an appellation reputedly first coined by the Mughal emperor Jahangir.[17] For Kashmiris, by which term I indicate native speakers of *Koshur,* the language of the Valley, "Kashmir" is the Valley, to be distinguished from the surrounding areas "Ladakh," "Jammu," "Punjab," from "Jammu Kashmir" (the Indian state, also the pre-1947 entity), and from "India" (the geographic area south of the Pir Panjal range; also the nation). But to some of them, "Kashmir" is also a dream of *aazadi* (freedom). It is also necessary to comment here on the qualifier "some." There are at least as many Kashmiri subject-positions as there are political viewpoints on Kashmir. Rather than incessantly modulating "Kashmiri" through qualifying adjectives ("some," "the majority of," and so on), I ask the reader to take as a default position my use of "Kashmiri" as marked by divergence, heterogeneity, and dissent. In and through heterogeneity, and in and through these multiple and overlapping "Kashmirs," is the territory of desire constituted.

Territory: Limits of the Nation

Jammu and Kashmir, of which the Kashmir Valley is a part, is territorially disputed between India and Pakistan.[18] This dispute began officially in 1947 with the birth of the two nation-states out of former British India. The violence surrounding the event known as the Partition is now getting increasing acknowledgment within academic as well as popular domains.[19] But 1947 did not only mean the surgical cut of the Radcliffe Line and a new beginning, however painful, for the masses of the Subcontinent—citizens now either of a secular, multireligious India or of the Muslim nation of Pakistan.[20] Interspersed within British India were numerous "princely states," nominally ruled by "maharajas" in a feudal relationship to the British Empire that indirectly controlled them.[21] There were further questions about which nation-state *they* would be part of. Jammu and Kashmir, the largest of the princely states, ruled by the Hindu Dogra dynasty but comprising largely Muslim subjects and territorially abutting both India and Pakistan, could have gone either way. In fact, the Maharaja entertained alternative hopes of an independent nation of Jammu and Kashmir. In this dream, although not in his continuing suzerainty, his desires coincided with those of Sheikh Abdullah, the charismatic leader of a populist, anti-Dogra movement that had arisen within Jammu and Kashmir by the 1920s.[22] In the heated post-Partition atmosphere, however, any notions of an independent Jammu and Kashmir were completely untenable.

In late 1947, tribesmen from the North–West Frontier Province of Pakistan crossed over into the Northern Areas of Jammu and Kashmir to seize control of the latter on behalf of their new nation. India, on its part, airlifted troops from its newly constituted army into Srinagar to fight the Maharaja's battle. Barely six months into independence, in early 1948, therefore, India and Pakistan fought their first of four wars over territory, all of which have involved, directly or indirectly, Jammu and Kashmir.[23] The results of 1947–48 were far reaching for South Asian geopolitics. The situation had called for a quick response from the people of Jammu and Kashmir; fatefully, the Maharaja responded on their behalf by agreeing to accede to India as an emergency measure. But in reality, the 1948 war was decisive only in heralding indecision as the new status quo. India demanded that Pakistan withdraw all those (army, as well as tribesmen) who had crossed into Jammu and Kashmir. Pakistan demanded that India uphold the promise of the plebiscite that it had made to the people of

Jammu and Kashmir when the Maharaja agreed to temporary accession to the Indian Union. Neither side has fulfilled these demands. Instead, what has prevailed is the violent tension and endemic irresolution produced by the Line of Control (LOC), the de facto border that, from 1948 onward, divides Indian-administered Jammu and Kashmir from Azad Kashmir, its Pakistan-administered counterpart.

The LOC marks the limit of Pakistani incursion into Jammu and Kashmir territory in 1948 or, to put it from another perspective, the extent to which Pakistan had been able to recapture from India that territory which was rightfully its own. It therefore marks, too, the limit of both the nation-states concerned. But these limits themselves remain unclear. First fashioned by the United Nations on 1 January 1949 as the Ceasefire Line, the LOC took its present name and shape through the Simla Accord of 1972, which concluded the third war between India and Pakistan over the disputed territory. "Drawn and redrawn by battles and treaties, the line is identifiable by traces of blood, bullets, watchtowers, and ghost settlements left from recurring wars over Kashmir between India and Pakistan."[24] This de facto trail of blood and war cannot be collapsed with the de jure international border between India and Pakistan that runs in a northeasterly direction from the Arabian Sea coastline toward Kashmir. This latter line boldly cuts through the Rann of Kutch, the Thar Desert, and the Punjab, but begins visibly to falter as it approaches the "grey zone" of Jammu and Kashmir.[25] Here, coexisting multiple borders start to shed evidence of competing claims, longings, and histories. Even as the official Indo-Pak border is the visible trace of Partition, this "epistemic murk" yields the LOC as the occluded trace of the epistemic violence wreaked at the nation-state's limits.[26]

To unravel the difference between the occluded and the visible, let us consider briefly the epistemic work of the map in South Asia. The highly ocular nature of South Asian national feeling is concentrated in the map, the spatialization of the nation as "geo-body."[27] In this task of spatialization, the boundary is crucial: "A nation can be imagined without a word or other symbol or color on a map, but this is impossible if boundary lines, the symbol which forms the entity of a map or a nation, are excluded."[28] In South Asia, this universal axiom of nation-statehood—every nation needs a map, and every map needs boundaries—has been predicated on the traumas of Partition. Scholarship on Partition has increasingly revealed how post-1947 boundaries have impacted South Asian collective identities—religious, regional, ethno-linguistic, and, looming above these categories, the national. It is now apparent that "inventing boundaries" and "imagining communities" have worked hand-in-glove to naturalize the fiction of citizenship.[29] The territoriality of the nation-state, demarcated through the Radcliffe Commission's boundary lines, has sought to impose supreme epistemic control in creating the citizen-subject out of the individual. By working in both "pedagogic" and "performative" modes,[30] the map visualizes the State's insistence that national affiliation must supersede other forms of collective self-fashioning. However, if the Indo-Pak border on the map and, since 1971, the border between India and Bangladesh,[31] proclaim the resolution to 1947, the proliferation of overlapping borders around Jammu and Kashmir tells several different tales.

The official Indian map subsumes without comment or qualification the entirety of pre-1948 Jammu and Kashmir, the visual equivalent of the oft-echoed claim, "Kashmir is an integral part of India." Likewise, Pakistan's stand on Kashmir—that it represents the "unfinished business" of 1947—is graphically rendered by its official map being, literally, without an eastern edge. Around 78° E, in eastern Jammu and Kashmir, the tilted rectangle that is Pakistan's shape remains ostentatiously unbounded—an astounding rebuttal of the universal dependence of national maps on borders.[32] Pakistan's flaunting of the missing boundary line between its northern and southern borders points also to the added complication of China's claims on the northeastern part of Jammu and Kashmir.[33] International maps, which show the territories of India and Pakistan, and sometimes China, overlapping around Jammu and Kashmir, present further cartographic options.[34] Traversing this already confusing cartographic terrain is the LOC, which, if at all registered, appears as "a sequence of ellipses."[35] In some maps, it abruptly ceases or changes appearance (the dots become smaller, the line becomes straighter) around the Siachen glacier.[36] For at least some Kashmiris, moreover, this tangle of thick, thin, and broken lines effaces another ghostly map, that of a hoped-for independent Kashmir. Haunting all these maps is the irony of the cartographic image itself: a legacy of the British creation, in 1846, of the Dogra princely state of Jammu and Kashmir out of the ruins of the Sikh kingdom of Ranjit Singh, and its subsequent consolidation through the imperial machinations of "the Great Game."[37]

The LOC, a border that is not quite a border, is thus laminated with messages contrary to the map's usual iteration of the nation-state's boundedness. Its chronic presence-in-absence not only highlights how the nation-state's limits implicate its geographic peripheries as central to its self-fashioning; suspended between de facto and de jure status, it also actually embodies both India and Pakistan's continuing inability to confirm its borders by defeating rival claimants to its desired territory. But "the nation dreads dissent"; unsurprisingly, the LOC is "not an obvious spatial marker" within Indian and Pakistani pedagogic domains.[38] Its absence from domestic Indian maps is matched by the statutory warning stamped on every foreign publication featuring a map of South Asia: "The external boundaries of India as depicted on this map are neither correct nor authentic." In the Pakistani case, a stamp tersely declares "disputed territory" over Jammu and Kashmir. Such warnings enact "the violence of the archive" on the ideal reader, who must be drawn into the "pact of citizenship" by being taught to "forget" some things (and "never forget" others).[39] In repeatedly denying alternative cartographies, these "privileged intersection[s] of the topological and the nomological, of the place and the law" mark the aporia at the nation's heart.[40] This aporia, "an open wound," is where two worlds grate against each other and bleed: "[A]nd before a scab forms it hemorrhages again, the lifeblood of two worlds merging to form a third country."[41]

What might these worlds be for Jammu and Kashmir, and what is the third that exists beside them? On one level, they are India and Pakistan, with the LOC borderland itself the third, hemorrhaging country. On another, they are the disjunctive worlds that exist within the Indian nation, with "the third country" constituting the unpredictable forms taken when they grate against each other too long. In the winter of 1989, the discrepant spheres of Indian "geo-piety"[42] and Kashmiri self-assertion collided to blast a moment out of history. Announcing itself in Srinagar, the Kashmiri demand for aazadi was made through Kalashnikovs, grenades and bombs, kidnappings, mass demonstrations, and other materializations of revolutionary violence. This moment was to pass, however. The Indian nation-state swiftly rolled out its own violent apparatus of discipline and punishment, and Jammu and Kashmir soon acquired the dubious distinction of becoming the world's most heavily militarized zone. Everyday reality was radically altered through "crackdowns," "bunkers," "militants," "surrendered militants," and a whole gamut of military and paramilitary regimens.[43] Self-styled Kashmiri militants crossed and recrossed the LOC, obtaining training and support from camps in Azad Kashmir and beyond. Non-Kashmiri *mujahideen* also crossed over from Afghanistan to join the struggle in the name of Islam.[44] Disappeared youth, raped women, intracommunal breakdown, interrupted childhoods, traumatized soldiers, and above all the thickness of rumor turned the region into a veritable "space of death."[45]

"Hum kya chahte? Aazadi"(What do we want? Aazadi). What is this "aazadi" that, in the early 1990s, brought Kashmiris out on to the streets of Srinagar in the thousands? A Persian loan-word into North Indian languages, available to multilingual Kashmiris today in two distinct pronunciations, depending on whether they are speaking Koshur or Urdu, the fluctuating sound of"aazadi" mirrors its fluctuating sense. The word can signal complete independence—political freedom from both India and Pakistan, or freedom from India in order to integrate into the nation-state of Pakistan; or greater federal autonomy within the Indian Union (Article 370). In everyday speech, its precise meaning is often left undefined, and a general sense of "freedom to choose" signified. Notwithstanding apparent differences, then, aazadi means the interiorization of sovereignty as democracy, and democracy as individual freedom. On a collective level, aazadi indicates a yearning for a confident, well-defined Kashmiri identity, or *kashmiriyat* (Kashmiriness), a term I return to below. Aazadi, in short, compresses a present-tense denial of the right to identity, memory, and history, with a messianic aspiration toward a different future. It confers on to Kashmiris a folded temporality that compounds the political uncertainty crystallized around the LOC. But aazadi also threatens the foundational myth of the Indian nation as patriarchal "joint family." If adjustment of one's collective aspirations to the demands of this overarching structure is the basis of the pluralistic Indian Union, aazadi represents Kashmiri rejection of the demand to adjust.

Since the 1990s, however, the demand for aazadi has itself adjusted to the pragmatics of the everyday. Many of the original militants have "surrendered," whether to the Special Task Force or to the Indian media; others opt to participate in the federal electoral process and thus parley long-term with Delhi. Some of the founding members of the Jammu and Kashmir Liberation Front (JKLF), who continue to call for a secular, independent Jammu and Kashmir, have declared Gandhian nonviolence;[46] simultaneously, new pro-Pakistani, pro-Islamic, and pro-Indian voices compete ruthlessly for legitimacy. The conflict, initially one of ethnic self-assertion, seems to have now assumed a pan-Islamic aspect.[47] This latter development, undoubtedly linked to global politics post-9/11, also echoes the early twentieth-century collective mobilization of Kashmiris as Muslims against their Hindu Dogra rulers, and aligns the aazadi movement to persistent class-based instrumentalization of religion in Jammu and Kashmir.

Such instrumentalization has been exacerbated with the flight from the Valley of the small but high profile Kashmiri Pandit community in early 1990.[48] While the children of those who left are growing up in Jammu and Delhi in a state of self-conscious "exile," within Srinagar and its surrounding towns and villages, a parallel generation has grown up knowing little other than abnormal social conditions.[49] But superficially, as violence shades into low-grade, long-term attrition, there is normalcy. The LOC's uncertainties continue, as does the official Indian line: "Kashmir is the core of our nationhood."[50] Elections are held, tourists return, new modes of pleasure emerge. Thus while the closure of cinemas in Srinagar was an early consequence of the conflict, the South Asian ubiquity of nonterrestrial television means that Bollywood films, international cricket matches, tearjerker Indian serials, and reality TV shows all consolidate the webs of infrastructure, enjoyment, and mobility linking India to Jammu and Kashmir. Any visions of "Greater Kashmir" notwithstanding, on a daily basis such links embed the Valley ever more firmly within India, paralleling Azad Kashmir's continuing embeddedness within Pakistan.

Desire: The Camera and Kashmir

The unpredictable consequences of such contradictory embedding are exemplified in the runaway success of Qazi Touqeer, a teenager from Srinagar, within the inaugural run of Fame Gurukul (India's version of Fame Academy).[51] Week after week from July to October 2005, millions of text messages from across India returned to the Gurukul the contestant of some dubious singing talent but unmistakable charisma. His cocky persona, "exotic" looks, and unconventional hairstyle evoked hysteria and adulation on a scale that boded well for his progression toward the real dream: to be a Bollywood star. Fame Gurukul brought this dream within reach. The young man who grew up mimicking Indian film heroes in the Mughal Gardens of Srinagar, posing in front of a video camera held by his brother,[52] was soon ensconced in Bombay, with agents, a flashy car, and a fat contract with Sony Television, marketed and adored as the small-town hero who conquered the deterritorialized India of cable TV.[53] But Srinagar, lest we forget, is not your average Indian small town. The soldiers of the Indian army have not gone home, and neither, really, have the mujahideen. As Qazi, in mock-defiant response to simulated gunfire and a soldier's barked orders—"Who are you? Identify yourself!"—strutted, chanting, "Hero, I am a hero," he calibrated the change from the early 1990s, when to be a militant was the only way a Kashmiri youth could be in the national limelight, to 2005, when a Kashmiri reaches stardom through the camera rather than the Kalashnikov.[54]

As Qazi declares in "Hero," *"Arrey, public ne mujha chuna!"*—"Hey, it's the public that's chosen me!"—we may rightly wonder: *which* "public"? "At last the Valley has its own hero," was the praise showered on to Qazi Touqeer by none other than the Indian president.[55] For liberal India, Qazi's heroism was much more palatable than that of the angry young men of 1989, who are now "either dead, disillusioned or at the very least, older."[56] While Indian commentators gushed about his success as bringing Jammu and Kashmir into the "national mainstream," within Kashmir his success catalyzed public discussions about Kashmiriness, Muslimness, and the basic appropriateness of a Kashmiri winning Fame Gurukul.[57] These discrepant interpretations of the same phenomenon return us to Mbembe's understanding of the entangled public spheres of the postcolony, and the bargaining in the conceptual marketplace that arises as a potential consequence. "By dancing publicly for the benefit of power," does Qazi prove that (since) "this power is incontestable—precisely the better to play with it and modify it whenever possible?"[58] Or, as suggested by the sad but unsurprising postscript to Qazi's moment in the spotlight, is a Kashmiri winner of Fame Gurukul merely another instance of the blunting of revolutionary violence, its subsumption into the ideological apparatuses supporting the nation? Qazi's meteoric popularity can be disarticulated neither from the political relationship between India and Jammu and Kashmir, nor from the affective relationship between India and the Kashmir Valley. The intimate tyranny of this relationship—indeed, its mutually constitutive nature—crystallizes around a narcissistic chiasmus: Indian desire for the Kashmiri who desires India.

The Kashmiri who desires, and is desired by, the Indian "public" is, furthermore, a suppressed signifier of the territory of desire—the Valley he is seen as willingly leaving to seek fame in India, but which he is never quite removed from in the public('s) imagination. The libidinal economy I have identified was crucially dependent on Qazi being a contestant from the Valley of Kashmir. The nature of his participation in Fame Gurukul illustrates how the India's continuing access to the Valley, thanks to the decisions of 1948 and the de facto realities of the LOC, facilitates a circuit of desire between the Valley and the subcontinental plains, a circuit which those same realities have cut Pakistan off from. While the demands for Kashmiri independence from India were first formulated outside Jammu and Kashmir,[59] the lodestone for those demands was the Valley; thus the formation of the JKLF among Azad Kashmiris in Britain must be understood as the crystallization of diasporic desire around the Valley as a lost object. Likewise, when demands for Kashmiri aazadi were finally articulated for India from Jammu and Kashmir, they arose from the Valley. The Valley has remained the epicenter of the movement and attendant countermovements from 1989 onward. Although the popular anthropomorphizing of the map of India embodies the loss of Jammu and Kashmir, positioned at the nation's "head,"[60] as its ultimate loss of face, what this fear conceals and reveals is desire for the Kashmir Valley.

The roots of this desire, and its connection to postcolonial violence and postcolonial pleasure, lie in a distinct relationship between modernity, the Valley, and the work of the camera (as Qazi's "success" ironically reminds us). Not one of those to claim that "the beginning of a history for [colonized] societies was precisely colonialism,"[61] I do nevertheless contend that the beginning of "modernity" for South Asia was grounded in the colonial encounter. Needless to say, modernity here is not understood as a transhistorical category; rather, it functions as shorthand for the creation, from the nineteenth century onward, of new modes of subjectivity through rapidly evolving technologies of mechanical reproduction.[62] While these technologies were used within the British Empire for purposes of discipline, surveillance, and epistemological control over vast areas, they also predicated a modern colonial subjectivity. Thus, it is now recognized that the colonized subject fashioned itself as modern by posing for the camera;[63] that the postcolonial state used a visual colonial discourse of Indian antiquity to assert its archaeological lineage;[64] and that the interocularity of photography, chromolithography, and oleography constitutes the nuts and bolts of South Asian modernity.[65] Drawing on but also pushing beyond this consensus, I use the camera, "the machine opening up the optical unconscious,"[66] to shed light on not merely the colony's emergent modernity but also on the antecedents to the postcolony's discrepant modernities, as manifested in the earliest and most frequently photographed landscape in South Asia: the Valley.

While investigating the 1995 genocide of Tutsis by the Hutus, Mahmood Mamdani found a "synthesis between history, geography and politics" necessary in order to "show how the unthinkable became thinkable."[67] The long, fraught relationship between the camera and Kashmir is where I locate my version of this synthesis, adding "fantasy" to its already potent mix. During the latter half of the nineteenth century, the politics of imperial adventure known as the Great Game combined with the Valley's location at the demographic, cultural, and geographic heart of a newly cobbled together princely state, to make it particularly appropriate to the allied adventure of photography.[68] In the 1860s, the adventurer-photographers Samuel Bourne and John Burke first entered the Valley with an unwieldy yet heroic assortment of glass plates, chemicals, portable darkrooms, and other accoutrements of the photographic endeavor. During the next century, photographers, and the surveyors and archaeologists they often accompanied, were transformed into the tourist as domesticated imperial adventurer. The postcolonial inheritance of this tourism was augmented by a series of 1960s "Kashmir" films, which again coincided with new technologies of pleasure—Technicolor and rock-n-roll. These technologies gave a new spin to "falling in love," making the Valley the exemplary landscape of erotic desire for modern India.[69] Although the Valley's role of postcolonial playground for metropolitan youth was interrupted by the political violence of the 1990s, a new kind of Kashmir film soon emerged in step with that violence. Overlaying heterosexual romance with "cinepatriotism,"[70] it has recreated the Valley as cinematic battleground, criss-crossed by lovers, militants, the military, and mujahideen.

From the 1860s until the present day, therefore, the Valley as landscape has been subject to the camera's gaze like no other space in South Asia. To explicate how this gaze has helped construct the Valley as a desired space, we may look to Slavoj Žižek's elucidation of the "role of fantasy in the economy of desire," whereby "an empirical positively given object become[s] an object of desire . . . contain[ing] some x, some unknown quality," precisely "*by entering the framework of fantasy.*"[71] I would likewise assert that the Valley, an empirical, positively given space, became a territory of desire precisely when the lens of the camera, as the original framework of fantasy, was trained on it. In other words, the quality of desirability that South Asia associates with the Valley, and which has resulted in "the lure of the land(scape)" and its complicated geopolitics, can be traced to the ill-defined relationship between the princely state of Jammu and Kashmir and the British Empire, to the libidinal colonial economy of power, knowledge and control of which it was indirectly part, and to the camera's gaze that made that economy manifest. The camera's conversion of an earlier aesthetic response to the Valley, embodied in the Mughal emperors' cultivation of the Valley's slopes into elaborate terraced gardens and their patronizing of miniature artists who captured the Valley's vistas through latticed windows,[72] thus initiated not merely the move to technologies of mechanical reproduction; it inserted fantasy into the very heart of colonial modernity.[73]

While the fantasy of Kashmir indexes the development and complications of South Asian modernity, an irony lies in is its persistently elusive object of desire. The Valley as framed by modernity can be seen as always already lost at the inaugural moment of its framing. Zahid Chaudhary's reading of colonial photography as symptomatic of a "phantasmagoric aesthetic" that manages "the very structure of vision and visibility to re/produce the modern form of alienation," together with Susan Sontag's classic explication of photography as loss, helps underscore this reading of postcolonial India's desire for the Valley as figuring a founding absence.[74] While the emphasis on modernity endows my argument with a historical specificity, I seek to nuance it further through the psychoanalytical tool of the fetish, or signifier of a fundamental lack.[75] If postcolonial India's obsession with its territory of desire makes the Valley a fetish for the nation-state, the Valley in turn can assume the power of a counterfetish, a *maleficium,* that can potentially unmask the State as the master fetish.[76] Whether as fetish or as maleficium, the Valley draws attention to, while seeking to disguise, what Ranjana Khanna has termed "the secret embedded in nation-state formation."[77] Thus, the Valley as a territory of desire itself arguably embodies the secret of nation-statehood—that, in Khanna's words, it is "constituted through the colonial relation." However, the relationship of indirect rule between the princely state of Jammu and Kashmir and British India complicates this interpretation somewhat, even as it complicates the mechanism for the transmission of affect offered by Khanna's characterization of the "secret" as "phantom:" a transgenerationally transmitted symptom of "an inaccessible remainder that is the kernel of melancholia, unknown, inassimilable, interruptive, and present."[78]

Khanna's argument that the "concept of nation-statehood needed to be radically reshaped if it is to survive without colonies, or without a conceded (colonial) other" ostensibly facilitates an "Orientalism"-style reading of the relationship between postcolonial India and the Kashmir Valley.[79] As an "othered" space within the postcolonial nation that has inherited the burden of colonial discourse, the Valley can indeed be seen as the conceded (postcolonial) other. But since it was never incorporated directly into British India, its relationship to postcolonial India is no straightforward colonial legacy. If the "secret" is the consequence of a trauma that, resisting assimilation, persists as the kernel of melancholia, then in fact the "epistemic murk" surrounding the Valley in postcolonial India speaks to the difficulties of locating that trauma squarely within the colonial–postcolonial axis. Neither in "the specter of the colonial that haunts the postcolonial nation,"[80] nor even in its violent birth in 1947 but, rather, in modernity itself is where I locate this trauma, that constantly displaces attention through the proliferation of new technologies of pleasure. Privileging modernity as a continually evolving phenomenon enables us to attribute the continuing conflict over territory to the Valley's function as the un-modern other for the modern Indian self. It also takes us beyond its two most usual explanations: the failure of democracy, and the "problem" of religion, both postcolonial continuations of Dogra denial of rights to their Kashmiri subjects. Kashmiri self-identifications as "Muslim" vis-à-vis rulers identified as "non-Muslim/Hindu/Indian," and the very demand for democratic rights, re-emerge as aspects of an aspirant modernity, whose strangulation is the consequence of the stubborn fantasy of nonmodern Kashmir.

To emphasize modernity, the consequent melancholia of which encrypts the secret and generates desire as its "phantom" symptom, is not to posit atavistically some arch-culprit for postcolonial conflict; the complications of an unevenly achieved modernity are a shared melancholic condition of the postcolonial world. Brought to bear on the Kashmir conflict, this perspective on modernity also rearticulates the concept of the "phantom" through the mutual, if often tortured embrace of Indian and Kashmiri. It is not only in desire for the Valley that Indians and Kashmiris find themselves united-but-opposed. Rather, such desire gestures toward the inability to disentangle the self from the other. Thus, even as Indians find detachment from the idea of Kashmir impossible, Kashmiris speak of aazadi and exude bitterness toward one India, while being fully embedded within the India of popular culture and its attendant discourses of representation and pleasure. As Qazi's ambitions and the momentary fame they subtended confirm, trajectories of pleasure entangle them ever more complexly with India as "the society of the spectacle."[81] This paradoxical duality is a specific aspect of the schizophrenic subject position of the Kashmiri as co-opted Indian citizen.[82] Yet, if in inviting the camera to focus on the selectively desirable Kashmiri body, Qazi can "toy with power" as much as collude with reality TV, it is because he destabilizes the camera's historic gaze on the desirable Kashmiri landscape. Like Deleuze and Guattari's concept of the "schizo," he "scrambles the codes."[83] Likewise, when the Kashmiri artist M.A. Mahboob paints a man with a camera lens on a tripod, he knowingly translates the camera's gaze on the Valley into another visual medium, and reinserts the non-Kashmiri eye into Kashmiri metacommentary.[84] If the gaze of the non-Kashmiri has framed the Valley as a territory of desire, it is by countering that gaze, not necessarily directly, but in oblique and fragmented proclamations of their claims to the Valley, that Kashmiris attempt to resist the hegemony of the camera.

Representation: The Body in the Text

Given that the earliest modern representations of the Valley have relied heavily on the camera, and given, too, the persistence of landscape in collective imaginings of Kashmir, a certain visual image has assumed primacy in generating desire for the Valley. This image foregrounds the Valley's landscape, and, occasionally, the ruin in the landscape; it prefers to eliminate Kashmiri people, monuments in use, and homes. These latter elements are by no means absent from nineteenth-century photographs of the Valley; however, they are progressively weeded out as the relationship between the camera and the Valley tightens and also expands from the photograph to the moving image.[85] I emphasize not only this visual and cinematic history but also its interaction, from the moment of its inception, with other kinds of texts, specially the written. Indeed, any inquiry into the accruing around the Valley of what Stephen Greenblatt has called "mimetic capital," and its gradual transformation into symbolic capital,[86] needs to consider the forms, and conditions, of interacting modes of representation. Furthermore, these interactions must include the dialogue between Kashmiri and Indian producers (and consumers) of texts. If we want to know how representations of the Valley have produced and sustained Indian desire for the Valley, how such desire may be differentiated from Kashmiri claims on the same space, and how such claims may relate to political resistance, then it is not the mere facts of intertextuality, interocularity, and intersubjectivity but the nodal points "quilting" these multiple fields of signification that must become the focus of scrutiny.[87]

It is not with texts as discrete and self-enclosed, then, but with texts as constituents of a long-standing discourse on Kashmir, that this book is concerned. This discourse, which constructs the Valley's landscape as paradise on earth, operates in ways similar to the nineteenth-century operation of the "picturesque"; more contemporaneously, it recalls the dehistoricization of architecture in the Israel–Palestinian conflict.[88] While it was the Mughal emperors who, reportedly, first bestowed the divine epithet on to the Valley, the technologies of modernity converted description into discourse. My understanding of "discourse" thus draws on Edward Said's re-articulation of Michel Foucault's argument for the links between textual representation and political power. Foucault equates knowledge with power, and modern technologies of production, dissemination, and surveillance with control. Said, particularly in *Orientalism,* applies this equation to understand the controlling and subjugating work of Empire.[89] The knowledge–power equation further allows us to seek possibilities of political resistance in the seizing control of representation (though neither Foucault nor Said focus on this possibility). We can thus argue that while representations of Kashmir constitute, over the long term, the discourse of the paradisiacal Valley (itself an inherited construct), Kashmiris have also used representation to insert themselves within this discourse. In fact, Kashmiri and non-Kashmiri representations of the Valley are discursively braided together, and it is this entanglement that pushes the "language, counter-memory and practice" of Kashmiri resistance back to that same discourse of the Valley as territory of desire.[90] "Discourse" is thus not a seamless web through which power is uniformly diffused; rather, it is striated, fragmented, and shot through with uneven articulations of claim and counterclaim.

To critique, but also to find within this unevenness possibilities of resistance and redemption, is the task of the cultural critic: "As we reckon with the loss and gain of place, we may discover, *through the force of interpretation,* forms of absence—of pain, of fear, of guilt, of desire."[91] It is toward such ideally forceful interpretation that I deploy tools from literary studies, trauma studies, histories of Indian modernity, political and philosophical approaches to state violence, and fieldwork in Srinagar. Such conceptual eclecticism, while part and parcel of literary studies now, has proved additionally relevant in my struggles, as critic, to reconcile the worlds within the text with those without. So I have learned to situate my reading of both Kashmiri and non-Kashmiri claims over the Valley within a thick description of the inner life of a conflict zone—not as an aspiring anthropologist but as a literary and cultural historian who maps what people say about Kashmir against their more conscious, creative representations of Kashmir. Through conversation and observation, I have re-read the Kashmiri collective psyche in terms of resistance and survival rather than merely trauma and victimhood, while mining awareness of my own subject position in order to analyze Indian attitudes toward the Kashmir Valley as imprinted by past and present traumas. While materialist approaches pointed to the necessity of disaggregating the category of "Kashmiri" in terms of class, the symptomatic reading of the cultural text revealed cross-cutting axes of affect, longing, and desire. As Michael Taussig found in the Putumayo districts of the Amazon, "[T]he problem of interpretation turned out to be an essential component of what had to be interpreted, just as resistance was necessary for control."[92]

The need for interpretative agility has benefited from psychoanalytical criticism's renewed focus on the material as the bodily that now increasingly overrides the traditionally uneasy relationship between Foucauldian and Freudian approaches.[93] This focus has helped me insert, within "discourse" and "representation," the uncomfortable fact of "bodies that splatter."[94] The evaporation of bodies from "recent historiography, anthropology, and feminist criticism inspired by Foucauldian, neo-Gramscian paradigms" has been lambasted by Mbembe: "These disciplines have reduced the complex phenomena of the state and power to 'discourses' and 'representations,' forgetting that discourses and representations have materiality."[95] But Mbembe himself does not abandon discourse and representation. On the one hand, "the signs, vocabulary and narratives that the *commandement* produces" are "symbols . . . officially invested with a surplus of meanings"; on the other, "the analyst must watch for the myriad ways ordinary people guide, deceive and toy with power instead of confronting it directly."[96] We need, therefore, to "examine how the world of meanings is produced and ordered, the types of institutions, the knowledge, the norms, and practices structuring this new common sense, the light that the use of visual imagery and *discourse* throws on the nature of domination and subordination."[97] Likewise, while examining how the meaning of "Kashmir" has been produced, ordered, and institutionally perpetuated, it is the knowledge that "the champions of state power" not only "invent entire constellations of ideas, a distinctive set of cultural repertoires, and powerfully evocative concepts, but [that] they also resort, if necessary, to the systematic application of pain,"[98] that keeps materiality firmly in the foreground. This relationship between pain, the body, and power underscores my understanding of materiality primarily as corporeality.

A persistent and painful *contingency,* "the question of being touched, again," thus returns discourse and representation to the meeting ground of biopolitics and necropolitics, into the "space of death" as "threshold for illumination as well as extinction."[99] Any consideration of how the Valley has been represented cannot allow materiality, both as the shackles of class and as the touch of the body, to slip out of the frame; rather, as Taussig notes, to "ponder mimesis" in this murky zone is to "become sooner or later caught, like the police and the modern state with their fingerprinting devices, in sticky webs of copy and contact, image and bodily involvement in the image."[100] The framework of fantasy has so consistently subordinated bodies to the landscape that, today, two decades after 1989, the Kashmiri is actively and collectively scapegoated for having so inconveniently disrupted that pastoral serenity.[101] Any ethically informed discussion of the Valley's representation in modernity must, therefore, consider the circumstances under which representation ceases to be a "merely philosophical problem" of distinguishing fact from fiction, and instead, capitalizing on such "epistemic murk," becomes "a high powered medium of domination."[102] As Taussig concludes, "this problem of interpretation is decisive for terror, not only making effective counterdiscourse so difficult but also making the terribleness of death squads, disappearances and torture all the more effective in crippling of people's capacity to resist."[103] Yet, however difficult the circumstances might be, counterdiscourse does emerge. As the contrasting emphases of Kashmiri and non-Kashmiri representations of the Valley reveal, discursive elision of the body from the landscape is countered by Kashmiri insistence on the body in the landscape.

This return of the body to the landscape infuses representation with materiality while unlocking the meaning of that chimerical term, kashmiriyat. Like aazadi, it is a varyingly understood word, one that everyone interested in contemporary Kashmir invokes—whether to dismiss, deride, or reaffirm. For Kashmiris, kashmiriyat is invoked usually in the context of its perceived erosion, in confirmation of the "community-in-neglect."[104] The psychosocial repercussions of political conflict are attributed to the suspension of kashmiriyat, and aazadi relied upon to ensure its restoration; when the Kashmiris will have obtained aazadi, kashmiriyat will have returned to them. In contrast, liberal Indian discourse invokes kashmiriyat as a placebo; it is assimilated to another discourse around secularism, syncretism, and Sufism that seeks to eject all that is troubling about Islam to the national imaginary.[105] Because kashmiriyat so easily signifies a malleable Islam that sits yieldingly with a benign Hinduism, the specter of its endangerment causes disproportionate alarm in the Indian public sphere. Tears are shed routinely not for human rights violations in the Valley but for kashmiriyat's putative destruction, with the added implication that it is the Kashmiri as Muslim who, left to his own devices, is up to the usual mischief. Precisely because every inquiry into contemporary Kashmir gets thus shunted toward overdetermined South Asian narratives of religion-driven partialities and schisms, I refrain from privileging "Islam" with causal force. Islam emerges instead through the interstices of identity politics between different constituencies within Kashmir, Jammu and Kashmir, and India, articulated frequently through the vocabulary of Sufi Islam—either to defuse its significations of a threatening otherness or, more productively (as I explicate shortly), to reinsert spirituality into the praxis of the everyday. Rather than reiterate reductionist understandings of kashmiriyat, Sufism, and Islam, then, I read the struggle over their meanings, so visible in their variegated mobilizations, as intrinsic to the struggle over territory, desire, and representation.

Accordingly, invocations of these concepts by Kashmiris should be seen as signaling attempts to regain control over the landscape itself. When Kashmiri poet Rahman Rahi, in my first epigraph, makes Srinagar's Zabarvan hills a psychosomatic messenger for his inner turmoil, he reclaims the mountains from the consumerist circuit of photography, cinema, and tourism for spiritual nourishment of the depleted Kashmiri self. For the Kashmiri cultural producer, such reclaiming implies a need not to celebrate the paradise on earth, but to commemorate the landscape's staining by Kashmiri blood, the "sheer rubies on the Himalayan snow."[106] This Kashmiri body in the landscape is now a body in pain, a body that bears scars of multiple registers of violence—physical, epistemic, psychosomatic, nostalgic. The body that intrudes into and distorts the collective Indian fantasy of the pastoral Valley of Kashmir is the key unlocking the meaning of Kashmiri demands for aazadi, including those now tied to Islamist self-assertion, and of Kashmiri declarations of kashmiriyat. If "political revolutionary violence is a form of melancholia, in unconscious response, perhaps, to the loss of an ideal, [which is] the right of subjecthood and the right not to be exploited,"[107] then the violent uprisings of 1989 are responses to the impossible conditions of existing only in desubjectified absence, as the disposable bodies evacuated from the nation's pastoral fantasy. We thus cannot disengage Kashmiri "political" attempts at self-representation from their "creative" or "aesthetic" counterparts. Likewise, Indian representations of the Valley as a beautiful, *framed* landscape can be disengaged neither from the federal democratic structure that frames political aspirations nor from "the official common sense of political economy" into which reality has "to be squeezed willy-nilly."[108] If Indian representations of the Kashmir Valley perpetuate three sorts of violence—the violence of the founding moment, the violence of legitimizing authority, and the violence of maintaining authority, Kashmiri counter-representations complicate this violence.[109] Together, they must be read against and to each other, as texts whose dissonance can prick the collective consciousness into what Khanna calls "critical melancholia."[110]

When Khanna suggests that melancholia, or the inability of the psyche to work through traumatic loss, might be the "basis for an ethico-political understanding of colonial pasts, postcolonial presents, and utopian futures," she resurrects melancholia from being psychoanalytical theory's poor cousin of mourning, seen as the successful integration of traumatic into narrative memory.[111] She thereby undermines traditional psychoanalytical reliance on the "healing power" of narrative and testimony, and the relegation of obsessions and repetitions to melancholia as an unproductive failure to narrate. Khanna's move resonates with my own understanding of South Asian history as a multiply traumatized domain, where narrative itself as a deeply contested site.[112] In consonance, therefore, with her search for critical melancholia, I advocate the reconciliatory power of non-narrative, fragmentary responses to conflict, such as the artwork, the lyric poem, and the poetic documentary. In further "defense of the fragment,"[113] I do not disguise the arbitrary ways in which I came upon much of this material; rather, I let those gaps and discontinuities illustrate the uncertainties and "logistical murk" that beset daily life in Jammu and Kashmir, and the difficulty of converting into "scholarly standards" those protean conversations in homes and offices over Kashmiri tea, on horseback across slippery slopes, and on *shikaras* (small Kashmiri boats) gliding through mottled lakes. Thus, I have willingly allowed the contingency of working with people's aspirations, anger, and desires to overcome the academic pursuit of "the whole picture." Indeed, its methodological reflection is the frequency with which I interrupt my own scholarly discourse through strategic recourse to the anecdote.[114]

The Argument, and the Rem(a)inder

From this assemblage of diverse Kashmiri and non-Kashmiri representations of the Valley as a territory of desire, I do, however, attempt to construct an argument. This argument takes the shape of two parts, termed "The Making of Paradise" and "Poetics of Dispossession." Part I, comprising three chapters, broadly focuses on the Valley's reconstruction as a "paradise on earth" through modern technologies of photography and cinema, in conjunction with scholarly discourse on the Valley's antiquity and its relationship to the development of tourism in Kashmir. Part II, also comprising three chapters, attempts to show how a poetic practice, again broadly conceived, might shatter this discourse and, through the experience of dispossession, reassemble it in philosophically and ethically illuminating ways. The book's Hinge, "Toward Unmaking," is, literally, a hinge between these two sections, bringing together the work of a contemporary Kashmiri artist with a particular nationalist discourse of Kashmiri handicraft. Its contrapunctal nature anticipates the book's movement toward intellectual and creative conversations between Kashmiris and non-Kashmiris as a means to greater mutual understanding. This movement culminates in Part II, the three constituent chapters of which seek to convince the reader of the viability of art practice as an alternative to militaristic and nationalist responses to political conflict. A glance back at the table of contents will provide graphic confirmation of the various symmetries and oppositions I have outlined here; I now provide some further orientation.

Chapter 1, "Masks of Desire," plunges the reader into the heart of the book's inquiry: collective desire. The cinematic apparatus of Bollywood is examined as the nation's major mechanism for mobilizing desire for Kashmir. Through two popular post-1989 films, and by reading in particular their surface anxieties against intertextuality with films from the 1960s, I offer a history of Bollywood's Kashmir obsession that enables us explore what desire might conceal. A recent documentary from Kashmir helps me complicate the mutually constitutive nature of Indian and Kashmiri desire through the resistive power of Kashmiri counterdiscourse. In chapter 2, "Framing Fantasy," I reconstruct the genealogy of fantasy that links these films, imprinted with the trauma of losing the object of desire, to the nineteenth-century history of photographing the Kashmir Valley. The photographic framing of fantasy is itself framed through analysis of contemporary, Kashmiri uses of photographs of conflict. This hidden history of the camera in Kashmir enables me interrogate the nexus between consumption, archiving, and value that underwrites the history of pastoral escape to the Valley as a corollary of Indian modernity. Chapter 3, "Modern Nation, Antique Land," views this history against the relationship between emergent tourism and academic representations of the Valley. The scholarly investment in the Valley as a source of an Indic antiquity, and its complicity with the Valley's development as a paradise for imperial and, after 1947, domestic tourism is also revealed as a consequence of the complex collaboration between Kashmir's Dogra rulers and the British Empire.

How might this multifaceted discursive history be understood as sustaining collective desire in the postcolonial nation, on the one hand, and as excluding constituencies within the nation, on the other? How, materially and affectively, might we move from desire to contestation and resistance? These questions are approached in the single chapter within the Hinge section, entitled "Fetish of Paradise." Here, the postcolonial discourse on and consumption of Kashmiri handicraft, itself implicated within the construction of Kashmir as pastoral fantasy, is interrupted through an affective political reading of the Kashmiri craft object via Kashmiri artist Masood Hussain's use of traditional papier maché techniques. Through the analytical tool of the fetish, I unpack handicraft as a signifier of Kashmiriness for Indians and Kashmiris, connect desire for Kashmir to the enduring trauma of modernity, and examine how Kashmiri self-fashioning through handicraft—by both artisan and studio artist—negotiates between appropriation, re-appropriation, irony, and a critical melancholia.

In "The Poetics of Dispossession," the book's second part, the possibilities and limits of Kashmiri counter-representation are plotted on a matrix traversed by the word, the voice and the thing. Chapter 4, "Conscripting Silence," analyzes images of silencing and unreadability in Kashmiri literature written in Urdu, English, and Koshur. Using Kashmiri multilingualism to illuminate the notion of kashmiriyat, I read these texts as allegories not of trauma but of voice. Responding to these writers' insistence on reservoirs of oral and bodily expression, I relocate survival and resistance in the fact of orality. Chapter 5, "The Other Possibility", turns to the cultural production of Kashmiri Pandits (Hindus) who left the Valley in 1989 under still controversial circumstances, to examine thereby Pandit and Muslim rival claims on a vision of the Valley's spirituality, tied to the topography and cultural practices of the Valley. Through this bifurcation of an imagined composite heritage, I foreground the problems inherent in the narrative form, but demonstrate through the work of Pandit sculptor Rajendar Tiku what he calls "the other possibility"—spiritually resonant, non-narrative, nonverbal alternatives to memorializing shared conflict. In the final chapter, "New Maps of Longing," I analyze Indian artist Nilima Sheikh's "Kashmir Paintings," an evolving series that responds to Kashmiri poet Agha Shahid Ali and her own travels in the Valley. In lieu of a conclusion, with its delusional promises of closure and solution, I use this "dialogue" to theorize the possible transcendence of territorial desire for the Valley through the reconciliatory and redemptive power of the artwork.

From the Hinge to Part II, my argument moves incrementally toward valorizing the object over the text, the image over the word, the lyric and the fragment over the linear sequence. This is not the literary critic's move into the ivory tower of indulgent theorizing; rather, this valorization emerges out of the ways in which differently situated Kashmiris seek legitimacy through specifically chosen modes of representation. The Kashmiri artisan, who creates things, is emulated by the poet, from a different class background, who works with words; the divisiveness of language, inescapable for the writer, is bypassed by the sculptor, who infuses into his work the spirituality of sacred objects. My attempts not merely to analyze but also to break through the surfaces of mimesis and representation are accompanied by the increasing prominence I grant to a range of contemporary South Asian spiritualities broadly inspired by Sufism. As my narrative will divulge, a surprising number of the actors in this piece turn to Sufi expressive and contemplative practices to infuse their works with spiritual resonance. Rather than see such Sufi Islam as standing outside of capitalism and modernity, I take cues from my sources to rethink Sufism as an antidote *and* product of the same modernity. Kashmiri cultural practices that return to Sufism clearly do so in an effort to circumvent the divisiveness of religion in South Asia, and in this move they are neither unique nor strange among South Asians. They do so, moreover, while fully cognizant of the hardening of class hierarchies around Kashmiri Sufi lineages, and the open enmeshing of politics and spirituality around Sufi shrines. Nevertheless, their deliberate rerouting of Islam, kashmiriyat, and even the quest for aazadi through a Sufi vein indicates to us the potential, if not manifest power, of spirituality in attempts toward healing and reconciliation both within Kashmiri society and between Kashmiri and Indian constituencies.

Inevitably, perhaps, my analysis will invite critiques of exclusivity, directed toward the privileged class positions that several of the cultural producers I engage with occupy, and the luxury of intellectual and spiritual choices that is theirs, whether in metropolitan India or in Jammu and Kashmir. I make no excuse for this selectivity other than the fact that the self-conscious cultural text—literary, visual, cinematic—is bound by its own circumstances of production and consumption. In the words of Theodor Adorno, "art neutralizes force as much as makes it worse: its innocence is its guilt."[115] Yet this innocent guilt leaves traces that enable us to extract from it the conditions of its possible redemption. The conversations that our elite artists and poets from Kashmir conduct with their perceived non-elite Kashmiri others, even if ventriloquized or imagined, wedge open a door. Sometimes, as with our Kashmiri artisans in the hinge chapter, or the collagist of photographs of dead Kashmiri men in chapter 3, it is those "others" who are revealed as deciding whether that door should remain open or be closed. In other words, materialist awareness of class positioning and contestations over religious affiliation underpin my analysis; but, superseding that awareness is my conviction that another materiality, that of the body, has to be given its rightful place in this story, and, that, furthermore, it hijacks the story through a certain tending toward the sacral. By acknowledging these links between the material and the spiritual, I hope this analysis of conflict draws some quiet lessons from those whom conflict has tangibly affected.

Especially in South Asia today, where contestations over postcolonial boundaries have wreaked havoc on the emotional, political and economic security of millions, we need diverse approaches to conflict and its resolution. Founded on the conviction that aesthetic and cultural responses to political conflict offer valuable clues to its genesis and growth, this book offers one such approach. I relocate "history" from high politics to the ways in which "Kashmir" has come to occupy a particular position in the Indian national imaginary. Rather than mimic the exclusionary moves of Indian and Pakistani wrangling over Kashmir, and leaving, as far as possible, similar reductionist wrangling over Hinduism and Islam, I follow contemporary Kashmiri voices in uncovering the discursive patterns shaping the relationship between Indians and Kashmiris. By bringing together texts *about* Kashmir with texts *from* Kashmir, I offer a model for dialogue between creative intellectuals representing opposing points of view within the nation-state. The cultural practitioner and producer is, I believe, crucial in transforming the postcolonial public sphere through compassion, restored agency, and greater democratic responsibility. If citizenship is a fiction, the individuals that comprise a readership, or an audience, are as bound together through the negotiation of autonomy as are citizens of a democracy. Creative responses to the Valley reveal how desire, the force that cements the group, might also be read against the grain. Thus may we demystify the naturalized fictions that support the nation's structures of power at the cost of the dignity of those the nation claims as its own.

However, when analysis is over, and landscape revealed as thoroughly constructed, is there anything that remains? When the text has been scrutinized as discourse, does anything transcendent survive? When the information has been gathered, do human interactions retain value? Here, I will risk offering the much-maligned word "beauty." Like Agha Shahid Ali's "blessed word," which exists, unstated, beyond the margins of the poem bearing that name, I use "beauty" as a cipher, to signal all those moments when I, as "caught by history" as anyone else,[116] could still find myself, momentarily, uplifted. Thus, what remain impossible to subject to analysis are my own memories of this celebrated, tragic landscape. Although hyper-aware of "territory," "desire," and "representation," I nevertheless cannot deny the materiality of my own experience within the landscape, especially as I remember moments I sat wrestling with my thoughts on early mornings and late evenings on the deck of a Dal Lake houseboat, with the sun's rays on the surrounding mountains. While acknowledging the violent processes of modernity that have made possible my presence there, I think it important to leave the elusive quality of "beauty," particularly as manifested in this topography, as remainder and as reminder.

Part I

The Making of Paradise

One

Masks of Desire

The mask is not simply hiding the real state of things; the ideological distortion is written into its very essence.

—Slavoj Žižek, *Sublime Object of Ideology*

Wars are not fought with guns, Altaaf, they are fought with cameras.

—*Mission Kashmir*

In 2001, when Bollywood star Hrithik Roshan was riding a wave of adulation, the film *Mission Kashmir* (dir. Vidhu Vinod Chopra, 2001) hit the screens with his portrayal of Altaaf, a Kashmiri whose life is a battleground between good and bad father figures. Witness to the decimation of his family during a crackdown, the orphaned Altaaf is subsequently fostered by the same police officer, Inayat Khan, who had commandeered that operation, and whose own son has died because of Kashmiri militancy. Haunted by recurrent dreams of a man in a balaclava, Altaaf discovers the same balaclava in Khan's bedroom. Khan thus unmasked, the boy runs away, returns, transformed, as the older terrorist. Manipulated by the mercenary Afghan *jihadi* Hilal Kohistani (himself the puppet of Pakistani bureaucrats, in turn the playthings of an Osama Bin Laden figure), Altaaf's desire for revenge conflates struggle against the good father with Kashmiri struggles against the Indian nation-state (and his final rejection of the bad father with the rejection of Islam and Pakistan). But *Mission Kashmir,* directed by a non-Kashmiri who grew up in Kashmir, goes beyond simply plotting the Kashmir issue onto an

Oedipal struggle between the nation and its dissidents. Its fantasies of what Slavoj Žižek calls the "transcendent other country" map Altaaf's desire for Khan's wife, Neelima, onto his childhood sweetheart Sufi's desire for him, and enfold, through idyllic games of cricket, the nation into the family; at the same time, they jostle with nightmares of masks, dangerously open windows, and explosions. Out of this duality emerges a deeper anxiety that sporadically erupts through knowing comments inserted into the mouths of its characters.[1]

This anxiety concerns the power of the camera. Hence, my second epigraph: a line of dialogue assigned to one of Altaaf's terrorist companions, watching television even as Altaaf polishes a gun. In this chapter, I link *Mission Kashmir*'s manifest preoccupation with the traumatic impact of the Kashmir conflict on the national imaginary with its latent, discomfiting realization that wars are fought and won with the camera rather than the gun. This analysis, which unveils not the secret content hidden by the film's form but "the secret of the form itself,"[2] considers *Mission Kashmir* as a self-conscious moment within a long history of the articulation of Indian desire for the Kashmir Valley through the cinematic apparatus we now call "Bollywood." The film offers a metacinematic memory of a lost Kashmir, as well as a reflection on cinema's role in precipitating that loss. Loss is configured in this film through cross-cutting axes of desire—between Altaaf and Inayat Khan, Altaaf and Neelima, Altaaf and Sufi, Inayat Khan and Neelima, even Altaaf and Hilal Kohistani. These tangled circuits superimpose on the topography of the Valley a tortured psychic topography of trauma, memory, and longing. While arguably all Bollywood films on Kashmir draw on similar circuits and topographies, the self-consciousness of *Mission Kashmir* makes it exemplary of the processes I wish to probe here.

In this chapter, I use *Mission Kashmir* to extract, from Bollywood's Kashmir obsession, the relationship between Indian popular cinema and the mobilization of national desire. South Asian popular cinema has always been a potent vehicle for "the transmission of affect," whereby disparate individuals willingly surrender their autonomy for the pleasures of the mass.[3] Bollywood films in particular are repositories of cultural memory around which group identification, including that elusive "national feeling,"[4] crystallizes. The volatile theatre they constitute for the miming of contestations over the "State" as both the "site of demand and the stake of the struggle,"[5] also invariably reaffirms the sanctity and salience of "nation." This understanding of Bollywood helps us reconstruct and explicate its historical use of the Valley to construct a postcolonial modernity.

I unlock the mutual implication of that cinematic genealogy and the Kashmir conflict through an examination of *Mission Kashmir*'s emphasis on masking. Relying, like Žižek, on the concept of the mask to theorize the interdependence of fantasy and ideology,[6] I read this emphasis as pointing to the homology between the mask of the cinematic apparatus and the mask of the State. Behind both masks stands not reality but further fantasy (or nightmare): the nation's ideological reliance on Kashmir as its territory of desire. Wars are indeed fought and won through the camera, therefore, but can the camera bring redemption? This question, which haunts *Mission Kashmir,* impacts other, post-1989, popular films that circle around desire for Kashmir and fear of its imminent loss. It also permeates recent Kashmiri attempts to seek freedom through training an indigenous cinematic gaze on the Valley.

Double Vision

Mission Kashmir opens with the image of a canopied shikara exploding on the Dal Lake. For a brief second before this explosion, we see the small boat silhouetted against the mountains, poised on the lake's tranquil waters. The colors are misty blue-gray, suggestive of twilight or dawn. As the shikara blows up, these colors are replaced by bright, theatrical flames that billow outward to fill the screen. The camera draws back, showing the same mountains and lake, though now irrevocably changed. The opening credits begin to roll, white letters dissolving into smoke-like effects, even as a voice chants on the soundtrack "*Dhua dhua, dhua hi dhua*" (Smoke, smoke, nothing but smoke).[7] Uniformed men race across the jetties and rickety wooden platforms that connect the Dal Lake's houseboats. As one of them reaches the extremity of a jetty, his superior, whom audiences recognize as established Bollywood actor Sanjay Dutt, comes into view, sardonically chastizing the impetuousness that has led this would-be hero right into the trap of an IED (improvised explosive device). The true hero, Dutt, now established as Special Superintendent of Police (SSP) Inayat Khan, rescues him, risking his own life, even as the platform blows up in another explosion. Thus does *Mission Kashmir* dramatically introduce its double vision: a constant juxtaposition of "what is" with "what had been" or, even, "what might have been."

This double vision solicits from viewers an awareness of various technologies of representation through which Kashmir is seen, remembered, and then forgotten. The first time we see the boy Altaaf, he is engrossed in sketching the mountains surrounding the Dal Lake, upon which his houseboat home is anchored. His childish attempts at "representing Kashmir" are interrupted by the police raid, led by Inayat Khan, on his houseboat, where the militant Malik-ul-Khan has taken shelter. Altaaf's entire family becomes collateral damage, and he ends up being fostered by Inayat Khan and his wife, Neelima. With Altaaf ensconced in the Khans' beautiful home, the subject of his sketching shifts from the Valley's landscape to a man's face covered by a black balaclava. We hear his furious scribbling with crayons before we see him sitting amid hundreds of his new creations. This repeated image is a psychosomatic imprint of the moment when the balaclava-clad Inayat Khan clamped shut Altaaf's mouth, even as his family fell to the hail of bullets around him. It becomes not only a way to counteract that silencing but also a response to the trauma of being silenced. Reflecting the difficulty of healing trauma by finding a new narrative to remember it through, Altaaf's abruptly changed artwork embodies the ongoing struggle between the traumatic event and the work of memory.

At the end of the police raid, the camera focuses on Altaaf's sketch of a shikara sinking slowly into the water. A disappearing remnant of his pre-raid life, it contrasts with the only post-raid pictures that Altaaf can make. His sketches of the lake become encoded as the innocent "before"—the shikara before it blows up—and his sketches of the masked man become similarly encoded as the "after"—the explosion that shatters innocence. But it is only the knowledge of the "after" that renders the "before" meaningful. Hence, *Mission Kashmir*'s double vision is essentially retrospective and melancholic.[8] It uses the present to recognize the past as having been a different, happier time, but those memories also color the present and make its full enjoyment impossible. This recognition stamps the Khans' attempts to make good, through Altaaf, the loss of their son Irfaan. Inayat Khan's manhunt for Malik-ul-Khan had been motivated by more than professional concerns. Irfaan, the same age as Altaaf, had succumbed to injuries sustained after a fall, because Malik-ul-Khan had issued a *fatwa* (edict) on Kashmiri doctors treating Indian security forces and their families.[9] Altaaf enters the Khan family as an undisguised replacement for Irfaan. He is given Irfaan's clothes, Irfaan's room, and Irfaan's favorite biscuits. Yet, as suggested by the different place at the dining table he is assigned, there remains a melancholic misalignment between the loss and its replacement.

Again, double vision confirms this misalignment. As Neelima sings a lullaby to Altaaf, whose sleep is rent by nightmares of the sound of gunfire and the sight of the masked man, Irfaan re-enters the very bedroom window through which he had fallen to his death. In a dream sequence, he plays with her, teases her, sings with her, but ultimately disappears through the same window. Before he disappears, he passes a cricket ball to the sleeping Altaaf who sits up in bed to catch it. This symbolic relay anticipates the importance of cricket as a familial and national bonding game.[10] Altaaf finally calls Inayat Khan *Baba* ("Daddy") while playing cricket and, in the film's concluding shot, a game of cricket between the Khans, Altaaf, and Sufi marks the "happily ever after." But as *Mission Kashmir* attempts to integrate Altaaf, the Kashmiri boy, into the family that, with the Muslim father, the Hindu mother, and the "good" Kashmiri Muslim girlfriend, mirrors an ideal vision of the secular nation,[11] its own representative mechanisms remind us that this is only a fantasy of integration. The closing image of the family at cricket is given to us in a crayon sketch, while a suffusing of backlight and heightening of color—a visual register recalling what has been called the "xeno-realism" of Indian Bazaar art[12]—keeps the lullaby dream-sequence and its own happy ending (the relay of the cricket ball) firmly in the realm of fantasy.

The grip of fantasy is reiterated in each song sequence of the film, which consistently uses xeno-realist chromatics to foreground its status as a crafted act of representation. The gap between representation and reality that thereby opens up is particularly marked in two songs that insert lines from Kashmiri lyrics within their own choruses, *Bhumbro* (O Bumblebee) and *Hrind Poshmal gindne drai lo lo* (O Intoxicated Ones, Poshmal, drunk [on spring], has come out to play).[13] Both are presented as studio creations, made for television by Sufi, a woman whose childhood dream of "organizing programs" has finally come true with her job in Doordrshan Srinagar.[14] *Bhumbro* is additionally the moment when Altaaf, returning to Srinagar after maturing as a militant across the Line of Control (LOC), encounters Sufi again. Having discovered via a television talk show, featuring Inayat Khan (now Inspector General of Police), that the host is his old playmate, Altaaf seeks her out in the Doordarshan studios. Stumbling into a performance of *Bhumbro* with Sufi at center stage, he is mistaken as one of the male dancers. Altaaf slides easily into this role, revealing his true self to Sufi during the performance. The lyrics reiterate the slippage between make-believe and truth. Pointing to the henna on her palms, Sufi sings, "All other colors are false, only the color of henna is the truth," a metacomment on the xeno-realist visuality of the set and lighting. The song sequence's ultrastaged nature exposes itself again in *Hrind Poshmal.*

As Altaaf and a troupe dance through a kitschy set depicting "Kashmir," singing of music's restoration of love, peace, and harmony, we see Sufi watching them on an editor's TV screen.

Highlighting the gap between the adult militant and the innocent boy, the songs also contrast the audience's knowledge of this gap with Sufi's innocence. We have seen what she has not: Altaaf's postcrackdown rescue, his postrescue realization of his foster father's identity; and his recruitment by Kohistani, the Afghan who fights in Kashmir on behalf of India's enemies. In *Hrind Poshmal,* scenes of Sufi's absorption in the television image knowingly alternate with scenes of Altaaf directing a terrorist strike against the Srinagar TV tower. As Inayat Khan and his officers rush to evacuate the Mughal Gardens in anticipation of the explosion, they disrupt a children's open-air painting competition. This reminder of the film's equation between artwork and innocence accentuates the split within Altaaf. The impossibility of closing the gap is figured in the song, *Sochon ki jheelon ka shahar ho* (imagine a city of lakes) that marks Sufi's rejection of Altaaf's new convictions. After a long look, cast by Altaaf at his framed sketch of the Lake, the song begins, initially returning to them playing by the houseboat deck just before the crackdown. Again, the colors shift to the lurid hues of Bazaar art, and the houseboat deck shades into a studio set even kitschier than that of *Hrind Poshmal.* Although Sufi and Altaaf attempt to reclaim their childhood in the setting of improbably orange sunsets and red Chinar trees, a closing refrain from *Bhumbro* sung by children dancing in simulated snow confirms the futility of fantasy.

Mission Kashmir's double vision thus clarifies the drive to fantasize as the flight from, as well as the masking of, reality, with the strategic overexaggeration of color drawing attention to representation as mask. Offsetting the nightmare of the mask, however, is the fantasy of the open window, the scene not only of the original loss of Irfaan but of his momentary return in the lullaby sequence to pass the cricket ball to Altaaf. The fantasies of Žižek's "transcendent other country" suggested by the window constantly alternate with nightmares of the mask that unmasks fantasy itself.[15] As Sufi sings to Altaaf during a shikara ride on the Lake after they have rediscovered each other, "This is a world of dreams/just try and see it through my eyes." But Altaaf's old nightmare interrupts her fantasy of love both visually and aurally. As images of the masked man and gagged boy crowd out the vistas of the Lake, a male chorus sings, "The dense smoke begins to clear; but look, the fog remains everywhere." The song's abrupt ending (a panoramic view of Srinagar and Altaaf's capitulation, "This is a world of dreams/I have seen it through your eyes") momentarily reconciles their different ways of seeing but exposes its fragility. The film thus admits its own stake in effecting this reconciliation, as if, with Altaaf's continuing inability to see with Sufi, the possibilities of an entire "world of dreams" are too unbearably held at ransom.

Love in Kashmir

It is no accident that Sufi's vision encompasses the view of the Dal Lake and the mountains as seen from a shikara. While fulfilling her promise to return Altaaf to the shikara of his childhood, this setting and perspective also establishes her as custodian of the Bollywood tradition that I call Love in Kashmir. Hers is a love song to Altaaf, and the rose that he takes from a shikara laden with blooms and offers her, a classic moment of Bollywood courtship—albeit one cut through by nightmares that threaten its reincorporation into another history. *Mission Kashmir* mobilizes its double vision into intertextually reminding its audience of a shared cinematic experience. In juxtaposing Altaaf's and Sufi's contrasting responses to the landscape of the Valley, moreover, the film also grapples with the violence and geopolitics that has converted, since 1989, that experience into a memory. The acknowledgment of that violence through the cinematic apparatus does not preclude its assimilation into a more amenable narrative; thus the film explicates Altaaf's desire for aazadi as his anger with Inayat Khan, which, once defused, reunites Indians and Kashmiris into one happy family. As we have noted, however, the closing crayon sketch undermines the happy ending, where Altaaf rejects militancy and joins the Khans with Sufi at his side. Love in Kashmir remains a construct, a fragile hope offsetting an underlying fear that Altaaf's is not an inability but a refusal to see with Sufi.

In Sufi's song in particular, then, we may locate *Mission Kashmir*'s debt to *and* reappraisal of Kashmir's privileged place within Bollywood. The lovers on the shikara in *Mission Kashmir* compress a long history of Bollywood's vision of the Valley as the "eroticized landscape of the mind in the social imaginary of Indians," whereby "as a place for honeymooners and lovers [it] was translated by the Bombay film into a symbol of purity and unspoiled nature."[16] The key figure here is the flamboyant actor Shammi Kapoor, who, together with a series of Indian Audrey Hepburns, made the 1960s the decade when "Kashmir, colour and bouffant hairstyles ruled the silver screen."[17] All depictions of shikaras in Bollywood can be traced back to the super-hit song, *Tareef karoon kya uski, jisne tumhe banaya* (what praise shall I shower on the one who created you), sung by Shammi Kapoor as Bombay Boy Rajiv to Sharmila Tagore, playing Champa, *Kashmir Ki Kali* (bud of Kashmir) in the 1963 film of that name. Rajiv, leaning, lurching and jerking on one shikara in the trademark Shammi Kapoor style, and Champa, shy and delicate, clad in ethnic Kashmiri dress, on another, with the camera shifting from aerial scenes of a choreographed "shikara ballet" on the Lake, to the mountains, and back to their faces—of such scenes is the very fabric of Bollywood nostalgia woven, and a very specific sixties ethos, combining excitement, modernity, youthfulness, and escape, still palpable.[18]

Preceding *Kashmir Ki Kali,* however, was a protracted yell, "Ya-hoo!," and a body-turned-projectile hurling down the snowy slopes of the Kashmir Valley. The body and the yell, which inaugurated in 1961 both Indian pop culture and its phanstasmatic relation with Kashmir, belonged to Shammi in his new avatar as "Indian Elvis of Filmistan."[19] The film in question, *Junglee* (The savage one; dir. Subodh Mukherji, 1961), captured together, for the first time and in color, the Kashmir Valley and the antics of a robust Shammi and a gamine Saira Bano. The glories of Eastmancolor provided a heightening filter for this new simultaneity of two different kinds of pleasures: the long-acknowledged beauty of the Kashmir Valley, a space where, in the words of Jawaharlal Nehru, "loveliness reigns and an enchantment steals over the senses,"[20] and the more contemporary excitements of hula hoops, waterskiing, rock-and-roll, and tennis whites. As that famous scene from *Junglee* still conveys, such youthful exuberance obtained spectacular expression through the topography of the Kashmir Valley, heightening the drama of its mountains, meadows, rushing brooks, rippling lakes and, above all, snow. This announcement of the Valley as the locus for novel modes of leisure and pleasure was thus intimately tied to the novelty of cinema in color. The formula was a resounding box-office success, and it was soon repeated in *Kashmir Ki Kali,* whose title cites a song sung by Saira Bano in *Junglee: Kashmir ki kali hoon main* (I am the bud of Kashmir).

Several similar "Kashmir films" followed in the first half of the decade, both with and without Shammi Kapoor in the male lead. Their highly patterned nature reminds us today of the pleasures and anxieties they solicited in order to bring forth a national audience through the affective use of the Valley's topography. Close-ups of snow, cascading water, and meadow flowers, and panoramic panned shots of mountain ranges and pine forests, worked with songs ranging from neotraditional *ghazal* (Urdu love song) to rock-and-roll to evoke an entire gamut of romance moods.

Through repetition across films, views of particular Valley locations came to signify different stages of courtship: the meadows of Gulmarg and Pahalgam, surrounded by looming mountains, emerged as settings for the declaration of love, while a shikara ride on the Dal Lake was consonant with the communication of reciprocity. But as the Valley becomes entangled in the production of "love," love itself becomes more than an emotion. By setting trends in clothes, hairstyles, and leisure-time activities, these films merged love with the creation of a cosmopolitan savoir-faire for an emergent middle class. Gone are the nationalist melodramas of the 1950s in high-voltage black and white:[21] as the medium changes to candyfloss color, the message moves to fun and romance in the Valley. By locating the transformation of an entire generation in Kashmir, cinema rendered it a pastoral space where the idea of a new Indian could materialize, and a new kind of youthful identity—the Indian equivalent of postwar baby-boomers—emerge.

This meaning of the Kashmir Valley was emphasized through two key narrative ingredients of classic pastoral drama:[22] escape and plot twists around multiple identities. The 1960s Kashmir films always involve the arrival of at least one protagonist to the Valley, along with his or her same-sex companions, from Bombay, Delhi, or Calcutta. This arrival is coded as escape from parental authority, which comic scenes adjudge as misplaced. Thus, in both *Junglee* and *Kashmir Ki Kali,* Shammi Kapoor plays a rich industrialist lad who escapes the clutches of an overauthoritarian mother via a holiday in Kashmir. As Rajiv, a.k.a. Shammi, motors along winding mountain roads in *Kashmir Ki Kali,* pausing to splash himself with water from a stream, lifting his face to the breeze, we recall how, in *Junglee*, the touch and feel of nature similarly predisposed the spirit of the plains dweller toward romance. Once in Kashmir, the protagonist, often in disguise, typically falls in love with an inhabitant of the Kashmir Valley, who is then inevitably revealed as being originally *not* from Kashmir. The films thus endlessly complicate basic boy-meets-girl plots: doublings and disguises, concealed and mistaken identities, missing children, changelings, substituted fathers, and overauthoritarian mothers. These convolutions, together with compulsive temporary escapes from the metropolis, authority, and convention, all in the name of falling in love, complexly implicate the Valley in the expression of a totalizing modern subjectivity centered in the cities of the plains.

A new postcolonial identity for urban Indians is thereby created through these films, with recurrent comic episodes around disguise and masquerade emphasizing the Valley's transformative potential for metropolitan youth. But this postcolonial playground, and its consequent role in destabilizing and reconstituting identity, is effective precisely because of its spatial disjunction from metropolitan India. The heterosexual couple that forms through the encounter of single-sex groups holidaying in the Valley must return to the city with their newly articulated subjectivities. The dialectic between city and Valley emphasizes this identity as comprising a cleaned-up version of industrial capitalism—an ideal marriage between Gandhian agrarian and Nehruvian socialist impulses.[23] While the city begins as bastion of capitalist greed and Westernization, the protagonist's removal to Kashmir exposes him or her to a premodern, paracapitalist "purity," which the new couple then carries back to reform the metropolis and the nation. These films thus articulate pastoral escape to Kashmir as a corollary to, rather than a critique of, metropolitan modernity. The Valley's potential to induce "falling in love" and its consequent ability to free young people from family obligations helps articulate a modern subjectivity through and in desire, where desire for the other is metonymic with desire for the landscape of otherness. While the Kashmiri as other ultimately turns out to be a reassuring version of the self (through the tropes of mistaken identity), the Kashmiri landscape where this recognition is managed remains the *unincorporated* space of transformation within the reconstituted modern imaginary.

These trends set by the 1960s Kashmir films evolved into a stock formula whereby the visual setting of the Kashmir Valley itself became a compressed signifier for heterosexual romance. Throughout the 1970s and 1980s, similar conjunctions of landscape, narrative, and holiday recurred within romantic song sequences in films—for instance, in *Bemisaal* (Incomparable; dir. Hrishikesh Mukherji, 1982) and *Bobby* (dir. Raj Kapoor, 1973). There is decreasing interest in conferring narrative rationale to the song sequence filmed in the Valley: the mere visual fact of finding oneself, with a beloved, in Kashmir, becomes its own justification. Whenever a film shifted its camera lens to the Valley, where its hero and heroine threw snowballs at each other, rode horses through the meadows, gazed into each others' eyes under the magnificent Himalayas, and sung amorous songs to each other in a shikara, the message was unambiguous: it was time to say "I love you" in English, time to be modern, cosmopolitan, and free. The 1960s Kashmir films bequeathed to the nation a new space for love, where desire itself was articulated through translation to Kashmir. The exuberant response of the protagonists and audience to the Valley's natural beauty, that superficially suggests a nation in love *with* Kashmir, is in the end a camouflage for the staging of love *in* Kashmir. As the games of mistaken identity reveal, moreover, Kashmiris never figure in this mise-en-scène as individuals in their own right. The postcolonial playground, itself a space disjunct from the nation, is sustained through their neocolonial erasure from the landscape of love.

Averting the Gaze

The wildly popular and still memorable 1960s Kashmir films touched a national chord in their use of the Valley to forge, through cinematic spectacle, a version of Benedict Anderson's "imagined community."[24] Not unexpectedly, the pastoral Kashmir they offered for the modern nation's cinematic consumption sharply diverged from the actual political situation then prevalent in Jammu and Kashmir. The period spanning the official birth of the Kashmir dispute in 1947 and the agreement between India and Pakistan to maintain the status quo of irresolution through the Tashkent Agreement and Simla Accord of 1972 was a volatile one for the region's status following the decolonization of British India. The seizing of the Valley's westward margins by Pakistan in 1948, and its new identity as Azad Kashmir, had rendered India's hold on Kashmir exceedingly vulnerable. This vulnerability, together with Nehru's promises of a plebiscite, the immeasurable political charisma of the first Kashmiri Prime Minister Sheikh Abdullah, and Kashmiri shock at his imprisonment by his own forces, at India's behest, in 1953, can be grasped only by shedding a presentist view of the Kashmir conflict as a frozen impasse. Jammu and Kashmir during the decade following these events then emerges as an altogether more unpredictable entity. This volatility was further exacerbated by the nascent condition of the overall federal structure of the Indian Union.

Electoral politics today bestows clarity on the ways in which federalism works as a mechanism for power sharing between regional and national interests in India, and as a bargaining tool for bringing regional cultural capital to the national table.[25] However, these now obvious aspects of the center-state relationship were in the process of evolution during the 1960s.[26] A window into this formative moment is offered by the Kashmir films, which cannot be disarticulated from intranational issues of power, representation and cultural belonging. They reflect both Nehru's re-organization, along linguistic lines, of the provincial divisions inherited from British rule, as well as the anxieties generated by contestations of that project. These newer contestations competed with the fissures along religious identity that not so long ago had caused the conflagrations of Partition. Thus opening views of New Delhi's India Gate, large maps of India showing India's new provincial divisions, comic subplots fuelled by the new mantra, "national integration," tasteless jokes featuring stereotypes of the South Indian, slapstick concerning Muslims and their alleged predilections—these emphases across the films ask to be read as symptoms of nationwide anxieties over language, religion and regionalism. Together with the films' preoccupations with lineage and authority, they remind us of the specific postcolonial shape being taken by the multiethnolingual, multireligious Indian Union even as neonormative groups within the nation attempted to formulate a balance of power between centrifugal and centripetal tendencies.

Of course, the biggest "problem" for national integration as the decade unfolded, whether to do with ethnicity, religion, federal structure, or national sovereignty, was Jammu and Kashmir itself. The 1960s cinematic performance of the Valley and its relationship with the rest of India is not merely evidence for, but itself an articulation of how, the politics of emergent federalism interacted with the major political events which arose from the uncertain status of Jammu and Kashmir in the 1960s. These events led to Jammu and Kashmir's full transformation by 1965, from an extremely problematic princely state of British India, into one of federal India's constituent units. This perspective lends immense saliency to the films' metanarrative of transformation and mistaken identity, and complicates their emphasis on mediating between tradition, whose repository is genealogy, and modernity, invested in the young individual. Their increasing obsession with displaced and misplaced Kashmiris echoes the controversies surrounding Jammu and Kashmir's special status, enshrined in Article 370 of the Indian Constitution, drawing attention particularly to the bar on land purchase in Jammu and Kashmir to those born outside its boundaries (as defined by India).[27] Through narrative and symptomatic repetitions, then, the films reveal how the overlapping of separate nation-building concerns—not only the gradual rearrangement of multiple collective identities and desires under the umbrella of an avowedly multiethnic, multireligious nation but also the relationship between India and Pakistan—had caught Jammu and Kashmir in an unenviable pincer-grip long before the 1980s.

Following his imprisonment in 1953, Sheikh Abdullah was replaced by a prime minister far more compliant with New Delhi's political plan for Jammu and Kashmir. As Kashmiri writer P. N. Bazaz remarked at the time, "[I]n almost every public utterance, Bakshi Ghulam Mohammed in season and out of season declared that Kashmir had finally and irrevocably decided to remain within India; the only problem facing the State was, in his opinion, to liberate that part of the country which was in the occupation of Pakistan."[28] But popular Kashmiri opinion hardly reflected "an increasing enchantment" with this prospect.[29] "With hindsight," remarks a recent commentator, "it is all too easy to recognize that the calm of the late 1950s and early 1960s was deceptive, and that the underlying causes of the Kashmir issue were effectively ignored, as opposed to resolved."[30] Reporting to Nehru on a visit to the Valley after a hiatus of fifteen years, Bazaz admitted in 1962 that, while "there is little doubt that Kashmir has, economically speaking, made an advance since 1947, the people are unhappy and restless."[31] Their restlessness culminated in massive popular demonstrations triggered by the disappearance, in 1963, of a sacred relic held at Srinagar's Hazrabal Mosque, a highly symbolic space for the expression of Kashmiri political identity.[32] This collective response, seemingly out of all proportion to the event, actually performed a crucial moment in the consolidation of Kashmiri self-identification as "a community-in-neglect."[33]

The uncertainty of life in a state cleft by a de facto international border, together with the unfulfilled promise of a plebiscite, cannot have made for a healthy collective psyche. There were other, worsening issues. In October 1963, the sycophantic reign of Bakshi Ghulam Mohammed ended, ringing in crucial symbolic changes concerning Jammu and Kashmir's relationship to in the Indian Union. As with all other states of India, Jammu and Kashmir would henceforth be headed by a governor and chief minister, rather than a head of state and prime minister. These and other changes emanating from Delhi, aimed at the eventual erosion of Article 370, resulted in "a demonstrable diminution of the faith which the people of Kashmir had pinned on India."[34] Nehru died on 27 May 1964, sealing the fate for talks with Sheikh Abdullah, still considered by Kashmiris as their legitimate leader. Sensing the confusions, Pakistan stepped up its claims on the region in the international arena, while, "by the beginning of 1965, the Indian attitude to Kashmir had hardened to a point which made compromise seem most unlikely."[35] In 1965, the second war over Kashmir was fought by India and Pakistan, and the Ceasefire Line, which was to be rechristened the LOC in 1972, consolidated. As the war came to a close with Russian, Cold-War–influenced intervention, it would seem that the region's fate was decided as one caught between two antagonistic nations.

The second Indo-Pak war made the political integration of Jammu and Kashmir into the Indian Union even more imperative for the Indian Union. Less might be said about the success of what Bazaz termed its "emotional integration."[36] As Sheikh Abdullah impassionedly pointed out even as India and Pakistan went to war, "The commitments made by both countries aside, the vital interests of the people of Jammu and Kashmir do not seem to have been heeded sufficiently. Indeed, over these long years, they have suffered incalculable harm and pain. The uncertainty to which they have been subjected has eaten into their very vitals, and until it is removed no progress in any sphere—administrative, political or otherwise—can be achieved."[37] This failure of emotional integration must be borne in mind when reviewing the Valley's cinematic performance during a vulnerable pause following post-Independence euphoria. Between 1961 and 1965, the disjunction between the cinematic and the "real" Kashmir became increasingly glaring. While these films of the early 1960s used the Valley as a space where the individuated, modern, Indian subject emerged while grappling with the ideological demands of the nation-state, this was the very moment that Jammu and Kashmir was undergoing a most traumatic encounter with those same demands.

Did the 1960s Kashmir films deliberately ignore the politics of the Valley while promoting its pleasures? I would rather see those pleasures as compromised by politics from their inception. The films' celebratory self-fashioning of a new Indian modernity made it impossible for them to openly acknowledge their libidinal economies. There are, however, indirect traces: the increasingly over-wrought narratives, specular splittings and doublings, and improbable endings offer symptomatic responses to the mounting pressure of political events in the Kashmir Valley. The films' heavy recourse to masquerade and disguise itself becomes a disguised acknowledgment of this disjunction, and of their own role in masking the truth about Jammu and Kashmir. Their disarming innocence is the imprint of two levels of fantasy: that the Kashmir Valley was a pastoral space emptied of popular unrest or political aspirations; and that this fantasy of Kashmir, being disseminated through and enjoyed by Indian audiences, was itself reality. As the protagonist of *Aarzoo* (Desire; dir. Ramanand Sagar, 1965) warns his sister while revealing to her the loss of his leg in an accident in Kashmir: "[Y]ou will not be able to face the truth." Heeding its own warning, the camera averts its gaze from his exposed stump—shielding its audience from truths that remain ultimately unspoken. When Bollywood returned to Love in Kashmir in the clearly troubled 1990s, these masks of desire continued to shape collective memory about the supposed tranquility of 1960s Kashmir.

The Rose-Tainted Lens

In 1994, a new Kashmir film for changed times appeared: *Roja* (The rose), directed by Tamil filmmaker Mani Ratnam. Its portrayal of a South Indian middle-class couple caught in Kashmiri separatism offered "a double allusion—allusion to loss, evoking previous Hindi films set in Kashmir (the industry now being deprived of a locale that could be used in any film to create instant magic); and indicating to the middle-class tourists from other parts of India that they can no longer visit Kashmir, a place of ravishing natural beauty—as the camera insistently points out—that should be rightfully 'ours' but has now been made inaccessible by the activity of anti-nationals."[38] The eponymous Roja, a small-town innocent, finds herself alone in strife-torn Kashmir, her husband Rishi, a cryptographer with the Indian army, kidnapped by militants. Evoking then-recent memories of the kidnapping of the Indian Home Minister's daughter by the JKLF, the film depicts Roja's triumph over bureaucracy and militancy in her eventual rescue of Rishi. Lacing this feel-good narrative is a heady obeisance to the dominant values of 1990s India: resurgent Hindu nationalism and a glitzy, post-liberalization consumerism. Fittingly, its catchy soundtrack circulated through the new private television channels, bringing the film nationwide attention. This unexpected, pan-Indian success laid bare the collusion between "the secret politics of our desires" and *Roja*'s flamboyant connection of Hindutva-style public culture to an inherited imagining of Kashmir.[39]

Through *Roja* and the intellectual debate it provoked, violence and geopolitics finally intervened within Kashmir's cinematic performance.[40] But critics and apologists alike failed to note the film's melancholic undercurrent. Political violence had made filming in the Valley impossible, and Mani Ratnam simulated its topography by turning to the adjoining Himalayan foothills. While the snow-capped mountains and pine trees were convincing enough, the absence of the signature lake and shikara reveals a central lack that disfigures the entire narrative. Roja and Rishi convert their arranged marriage into "modern love" while he is posted to Kashmir immediately after their wedding, but it is Kashmir, too, that interrupts their domestic bliss. The cryptographer's assignment can double as a honeymoon destination only by dint of a cinematic memory of Love in Kashmir; but the reality of 1990s Kashmir insists on an altered narrative of danger and desire. A new Kashmiri character appears: the terrorist, whose ability to solicit from an audience an ambivalent fascination is dissipated by splitting him into "good" and "bad" versions. Thus, the terrorist Liaqat Khan is redeemed as he lets Rishi go, but his compatriot Wasim Khan remains a threat to the nation and the narrative. Like his dumb-mute sister's silence, his final cry, "We shall have our aazadi," releases an excess that escapes closure. Rendered however subservient to the need for Rishi's and Roja's happy ending, the film's terrorists nevertheless signify that something has changed forever in the Indian fantasy of Kashmir.

Roja's return to this fantasy is thus a masked realization of the impossibility of return. A contemporaneous response to the violence in Jammu and Kashmir, it also marks cinema's attempt to reclaim what was in the process of being lost to the national imaginary through Kashmiri rejection of the nation. Additionally significant is that cinema's renewed interest in Kashmir was catalyzed by a product of a regional film industry, whose competition with Bollywood parallels political contestations between Northern and Southern India.[41] Mani Ratnam's successful penetration of the national market with *Roja*—a first for a Tamil film—points not only to his timely capture of an older territory of desire hitherto dominated by Bollywood; it also revives the power of this cinematic Kashmir to forge a national identity. In staking a claim to a region geographically distant from Tamil Nadu, and through mutual incorporation of the South Indian subject and the current political conflict, *Roja* mines the cinematic legacy of a pastoral Kashmir that perpetuates the Indian modern. Suspended between fact and fantasy, Kashmir enables the maturation both of provincial girl into modern Indian woman, and of marital desire. The film's strong investment in the metonymy of couple and nation is founded on its struggle to appropriate Kashmiri anger and exonerate State brutality. *Roja* invited audiences across India to participate in overt collective fantasy as well as covert collective trauma.

As in the 1960s, popular cinema monitored and articulated national feeling through turning to Kashmir, but the stakes were now immeasurably higher. While the 1960s films averted their gaze from the political complications in Jammu and Kashmir, the "cinepatriotism" triggered by *Roja* returned obsessively to them.[42] *Junglee* and its successors had exemplified how Bollywood's indispensable role in forging the imagined community of the nation was always already sustained at the cost of real communities. *Roja* and its successors continue to play out—albeit through varying degrees of self-consciousness—this complex relationship between political and cultural forms of representation in a less innocent age. The new concatenations of "pleasure and the nation,"[43] so charmingly enacted through the hula hoops, tennis whites, and motor cars of the 1960s, may now appear dated, but the price paid for the modern Indian created thereby has reappeared in the guns that accompany the roses of the post-1989 Kashmir film. Read against the grain, *Roja*'s affirmative politics reveal cinema's inability to tear itself away from the impact of aazadi, made even more potent through its pairing with another lethal word, jihad. As films after *Roja* confirm, the Kashmiri who wants aazadi in the name of jihad is repackaged as the Kashmiri whose otherness has transformed into a dangerous, *Muslim* alterity. This figure becomes a focus of desire cathected from the ravaged landscape, but only in narrative modes where closure and gender politics can rehabilitate him within the nation's metanarrative, *and* evacuate him from the nation's space of fantasy.

It is an awareness of this inescapable politics of representation that colors the double vision of *Mission Kashmir*—what we may now term its "rose-tainted lens." *Mission Kashmir*'s problems with seeing emerge intrinsically related to its cinematic metamemory. The rose that Altaaf, momentarily succumbing to Sufi's plea for love in Kashmir, presents to her alludes to both the 1960s *Kashmir Ki Kalis* and Mani Ratnam's *Roja*. But the thorn that pricks Sufi's thumb passes silent commentary on those earlier films. The all-too-real rose contrasts with its plastic counterpart depicted in the 1965 superhit, *Jab Jab Phool Khile* (Whenever flowers may bloom; dir. Suraj Prakash). That plastic rose was clutched by a doll, a miniature version of the protagonist Raja, a "simple" Kashmiri houseboat owner. Raja presents this doll as souvenir to Rita, a "modern" Bombay woman holidaying on his houseboat.[44] Even as the diminutive doll exposes the disturbing power relations set up between the unsophisticated Kashmiri man and the metropolitan Indian woman, its rose links those relations to the fetish's work of endless substitution. The plastic rose stands in for the real rose, which stands in for the gardens of the paradise on earth, which stands for the nation's collective desire. The same chain of substitutions reified by its plastic-ness is demystified, forty years later, by *Mission Kashmir*'s thorny rose: a counterfetish that tries to reinstate the Kashmiri within the landscape of desire.[45]

The Oedipal struggle between Altaaf and his good and bad father figures (Khan and Kohistani) replicates *Mission Kashmir*'s own "anxiety of influence" as it struggles to diverge from its cinematic predecessors. This struggle overwhelms the attempts by its makers—director Vidhu Vinod Chopra, scriptwriter Vikram Chandra, and actors Hrithik Roshan, Sanjay Dutt, and Preity Zinta—to portray sympathetically the traumatized Kashmiri. The scarring of Altaaf competes with the scarred landscape, so that the film's overriding trauma emerges as the nation's feared loss of its territory of desire, the idyllic Kashmir of 1960s Bollywood. Also the prime mover in *Roja*, this fear reappears in another recent Kashmir film, . . . *Yahaan* (. . . Here; dir. Shoojit Sircar, 2004), which details the romance between Aman, an Indian army officer in Srinagar and Ada, a Kashmiri girl. . . . *Yahaan* blatantly interprets the Kashmir conflict as an impediment to modernity (conceived of in overwhelmingly consumerist terms) and romance: the first song shows Ada longing, in the same breath, for love and blue jeans. When Aman, stationed in an army bunker below Ada's bedroom window, remarks, "[C]an't believe that Shammi Kapoor once used to dance here," Ada's eavesdropping younger sibling asks, "[W]ho is this Shammi Kapoor and why did he once dance here?" Amnesia about Kashmir's cinematic past, the film suggests, is the cause of Kashmiri disaffection; the savior is the Indian hero who protects the Kashmiris, romances the Kashmiri heroine, and revives, with her, a submerged memory of Love in Kashmir.

In. . . *Yahaan*, as with *Roja*, conflict is explicated by two cinematic conventions: the workings of the romance plot, and the need for romance. Simultaneously, celebration of the new Indian media deflects attention from the cinematic camera to the camera of reportage. As critics have noted, the conspicuous consumption that, through economic liberalization and the advertising industry, has gone hand-in-glove with media expansion, furnishes *Roja*'s deepest allegiances and pleasures. . . . *Yahaan*, directed by a maker of ad films, goes a step further: here, redemption comes through a private news channel that enables Ada to declare her love for Aman on live television, facilitate the army's victory over militants, and chastize the Valley for "forgetting how to love." *Mission Kashmir* ostensibly shares this vision of the camera as barometer of national feeling: Sufi, we remember, works for national television, while Altaaf targets the nation through the TV tower. But *Mission Kashmir*'s song sequences—those essential components of Bollywood's desiring machines—double as pieces Sufi choreographs for television. By thus collapsing film and television (and thus prescient of Qazi's success in Fame Gurukul), and through its characters' comments on the camera's power (witness this chapter's second epigraph), the film acknowledges its limitations as an instrument of critique. The compromised rose-tainted lens is the truth that swirls around *Mission Kashmir*'s fixation with the black balaclava. While *Roja* was driven by the cryptographic imperative to crack the code, *Mission Kashmir* insists that the mask is the reality that needs to be deciphered.

My Burnt-Out Love

Mani Ratnam's choice of a cryptographer for protagonist may well have been inadvertent, but it resonates suggestively with what revisionist psychoanalysts Nicholas Abraham and Maria Torok have termed "cryptonymy."[46] Following Abraham and Torok, we may read Rishi's cryptographic mission as voicing a response not merely to the needs of national security, but to the trauma of the threat to security. The Kashmiri who resists the nation's desire for Kashmir then emerges as a version of Abraham and Torok's "phantom." Popular cinema presents him as the residue that, refusing assimilation, is uncomfortably and forcibly incorporated within the nation's body—the kind of embrace that, as Mani Ratnam would later admit through an infinitely more radical film about separatism and the nation, is ultimately deadly.[47] This reading retrieves from *Roja* that submerged streak of melancholia I have earlier claimed for it. Nevertheless, and despite the consequent interlocking of Kashmiri and Indian traumas, this melancholia remains in the film a wholly Indian affliction, in keeping with its lack of "critical edge."[48] In comparison, *Mission Kashmir*'s insistence that the mask is the meaning, and that meaning is trauma, enables it to approach a level of "critical melancholia." Yet it too cannot break through its representational codes to privilege a Kashmiri viewpoint. The balaclava, as material trace of trauma, circulates back and forth between Inayat Khan and Altaaf, but it blocks access to any underlying reality. Can a camera wielded by a Kashmiri, and a film that eschews Bollywood's pyrotechnics for documentary's purported sobriety, reveal anything different?

Popular cinema's continuing inability to leave behind its self-referential fantasy of Love in Kashmir may now be contrasted to a Kashmiri filmmaker's perspective. "My love is burnt out," flatly declares the narrator of the documentary film *Paradise on a River of Hell*. The voice is that of one of its two directors, Abir Bazaz, who by the time of its making, had left Srinagar's "wretched desolation" to study mass communications at Jamia Millia Islamia, a Delhi university.[49] One of the many young Kashmiris who arrived in Delhi during the worst years of conflict, Bazaz exemplifies their status, described in the introduction, as co-opted Indian citizens. Like the poem by Agha Shahid Ali that opens that chapter, it sees "Kashmir from New Delhi" through immense imaginative work, by "willing to glass" the mountains that separate the exile from Kashmir.[50] This constricted subject-position can, however, also free—as the film (like the poem) testifies through its making and circulation. A collaboration between a Kashmiri and an Indian student, commissioned by and broadcast on national television, winner of awards at South Asian film festivals, and screened repeatedly in India and abroad, "Paradise on a River of Hell" brings to wider view a deeply personal, Kashmiri attempt to re-enter the trauma that shaped an entire generation's adolescence.[51] Like *Mission Kashmir,* it repeatedly turns to images of windows and apertures, but what is retrieved and framed thereby is a very different memorialization of the 1990s.

Unlike some postmodern attempts at memorializing trauma, this film is not formally fractured.[52] Rather, its collage-like juxtaposition of scenes—of Srinagar's rubble, empty streets and deserted houses, and, radiating outward from Srinagar, of pine forests, ancient ruins, Sufi shrines, and villages as sites of contemporary atrocity—convey a painful lyricism that echoes in the soundtrack's Kashmiri Sufi and folk music. This striving toward wholeness embodies a desire to excavate aspects of the 1990s in danger of being forgotten: the euphoria of the movement for aazadi, and the brutal retaliation by the Indian State. But, particularly through the English-speaking narrator, the film also records the disillusionment Kashmiris experienced as the movement lost momentum through a lack of ideological cohesion, and their bewilderment as prized aspects of their culture fell apart under pressure of events. It thus mounts a critique internal to Jammu and Kashmir, seeking solutions not for a rapprochement of Kashmir and India but for the internal healing of Kashmiri society. "I must learn to speak for myself, in Kashmiri," says Bazaz in an earlier film of his, *Kun'ear*—which explores discourses around the Kashmiri language—"that is aazadi."[53] This sentiment elucidates the wider purpose of *Paradise on A River of Hell*. Speaking for oneself in Kashmiri becomes a metaphor for presenting, through the language of cinema (albeit, ironically, glossed in English) an alternative, Kashmiri understanding of the 1990s, that implies in turn alternative commemorations, alternative definitions, and alternative genealogies for that decade.

Paradise on A River of Hell thereby gains an intertextuality very different from that seen in Bollywood's Kashmir films. The account of Kashmir by Walter Lawrence, first British Settlement Officer in the state of Jammu and Kashmir, yields a reference to Kashmiri Hopscotch, "one of whose squares is hell," that connects with the film's title, itself a line borrowed from Agha Shahid Ali's poem "Farewell."[54] Such echoes reinsert Ali, English-language poet fêted in America, into a specifically Kashmiri "horizon of expectations," formed here by a continuing, widely diffused, and often intimate familiarity with early European commentators on Kashmir.[55] Similarly, just before the camera pans Bijbehara—"an ancient seat of Sanskrit learning," the narrator tells us, but "now the name of a massacre"—a Sanskrit *shloka* (sacred verse) sounds a warning: "Listen, O King—the deer you chase is the deer from the cloister—don't kill her, don't kill her." Explicated through subtitles, this warning is appropriate to both statist and anti-State actors in the Kashmir conflict and, like the narrator's careful phrasing, eschews blame mongering for a powerful contrast between Kashmir's cultural past and its devastated present. Medieval Kashmiri Sufi poets—Lal Ded, Habba Khatoon, and Noor-ud-Din—are likewise quoted, not to pander to liberal Indian sensibilities concerning "good Islam," but to offer understated commentary on the intimate connection between violence and desire, and to urge for a philosophy of forbearance and renunciation tinged with messianic hope.

This strategy is best demonstrated by the film's closing image of Tsrar-e-Sharif, the Sufi shrine of Noor-ud-Din. On 11 March 1995, the shrine's fragile wooden structure, including its delicate decorative fretwork, was totally gutted in a confrontation between militants hiding inside and Indian security forces outside.[56] For Kashmiris, Hindus, and Muslims alike, this destruction of Tsrar has served as an apocalyptic portent of the end of that intricate system of intrasocietal checks and balances that can be summed up as "kashmiriyat." Yet, as Ali imagines Sheikh Noor-ud-Din reminding him, "On the pyre the phoenix is dear to destiny."[57] Stitching this quote from Shahid to a verse by Lal Ded, while visually foregrounding a potter at his wheel in front of the restored shrine, Bazaz retrieves out of catastrophe a call for the restoration of morality:

> That Lalla of Padmapora drank divine nectar
> Face to face with Shiva
> O Lord, bestow on me the same grace.

> My spirited guru renounced the world in true recognition
> The way the pupil outshone the master
> O Lord, bestow on me the same grace.

By opening and closing his film with references to his grandmother, following whose footsteps the narrator approaches Tsrar, Bazaz further revivifies a notional kashmiriyat by grounding its traditional signifiers in the sites, emotions and experiences of 1990s Kashmir. As "alienation" is redefined as "learning to think through pain," kashmiriyat, too, re-emerges as the need to reassess what it has meant to inhabit, through the centuries, this territory of desire.

For Bazaz, such inhabiting implied civil coexistence between the different religious groups of Kashmir. Images of deserted Rainawari, the old Srinagar hub of Pandit life, stand as mute witnesses to a changed present, as does the Gurdwara at Chittisinghpora, a predominantly Sikh village whose inhabitants were almost completely wiped out by unidentified assailants on 21 March 2006.[58] Again, more eloquent than any verbal explanation is the visual emphasis on the brilliant blues and greens that frame the Gurdwara. This emphasis also appears as the camera lingers over a deserted Hindu temple on the banks of the river Jhelum in Rainawari. The focus on the urban conurbation along the Jhelum rather than the Dal Lake solicits a viewerly response very different from Bollywood's trademark panoramic view of Kashmir's mountains and water features. The sacred site reinstated in its immediate natural surroundings offers a truth alternative to the fluttering, fragmentary newspaper headline, declaring "the truth about Chittisinghpora," that the camera briefly focuses on as the Gurdwara gates slowly close. The image of a silhouetted Sikh boy framed by these gates blends into that of a Sufi shrine full of supplicating Muslim women, suggesting the filmmaker's need to affirm a sense of continuing spiritual holism that fights the version of truth proclaimed by the newspaper.

Yet, this holism, suggested by the visual seamlessness and its contrast with the artfully placed newspaper fragment, is ultimately simulated by the camera and editing technique. If, as the narrator says, again quoting Shahid, "there is in Kashmir a longing for the blessed word to come from Tsrar-e-sharif,"[59] this longing is realized through the work of film. The mask of representation reappears, its ubiquity only heightened by Bazaz's vigilance. As the narrator approaches the village infamous for the mass rape of its womenfolk by Indian security forces in 1990, he admits, "I can't summon the courage to go to Kunanposhpora, so the village is passed by."[60]

Peering gingerly through the camera, uncertain about invading the site of trauma while trying to retrieve it for Kashmiri collective identity, the void Bazaz leaves is ultimately defined by the camera's abstinence. As the camera proffers swirling color images of Kashmir's ancient Hindu temples, the narrator remembers his first encounter with those sites through yet another camera: "I can never forget a madman I had seen on TV haunt these ruins. Madness lurks somewhere in these shadows—the saffron link to my past."[61] Another, monochrome link to more recent pasts is offered by a close-up shot of black-and-white photographs placed under the Jhelum's waters. Through the wavering optics we discern images of mass demonstrations and raised fists. These barely identifiable remnants of the turbulent 1990s, deliberately obfuscated by submergence in the river, suggest that Bazaz's attempted reinsertion of the Kashmiri into the landscape is tied to memory work that cannot be disentangled from its production and perpetuation by the camera.

It is the photograph that provides further clues as to why the Kashmir Valley, in particular, offered its landscape as the nation's territory of desire. The obsessions that "lurk somewhere in the shadows" of Bazaz's film speak back to, but also share, the melancholia that lurks in the shadows of popular cinema's celebration, through the Valley, of modernity, postcoloniality, and the necessity of the nation. The submerged but still visible photographs of Bazaz's film reveal to us the roots of this melancholia by reminding us that photography, which seeks to pin down and fix its subject, also records the infinite fragility of the moment. Bazaz's insertion of the photographs within his film exposes to view the competition and collaboration between cinema, the moving image, and its still counterpart, the photograph, cinema's progenitor and companion in modernity. While cinema, it has been argued, is better equipped to reveal the play of fetishism, then the photograph, with its connotations of death, loss and desire, and its physical portability, is the fetish *par excellence*.[62] In the next chapter, such theorizations of the photograph will help us understand the work of the first photographers in Jammu and Kashmir as initiating the relationship between modernity, framing and desire that still marks the Valley as a represented space, as well as recent Kashmiri uses of the photograph that grapple with this complex and contradictory legacy.

Two

Framing Fantasy

Kashmir shrinks into my mailbox,
My home a neat four by six inches.
I always loved neatness. Now I hold
The half-inch Himalayas in my hand.

—Agha Shahid Ali, "Postcard from Kashmir," 1987

I hope presently to extend my travels to Kashmir, where,
according to Tom Moore,
If there be an Elysium on earth
It is this! It is this!
and where I hope to find and produce pictures which
I shall not be ashamed to send to England.

—Samuel Bourne,
"Photography in the East," 1863

"Speak, Shafika," prompts an off-camera voice. And Shafika, a young and very pretty Kashmiri woman, begins her story: how her husband Muhammad ("Hammeh"), an auto-rickshaw driver, was arrested on 22 October 2000; how she and her children keep waiting for his return; how she has no idea whether he is dead or alive. For Hammeh is one of Jammu and Kashmir's "disappeared," and Shafika, one of the countless Kashmiri "half-widows" who dwell in a limbo defined by emotional turmoil, the Indian State, and Shariat law.[1] As Shafika speaks in Kashmiri-accented Urdu to the makers of *Waiting* (dir. Shabnam Ara and

Atul Gupta, Delhi Bioscope, 2005), a documentary film on disappeared Kashmiris, the camera flits between her face and a small color snapshot of the couple in happier times, smiling at another camera, her arm lightly placed on his. "I waited and waited," says Shafika, while our gaze moves to a clock on the wall and rests on soldiers seen through an auto-rickshaw's rearview mirror on the boulevard fringing the Dal Lake. One of their children speaks about the father's arrest; another displays a leaflet about the disappeared produced by the Kashmiri organization and resource center, The Association of Parents of Disappeared People (APDP).[2] We return to the photo of Shafika and husband; it dissolves into an identikit image, that itself becomes transposed on to a poster for the APDP. Simultaneously, we hear the then director of APDP, Parvez Imroz, explaining, in English: "Every [army] camp is a detention centre. They detain them, they interrogate them, they torture them, then they make them disappeared." In the course of the film, photographs of disappeared Kashmiris, including images of photographs reproduced on the front pages of local newspapers, recur.

The complex layering of media in *Waiting* elaborates on the previous chapter's concluding emphasis on "the diegetic interpolation of still photographs in narrative films," particularly when, as Catherine Grant comments in the contexts of similar interpolation in films on the Argentinian disappeared, "both the photographs and the films are especially loaded with political and emotional significance."[3] The disappeared Kashmiri speaks both for political uncertainty and the erasure of Kashmiris from popular cinematic representations of the Valley. Do these "still moving images," to use Grant's phrase for photographs inserted into documentary films, succeed in reinstating Kashmiri subjects into the narratives and the territory from which they have been erased? Or does their emphasis on multiplicity and excess fall equal prey to the photograph's "work as a fetish" and cinema as "an extraordinary activator of fetishism?"[4] The photographs in *Waiting* oscillate endlessly between an attempted re-subjectification of Kashmiris, and their inadvertent objectification as they become "hauntingly re-reified."[5] Yet the thin line they tread also interrupts and traverses the fantasy of the territory of desire. They demand that we re-engage with a history whose broad contours are outlined by my epigraphs: the history of the camera in Kashmir. The turbulent 1990s have necessitated an aesthetic and political shift from the quiet voicing, in "Postcard from Kashmir,"[6] of landscape photography's pervasive ironies, to the more radical superimposition of the body's traces on the landscape, as seen in documentary films such as

Waiting and *Paradise on a River of Hell*. This shift notwithstanding, Ali's wry acknowledgement of the photograph's shrinkage of the grandest of landscapes remains a poignant commentary on the excitement, expectation and sense of adventure attendant on early photography in Kashmir.

This chapter examines the work of Kashmir's first photographers, Samuel Bourne and John Burke, including Bourne's celebrated narrative dispatches from the Himalayas to the nascent *British Journal of Photography*.[7] I argue that theirs were the original frames of fantasy, when the rumor of Kashmir was verified and transformed by the camera as the touchstone of modernity. As the above epigraph from Bourne attests, Kashmir, designated by the Mughals as "Elysium on earth" had already entered the European imagination through *Lalla Rookh,* Thomas Moore's "Oriental Romance."[8] Photography translated this idyllic depiction of Kashmir from a verbal to a visual domain, thereby insuring its further dissemination; but it also inaugurated, through the photographer's relationship to Kashmir, a completely new mode of collective self-fashioning. As indicated by the commercial circulation of these early photographs and their compilation into handsome albums still extant in private and national archives, this self-fashioning was shaped by consumerism as much as adventure. The entanglement of photography with the imperatives of commerce, nostalgia, and colonial control produced the imperial prototype of the Valley as a transformative space. In the early twentieth century, photography in Kashmir was gradually domesticated through growing tourism on the one hand, and the Dogra-British political relationship on the other. This is the legacy that, in the 1960s, the decolonized nation refashions into the postcolonial playground of cinema. It is also a legacy of fantasy that, read now against an alternative, hidden history of the camera in post-1989 Kashmir, calls for its own ethical reframing.

A Strange, Confined Space

An innocuous-looking pink plastic box rests in the office of Majlis, a Bombay-based NGO interested in civil society issues.[9] The kind one might use to pack lunch, it is stuffed with small photographs, mostly black and white snapshots. A Kashmiri photographer had taken them for local newspapers during the 1990s. Seemingly wishing to remove their material presence from his current life, he handed them over to Majlis workers, visiting Srinagar in 2004, who have kept them in their Bombay premises ever since.[10] These photographs now spill out of their plastic container across the low glass table in Majlis's front room, where I sit with my laptop. There are images here of massive demonstrations, shuttered streets with furtive policemen in the corner of the frame, women with children, resistance leaders addressing crowds of tens of thousands. There are blood-splattered bodies lying on the street, being poked with rifle butts. Uniformed officers round up men while women sit in a huddle. A corpse sprawls across a deserted street with his head in the gutter while uniformed men look away. Another body lies on the snow, surrounded by a *kangri,* a blanket, and three *pheran*-clad men who crouch, looking up at the camera.[11] I cannot read their expressions. Neither can I read the captions, in *nastaliq* script, that are scrawled on the back of some of these photographs. I cannot even make out whether they are written in Kashmiri or Urdu—though they inform me at Majlis that it is the latter.

Maljis has got native speakers of Urdu and, latterly, of Koshur (Kashmiri), to translate the captions. But even when this project is completed, the photographs will remain "silent rectangles of paper," compressing, into their "strange and confined space,"[12] an inwardness of conflict that is compressed further into the strange confinement of the pink plastic box. The resistance to interpretation signaled by this extreme lamination is exemplified by some of the photographs being stuck back to back with glue. Access to any possible caption behind the image is blocked, and, instead, new palimpsests created: on one side, a bandaged man and child lying in shabby domestic surroundings, on another, a woman contemplating a home reduced to rubble; two overturned scooters, one rider (in a checked shirt) sprawled on the road, blood flowing from his head, stuck to the snapshot of a young bearded man (open-necked white shirt, camouflage jacket), almost smiling, in his eyes perhaps a quizzical hope. Another pair: the silent screams of mourning women, juxtaposed against a half-mocking youth looking at the camera, while a police officer with cocked rifle looks in another direction, avoiding the camera's gaze. The multiplicity of looks, conjoined with the mobilized emotion of women mourning an unknown dead person, proclaims a complex status generated by photography's relationship to the moment it seeks to record. This relationship has been thoroughly theorized in terms of witnessing, memorial work, and loss;[13] yet the cryptic character of these images visibly challenges the academic task of unlocking their meaning.

But isn't it precisely this untranslatable quality, this liminal position between opacity and transparency that analysis must grapple with? To use Kaja Silverman's apt phrase, these photographs are the "threshold of the visible world."[14] So psychologically pressing were they that the person who took them was ultimately compelled to exorcise their traces. Rather than destroy them, however, he took the opportunity to hand them over to Majlis. Through their transfer, the photographs became more than an indexical record of the situation within Kashmir from the 1990s onward. Rather than merely attest the loss of moments past, they now constitute a peculiar gain. A mobile site of memory, they do different kinds of memory work in different spaces. For the Kashmiri, they had signaled the unbearable weight of remembering; in Majlis, they offered the means to remember anew. The Majlis representatives had traveled to Srinagar as part of a broader project: the creation of *Godaam* (Urdu: warehouse),[15] an archive of predominantly visual material relating to the Kashmir conflict—documentary films, television footage, and press photographs from Kashmir, photographs or videos of family holidays in Kashmir. Through Godaam—for instance, through public workshops structured around its growing material—Majlis had hoped to nurture within civil society a politically responsible awareness of the history of the Kashmir issue. Their anticipated work took unexpected new direction, however, when physically touched by the photographs taken by a Kashmiri for local consumption. This tangibility points to the photograph as material survivor, whose uncanny persistence overshadows Godaam's practical utility as a repository of collective memory.

Most obviously, copyright issues surrounding the reproduction of these photographs remain murky, so that as of now, academic references to them (such as my own here) must remain ekphrastic.[16] To view these photographs, one has to travel to Bombay, seek an appointment with Majlis, take them out of their humdrum container, and stuff them back in after seeing them in a busy room where people conduct the daily business of an Indian NGO. Alternatively, one can travel, as I also did, to Srinagar in search of other such photographs. The story of that journey will enable me, later in this chapter, to theorize further the relationship between the photograph and value. For the moment, I should merely like to emphasize the ironic similarities between the pink plastic box and the carefully, almost religiously guarded albums and boxes of early photographs of Kashmir in national and private archives across the world. While occupying opposite ends of the value spectrum, they nevertheless both demand from would-be viewers awareness of their existence and the willingness, if not ability, to go *to* them to experience their materiality. There is an esoteric quality to both kinds of Kashmir photographs, but those in the pink plastic box are hyperesoteric, gaining their inaccessibility from being the flotsam of History. They cannot be known directly from circulation through mechanical reproduction; they are deemed fit for neither coffee-table books nor national collections; they do not belong to any canonized photographic lineage. Their contingent transfer from a Srinagar photographer's *godaam* to an alternative metropolitan "archive" valorized by the adoption of that same vernacular term confirms, albeit while entangling, the discrepant and unequal public spheres within the nation that I discussed in the Introduction.

In the case of Kashmir, this discrepancy must be aligned above all to discrepant understandings of the same territory, shaped by the power of certain kinds of visual representations. Godaam is meant to be an alternative archive: but alternative to what exactly? Once again, the flower-laden shikara on the Dal Lake, a clichéd signifier of the Valley, offers us a clue. We have examined the cinematic history of this image in chapter 1. Some version of it adorns the covers of countless books on Kashmir.[17] In the pink plastic box, however, I came across a different kind of shikara photograph. This is a black-and-white snapshot of a shikara with "River Police" stamped on its side, bearing three watchful, conspicuously armed policemen against a blurred backdrop of houseboats. It reminded me of a fish-eye view, in color, of a similar River Police shikara, reproduced in a photo-essay in the magazine *Gallerie*'s special issue on Kashmir.[18] That same photograph was framed and hung on a white wall as part of the art exhibition on Kashmir, curated by *Gallerie*'s editor, discussed in my Introduction.[19] Like its companion photographs in the photo-essay and the exhibition, it highlighted Kashmir's natural beauty through color and composition while seeking to undercut it through an overt reference to political conflict. Any radical commentary hoped for by this contrast of expectations was, however, forestalled by the high quality magazine and the immaculate exhibition space. Such privileged framing conditions cement rather than rupture the photographs' position within a discourse of aesthetic value that has accrued around images of the Valley's topography—an issue I shall return to at the close of this chapter.

As I have been arguing, furthermore, this discourse is intimately linked to the generation of desire through the self-fashioning of a modern Indian self. In an account of photography and modernity in India, Christopher Pinney describes a small town studio in Nagda in Central India that offers various fantasy backdrops for its customers to pose against. These include hybrid, over-painted vistas of English-style country houses in tropical surroundings, each vista separated from the one immediately behind it by means of a curtain. Beyond the final curtain lies, in Pinney's words, "the pièce de résistance in this chamber of dreams[:] the great expanse of the Dal Lake in Kashmir . . . shimmering beneath cascading pine-encrusted mountains, illuminated by efflorescent skies, and all offset by a foreground luxuriating in multicolored meadow flowers, a perennial location of dance sequences in Hindi movies."[20] In the previous chapter, I have elaborated on the connections between such dance sequences, modernity, and desire; we can now push forward these conclusions to the consideration of the work of photography. Most significant in this context is Pinney's color plate of an inhabitant of Nagda, clad in "modern attire" of shirt and trousers, posing before this, or another very similar, lurid, "xeno-real" scene (complete with shikara). The plate is dated 1991,[21] a year when the Lake would have swarmed with River Police shikaras and army motorboats. For Pinney, "The vitality and potency of the local space that photography occupies is a place where faces can easily become masks and where photography is translated as a complex theatrical idiom."[22] If the backdrop of the Dal Lake becomes a "mask of desire," closely allied to the work of popular cinema, then photographs such as those in the pink plastic box become the trigger for unmasking the constructed selectivity of that process.

The Witchery of Lake and Mountain

A direct line of fantasy connects the backdrop of the Nagda studio, the cinematic shikara rides that it alludes to, and the imaginings of a mid-nineteenth–century Shropshire Lad who, while working as a bank clerk in Nottingham, was not afraid to dream of "the objects and . . . the sublime future" of photography: "If it is possible for any species of art as it hung continually before us to embody in itself the grand sentiment, "a thing of beauty is a joy forever," such a picture, we may imagine, would be a photograph of large dimensions of some magnificent autumnal landscape, in which were combined every element of the grand, the picturesque and the sublime, as seen in the bewitching light and soft effulgence of a gorgeous sunset, and in which [i.e., the photo] the wondrous reality of every colour, tint, and hue of the grand original was beheld."[23] Addressing thus the newly formed Nottingham Photographic Society in 1860 on "some of the requisites necessary for producing a good photograph," Samuel

Bourne's already discernible sense of high adventure and panoramic vision illustrates photography's seductive pull on a young man eager to reach out beyond life in a provincial English town. His ambition soon outstripped his first subject, the Lake District.[24] Most probably inspired by Francis Frith's photographs of Egypt and the Palestine exhibited in Nottingham in 1859, and having won second prize in "a mammoth competitive examination for Nottingham Photographic Society,"[25] Bourne realized that he could achieve greater distinction by turning to another Oriental space that was rapidly proving to be fertile ground for this new art.

In 1863, Samuel Bourne, photographer-adventurer come lately to India, took the long road from Simla, summer capital of the British Raj, to the Western Himalayas. His reason? "Wanderings," in the manner of earlier Company artists, "in the search of the [Indian] picturesque," [26] but accompanied now with a camera rather than paintbrush. Scarcely two decades since photography had been invented it was already irresistible as a pursuit in both Europe and the colonies, its central attraction its capacity seemingly to fix the truth through the "penetrating eye of the camera."[27] Photography was amenable to both older-style peregrinations in the Lake District and Scottish Highlands, as Bourne's own early career attests, and to metropolitan demands for surveillance and control. But photography's technologizing of the gaze gained even more significance in the colonial domain. Here, "an uncertain world of . . . slippery facts" was rescued by photography's "indexicality and superiority over more equivocal signs."[28] This "yearning for the index" gathered particular force through the British attempt to "transcend the symbolic vagaries of encounter with India."[29] As historians of the colonial visual have amply documented, from the 1850s onward ethnographic and architectural photography had begun to enjoy great currency in India, even as the colonial subject enthusiastically took to the lens in order to perform a modern self through mimicking the master.[30] But while the click of the shutter collapsed the gap between representation and reality with scientific precision, the cumbersome developing process retained more than a hint of alchemy. It is these mysteries of the modern, inherent within the material transformations enabled by the photograph, that I want to emphasize through Bourne's search for the Holy Grail of photographic perfection.

Bourne's career exemplifies both the pragmatic and alchemical aspects of early Indian photography. Like his predecessor William Hodges, pioneer of the Indian picturesque, he was the quintessential artist of Empire,[31] with a keen eye for composition, as well as commerce. In Simla, he joined

Charles Shepherd, an established studio photographer.[32] The resultant photographic firm, Bourne and Shepherd, soon amassed a catalogue of photographs that ran into the thousands. As I shall discuss in a later section, these catalogues offered colonial and metropolitan subjects the chance to become connoisseur-customers of the photographic view. Furthermore, Bourne's methodically assembled photographs of urban architecture and ethnographic portraits from across India elicited "a pleasurable response in accordance with artistic preferences of the day," while "advancing the medium for scientific and archaeological documentation on the subcontinent."[33] But it was "the superb technical and artistic qualities of Bourne's images of the Indian landscape," showcased through his three Himalayan journeys of 1863, 1866, and 1869, that "creat[ed] an immediate sensation among his peers."[34] Combining extreme endurance, enormous stamina and aesthetic appreciation, Bourne pushed the European boundaries of high-altitude survival, as well as high altitude photography. His spectacular achievements in the Western Himalayas still await widespread recognition. Particularly pertinent to this inquiry is the special place that Kashmir, and what he called its "witchery of lake and mountain,"[35] occupied therein. Bourne's fascination with photographing Kashmir offers deeper understanding not only of his "clear repercussions for future professional and serious amateur enterprise in India,"[36] but also of his foundational role in the modern visualization of the Valley.

Bourne's Himalayan journeys began at Simla (today, "Shimla"), a colonial hill station and gateway to the still relatively inaccessible regions that had recently become the princely state of Jammu and Kashmir.[37] But it excited in Bourne neither the photographer nor the adventurer. "I must confess to my disappointment with Simla," he declared, "its great defect to the photographer is its lack of water: there are no lakes, no rivers, and scarcely anything like a stream in this locality, neither is there a single object of architectural interest."[38] This visual monotony combined with the "unvaried surface of barren rock and sand" on the road to Simla to generate considerable skepticism about what awaited further journeying: "I have no doubt that in some part of the Himalayas grand and striking views are to be found, as I hope ere long to verify; but they would consist chiefly of ravines, passes and mountain ranges—without verdure, without foliage, and without water."[39] Bourne's earliest photographs from Simla certainly have a somewhat dutiful air;[40] later in the year, as he ventured forth to "Thibet and the frontiers of Chinese Tartary," his excitement at more variegated topography produced more dramatic images. But here, too, the topography soon became "uninteresting," with "all vegetation having ceased," leaving "nothing but bare mountains with great camel-back ridges."[41] Throughout 1863, inspired particularly by the rhapsodies of *Lalla Rookh*, Bourne kept hoping for a different experience in Kashmir.

In November 1866, accompanied by no more reliable a guide than Montgomerie's *Great Trigonometric Survey*, and by the mandatory posse of sixty-odd coolies bearing photographic and nutritional supplies, Bourne finally trudged up the road from the kingdom of Chumba to face the prize he was after:

> My first glimpse of the Vale of Kashmir, which stretched away to the north like a level plain, with here and there a bright shining patch shining through the haze, like silver, the reflections from sheets of water. Bounding the valley on the west were seen the snowy slopes of the great pir panjal range, forming almost from the spot where I stood, an unbroken line of snow-clad peaks till hidden from view by the haze of distance. To the right, other pyramids of snow rose on the view in glorious and boundless succession. . . . What a scene was the whole to look upon; and what a puny thing I felt standing of that crest of snow!—a mere atom, and scarcely that, in so stupendous a world![42]

The "wild and untrodden Himalayas" heightened Bourne's standard Victorian appreciation for the sublime but, as he descended toward Srinagar, the vertiginous sense of estrangement induced by "this sublime panorama" was gradually tempered with palpable nostalgia: "The freshness, fertility, verdure and sylvan beauty of Kashmir is very great, and seems to remind one very forcibly of the hills and valleys, green fields, parks and pastures of England."[43] Bourne's weekly report from the Himalayas reveals that even as the search for the sublime battles with a delight in the picturesque, this dialectic itself was driven by a longing for what he had left behind. "If he could only transport English scenery under these exquisite skies," he had asked rhetorically of the Photographer in the East, "what pictures would he not produce!"[44] Now, with the uncannily familiar landscape of Kashmir at hand, replete with the water features his aesthetic sense so craved, he could work to realize this desire.

Bourne took hundreds of photographs in the Valley.[45] While his photographic feats in the Higher Himalayas produced dazzling landscapes where the "serrated edge between the light and the dark symbolized the treacherous edge he [had to] explore,"[46] the Valley coaxed from him the most tranquil and soft chiaroscuros. Often by accident, he discovered the technical adjustments needed to capture precise shades of light, cloud and mist;[47] the result is a body of visual poetry. His more dramatic images of passes, mountains, and valleys radiating outward from Srinagar, such as those of the Sind Valley near Sonamarg and the towering rocks of the Zojila Pass leading to Ladakh, offer the perfect sublime foil to the serenely picturesque images taken from the Third Bridge over the Jhelum River,

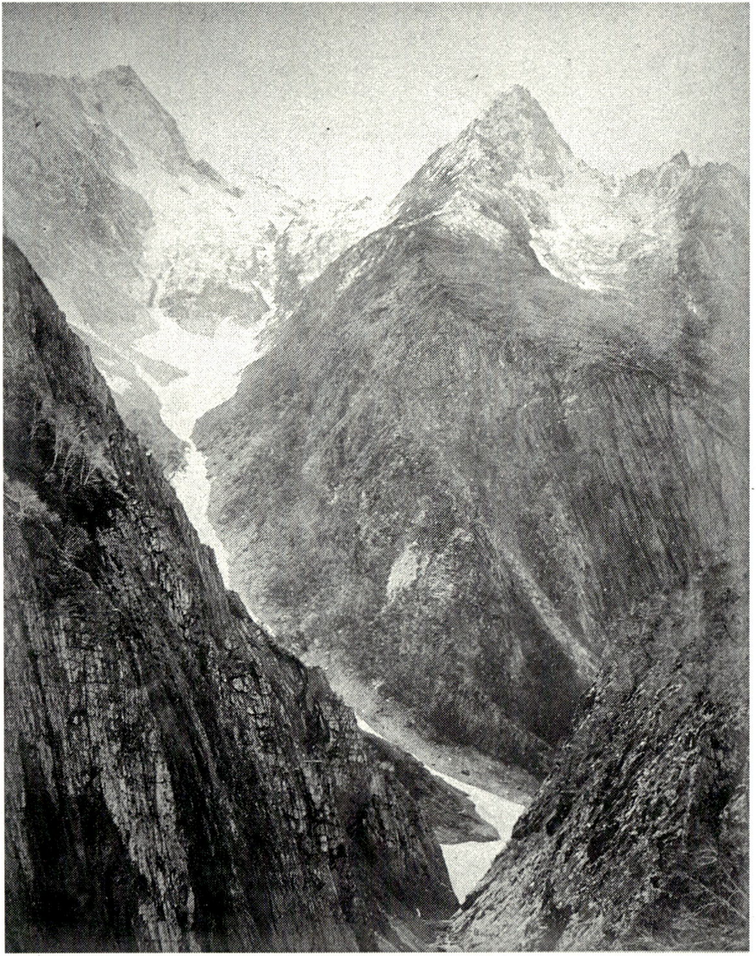

Samuel Bourne, *Zojji-la Pass,* 1864. Albumen print, 295 × 240 mm, photographer's reference no. 990 (ACP 95.0109-00054). A handwritten caption on the page identifies the image as "View in Zoffi-La Pass."

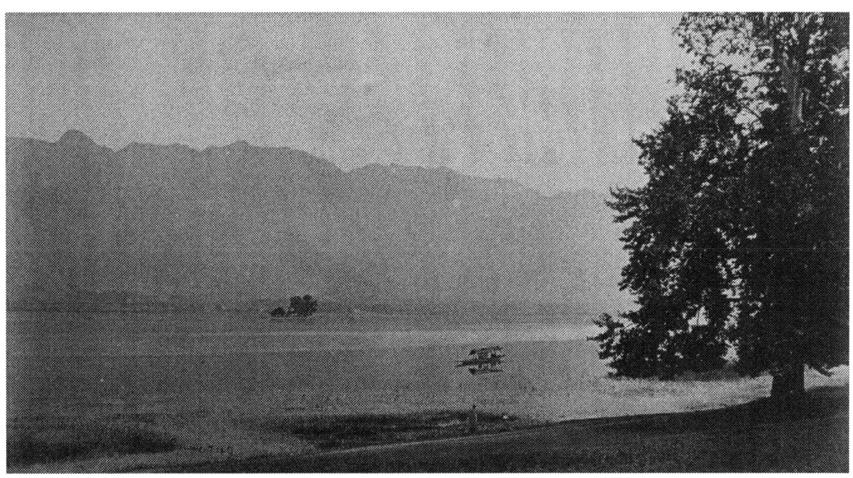

Samuel Bourne, *Lake in Srinagar, Kashmir,* 1864. Albumen print, 190 × 102 mm, photographer's reference no. 749 (ACP D2003.60.0001-00043). A handwritten caption on the page identifies the image as "Isle of Chumars from Nasib Bagh."

the Dhul and Mar Canals that cut through the city, the Shalimar Gardens overlooking the Lake, and the Lake itself.[48] Above all, Bourne was the first and the supreme photographer of the Dal Lake and the shikara. He never tired of photographing the Lake and its boat life from myriad angles; often, he would photograph it from the same vantage point, shifting ever so slightly to grasp yet another nuance.[49] As Gary Sampson observes, he embodied "the artist as creator of dreams or myths, who employs the camera in a way that romanticizes the natural environment."[50] Sampson finds Bourne's "mythical quality" equally present in all "his picturesque imagery"—be they "views of Ootacamund, Srinagar or the Himalayan hill stations." I want to argue, however, for its heightened presence in Bourne's Valley views.

On the Edge of Adventure

As Sampson's comments remind us, Bourne successfully photographed several hill stations and their surrounding landscapes, such as Ootacamund in the Nilgiri Hills, Darjeeling in North Bengal, and even other sites where water and mountain came together, such as Nainital in the Garhwal region. How did his photography come to confer on Kashmir in particular an affective aura different from that developing around South Asian mountain regions in general? This extra edge I would locate in the conjunction of an inherited tradition of landscape eulogy with a historically strategic location. The creation in 1846 of the independent kingdom of Jammu and Kashmir enhanced the Valley's threshold status at the crossroads of the Eastern and Western Himalayas, of the cultures and economies of East, Central, and South Asia, and, most significantly for the nineteenth century, of Russian and British imperial interests. Commercial as well as military imperatives fuelled Britain's ambitions in Inner Asia: Chinese Turkestan was the source of fine *pashm* wool, from which the fabled pashmina shawls of Kashmir were woven, and the trade routes for its outward passage were jealously guarded by the Maharaja of Kashmir.[51] Snaking through narrow valleys and high passes, these ancient routes made Srinagar vital for entering Central Asia through the intervening regions of Ladakh, Gilgit, and Hunza. Whether to cozy up to the Maharaja, then, or to lay hands by any other means on the ibex's undercoat, all the while keeping one eye on the Tsar—for these various reasons the Valley by the second half of the century was being criss-crossed by camera-bearing adventurers, explorers, and British agents.

The earliest uses of the camera in Kashmir were, in fact, purely pragmatic. Working on behalf of the British government in the 1850s, Captains Philip Egerton and Melville Clarke had trekked around the Valley seeking alternative access to Yarkand and its pashm wool via Spiti. With rudimentary cameras, they took photographs of the region and its people that were subsequently inserted into their published reports. But these have an ad hoc and, in the case of Egerton's work, a rather blurred air about them; they conspicuously lack what Arthur Ollman, in discussing Bourne's work, calls the controlling "abstraction" of the rectangular frame of the photograph.[52] However, in the decade following these initial photographic forays, the rapid understanding of photography's special features—not only its usefulness as a tool for recording reality but also its potential to create a shimmering relationship between reality and myth—worked in tandem with the growing adventure of Kashmir. A penchant for high altitude landscape photography, as well as excitement generated by the Great Game, or "the colliding British and Russian struggles for influence over Afghanistan and Central Asia during the nineteenth century,"[53] pulled photographers of different inclinations toward the Valley. Thus, the frame of fantasy imposed on Kashmir by Bourne, aficionado of the Himalayan landscape, must be seen alongside the competing but complementary frames created by the leading photographer of the Great Game, John

Burke. Even as the major events leading to substantial British presence in the Western Himalayas—the First Afghan War and the First and Second Sikh Wars—had also created the state of Jammu and Kashmir,[54] so did Burke's interest in photographing the Great Game inevitably draw him to the Valley and its environs.

In 1857, would-be paparazzo Felix Beato had rushed from Europe to photograph "the Sepoy Mutiny." In a pre–jet-engine age, he was beaten by time.[55] No such disadvantage faced the young Irishman Burke as, from his conveniently close base in the hill station of Murree, he traveled with his equipment to photograph the events that formed the larger canvas of the Great Game, from the Amballa Campaign (1863) to the Second Afghan War (1878–80).[56] In partnership with the older William Baker, just as Bourne had partnered with Shepherd, Burke's photographs helped make Baker and Burke the leading photographic establishment in the northwestern swathe of British rule in the Subcontinent. The arc of their influence—Lahore, Peshawar, Rawalpindi, and Murree—diverged from Bourne and Shepherd's focus on the cities of the Indo-Gangetic plains—Agra, Delhi, Lucknow, Calcutta. But the separate styles, motivations, and geographic constituencies of Bourne and Burke intersected at the Valley of Kashmir, layering it with multiple and overlapping resonances. Like Bourne, Burke took several hundred photographs in and around Srinagar. But these are compositionally different, even when they focus on similar subjects. A denser, more crowded aspect obtains in Burke's Srinagar photographs: we see, close-up, the texture of the brick and timber houses, the narrowness of the Mar Canal, the rowers of shikaras.[57] Where Bourne sought tranquility, Burke sought dynamism. This live quality of his photographs, no doubt arising from his interest in photographing war, also resulted in several fine ethnographic portraits that managed to overcome the practical difficulties consequent on the length of time it took to take a photograph. The same restless naiveté toward posing for the camera that Bourne found somewhat tiresome while photographing Kashmiri subjects,[58] is successfully mined in Burke's sympathetic studies of Kashmiris.

Burke was also a key player in another important aspect of British adventure in Jammu and Kashmir. As Bourne's use of *The Great Trigonometric Survey* suggests, Kashmir, although not officially part of Empire, was subject to its typical obsessions with surveying and textualizing.[59] As part of the same impetus, in 1868 the Archaeological Survey of India sent its Superintendent of the North–West Provinces, Henry Hardy Cole, to take archaeological stock of Jammu and Kashmir. In the report that ensued a

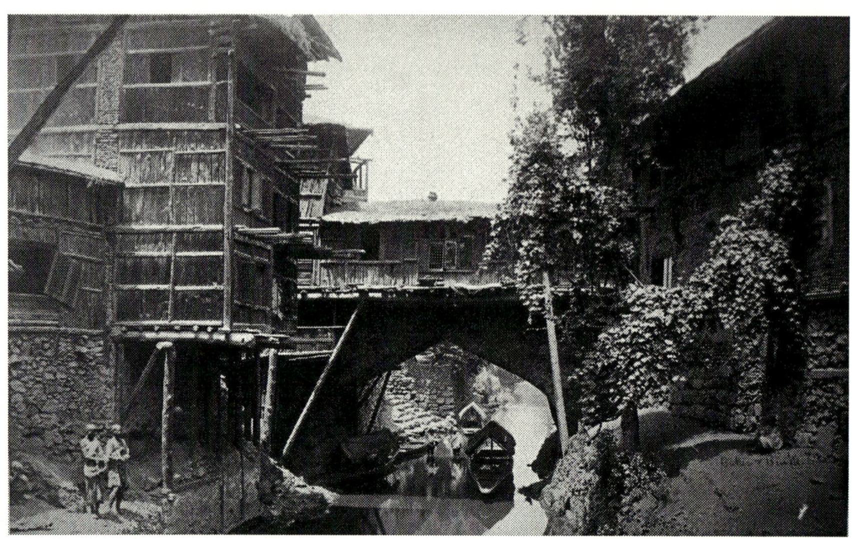

Baker and Burke, *Old Bridge on the Mar Canal,* c. 1863. Albumen print, 115 × 118 mm, photographer's reference no. 681 (ACP 95.0109-00003). A handwritten caption below the print identifies the image as "in Srinagar City."

year later, *Illustrations of Ancient Buildings of Kashmir,* the said illustrations comprised high quality photographs by Burke himself, whom Cole commends warmly in his preface: "Mr Burke, a photographer of Murree and Peshawur, formed one of our party. The zeal which he displayed in our work, and the successful manner in which he completed it, entitle him to great credit."[60] Burke's photographs of the ancient Hindu temples of Martand, Avantipore, Pattan and other smaller sites reiterate his sensitivity to architectural texture and detail. Like Bourne's photographs of the Dal from several different angles, Burke's repeated views of the same sites, while no doubt executed at Cole's behest, facilitates a relationship with the subject matter marked by astonishing elaboration and depth. His panoramic views of the ruin in the landscape are reminiscent of *Ozymandias,* Shelley's poetic rumination on the remnants of ancient Egypt, and whose echo we also hear in Cole's prose: "Scarcely anything remains apart from the foundations and the outlines of the colonnades of two temples."[61] But he also fills the frame with close-ups of, for instance, a single arch. The latter images reiterate Cole's frequent recourse to the past conditional tense to imagine what the sites would have looked like centuries ago.

This movement between the desire for emptiness and the desire for plenitude suggests that for Burke, as much for Bourne, photographing Kashmir was underscored by the pull of nostalgia. An essential element in the Romantic cast of mind, the powerful sentiment of nostalgia—for the ruin in the landscape, for the picturesque view framed by the mountains that themselves promised the experience of the sublime—was honed by the Victorians through the outreach of the Empire.[62] Evoking what was already absent (the ancient temple, the English countryside), their photographs are born out of a self-aware desire for traces of different pasts, constituted through and in technological innovation. This imbrication of modernity, longing and loss gradually drew Kashmir into a collective imperial imaginary, even as its political and geographical status helped maintain a certain liminal wildness. Nostalgia thus collaborated with the struggle for the cartographic definition of a frontier region that was being played out through the Great Game. In this repositioning of Kashmir, our photographers' separate but convergent itineraries played a crucial role. Burke approached Srinagar eastward from Murree; Bourne did so westwards from Simla. Both were strongholds of the Raj, comfort and contact zones that photographers as well as allied adventurers could step out of and assuredly return to. Psychologically, therefore, these and other routes to the Valley from the Himalayan foothills increasingly secured it within the ambit of Empire. Photography is not merely evidence for the region's gradual detachment from existing geocultural affiliations with Central and Inner Asia and its concomitant enmeshing within British India; it is the basic machinery for what Omar Khan, discussing the legacy of Burke, calls the "colonial imagination's conquest of Kashmir."[63]

Furthermore, the Kashmir photographs of Bourne and Burke also pin down, through glass plate and collodion, each phase of their adventures through the intermediary spaces between the plains and the hills; hence, the importance placed, by both photographers, on landmarks en route. But the mutually consolidating roles of periphery and centre shift once again in the Valley, as a new centre is created in Srinagar for the photographic exploration of the ancillary river valleys and, through them, the higher mountains. In this manner, to cite Ollman's observation on Bourne, are the Himalayas rendered "obtainable and conquerable."[64] Their resultant reduction in size—a process that will culminate in the "half-inch Himalayas" of my first epigraph—also functions as frame for the photographic transformation of Srinagar. The photographers admit to its lanes and houses being fetid, foul, and cramped; its inhabitants are declared poor and unwashed.[65] And yet, in photographs they are rendered dignified and attractive, their dwellings satisfyingly picturesque, a foil to the sublime that is generated by photographs of the mountains, lakes, valleys, and rivers, and to the antiquity crystallized in Kashmir's ruins. Kashmir emerges thereby as the perfect aesthetic composite. Khan's appraisal of the role played here by geography and politics—"just beyond British Control and ruled by a Maharajah, Kashmir fed a romantic Orientalist appetite"[66]—is thus insufficient explanation for the particularity of Kashmir's development into a territory of desire. The "just beyond" is, in fact, the key to this mystery. Not merely, as Khan observes, "although," but, in fact, *because* "Kashmir was outside the British Raj and visited by less than 1000 Europeans each year during the 1860s, its visual beauty was the best selling consumer photographic subject."[67]

Mimesis, Consumption, and Value

In considering how a place "just beyond" the pale of British India could nevertheless become a "best selling consumer photographic subject," Khan posits a fairly straightforward relationship between photography and value:

> The catalogues of firms like Bourne and Shepherd of Calcutta and Baker and Burke of the Punjab offered more photographs of Kashmir than any other location in India. These firms were responding to the demands of the many people who could not travel there—customers in the hot plains who yearned for images of cool scenery. . . . [T]hese demands fuelled the popularity of photographs of Kashmir, whose landscape photographers would capture on glass plates and submit to various all-India photographic competitions in the quest to win coveted gold medals.[68]

Returning to Slavoj Žižek's insistence on the primacy of the *frame* in the creation of fantasy, I want to reverse Khan's understanding of customer demands as the cause, and photography as the effect, of desire for Kashmir. Bourne and Burke were not the first to send dispatches about Kashmir's beauty to the outside world; neither were theirs the first attempts at reproducing that beauty through "mimesis," or artful representation. Their predecessors ranged from the Mughals and their artists to a long line of Europeans travelers from Bernier onward, including those of the armchair variety such as Thomas Moore, author of *Lalla Rookh*.[69] What Bourne and Burke do pioneer is the simultaneous aesthetic and commercial development of a new mimetic technology. Not just photography, therefore, but the practices of consumption it engendered augmented the value of Kashmir and transformed it from landscape to fantasy.

A helpful formulation in this context is what Stephen Greenblatt has called "mimetic capital."[70] Like goods within an economy, representations accrue value as they circulate within the public sphere. In the case of photography, Walter Benjamin's emphasis on the "mechanical reproduction" of the modern artwork explicates further how such mimetic capital may be generated.[71] The photograph's infinite reproducibility from the template of the negative annuls the distinction between "copy" and "original," placing it in a very different circuit of value from the painting. Photography enlarged the circle of connoisseurship through commercialization,[72] as is made clear by the separation of photographer and consumer during its earliest days. Bourne and Burke did not take photographs to please themselves alone; they were made commercially available through the catalogues of their respective firms.[73] Each photograph entered these catalogues as a number and a caption, which, in the absence of the photographs themselves, guided potential customers in both India and Britain in formulating their order. The catalogues also contained pricing information: in general, photographs cost between Re 1 to Rs 8 depending on size and format, with discounts available for bulk orders. Prices were not the only index to the level of competition between the two firms. Also announced were the medals won by their respective photographers in exhibitions organized by colonial photographic societies. Accompanying offers of framing and mounting services further assured customers of the photographs' material value. By offering a forum for self-advertisement, therefore, as well as through details of pricing and presentation, these catalogues facilitated the generation of mimetic capital. For several reasons, value most accumulated thereby around views of Kashmir.

The initial focus on Kashmir as photographic subject was undoubtedly predicated on the separate yet overlapping predilections of Bourne and Burke. But the steady lead in terms of numbers that the Kashmir photographs maintained in the catalogues,[74] together with the prizes and medals they regularly attracted, confirms the working of a spiraling circuit of value rather than the linear chain of demand and supply postulated by Khan. A taste for Kashmir was not only being created but accelerated through this interaction of photographers and consumers. It was further enhanced through the nascent practice of albums and scrapbooks, in which photographs could be arranged in thematic clusters. The firms contributed to the formation of consumer taste through actively intervening in album compilation.[75] A large number of these albums survive today in archives.[76] Usually of English make, most are in excellent condition, testifying to the high quality of their Moroccan leather bindings and thick pages. Their value is further proclaimed by gilt monograms and album locks. The photographs within often concentrate on work by Bourne and Burke, and they are accompanied by handsomely handwritten captions, echoing the formulations of the catalogues from which the albums were compiled. Typically, the photographs include landscape and architectural views from across British India, and sometimes from across Asia. Even in such eclectic collections, however, Kashmir views regularly preponderate. Album after album yields the same images of the Dal Lake with shikaras, the Jhelum from the Third Bridge flanked by houseboats and the shrine of Shah Hamdani, the chinar trees and poplar avenues, the Sind Valley and the Zojila Pass, and the temples of Martand and Avantipur.[77]

Through not merely repetition but also their spatial arrangement, these albums foster a viewerly engagement that mimics Bourne and Burke's actual journeys to and around Srinagar. Their owners could have included, as Khan suggests, would-be visitors to Kashmir. But they definitely included those who had themselves been there and wanted portable, assorted memories of their Kashmir adventures. Thus, the format of the albums made proto-postcards of their constituent photographs.[78] In step with landscape's gradual conversion to the "half-inch" souvenir, furthermore, solitary adventure was domesticated into tourism.[79] The majority of pre-1890s, Kashmir-centric albums of known provenance belonged to members of army regiments of the North-West Frontier Province adventuring in Kashmir.[80] By the turn of the century, these lone male travelers who compiled their albums through photographers' catalogues began bringing to the Valley their memsahibs and their field cameras.[81] Photograph sizes shrank further, professional and amateur successors to the early photographers emerged, but the views remained unchanged. Simultaneously, the Raj's relationship to Dogra rule became formalized through the stationing, in Srinagar, of Collectors and Residents.[82] As we shall see in chapter 3, this relationship made the Valley a space for imperial relaxation as well as imperial adventure.[83] Visual record of this Dogra-British collaboration exists in the photographs of official visits, entourages, and shooting expeditions that increasingly crowd the albums alongside the established landscape and architecture views.[84] In an album commemorating the 1902 Kashmir visit of Lord and Lady Ampthill and Suite, we find a portrait of a handsome *barasingha*, or "twelve-antlered" Kashmiri stag in a garden, tethered to a post that remains outside the frame:[85] a poignant allegory of the commodification of Kashmir through photography, and its harnessing into a subject of collective desire.

The domestication of adventure in Kashmir during the first half of the nineteenth century invites a reassessment of the relationship of fantasy, photography, and value. If the liminality of Kashmir and the frame of the photograph worked together to create a space of fantasy where "the serrated edge" fashioned the imperial, adventuring self, should not its

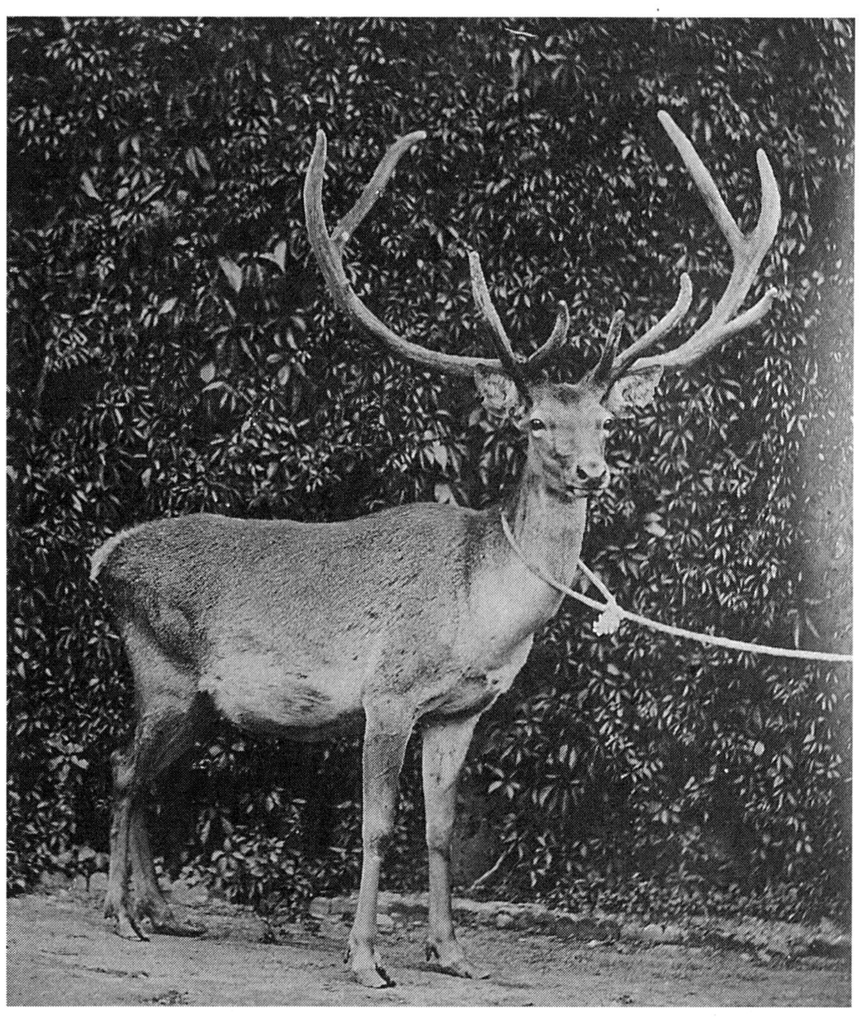

Diwan Alimchand, *A Stag in the Garden of Sir Amar Singh,* 1904. Silver gelatin print, 206 × 180 mm (ACP D2003.60.0001-00058).

increasing accessibility have diminished the value of the "just beyond"? However, value was retained through the logic of mimetic capital. The albums of Kashmir views are tangible evidence that circulation of the representation enhanced the aura of the thing represented. In fact, emergent tourism helped keep this aura intact by tacitly blurring fantasy and reality. As the writings of Bourne attest, the photographic fantasy of Kashmir always included a strong domestic element. The longing for England it embodied was increasingly fulfilled through the infrastructure of tourism. In course of the first half of the twentieth century, an entire social season sprang up around Srinagar and Gulmarg, whose consequences we shall examine in the following chapter. The continuing popularity of photography in Kashmir, and the establishment in particular of the landscape views first framed by Bourne's camera, ensured that the fantasy of Kashmir not only survived but evolved into one of pastoral escape in the shadow of the Himalayas. As the landscape becomes further framed into domestic views, there is decreasing room for the urban geography of those areas of Srinagar where tourists, now moored to their increasingly opulent houseboats, did not venture. As the bridges, overhanging houses, Mar Canal views and ethnographic portraits receded from albums, increasing prominence was secured by landscapes of the Lake and of the social life centered round the clubs of Srinagar and Gulmarg.

The architectural views of Srinagar, in the meanwhile, fed into an increasingly interested appreciation of Kashmir's pre-Islamic past. In 1898, Maharaja Pratap Singh converted the Ranbir Singh Palace in Srinagar into the Pratap Singh Museum. Today, in the first gallery of the dusty and neglected State Museum, statuary from Kashmir's Buddhist and Hindu sites is still prominent. Clearly geared toward establishing Dogra legitimacy among the Valley's Muslim majority population, the emergent prominence of Kashmiri antiquity had long-lasting consequences on popular visualizations of Kashmir. By the 1920s, photographs of the ancient monuments of Kashmir moved firmly into the province of the Government Department of Archaeology and Antiquities. The circulation of these photographs within a growing archaeological discourse confers another category of value on Kashmir—that of its ancient civilization. The landscape evolved into the pastoral fantasies of 1960s Bollywood that we have explored in the previous chapter. What happened to the ruin in the Kashmiri landscape shall be revealed in the subsequent one. Here, I want to emphasize that the division of representative freight fractured but did not diminish value. Rather, as the *idea* of Kashmir became important to different constituencies, its resonance multiplied. In the case of Kashmir photographs, this resonance has been heightened by archival practices outside Kashmir. Reverentially preserved in the great libraries and museums of the UK, and acquired by private collectors through familiarity with the international auction circuit, the photographs of Bourne, Burke, and their followers are precious objects today. Irradiated by the ideological potencies of the archive and the art market, their incremental value drives another wedge between what one Kashmiri blogger calls the "Srinagar you see"—a photograph of the Dal Lake, and the "Srinagar we see"—a crowded, potholed Srinagar road.[86]

The View from Kashmir

Yet another manifestation of the disjunction between Kashmir and centers of privilege in decolonized India, this discrepancy highlights how the concept of Kashmir views continues to play into intranational discourses and practices of value. As I finished writing this chapter, an exhibition entitled *Kashmir Views* opened at the very nice India Habitat Centre in New Delhi.[87] It comprised photographs of Kashmir taken by Ram Chand Mehta (1910–94), a Kashmiri photographer-entrepreneur of Punjabi origin, the youngest of three brothers who in 1918 founded Mahattas, Srinagar's premier photo studio. Heavily patronized by Valley's indigenous and variously expatriate elite from the 1930s onward, Mahattas is now run by his son Jagdish Mehta, and stands as faded remnant of an older era. The grandsons, whose brainchild the exhibition was, have expanded into the Delhi-based Mahattas Multimedia, including its subsidiary IndiaPictures.com, "India's leading Photo stock company."[88] With curatorial and entrepreneurial inputs, IndiaPictures.com digitally reprinted from R. C.'s original negatives 140 black-and-white photographs in varying formats. The varied fare, ranging from the 1930s to the 1950s, included portraits of rural Kashmiris outdoors and elite Kashmiris in the studio, and a few political photographs from the 1960s. Predictably, the bulk constituted landscape and Srinagar views in the Bourne-Burke tradition, albeit often reinterpreted through the framing devices of cornices, latticework and window arches. Now elegantly re-framed in brown wood, they were exhibited alongside old field cameras, bric-a-brac from the developing process, hand-written letters, and two hats belonging to the photographer. The photographs' status as *old* objects, sharing the patina of the "now-antique" studio paraphernalia,[89] was thereby asserted.

As a clearly retrospective exhibition, Kashmir Views revealed the complex consequences that photography's combination of aesthetic, nostalgic, and commercial considerations has left on Kashmir. The photographs were competitively priced and they found buyers with ease. This value derived from their mimetic and therefore symbolic capital. The organizers emphasized the grandsons' tribute to their pioneering grandfather, the loving labor of their retrieval: "The photographs lay buried in the attic of his studio on the Jhelum; they have now been recovered and dusted."[90] This statement appears to be somewhat embroidered; reportedly, they lay buried in the godaam (once again, that word) of a Kashmiri Muslim printer, a long-term employee of Mahattas.[91] If true, his elision from the publicity material joins the inclusion of hats and portraits of ladies with bobbed hair to trace the lineaments of a familiar Anglophone-elite collaboration. An even starker commentary on the brokers of power radiated from a photograph of the Maharani of Kashmir in Western male attire, complete with bowler hat, tie, and rifle, sitting astride a felled barasingha whose testicles loll obscenely into view. No mere allegory, as with the previously discussed stag, this is a statement of the multiple shoot. The photographer's camera confirms the potency of the cross-dressing Maharani's rifle. Photography is here the relay of power. This relay continued within the wider frame of the exhibition's opening ceremony, whose chief guest was Jagmohan, the controversial and, for many, infamous governor of Jammu and Kashmir during the early 1990s.[92] The speeches at that ceremony praised the successful photographic retrieval of Kashmir at a time when it was still "paradise on earth," "beautiful, innocent and immaculate."[93]

The claim is inaccurate. The Valley from the 1930s to the 1950s was as removed from the tranquility of these photographs as its 1960s counterpart was from the pastoral playground of Bollywood's Kashmir films. The anglicized photographer's admittedly exquisite photographs of rural Kashmiris recall the grassroots rebellion against the Dogra regime and its elites spearheaded by Sheikh Abdullah in 1931 that led to the momentous land reforms of the 1950s under his "New Kashmir" manifesto.[94] In R. C.'s Srinagar photographed we glimpse history in the making: the class antagonisms that fifty years later re-emerged with Srinagar youths seizing, through the gun, legitimacy *within* as much as *for* Kashmir; the new houseboats for tourists alongside older *doonga* boats housing the Lake dwellers, now transformed into houseboat servants. But only to the informed do these photographs evidence the Valley's high politics, microhistories, and urban geographies. To the average viewer and buyer, they were valuable precisely because they seemed removed from "history." The selection, framing and consumption of the photographs were motivated by a deeply internalized self-censorship that was convinced of its own disinterestedness.[95] R. C.'s corpus might well have included traces of views from rather than of Kashmir; but Kashmir Views valorized the fiction of the absent photographic I/eye: hence its exclusion of photographs where R. C.'s own shadow tellingly fell across panoramic shots of landscape.[96] Through the curatorial decision to highlight "beauty" without acknowledging its constructedness, the exhibition perpetuated the fantasy that Bollywood is invested in protecting, while revealing photography's somewhat different, but also complementary mode of doing so. While the individual surrenders to the collectivity of a cinema audience, he or she regains the illusion of autonomy through the contemplation, purchase and display of the "art photograph." That the earliest purchases were made by Jammu and Kashmir Bank and Jammu and Kashmir Tourism suggests the constituencies within Kashmir, invariably congruent with a perpetuation of class-based bastions of power, that wish to share in this mode of investing in the Kashmir fantasy.

But within Srinagar are also less privileged constituencies who resist such investment by valorizing very different kinds of "Kashmir views."[97] In Srinagar's Batmaloo neighborhood, next to the Sufi shrine of Dawood Sahib, is the tiny office of a breakaway resistance group termed Islamic League of Students (ILS). I had heard that they possessed photographs of the 1990s such as those now in Majlis's Godaam. As I sat discussing India's role in Kashmir with ILS leader Shakeel Bakshi, his assistants brought to us what looks like rolled-up banners. These unfurled across the patterned carpeting to reveal photographs stuck on them in the manner of posters. Thanks to my apprenticeship with the pink plastic box, I recognized the scenes of demonstration, carnage, bullets and blood enacted on the Kashmiri male body. I observed wounded, mutilated corpses on funeral biers garlanded and dressed like bridegrooms—their martyrdom being celebrated, not mourned. There were photographs, too, of these very posters mounted on poles in a marquee—the record of their display the previous year during the *urs* (annual feast) of Dawood Sahib. As with any subcontinental shrine, the urs takes the form of a local *mela* (fair), drawing devotees of the saint in question into a tightly felt community of shared love and reverence. Exhibiting such disturbing photographs in this sacral space was clearly a conscious decision, aiming to tap into the urs as reservoir of spiritual affect. Without that context of shared purpose, viewing these photographs of the wounded Kashmiri body collective was, for me, dangerously akin to a pornographic enjoyment of the spectacle of violence. Sensing my discomfort, Bakshi signaled that the posters be re-rolled out of sight.

This "exhibition" had had but a brief life.[98] The urs had been stormed by local police (part of the power "sandwich" according to Bakshi, whereby the police and the judicial machinery of Jammu and Kashmir are under "unified control"—"and this is what we call democracy!"). The posters were quickly rolled up and transported to a hiding place nearby—another godaam?—from where, presumably, they had now been retrieved for me. The significance of the poster format dawned on me: in Bakshi's words, "we had to keep the photographs mobile" and yet ever-ready for display. There are, allegedly, video recordings of the 1990s, too, secreted away somewhere. "One day when we are free. . . ." His voice tailed off. For now, the mere survival of these photographs is, for him, a fact of history. "They" did not want Kashmiris to maintain any relationship with *tarikh* (Urdu: history). By bringing them out of hiding, Bakshi seeks to reinsert Kashmiris into history, but through the restoration of morality. They are mnemonic devices aimed at the spiritual and political reawakening of a new generation weaned away from Kashmir through the relentless promotion of "national interest" by the media and satellite TV in collusion with the "establishment." The photographs in the shrine resist this unholy collaboration that grinds down morality and promotes amnesia regarding the 'sacrifices" of the generation of 1989. I was reminded of Agha Shahid Ali's poem "Farewell" which pits "my memory" against "your history," while cognizant that Bakshi would certainly consider Kashmiri families such as his, and the proprietors of Mahattas, as prime perpetuators of the elite collaborations that mark the advent of colonial modernity, and of the camera, in Kashmir.

The photographs in the shrine present more than an alternative history. They are a material alternative to history itself. If their custodianship is "a game of hide-and-seek, a love-longing, an ardent desire," their placement in the shrine converts them into *taveez* (amulets) that transmit the saint's spiritual, healing power to the wearers' body.[99] Their healing potential is aimed at reconstituting Kashmiri selfhood, whose "dilution" Bakshi astutely points out as being linked to the Indian establishment's appropriation of the word kashmiriyat—in any case an inadequate linguistic cipher for a complex of values that is best left "a dash-dash-dash." Placing the photographs in the shrine is an attempt toward kashmiriyat's corporeal rather than linguistic replenishment as well as an acknowledgment of replenishment's impossibility. The body is thereby returned not to the landscape but to the urban site of the Kashmiri shrine, even as "Kashmir views" are transformed through a predominantly architectural vocabulary. Bakshi opened our conversation by quoting the Kashmiri modernist poet Mahjoor: "O Nightingale, fluttering in your cage! Who will free you? You have to create, with your own hands, the *tools* [my emphasis] for your aazadi."[100] Metaphors of construction crowd his vision of free Kashmir: "I am a mason [*sinan*] whose hands contribute to building a secure habitation for Kashmiris. In the absence of security, what use are these lakes and gardens [*aab-e-gulzar*]?" Questioned on the camera's promotion of these very lakes and gardens, he responded: "people sit at home watching readymade images. It is a wholly different matter if someone reaches beyond the image to reality. Everyone listens to the *saaz* [a stringed instrument]. We are grateful if even one person listens for the suffering of its strings."

This chapter has tried to rise to the challenge that Shakeel Bakshi sets out through the analogy of the mellifluous saaz and its suffering strings. By beginning and ending with Kashmiri uses and, undoubtedly for some, misuse of photographs of conflict, I have sought to destabilize what Partha Chatterjee calls the "consensual form of a convention:" in this case, postcolonial India's celebration, through the inheritance of a colonial visual discourse, of the "natural" beauty of Kashmir. The "commonsensical obviousness of every conventional practice" means that "when we try to decode the underlying order of meanings, we do not imply that the artists or publishers or teachers participating in the practice are conscious of that underlying structure, or even curious about it."[101] It is equally unnecessary to hold the first photographers of Kashmir culpable for the "innocent guilt" of their art.[102] Yet there is an undeniable continuity between their Kashmir views and the frames of fantasy still imposed on the Valley in contemporary India. Through the potent relationship between fantasy and value, photographs of "paradisiacal" Kashmir are constantly susceptible to easy alignment with the orthopedic regimes of the nation-state. The persistence of the godaam, with its connotations of unceremonious storage, alternative sites of valorization such as the Sufi shrine, and the photograph as amulet all offer suggestive antidotes to fetishism and melancholia induced by the official archive.[103] Their full significance will emerge in due course—but after we examine, in the next chapter, how photography interacted with academic discourse and domestic tourism to extract, out of the territory of desire, the modern nation's very own antique land.

Three

Modern Nation, Antique Land

All of us, I suppose, have varying pictures of our native land and no two persons will think exactly alike. When I think of India, I think of many things: of broad fields dotted with innumerable small villages; of towns and cities I have visited; of the magic of the rainy season which pours life into the dry parched-up land and converts it suddenly into a glistening expanse of beauty and greenery, of great rivers and flowing water; of the Khyber Pass in all its bleak surroundings; of the southern tip of India; of people, individually and in the mass; and above all, of the Himalayas, snow-capped, or some mountain valley in Kashmir in the spring, covered with new flowers, and with a brook bubbling and gurgling through it. We make and preserve the pictures of our choice, and so I have chosen this mountain background rather than the more normal picture of a hot, sub-tropical country.

—Jawaharlal Nehru, *The Discovery of India*

Incarcerated in the Ahmadnagar Jail during the 1940s, the future first Prime Minister of independent India and architect of its postcolonial modernity turned to Kashmir to "discover" his "native land" (here, a phrase that moves ambiguously between India and the Kashmir of his ancestors).[1] If, as has been commented upon in the context of postcolonial Egypt, "for a state to prove it was modern it helped if it could also prove it was ancient,"[2] then Nehru's articulation of modern-yet-ancient India pivoted on the image of Kashmir in springtime framed by the snow-capped Himalayas. As we have seen in chapter 2, this framed view of the Valley derives from the first photographers of

Kashmir. Thus Nehru's candid admission—that "we make and preserve the pictures of our choice"—reiterates not only the constructedness of writing the modern nation but also, in the case of his dream for India, the reliance of this process on the visualization of the Valley. While *The Discovery of India* illustrates that "the importance of the past for modern movements of political emancipation has been undeniable,"[3] my epigraph additionally reminds us that "to produce a past a state has to produce a place."[4] This place, where a fitting past for India crystallized, was for Nehru none other than the Valley of Kashmir, elsewhere eulogized by him as "a favoured spot . . . where loveliness dwells and an enchantment steals over the senses."[5]

What enabled the Valley to offer so crucial a foil to "the more normal picture of a hot, sub-tropical country?" Underlying Nehru's invocations of Kashmir in *The Discovery of India* is the powerful perception of a landscape whose desirability is intimately connected to its organic relationship with an ancient culture. In this chapter, I explore the textual discourses that worked with the camera to produce the Valley as a space of natural beauty as well as venerable ancientness. As suggested by my epigraph's position within Nehru's account of India, this valorization of Kashmir was closely linked to the production of the modern nation. But the discursive linkage is not so much Nehru's invention as his inheritance: a legacy of the collaboration between the Dogra Maharajas of Kashmir and a veritable battalion of European scholars who visited Kashmir from the 1870s onward to study its Sanskrit manuscripts and its Hindu and Buddhist material remains. Spurred on by archaeological interest in the region's pre-Islamic architecture, and by linguistic research conducted by missionaries in Srinagar, these Indologists laid the foundation for a potent imagining of ancient Kashmir that grounded its Hindu elites in the Valley's topography and history, but dismissed its Muslim masses as latter-day interlopers. The Indologist's quest for antiquity also brought him in competition with the tourist for control over the Valley. This chapter traces how the struggle between tourism and academic esotericism heightened the Valley's significance for postcolonial India.

While the previous two chapters have looked to the visual image, then, this chapter foregrounds the written word. Memoirs, guidebooks, the accounts of Valley life left by the increasingly complex array of imperial personnel stationed there, and the "chits" (testimonials) rendered by them to the ancestors of today's houseboat owners, all play their part, as does the Indological production of grammars, dictionaries, critical editions, and inventories of Sanskrit manuscripts. While these latter bristle with prefaces, introductions, forewords and frontispieces—the collective apparatus that Gérard Genette has called the "paratext"—the travelogues and memoirs I examine are also reinforced with maps, appendices and photographs.[6] My analysis attends to these paratexts that fortify and shield the text "in its naked state." I do so not only to expose the paratext as "the bearer of an authorial commentary either more or less legitimated by the author" but also to map these strategies of legitimization on to the political games being played out during and immediately beyond Dogra rule (1846–1947). The paratext's role in breaking "the text's sealed frontier by constituting the threshold between the interior and the exterior" mirrors Kashmir's threshold position during this period. Yet paratext and territory of desire alike are "zones not just of transition but of transaction, the privileged site of a pragmatics and of a strategy." The transactions conducted through these fringe zones augmented the sense of the Valley as an exceptional space, and provided the rationale for its transfer from colonial fantasy to national(ist) necessity.

Storehouse of Antiquity

1888 was a meaningful year for Kashmir. George Eastman launched the Kodak, thereby inaugurating the transformation from extreme to easy photography that would also constitute a definitive step toward the emergence of the mass tourist.[7] It was the year, too, when a Hungarian scholar traveled to Srinagar from Lahore, where he had arrived only six months before.[8] His name was Marc Aurel Stein; his motivation was the ultimate Orientalist dream—the pursuit of ancient manuscripts. Like Bourne and Burke, Stein used Kashmir to springboard from a life of provincial obscurity in Europe to high adventure in Asia, but it was not the camera, already poised to lose some of its edgy glamour, that was to be his modus operandi. In his fifty-year association with the Valley, Stein certainly took several photographs. Now preserved in the British Library, they reveal him only secondarily concerned with the photographic framing of the Valley. Rather, catalogued and neatly labeled in identical grey cloth bound albums, Stein's photographs embody the subordination of camera and landscape to his scholarly project—the philological capture of Kashmir's past, and its conversion from a medley of badly copied manuscripts and oral transmission into the more "reliable" record of edition, catalogue, and commentary.[9] Part of the Orientalist endeavor to create through "monumental texts," the "critical edition" of India's ancient past, and part of his own interest in the Silk Road's material history,[10] Stein's involvement with a specifically *Kashmiri* antiquity nevertheless demands separate reassessment for the lasting impact it was to have on nationalist perceptions of the Valley.

From 1888 onward, Kashmir facilitated Stein's annual escape from his professional commitments in Lahore's Oriental College and Punjab University. Over several summer vacations camped in Mohandmarg, an alpine meadow north of Srinagar, he pored over manuscripts of Kalhana's *Rajatarangini,* a Sanskrit chronicle of Kashmir's pre-Islamic rulers, working out their interrelationships to prepare an authoritative edition and commentary. This magisterial three-volume work appeared in 1900; it was preceded, in 1894, by a catalogue of all the Sanskrit manuscripts in the Maharaja of Kashmir's possession. The catalyst for both works was Stein's initial encounter with the Valley. "It was in the summer of 1888," he declares in the first sentence of the *Rajatarangini*'s Introduction, "on my first visit to Kasmir [sic], that I was attracted to the task which the present work is intended to complete."[11] His Preface to the Catalogue likewise opens with "the autumn of the year 1888, when on returning from a journey to Kashmir I took occasion to visit the Dogra capital [Jammu] and to inspect its Sanskrit library."[12] That momentous first visit to Jammu and Kashmir was generated by Stein's early exposure to the towering edifice of German scholarship on India. Although cerebral rather than territorial acquisitiveness fuelled German Indology, it manifestly consolidated British imperial interests through the discursive power of Orientalism.[13] The Orientalist web that stretched from Asia to Europe brought together Stein, an impressionable and ambitious Central European student, and Georg Bühler, formidable German professor of Indology, at the University of Leipzig's lecture theatres during 1879–80. It was Bühler who alerted Stein to the *Rajatarangini*'s existence, and tipped him off about "one of the great store-houses of Sanskrit Literature in India."[14]

Used by Stein to describe Jammu's immensely symbolic Raghunathji Temple,[15] the phrase "great storehouse" could well apply to the Indologist valorization of Kashmir. The concept of the godaam reappears—not in antithesis to the archive, as in the previous chapter, but as proto-archive itself. In 1875, the British Government deputed Bühler to search for Sanskrit manuscripts that might lie, awaiting scholarly scrutiny, in indigenous storehouses. He responded with alacrity. "The order of Government to proceed on a tour to Kasmir, Rajputana and Central India in search of Sanskrit MSS. reached me on July 18th, 1875. I started from Surat the following day." Thus begins his "Personal Narrative," the first section of his "Detailed Report" of this expedition, later published in the Bombay Branch of the Asiatic Society Journal.[16] Bühler's account reflects the single-mindedness of his mission: the extraction of raw data for the Indology machine. Not the Valley's landscape, but the etymological challenges its place-names posed to a scholar of Sanskrit, thrilled him. Topography is viewed through the filter of philology; people are important only as native informants. "On the 20th of October, three hundred MSS. had been packed securely in eighteen tin-lined boxes, a general list had been prepared, and the accounts with the writers and sellers of MSS. had been settled."[17] Bühler was ready to leave the great storehouse, albeit after a detour to the temples of Avantipur and Martand. His companions were "a Kasmirian [sic] singer who knew some of the old songs in which I was interested, and a Mahomedan munshi who had studied Kasmiri [sic] in a scholarly manner and who had assisted the late Dr. Elmslie in the compilation of his vocabulary."

As this last detail suggests, Bühler's Indology took a specifically Kashmiri turn under the influence of the work done by Europeans already in the Valley. Through information gathered by traveler-players of the Great Game, preliminary observations about Kashmir's pre-Islamic material remains had begun to permeate the new Orientalist journals. On the basis of reports by William Moorcroft, "the first Englishman to enter the Valley," H. H. Wilson translated the *Rajatarangini* for the *Transactions of the Asiatic Society* as early as 1825, although it was marred by conjecture and mistakes.[18] Likewise, Alexander Cunningham's accounts of the temples of Kashmir motivated the later, more thorough archaeological survey led by H. H. Cole.[19] But most crucial to Indological scholarship, given its linguistic orientation, were the Christian missionaries, since the 1860s the one prominent group of Europeans in Kashmir other than "the officers of the sword and pen."[20] As with all imperially sanctioned missionary work, theirs were the first pragmatic attempts to master the local language. Thus, the aforementioned Dr. Elmslie had authored the first "vocabulary of the Kashmiri language," based on materials "collected . . . while discharging his duties as a medical missionary."[21] In 1888, the Society for the Promotion of Christian Knowledge (SPCK) in London published T. R. Wade's *Grammar of the Kashmiri Language,* compiled "from notes . . . made whilst labouring [for] the Church Missionary Society for some years in Kashmir."[22] In the words of another active missionary in the 1880s, J. Hinton Knowles, "the vocation of a missionary brings one into close and constant touch with the people." His compendia of Kashmiri proverbs and folktales resulted from "the opportunities afforded [him] through a four years" residence in the valley," including "two long quiet winters" filled with "many hours of labour, study and anxiety."[23]

Knowles's work on the oral resources of Kashmiri contributed to the growing scholarly construction of Kashmir as a storehouse not merely of manuscripts but also of orality. The philologist decoding Sanskrit and the missionary decoding the vernacular were united in their reliance on oral transmission, the corrupter of pristine originals but also the badge of their continued currency. The hunt for the oral diverted the Sanskrit specialist to the vernacular: from Brahmins Stein solicited memorized versions of the *Rajatarangini,* but from the Muslim professional storyteller Hatim, Kashmiri folktales after the manner of Knowles. Value accumulated from the study of Sanskrit flowed into awakening interest in Kashmiri, not for its own sake but for what it might mean for Kashmir's imaginative status. Stein's work on the *Rajatarangini* had confirmed its importance as ancient India's only "legitimate" historiography (the rest of its literature being comprised of what the British dismissed as "myth" and "fable").[24] Thanks to Stein and Kalhana, Kashmir could be flagged as the fount of a learned antiquity, enhanced further by its sculpture being, like that of the Gandhara tradition in Afghanistan, distinctly Greco-Buddhist.[25] Now the Kashmiri language, too, appeared striated with unchanged ancientness. "The ancient Indian system by which literature is recorded not on paper but on the memory, and carried down from generation to generation of teachers and pupils, is still in complete survival in Kashmir." Thus opined Lionel Barnett in 1920 while introducing a collection of the sayings of Lal Ded, "mystic poetess of ancient Kashmir," coedited and translated for the Asiatic Society by himself and the eminent linguist Sir George Grierson.[26]

Verses attributed to the fourteenth-century Kashmiri poet Lalla (Lal Ded) had been already collected by Knowles via his proverb-hunting. That they could subsequently attract separate interest is fruit of the conversation between Sanskritists and missionaries. Between 1896 and 1899 Grierson, ultimately author of a two-volume dictionary of Kashmiri, wrote several technical essays on Kashmiri for the Asiatic Society that were quickly republished as a collection. Its introduction enthusiastically commended Kashmiri to the comparative philologist: "A study of Kaçmiri [sic] is an essential preliminary to any enquiry which deals comparatively with the mutual relations of the modern Aryan languages."[27] This assertion of the wider importance of Kashmiri is echoed a year later in Stein's claims for Kashmir:

> From the high mountain plateau which my camp once more occupies, almost the whole of Kasmir lies before me, from the ice-capped peaks of the northern range to the long snowy line of the Pir Pantsal,—a little world of its own, enclosed by mighty mountain ramparts. Small indeed the country may seem, by the side of the great plains that extend in the south, and confined the history of which it was the scene. And yet, just as the natural attractions of the Valley have won it fame far beyond the frontiers of India, thus too the interest attaching to its history far exceeds the narrow geographical limits.[28]

Shaping both endeavors is the shared Guru, the recently deceased Bühler, to whose memory Stein and Grierson respectfully dedicated their respective labors on Kalhana and Kashmiri.[29] Through such labors, ancient and contemporary Kashmir became linked for "the philologist, the ethnologist, the antiquarian, the student of folklore and the general reader" (a list I borrow from Knowles) as a densely packed storehouse of antiquity.[30] However, there were others beyond this litany of interested parties who benefited from that construction.

The Kashmir Durbar

Reading the paratexts of the books on Kashmiri antiquities produced from the 1870s onwards, one is struck by the feeling of being in a perpetual tea party. Through acknowledgements, dedications and footnotes emerges the circle of Kashmir enthusiasts, the "white Pandits" of Srinagar around the turn of the century:[31] Stein, Grierson, Knowles, the medical missionaries Ernest and Arthur Neve and Canon Tyndale-Biscoe who followed in the footsteps of Knowles and Wade, the archaeologist-explorer (and later Resident of Kashmir) Francis Younghusband, the Settlement Officer Walter Lawrence. They all wrote copiously—the Neves, Tyndale-Biscoe, Younghusband, and Lawrence adding to the scholarly literature popular accounts of the Valley's history, geography, and ethnography—and they all named each other in their prefatory material.[32] Also always thanked are the successive British Residents of Jammu and Kashmir during this period. The Resident's office ultimately derived from the Treaty of Amritsar between Gulab Singh and the British. After the death of the second Maharaja Ranbir Singh, the official British role in the State transformed from "Officer on Special Duty" to "Resident," reflecting an increased presence and influence.[33] Its symbolic and material marker was "one of the most charming houses in India—a regular English country house,"[34] the British Residency in Srinagar. In its beautiful garden and reception rooms the "white Pandits" met and discussed over cucumber sandwiches the antiquity of Kashmir. As Evelyn Battye, Personal Assistant to the Resident in 1939 remembers, "one autumn visitor of great interest was the fascinating teller of outback tales, Sir Mark Aurel Stein, the famed Anglo-Hungarian archaeologist and explorer of Chinese Turkestan, a still vigorous man then in his old age."[35]

Stein's was indeed a long relationship with the Residency—as attested by the acknowledgments recorded in his *Catalogue* and the *Rajataranngini*.[36] His access to the manuscripts of the Raghunathji Temple had been enabled by the then Resident, Colonel R. Parry Nisbet, on whose recommendation the Jammu and Kashmir State Council "approved" his plan for cataloguing the Temple's treasures. When Stein turned to the equally tricky task of collating the *Rajatarangini*'s manuscripts, many of which were in the possession of Kashmiri Pandit families, the Residents Col. Barr, Mr. Barnes and Col. Sir Talbot likewise stepped in to mediate on the scholar's behalf, although, as Stein also acknowledges, it was Walter Lawrence who gave him "initial advice." For both the catalogue and the edition, moreover, the mediation was between not Stein and the Kashmiris themselves, but Stein and the third Maharaja Pratap Singh; hence, the fulsome thanks rendered by the former to the latter's "spirit of true enlightenment [that] has readily given assent to the proposal for making the great collection formed by his father generally accessible for research."[37] Also thanked is Pratap Singh's brother, Raja Amar Singh, for his supporting role as Prime Minister of Jammu and Kashmir and hence the head of its State Council. For the preparation of the *Rajatarangini,* the help they proffered was rather more material: "His Highness the Maharaja and the State Council of Jammu and Kashmir had already given proof of their generous interest in my labours by sanctioning in 1891 a grant toward the publication of the Chronicle."[38] Similar thanks to Pratap Singh and Amar Singh are also recorded by Walter Lawrence and Francis Younghusband in their memoirs of the Valley.

Why would the Dogra princes be so forthcoming in their help to a motley crew of European enthusiasts? In answer we may point to a phrase which crops up regularly within these records of acknowledgments, the "Kashmir Durbar," where "durbar" translates as "imperial assemblage," "royal court," and "government of the princely state."[39] Pratap Singh's facilitation of Indological research on Kashmir was conducted not merely in the persona of the Maharaja but on behalf of his Durbar—a structure and concept whose very existence derived from a complex set of colonial appropriations and indigenous re-appropriations of precolonial enactments of sovereignty. The Mughal Durbar was the physical space where the Emperor congregated with his court, the spectacle of the congregation on behalf of the subjects, and a symbolic network of hierarchies and interdependencies—a multivalency the British Empire liberally borrowed from to satisfy its love of "ornamentalism."[40] The transfer of power from the East India Company to the Crown following the "mutiny" of 1847 culminated in the three imperial Durbars (1877, 1903, and 1911), which "served to nationalise a local ceremonial idiom by bringing together princely India and British India in week-long festivals of chivalric unity, feudal hierarchy and imperial subordination."[41] The relationship between British India and the Dogra Princely State—ties "if not of affection then of self-interest"[42]—signals the Kashmir Durbar as constituting an ambivalent sign of simultaneous deference and self-assertion. Simultaneously, it negotiated the tricky business of extracting legitimacy from a subject population the vast majority of whom was connected to the Dogras neither by ethnicity nor religion. This double act is best illustrated by work patronized by the Maharaja in the Kashmir Durbar's name.

The Dogra search for legitimacy in Jammu and Kashmir was based on their assertion, for themselves, a high-born Hindu-ness.[43] It was achieved by playing to British stereotypes of Rajput aristocracy on the one hand, and courting, on the other, the urban component of Valley's small but significant Kashmiri Pandit group. The flourishing Indological scholarship on Kashmir, facilitated through long-term scholarly presence in the Valley, confirms and clarifies the workings of this strategy. The Residents enhanced their power on the ground through brokering between the Maharajas and the scholars; the scholars got access to primary material whose critical apparatuses they wanted to create; the Maharajas received through that scholarship external validation of their claims to the Valley; the Pandits, whom they encouraged to share information with the European scholars, were hailed by all concerned as vestiges of the ancient, pre-Islamic culture of Kashmir. The European pursuit of antiquity thus locked the Dogras, the British administrators, the scholars, and the Pandits into a circle of mutual benefit. The circle soon widened to include other players. The creation, in 1898, of Srinagar's Sardar Pratap Singh Museum on the premises of Ranbir Singh's summer palace already affords a preview of Dogra responses to European scholarly practices. More was to follow: the establishment, in 1904, of the Durbar's Archaeological and Research Department, and the inauguration, in 1911, of the Kashmir Series of Texts and Studies,[44] a project that echoes the title, format and vision of the prolific "texts and studies" production beloved of German philological culture.

The circulation of the constituent volumes of the Kashmir Series of Texts and Studies demonstrates the Kashmir Durbar's shrewd understanding of the mechanisms whereby value accrued through the infrastructure of academia. If, in the previous chapter, we discussed the mimetic capital generated through the circulation of photographs, we may now consider here the parallel phenomenon of academic capital. The Series was published by the Kashmir Durbar's Archaeological and Research Department, edited by its director, J. C. Chatterji, a Bengali Brahmin with a Cambridge education, and printed at the Nirnaya-Sagar Press in Bombay.[45] The title pages of its volumes were in both Devanagari and English, and adorned with the Department's stamp, at the centre of which sat the Dogra crest. Each volume was priced in rupees and shillings, testifying international circulation, and, in anticipation of a pan-European readership, was available through Trübner and Co. and Luzac and Co. in London, Otto Harrassowitz in Leipzig, and Ernest Laroux in Paris. Clearly, the Durbar had taken pains to ensure the dissemination of the Series, a strategy already evident in the presentation of Stein's Catalogue of Manuscripts to Cambridge's University Library by none other than "His Highness the Maharaja of Kashmir," Pratap Singh.[46] An early ambition to infiltrate the academic bastions of Europe thus seems to have come to fruition with the Kashmir Series. While its packaging and carefully planned dissemination signals the Durbar's decision to promote a certain brand of scholarship, the contents of the Series exposes the connection between that promotion and Dogra self-fashioning as Hindu rulers of a Hindu State.

In this context, that only around four percent of Jammu and Kashmir's population was Hindu did not matter. Far more significant was that these Hindus were uniformly Brahmin. Between 1894, when Knowles casually contrasted "learned Pandit" to "ignorant Mussalman," and 1900, when Grierson asserted the "purity" of Pandit speech against its "contamination" by Kashmiri Muslims,[47] the Indologists had increasingly privileged Kashmir not merely as a Hindu enclave within a degenerate Muslim population but, in retrospect rather shamefully, as a "pure," Brahmin Hindu enclave. It was this privileging that the Dogras seized, themselves neither Kashmiri nor Brahmins but eager to ally with latter as joint custodians of a heritage buried under centuries of Muslim intervention and avowed decay. Their calculated exploitation of Indology's love affair with Brahminism is evident in their willingness to showcase, through the Kashmir Series, the Shaivite Hinduism of the Kashmiri Pandits—somewhat unexpected given their own Vaishnavite practice.[48] Thus the first volume was a critical edition of two Sanskrit handbooks of Shaivism, the *Sutras* of Vasu Gupta and the *Vimarshini* by Kshemaraja. In the preface, Chatterji acknowledged the different Pandits who had contributed to this task, thereby refashioning standard Indological practice into a new collaboration that anticipates the utility of Kashmir for a vision of Hindu India.[49] In 1912, a prospectus of the publications of the archaeological and research department was issued, revealing an ambitious editorial remit of over eighty similar Shaivite texts.[50] In the words of Pandit Mukunda Shastri, who edited for the Series "a rare work bearing on the Advaita Shaiva Philosophy of Kashmir": "Above all, it is the munificence of the Kashmir Darbar which, in fact, is to be applauded for the publication of such philosophical works, and deserves the heartfelt thanks of the students of Hindu Philosophy all over the world."[51]

Sacred Soil of Kashyapa

"The Valley of Kashmir is the holy land of the Hindus." Thus opens the chapter entitled "Archaeology" in Walter Lawrence's *The Valley of Kashmir,* clearly delineating the overlap between the project of constructing a Kashmiri antiquity and the reclaiming of the Kashmir Valley for Shaivite Hinduism. As Lawrence goes on to elaborate, "I have rarely been in any village which cannot show some relic of antiquity. Curious stone miniatures of the old Kashmiri temples, huge stone seats of Mahadeo [Shiva] inverted by pious Musalmans, Phallic emblems innumerable, and carved images heaped in grotesque confusion by some clear spring, have met me at every turn."[52] The insistent coupling of "relic of antiquity" with "village" and "spring" articulates Hinduism's primordial relationship with Kashmiri topography and political economy, while simultaneously alienating the "pious Musalman" from those relics. Thus the assertion of

Kashmir's importance to Hindus necessarily removes Muslim claims to the same territory—a result most ironic (but perhaps predictable) in a text that records its author's task of reforming the relationship between Kashmiri Muslim peasants and their largely Pandit landowners.[53] Granted, it was in the colonial interest to declare that relationship painfully oppressive; nevertheless, the historical obfuscation of its basic power dynamics is a consequence of the scholarly promotion of the links between Shaivism and the Kashmir Valley. That promotion increasingly heralded the Valley as a crucible for a Shaivism that heralded Kashmir's singularity while also somehow representing Hinduism at large. Between its geographic position and its putative role as guardian of Shaivite Hinduism developed a powerful homology, apparent already in Stein's emphasis on the Valley as a "little world enclosed by the ramparts" of the Pir Panjal range, but containing nevertheless a historical interest that "far exceeds [these] narrow geographical limits."[54]

Stein's scholarship was, in fact, absolutely crucial to this homology. The map of ancient Kashmir accompanying his edition of the *Rajatarangini* both conveys his understanding of the Kashmiri landscape as indelibly stamped by the traces of its pre-Islamic past, and superimposes this understanding on to the colonial practice of mapping and surveying—the map in question being recently enabled by the Great Trigonometric Survey of India. His many photographs of the actual stone blocks out of which Kashmiri temples were built co-opts another mechanism of colonial modernity into the retrieval and preservation of ancient Kashmir's lithographic traces. The photograph of the peak in the Pir Panjal called the Harmukh (Face of Shiva) that forms the frontispiece of the inaugural volume in the Kashmir Series demonstrates the wider utility of these transformations, into whose service even geology was marshaled.[55] Evidence from rocks and fossils was used to verify the legend of Kashmir's lacustrine origins, preserved both in the *Rajatarangini* and another Sanskrit text, the *Nilmatha Purana,* to which it was intertextually linked. The legend in question commemorated the emergence of the Valley through the draining of an immense lake by the sage Kashyapa in order to check the excesses of the demon Jalodhbhava who dwelt within it.[56] Support for it was also found in the etymological explication of Kashmir as *kashyapa-mar* or "Kashyapa's lake."[57] The preface of the twenty-second volume of the Kashmir Series appeals to both Sanskrit myth and paleonto-geology in its commendation that "the Kashmir Durbar as also those interested in the Philosophy of the sacred soil of Kashyapa are to be complimented on the appearance of this volume."[58]

The "highly abstruse and deeply philosophical nature" of the book in question metonymically colors the Valley from which its contents are seen to have sprung.[59] The cerebral and organic are seen as more than merely coexisting in Kashmiri Hinduism; together, they imbue the Valley with a prehistorical sacrality. If Kashmir thereby emerges as the "soil of Kashyapa," that soil's "sacredness" derives from an academic emphasis somewhat tangential to that of Sanskritic Indology (although fully compatible with it). Study of the Valley's Greco-Buddhist architecture had encouraged a loose but suggestive linkage between Kashmir, classical antiquity, and paganism. Alfred Foucher, French archaeologist and Stein's long-time rival, located "this special charm of Kashmir" in "the grouping of two kinds of beauty in the midst of a nature still animated with a mysterious life, which knows how to whisper close to our ear and make the pagan depths of us quiver." The two said beauties are, respectively, "its magnificent woods, the pure limpidity of its lakes, the splendor of its snowy mountain tops, the happy murmur of its myriad brooks sounding in the cool soft air," and "the grace or majesty of its ancient buildings." For Foucher, the grandeur of Martand recalled a Greek temple, the tiny shrine of Payar "the choragic monument of Lysiscrates," and "the gujar shepherds . . . the Sicilian shepherds in Theocritus."[60] In a nice inversion, Arcadia is declared "the Kashmir of Greece," whence Pan had fled "to escape persecution;" in Foucher's own flight of "mystic fancy," Pan, and classical antiquity, were "still living in the shadowy heart of the Kashmiri jungle" and in the lost valleys of the Himalayas." Such scholarly rhapsodizing on the *pantheistic* quality of Kashmir was easily mobilized into the construction of Kashmiri Shaivism as uniquely esoteric and spiritual.

Esotericism, however, was of little use if not made known to an audience beyond the scholarly. Foucher's florid imaginings of Kashmir appeared in 1933 within his introduction to a publication by the India Society, *Ancient Monuments of Kashmir*. Written by R. C. Kak, sometime director of the Kashmir Durbar's Department of Archaeology and Research, and himself a Kashmiri Pandit, the book was, unsurprisingly, "generously" funded by "the Government of HH the Maharaja of Jammu and Kashmir." Kak describes it in the preface as a digest of the "several valuable accounts published of the various classes of monuments in the Valley [but] . . . mostly scattered over Journals of learned Societies, Archaeological survey reports, and other similar publications, to which the general reader has not easy access."[61] While Kak's footnotes certainly reveal his diligent assimilation of Indological scholarship such as Stein's, he nevertheless goes beyond his masters in presenting, particularly in his chapter "Political History," the Islamic period in Kashmir as one of unmitigated plunder, barbarism, and iconoclasm. The privileging of the Valley's Hinduism is visually supported by the accompanying photographs: there are three of Kashmir's scenery and six of its Islamicate heritage (the Mughal gardens, the Hari Parbat, the Jama Masjid, Bud Shah's tomb and the Mosque of Akhun Mulla Shah); but these pale in comparison against the forty-seven photographs of terra-cotta tiles and medallions from pre-Islamic sites, and fifteen large plates of temples. Through this "handy, compact and easily accessible" work, then, "the sacred soil of Kashyapa" is popularized for the visitor who, "without desiring any great erudition, takes an intelligent interest in the subject of Archaeology."[62]

In this task, Kak is heartily commended by Francis Younghusband, celebrity explorer-archaeologist in the Stein tradition and, between 1906 and 1909, Resident in Srinagar. In a specially written foreword to *Ancient Monuments,* Younghusband eulogizes Kashmir's beauty by condensing diverse inherited discourses: the "girdle of snowy mountains" and the "primeval forests" hailed by Indologists, the "paradise of bliss" of the Mughals, the travelers who pine either "to go there" or "to go there again" in the manner of *Lalla Rookh*'s readers.[63] But he also insists that the enjoyment of this natural beauty should be properly accompanied by "study" (such as that now enabled by Kak's book) of the remains left in the Valley by the "great ones of India." This exhortation is echoed in Foucher's introductory remarks to *Ancient Monuments*: "not all the people who visit Kashmir go there only to hunt, or to fish or to dance. Some take with them to the Happy Valley interest of a more intellectual kind, and for them the India Society has had the excellent idea of publishing this volume by Mr. Ram Chandra Kak."[64] In his 1909 memoir-cum-guidebook, *Kashmir,* Younghusband had already mock-ruefully commented that "the pleasures of travel in Kashmir are surely and steadily deteriorating. . . . The visitor disposed to solitude more frequently encounters his fellow Britisher."[65] This increased accessibility of Kashmir to visitors more casual than hardy explorers, high altitude photographers and Great Game enthusiasts corresponds to the growth of international tourism at the turn of the century. Nevertheless, Younghusband's and Foucher's support for Kak goes beyond the intellectual panic that the change from the hard graft of travel into the cushioned ease of tourism has typically triggered.[66]

The emphasis on an intellectual approach to the Valley's natural resources, and the concomitant appeal to its archaeological remains, point to an emergent contestation over the sacred soil of Kashyapa somewhat more complex than the binary between the tourist and the traveler posited by historians of tourism.[67] *Ancient Monuments* needs to make the distinction between the superficial pursuit of hunting, fishing and dancing and the more worthy examination of Kashmir's ancient monuments in order to justify its own existence in the world. Its promise of accessibility lures the traveler into the world of esotericism while it remains firmly embedded within the discourses that constructed that esotericism in the first place. The Valley as a realm of Shaivism and a cradle of pantheistic antiquity had generated the need for exegesis or scholarly explication to the world at large. Precisely such exegesis created the "markers" required to solicit what has been termed "the touristic gaze."[68] "The many plates accompanying the volume will serve to remind the returned traveler of the beauty of Kashmiri sites and buildings, and to the intending traveller will give food for his imagination." Foucher's words here betray the permeation of the scholarly apparatus by the tourist's need for the souvenir.[69] The blurring induced by the welding together of photography and tourism is even more apparent in Younghusband's *Kashmir,* which had lamented the passing away of an old order of "virgin travel."[70] Younghusband's written account is nevertheless illustrated by soft watercolors (by one Major Molyneux) blatantly derivative of the photographic views established by Bourne and Burke. In these coexisting declarations of esotericism and practices of accessibility we glimpse the forging of alliances, as delicately balanced as that between the Dogras and the British, between groups with ostensibly opposing interests.

The Happy Valley

It was a cold spring afternoon in April 2004. Even as I had arrived in Srinagar to combine research with a workshop for students, conducted with a friend who taught political science at Srinagar's Government College for Women, the friend in question was struggling for his life in hospital after being shot repeatedly at close range by two unknown youths who had entered his home on the pretext of academic discussion. While, in the houseboat *H.B. Holiday Inn,* I grappled with the fragility and violence of contemporary Kashmir, its owners came up to me with a papier maché folder,[71] whose tattered covers could barely contain what looked like a bundle of frayed and yellowed documents. Knowing of my insatiable interest for all "old things" in Kashmir, they had correctly surmised it would offer some small means of distraction. Inside, I found several, variously-sized hand-written notes, many headed with the crests of army regiments. As I rifled through the material with increasing excitement, a familiar name suddenly leapt out: "Dr M. Aurel Stein." The signature executed in thick black pen, which I was to see several times in the future in more expected places, spread in a confident slant across an A5 sized, unheaded leaf of paper: "October 3rd, '88, Baramulla. Mohamdu boatman has been in my service for the last five weeks, during which he took me to Lake Manasbal, the Dhal and several points on the Viha't [or Vyeth, from "Vitasta," the Sanskrit name for the Jhelum]. He accompanied me also on small journeys inland and proved everywhere a useful servant. He has a quick perception and the wish to please. His boat was always very clean as well as his shikara."[72]

This uncanny trace left by a not-yet-famous Stein, in chance custody of the descendants of the boatman who facilitated his "antiquarian tours,"[73] returns us to the godaam as a humbler, but far more charged site of memorialization than the post-Imperial archive. As with the pink plastic box that taught me to interrogate the camera in Kashmir, a contingent encounter with a papier maché folder first alerted me to the deep connections between tourism and Kashmir's academic construction as an antique land. The *Holiday Inn* testimonials are as relentlessly palimpsestic as the Majlis photographs: covered with official stamps, numbered in different sequences by different pens, stuck to other sheets of paper on which are traced mysterious handprints. While these marks remain largely undecipherable, the testimonials do enable a basic reconstruction of three generations of boatmen (and vessels) between 1887 and the 1930s: Mohamdu of the 1880s, and his unnamed doonga boat; his son Rahmana of the 1900s, whose doonga had acquired the name "Alexandra"; and, by the 1930s, the grandson Khalika, owner of the *H.B. Eagle* and the *H.B. Golden Fleece* (and the father of the *Holiday Inn*'s current owner). The men are praised for their knowledge of hunting and fishing terrain, for skilful navigation, for cleanliness and affability, and, increasingly, for European-style cooking and fluency in English—skills summed up by that phrase beloved of Anglo-India, "a good bandobast." Fragmentary remnants of the houseboat's colonial origins, these "chits" are the material link between today's walnut-wood-paneled, sedentary leviathans bursting with noisy groups of middle-class Bengali and Gujarati tourists, and the mobile, reed-matted doonga boat so indispensable to our tireless Indologists.

That the houseboat, which now crystallizes the clichéd experience of Kashmir as the tourist's "Happy Valley," should share a genealogy with the pursuit of Kashmir's antiquity is entirely consonant with the historically close links between the heritage and tourism industries worldwide.[74] But the chasm between postcolonial India's continued promotion of the Valley as tourist paradise and the realities of daily life there—a chasm into which I was first thrust in April 2004—demands that we critically prise open those links. As Daniel Spurr has observed while discussing the case of Mexico, the relationship between the "cultivation of an aesthetic ideal" and "domination in the realms of concrete practice": "When Mexico is removed by interpretation from the actual consequences of political and economic power, the capitalist and the archaeologist can more readily go about their business."[75] For Kashmir, though, I would reverse this statement. It is the business of tourism—that iconic capitalist industry—in conjunction with philology and archaeology, which has contributed to Kashmir's removal, by interpretation, from materialist considerations. Let us then, "through the force of (counter-) interpretation,"[76] return the Indological construction of the Valley as a living, and, increasingly, a Hindu antique land, to the previous chapter's conclusions concerning the photographic framing of Kashmir's natural beauty. These two trajectories of representing Kashmir then emerge braided together with a third strand: the development of a tourist infrastructure for the Valley from the 1880s onward. It is this development, itself another by-product of the power struggle between the Dogras and the British, that rearticulated Kashmir as "the Happy Valley" and consolidated its framing as the territory of desire.

Gulab Singh's rule, the period of Dogra experimentation with modes of legitimacy,[77] was also when Europeans traversed Kashmir as explorers on cartographic reconnaissance missions. As Lieutenant-Colonel Torrens remarked in his "Travels in Ladak, Tartary and Kashmir" of 1862, although "European energy [had] before explored every portion of our intended route . . . it was known to but few—to an enterprising shikaree [i.e., sportsman] or two, a still rarer scientific traveler, or to the persevering members of the Indian Survey Department."[78] The consolidation of the Dogra Hindu state under Ranbir Singh coincided with the heyday of the photographer-explorers and their framing of the Valley as pastoral fantasy. Travel *to* Kashmir replaced travel *through* Kashmir. By Pratap Singh's time, there were far more European visitors here, including women. In 1879, Mrs. Murray Aysnley wrote of traveling from Lahore to Srinagar equipped with tents and servants, but, thanks to the British Officer's helpfulness, staying in a "bungalow for visitors" on the Jhelum's banks (the tents came in handy, however, when they moved to the Liddar Valley for a spot of shooting).[79] The increase both in the remit of activities for visitors, and in their formalization and regularization, reflects the power struggles between Pratap Singh and the British; the more they took away from him, the more rules and conditions he imposed. This tug-of-war is captured in the six appendices to Wakefield's *Happy Valley* of 1879, which compile information about routes to the Valley, tariffs for boat hire and postal rates alongside "rules for the guidance of officers and other travelers visiting the dominions of HH Runbeer Singh," "local rules for the guidance of visitors in Kashmir," and, most revealingly, the complete text of the Treaty of Amritsar.[80]

These appendices transform Wakefield's "sketches of Kashmir and Kashmiris" into a de facto guidebook that also calibrates the shift between the Great Game explorers and a newer breed of Kashmir enthusiasts. Just as the former had filled up the "great blank" between Kashmir and Ladakh,[81] the latter's demands were fast filling up an infrastructural blank. Those looking back, through their memoirs, on the last two decades of the century invariably recall this period as one of hectic change in the Valley, spurred on by the opening of the Suez Canal.[82] The doongas had expanded into houseboats with European-style bedrooms, bathrooms, pantries and reception rooms. Boatmen were serving memsahibs marmalade and toast at breakfast, scones at tea and puddings at dinner, European dry goods now being freely retailed from Cockburn's Agency in Srinagar. Letters and telegrams sent from Lahore and Rawalpindi instructed houseboat owners to receive their guests upstream at Baramulla, and keep the larder stocked and mattresses aired, while boatmen flourished headed notepaper and demanded signed contracts.[83] Alternative accommodation also developed; where Wakefield and Mrs. Murray could only point to tents and the possibility of visitors' bungalows, in 1904 *The Imperial Guide to India* was directing tourists to Nedou's Hotels in Srinagar and Gulmarg, the brainchild of Michael Nedou, an Austro-Hungarian entrepreneur whose enterprise equaled Stein's.[84] The alpine meadow of Gulmarg, in the 1870s already established as an escape from Srinagar's summer, had by the new century spawned a thriving social scene with balls, parties and picnics;[85] its facilities ranged from golf courses to hairdressers "just come out from London" and offering, at "Nedou's Hotel during the Gulmarg Season," the latest "permanent waving" and "point winding system" for "soft and long-lasting curls."[86]

Flapper haircuts, Thomas Cook's services, and, not to forget, Mahatta's Studio: by the 1920s the Valley was fully enmeshed in an international modernity—even if primarily to benefit those who thronged it in summer.[87] As M. M. Kaye fondly recollects of the 1920s and 1930s: "That was a wonderful time; sun-soaked and pine-scented days, and moonlit or star-spangled nights, laughter and dancing, and a band playing hit tunes of the day."[88] Photographs, now of social activities, interacted with memoirs to encase the Valley in thick memorialization: thus Kaye "had read Moore's *Lalla Rookh* and Younghusband's *Kashmir,* admired Molyneux's delightful watercolours and Mother's amateur efforts at copying them, seen endless snapshots in other people's albums as well as the ones Mother kept so carefully, and in general heard a great deal about the spectacular beauties of that favoured country."[89] Anticipation, experience and recollection fused into one enchanted continuum, effectively insulating the construct of "the Happy Valley" from gathering political events both in India and in Jammu and Kashmir. While the Bright Young Things "dance[d] until well after midnight at Nedou's Hotel or the Club, without a care in the world,"[90] a charismatic young Kashmiri Muslim called Sheikh Abdullah was rallying his fellow Kashmiris against Dogra rule, and another equally charismatic young Indian of Kashmiri Pandit extraction, Jawaharlal Nehru, was poised to plunge into anticolonial resistance. In the not-so-distant future lay their eventual love-hate relationship, and the fateful collision of their respective dreams and hopes. If today, eager plains-dwellers still flock to Gulmarg, despite the very real possibility of bombs exploding in their tourist buses,[91] then in that astonishingly persistent illusion of the Happy Valley lies their complex legacy.

Memoried Loveliness of Ages Past

Let us now return to that momentous work with which I began, Nehru's *Discovery of India,* and to my overarching concern with the relationship between India as "modern nation" and Kashmir as "antique land." I have demonstrated thus far the interrelationship between different genres of writing, different sorts of interests, and the emergent representation of the Valley as a territory of desire. I now want to suggest how this discursive accumulation of symbolic resources during the period of Dogra rule helped shape the postcolonial nation's sense of self. A crucial bridge between the colonial and the postcolonial is Nehru, himself from a high-profile family of émigré Pandits long settled in the city of Allahabad.[92] While Nehru's self-confessed "partiality" to the Valley of Kashmir has attained the status of urban legend, how Kashmir moves between Nehru's emotions and Nehru's prose demands fuller attention. Well known though *The Discovery of India* is as a foundational text for Nehruvian secularism,[93] we need to probe deeper the role of Kashmir therein in constructing that vision of India. Not coincidentally, substantial references to the Valley occur here in those highly sensitive textual positions, its beginning and its end. Consolidating this framing work of Kashmir for Nehru's extended argument is a seemingly matter-of-fact reference in the Postscript to a month-long trek in Kashmir. Here Nehru speaks with relief of finally escaping his post-prison whirl of political activities to Kashmir's "mountains and snow-covered peaks."[94] This reference to the Valley's therapeutic power at the edges of the text combines tellingly with the metaphysical and historical discussions within which it is elsewhere deployed.

The Discovery of India is driven by the urgent anticolonial need to possess a vibrant concept of India that could swirl together its "physical and geographic aspects," its "past" and its place in "the modern world."[95] An inherited idea of Kashmir manifests itself as an essential building block within this metanarrative. Seeking precolonial evidence for "the long panorama of India's history," Nehru has "journeyed through India in the company of mighty travellers from China and Western and Central Asia" and their reports; in particular, he has "wandered over the Himalayas, which are closely connected with old myth and legend, and which have influenced so much of our thought and literature."[96] Especially drawn to them through his "love of the mountains" and "kinship with Kashmir" he "saw there not only the life and vigour and beauty of the present, but also the memoried loveliness of ages past." Into this expressive phrase is condensed Kashmir as a storehouse of a living antiquity, as a place of extraordinary natural beauty, and as a layered site of collective memorialization. Thanks to such discursive and affective multivalency, Kashmir can enshrine "something living and vital" that redeems India despite "a progressive deterioration during centuries."[97] It furnishes the necessary connection between the past and present, a connection that, in its organic vigor, far surpasses "the books and old monuments and past cultural achievements [that] helped [him] produce some understanding of India."[98] Nehru's self-awareness here—that, as alienated member of the Anglophone elite class, he is capable of but also restricted to "producing"

India as "ancient palimpsest"—recurs in his later admission, reproduced in my epigraph, of "constructing pictures of his choice."

The deliberate insertion of Kashmir into Nehru's picture of India derives from his engagement with select, and by now, hopefully, recognizable aspects of Kashmiri geography and history. Kashmir is presented as the geographic limit case of the evolving Indian nation space, which was, at that very moment, being visualized as Bharat Mata (Mother India) in nationalist discourse.[99] The seductions of the Janus-faced "just beyond" that we noted in the previous chapter animates Nehru's interest in Kashmir's Central Asian links as well as his attempted enclosure of it within the spatial extent of India. Even as the postcolonial nation was to incorporate Kashmir into its geo-body by curving its borders around it, so too does Nehru discover his India by wrapping his first and final chapters around references to the Valley. Justification for this move comes from the Valley's hospitality to autochthonous Indic religions, Buddhism and Hinduism, that vertical connection between the histories of Kashmir and India having already been formulated through the emphases of the Indologists and the Kashmir Durbar. Historical depth and geographic positioning merge to make Kashmir one of India's remaining "favoured spots where we may still sense the mystery of nature, listen to the song of life and beauty, and draw vitality from it."[100] The lines are blurred between a soft Hinduism and Kashmir as a repository of a "pagan," "pantheistic outlook." No guesswork is needed to connect Nehru's flight of pantheistic fancy to the "mystic fancy" of Alfred Foucher. Substantial chunks from Foucher's introduction to Kak's *Ancient Monuments* appear in this chapter to support Nehru's evaluation of Kashmir as a "favoured spot" where "loveliness dwells and an enchantment steals over the senses."[101]

Nehru's eloquence sharpens Kashmir's contrast to the modern world's spiritual depletion. Presumably its brand of pantheistic "enchantment" is the same as that "enchantment" and "witchery" which once vivified India, and, once again, that "old enchantment that seems to be breaking today as she awakens to the present."[102] His own enchantment with this word fashions Kashmir as a promised antidote to India's yearned-for modernity. It is the antique land that, in retaining the quintessence of India, will enable the nation overcome the "signs of sterility and racial decadence" blighting "modern civilisation." The intellectual bedrock for Nehru's dreams of modernity, *The Discovery of India* also articulates his fears concerning "the competitive and acquisitive characteristics of modern capitalist society, the enthronement of wealth above everything else, and the continuous strain and the lack of security for many," [which] add to the ill-health of the mind and produce neurotic states." In hypothesizing "a saner and more balanced economic structure [that] would lead to an improvement of these conditions," Nehru is unambiguous about the necessity of "greater and more living contacts with the land and nature."[103] While he does not specify Kashmir at this point, his underlying assumptions are articulated in those 1960s films that play off Kashmir as pastoral fantasy against capitalist bastions such as Bombay. Nehru's mobilization of Kashmir for modern India proves equally useful for its postcolonial historiography; the passage that provides my epigraph also appears as frontispiece to S. C. Roy's *Early History of Kashmir,* whose foreword by historian K. N. Panikkar insists that "walled off by high mountains and endowed with unequalled natural beauty, Kashmir remained an inviolate sanctuary of Indian culture."[104]

If Kashmir furnished the essential complement to the modern nation which, thanks to its anticipated economic advancement, was deemed to have lost touch with nature and spirituality, academic work in post-1947 Jammu and Kashmir continued the Durbar's project of promoting the Valley's nature and spirituality by yoking it to Shaivism. *A Descriptive Analysis of The Kashmir Series of Texts and Studies,* issued in the 1950s by the Research and Publications Department of the Jammu and Kashmir Government, opens by asserting that of the eighty-seven volumes produced thus far by the Department, "no less than fifty-six, comprising sixty-four separate works, are just on the one subject of . . . the "Trika Shastra," or the Threefold Science," a distillation of the Shaivite philosophy that is the "greatest" of Kashmir's many "humanistic achievements."[105] Kashmiri Hinduism's relevance to Indian culture reappears in familiar conjunction with Shaivism's organic connection with Kashmir. The Trika "represents the Vedanta, the Sankhya, the Dharma and Vinaya of the Buddha and of the Vaisheshika-Nyaya, as well as all that is highest and noblest in the Vaishnava and Shakta schools, particularly the emotional discipline of supreme love and devotion *(bhakti)* and aesthetic appreciation." But, "like saffron," it is also Kashmir's "very own, growing nowhere else in India except Kashmir," and so "altogether unique to it." Visually supporting these opening statements are several black-and-white photographs of the Himalayas, Hindu temples of the Valley and Sanskrit epigraphs, interspersed with crude line drawings of Shiva: an arresting frontispiece image of Shiva Mahadeva in Tandava pose, another of his bust placed over an open book, and a third, larger bust placed over a plinth on which is written (in English), "Tantralok" (the abode of Tantra).[106]

This ostensibly strange combination of illustrations reveals a struggle broadly consonant with the 1950s as a time when, as Partha Chatterjee observes, "one is as yet unsure which way the plot will move." Analyzing similar drawings of historical monuments in 1950s Indian textbooks, Chatterjee posits the emergence, through them, "of an attitude of sacredness in connection with national icons diametrically opposed to that of the romantic." Unlike the photograph's "romantic anachronism," the drawing's "visual anachronism" decontextualizes "the real object," locating it "in an abstract and timeless space."[107] Here, the drawings are not even of a "real object" but of a Hindu god. The pedagogic equivalence bestowed on Shiva and Kashmir's temples enacts an intellectual decolonization that would ultimately insist on the epistemological equivalence of "myth" and "history."[108] A "yearning for the index" nevertheless persists, particularly in photographs of a measuring tape placed against fragments of stone carvings.[109] *A Descriptive Analysis* thus demonstrates the continued subscription to colonial-style empirical validation alongside a resurgent neo-traditionalism. Its pages capture a postcolonial reconstitution of colonial modernity through the best fit between the modern nation and Kashmir's "memoried loveliness." It also suggests new developments in Abdullah's post-Dogra administration, which empowered Kashmiri Muslims through land reforms and through breaking the Pandit monopoly on government jobs.[110] The deputy director of the Jammu and Kashmir Research Department now bears not a Pandit but a Muslim name (Sahibzada Hassan Shah). However, even as new entrants to the middle class in Jammu and Kashmir emerged to threaten established elites, the latter found succor in the nation's project of the best fit—not just in the realm of ideas, but in the structuring of a federated polity.

Until the 1990s, the British Residency in Srinagar housed a Handicrafts Centre run by the State Government of Jammu and Kashmir—a transformation the significance of which will unfold in chapter 4, but that, at the close of this one, offers a succinct comment on the postcolonial utility of pre-1947 structures of power. The state government's relationship to the central government in Delhi is seen by many in contemporary Kashmir as replicating the fraught collaboration between the Dogras and the British. The continuity lies in a perceived disregard for the people of the Valley, even while the Valley furnishes potent symbolic and affective resources for the nation. In 1999, the Residency was burnt in a mysterious act of arson, presaging the gutting of the Tourist Centre, next to which it stood, in April 2005; this latter, less mysterious act was perpetrated by Kashmiri militants protesting the reopening, by the state and central governments in conjunction with the government of Pakistan, of the Srinagar-Muzaffarabad Road, a route much traversed by pre-1947 travelers to Kashmir but interrupted by the Line of Control from 1948 onward.[111] Both these episodes exemplify the long-lasting impact of the European presence in Kashmir during Dogra-British rule, whereby the Valley became a hothouse of modernity though modernity failed to take root in it. Paradoxically, its very construction as a space of antiquity and beauty has been mobilized into a site of contestation. Equally amenable to Nehru's secularism and to political Hinduism of various shades, the territory of desire has also been variously internalized and contested by Kashmiris who seek to dialogue on equal terms with the Indian nation. It is that dialogue between discourse and counterdiscourse, hegemony and resistance that the remainder of the book focuses on.

Hinge

Toward Unmaking

Fetish of Paradise

In abnormal times extraordinary things blossom.

—Khazir Hassan Qasba, Kashmiri craftsman

He not only defetishizes; he reenchants.

—Michael Taussig, "Maleficium: State Fetishism"

In August 2005, I was in Srinagar, investigating the production of papier maché handicraft. The previous summer I had met at Government Art College in Srinagar a Kashmiri artist, Masood Hussain, who makes large bas-reliefs of papier maché.[1] Hussain's imaginative grappling with this Kashmiri craft tradition spoke to my desire to critique, through handicraft, the relationship between Kashmir, tourism, and the postcolonial nation. In Delhi the following year, a comprehensive exhibition of Hussain's works helped me to begin conceptualizing the Kashmiri souvenir as the nation's fetish. I arrived in Srinagar a few months later with some theoretical understanding of fetishism and some historical understanding of handicraft as nationalist project in India. I was nevertheless unprepared for what I discovered in the living room of Agha Ashraf Ali, educationist and father of a poet: a vase nearly six feet high, ostensibly porcelain but on closer inspection made of papier maché, and a bonsai-sized crab apple tree, bearing birds and blossoms, carved of Kashmiri walnut wood. Their exceptionality was illuminatingly emphasized by the master craftsmen who were their creators. As Khazir Hassan Qasba, maker of the crab apple tree, expressed in the aphorism I cited as my first epigraph to this chapter, these exquisite masterpieces, manifestations of an inner urge, "a flash of the soul," were signs of abnormality, of excess. Syed Hasan, the maker of the vase, agreed with him.[2] In these creations, however, I find also the work of "defetishization" and "reenchantment" that Michael Taussig, in my second epigraph, asserts.[3]

This "hinge" chapter unravels the connections between some prominent signifiers of Kashmir in the "abnormal times" of contemporary India: Kashmiri handicraft, Kashmir as territory of desire, and the Kashmir conflict. It thereby draws a line of continuity through the work of my previous chapters, and pulls that work toward the three chapters that will follow it. As I explained in the Introduction, it thus functions as a literal hinge within the book's extended argument: it moves forward where chapter 3 ends—with the beginnings of a nationalist discourse around Kashmir that promoted its purity and antiquity to supplement the modern Indian nation—while simultaneously anticipating my focus on Kashmiri counterdiscourse that shall be the subject of the remainder of the book. On the one hand, therefore, I examine here the importance of Kashmiri handicraft in discursively consolidating Kashmir's relationship to the nation. On the other, I use handicraft itself to show how Kashmiri creativity today grapples with the signifiers of exceptionality as subjugation. I take as exemplary here Masood Hussain's transformations of papier maché into multilayered condensates of an alternative Kashmiri history, a history the signposts of which are the wounded Kashmiri body, the fragility of Kashmiri culture, and the healing power of spirituality. But I place Hussain alongside contemporary Kashmiri craftsmen working in more anonymous ways with souvenir production for a vast domestic and international tourist and craft market. Bringing together the artist and the craftsman is the shared power of transformation, emanating from the common ground of the *karkhana* (Urdu: workshop), and restoring in both the depleted aura of the *karigar* (Urdu: workman, craftsman).

Under colonial industrialization, the karkhana or artisan workshop developed the new meaning of "factory."[4] Its companion word, karigar, has escaped a similar semantic trajectory, its association with karkhana having loosened. By examining the artist/artisan through the composite filter of the karkhana and karigar, I reconceptualize certain circuits of value that confer on objects the sheen of capital. Earlier, the godaam enabled us to dismantle the nexus between storage and value. Now, the karkhana and the karigar help reinstate buried connections between value and making. Hence, in this hinge, the theoretical utility of the concept of the fetish: in psychoanalytical theory the telltale substitute for an original loss, in Marxist usage the signifier of the commodity's lure through its alienation from labor *(kar),* but whose etymology returns us to the "handmade" and the talismanic.[5] Hussain's artwork helps me wrench out of the superficial veneer of the handmade papier maché souvenir an *affective* political reading of the craftwork in modernity and, particularly, of the Kashmiri craft object as traumatic reminder of the nation's disavowal of the Kashmir conflict. The psychosocial overlap between the souvenir and the fetish manifests itself as the alluring surface that both obscures history and announces this obscuring, and whose symptomatic correlate is the carapace or the "mask of desire." Through the fetish of paradise, then, I recapitulate my conceptual and historical arguments to probe deeper into Kashmir as the nation's phantasmatic topography.[6] Guided by the Kashmiri karigar, however, I also prise out of this topography a critical, even redemptive ability "to draw out the sacred quality of State power" as the master of all fetishes.[7]

Pain

During the summer of 1995, while living in New York, the late Agha Shahid Ali came across photographs of recent work by Masood Hussain—his contemporary in age and, like Ali had once been, an inhabitant of Srinagar. "One particular photograph made an emotional claim on me," wrote Ali later, and he asked Hussain, through friends, for permission to use it on the cover of his manuscript of poems, *The Country without a Post Office.* In his review of the 1998 Delhi exhibition of Hussain's works, which included the piece that made it to the book cover, Ali explains his choice: "Not only is it beautiful, but the cover further textures the poems and underscores, quite compellingly, the literal and metaphoric implications of the title." One image of a child "looking out from an enclosed space, possibly a hideout" becomes, in an allusion to Walter Benjamin, "Masood Hussain's angel of history, wearing many expressions at once—fear, longing, hope, curiosity, helplessness, resignation." If, however, "to see all this in a child's face" exemplifies how "in Masood's work, the political exists only by inhabiting the mystical," this insight is in turn enabled by his depiction of the child's hideout: "in parts barricaded with sculptured carvings of/from tree trunks, on all of them an incidental graffiti scrawl of Persian letters, the wounded wood in places sutured together, and at the base, a reminder of Kashmir's destroyed latticework." A *tasbih,* or Muslim rosary, hanging from the latticework, offers a further "hint of helpless prayer."[8]

Texture, latticework, prayer, the political, and the mystical: the significance of each of these elements will unfold gradually in this chapter. But by highlighting them Ali announces his own stake in explicating to Indian viewers a Kashmiri artist's work—a task that we see his father continuing today as, for instance, when he converts his home into a temporary exhibition space for Kashmiri master craftsmen. In endorsing Hussain's exhibition, Ali insists on a national visibility for Kashmiri artists, through which Kashmiri voices, otherwise as "trapped" as "the angel of history," can bring news to the outside of what has been happening in Kashmir. "In Masood Hussain's work, we are in the world of destroyed shrines, broken windows, crushed prayers." This "we" draws readers and viewers together toward the deeper meanings of such destruction: "What uncompromising reminders we are given of ruined latticework! Memory is brought to harbour passionately, so it may survive despite threats to it and the history behind it."[9] As with the "mobile photos" of Shakeel Bakshi, destruction, survival, and restoration alike are conducted here through the material incarnations of history and memory. Thus a key signifier for both Hussain and Ali is *panjr,*[10] the wooden latticeworked windows that adorn Kashmiri shrines and homes, but that, in post-1989 Srinagar, often dangle half-broken from their hinges, announcing abandonment and desolation. Despite, or because of, this visual fragility, artist and poet assert through latticework the resilient particularity of Kashmiri everyday life. For Ali, Hussain's representation of the ruined but still surviving materiality of latticework revives kashmiriyat itself—a concept to which "only artists and their sympathizers may now be entitled, for on political lips the term goes little beyond an irresponsible shibboleth."[11]

Underneath this visible signifier of kashmiriyat, however, lurks something which remains unspecified in Ali's eloquent reading: Hussain's *simulation* of latticework through papier maché. This technique of turning waste pulp into delicate, lacquered objets d'art decorated with stylized floral patterns was brought to Kashmir, along with other crafts traditions, from Central Asia during the fifteenth century under the patronage of Kashmiri ruler Zain-ul-Abedin.[12] Its secrets remained within Kashmiri Shia Muslim families descended from those original Central Asian artisans. Hussain, belonging to one such family, uses this inherited craft technique to create his large reliefs rather than the small bowls, frames, vases, and boxes that now saturate the craft and souvenir market. This transposition derived partly from practical considerations. Hussain early realized that exhibiting actual pieces of heavy lattice work was impractical and financially unviable, and that papier maché presented itself as a far more portable medium. But other aesthetic and political possibilities were fortuitously realized thereby, possibilities made manifest in Ali's own reference to papier maché in his poem "The Country without a Post Office":

> Again I've returned to this country
> where a minaret has been entombed.
> Someone soaks the wicks of clay lamps
> in mustard oil, each night climbs its steps
> to read messages scratched on the planets.
> His fingerprints cancel blank stamps
> in that archive for letters with doomed
> addresses, each home buried or empty.
>
> Empty? Because so many fled, ran away,
> and became refugees there, in the plains,
> where they must now will a final dewfall
> to turn the mountains to glass. They'll see
> us through them—see us frantically bury
> houses to save them from fire that, like a wall,
> caves in. The soldiers light it, hone the flames,
> burn our world to sudden papier maché
> inlaid with gold, then ash. When the muezzin
> died, the city was robbed of every call.[13]

Summoning the weight of a community's experience of violence, Ali moves the fragile flammability of papier maché from metaphoric substitute for the burnt houses to a metonymic contiguity with the Kashmir conflict itself.[14] Papier maché inlaid with gold, then ash . . . this verbal transformation parallels Hussain's material transformation of papier maché into wood.[15] Why, then, was Ali silent about this basic aspect of Hussain's art?

An explanation can be sought in the instantaneous, even jaded, recognition as "Kashmiri handicraft" that clings to papier maché products in urban India. On entering any Indian government emporium—more on this later in this chapter—dedicated either in its entirety or in part to Kashmiri handicraft, one is greeted by piles of papier maché boxes, bowls, candlesticks, vases, napkin rings, and (somewhat bizarrely) Easter eggs, daubed in gold and covered with hastily executed floral designs in colors frequently bordering on the lurid. Seemingly identical objects can be purchased in Kashmir, from private and government-run showrooms there, as well as from salesmen in shikaras bringing them by the sackloads to houseboats filled with haggling tourists. In Kashmir, papier maché is part of what Daniel MacCannell, in discussing the dynamics of tourism, calls the front region of "staged authenticity"; by the same token, latticework belongs to the back zone generally inaccessible to the tourist.[16] Papier maché products circulate within the national imaginary and national space in a manner that latticework, yoked to Kashmiri houses, cannot. Ali's was perhaps a strategic omission, calculated to highlight those Kashmiri crafts that, because still part of Kashmiri daily life and commercially unimportant, are hidden from outsider view, and downplay, likewise, those that have become overfamiliarized and overcommercialized. His own poem approximates papier maché to not the living Kashmiri habitus, but its destruction by Indian soldiers—although it remains ambiguous whether the Kashmiris "frantically burying" their homes offer a more satisfactory prognosis for cultural preservation during conflict.

And yet, the essence of Ali's lines resurfaced in a comment inscribed in the visitor's book for Hussain's most recent exhibition in Delhi: "I never knew papier maché could produce such pain," wrote a visitor with a Delhi address; "in solidarity with your people."[17] We return to the disjunct public spheres of the nation: the public sphere of the metropolitan Indian, who drops into art shows in the capital, and, in a manner recalling Roland Barthes's distinction between the *studium* and the *punctum,* finds herself unexpectedly moved; the public sphere of the Kashmiri artist, who chronicles his psychosocial world of devastation and conflict through his craft heritage and, now, the sphere of the Kashmiri poet in multiple exile, deterritorialized interpreter of his fellow Kashmiri creative intellectual.[18] But in this stray comment we also glimpse such disjunctions momentarily collapsing. The medium that was expected to induce anesthesia and amnesia (or which is retrospectively recognized as doing so) is able instead to produce pain and gnosis. Ali's coyness is confounded by the artwork's ability to shock this viewer into not merely relinquishing her preconceptions but actually gaining insight into the psychic dimensions of the Kashmir conflict, presented from a Kashmiri subject-position. The visitor's surprise at the empathetic potential of papier maché ratifies but also challenges Ali's reticence in mentioning the medium of Hussain's work. In fact, both that reticence and the viewer's sudden empathy pivot on his use of papier maché.

Nevertheless, this illuminating admission indisputably asserts the perceived opacity of the Kashmiri papier maché object and the fact that it is not normally read for signs of conflict and pain; rather, it solicits another kind of gaze altogether—that which is attracted by its surface gloss, its Islamicate patterning, and its portability. The first two characteristics recall Laura Mulvey's observation about the fetish: "In popular imagination, it glitters." The papier maché object's lacquered sheen and patterned surface exemplifies her understanding of the fetish as a "carapace, which hides ugliness and anxiety with beauty and desire," and whose brittle surface shields a wounded body. These superficial attractions thus enact the fetish's "seduction of belief to guard against the encroachment of knowledge."[19] In obscuring pain, the papier maché object confirms not only that "the fetish necessarily wants history to be overlooked" but that this overlooked history is that of its own making. What is this history? We can move toward an answer by connecting the attractions of papier maché's surface to its portability. Ironically, also the spur for Hussain's artwork, and rejected in the gigantic vase that I described in my introduction, its portability has made the papier maché object the exemplary Kashmiri souvenir: easy to sell, buy, and carry away. This ease also derives from, and ensures, papier maché's cheapness: their much higher economic value is another reason why both the vase and Hussain's reliefs are "extraordinary" encrustations of "abnormal" times.

Longing

Leaving the Kashmir Valley after a visit during the politically unsettled early 1950s, the British journalist and travel writer Pearce Gervis recalls, "[I]began to wish I had brought with me more of the arts of Kashmir, presents to give to those who had not been there, that they also might enjoy it." These "reminders of a really delightful land which so many have coveted, which some have captured for a while," can, unlike that land, be coveted *and* permanently captured by the acts of purchase and display. They concretely materialize the longings of departing travelers who, "at this stage of the journey promised themselves that one day they will return," and who invariably regret "that they had not taken a greater number of photographs, made more sketches or painted more pictures, and that they had not brought away with them more of the really beautiful things that are offered there at such fantastically low prices."[20] In the previous chapter we already saw photographs and sketches being mobilized, in Alfred Foucher's words, to "remind the returned traveller of the beauty of Kashmiri sites and buildings, and to the intending traveller . . . give food for his imagination."[21] I want to use Gervis's comments to consider objects that, unlike the amateur productions of the tourist's own labor, are available for consumption through purchase. To return to his words cited above, these arts of Kashmir are made to be sold, are useful in having no purpose other than display, are valuable because fantastically cheap, are purchased to be cast out of economic circulation, and are gifted not as reminders of past enjoyment but as substitutes for enjoyment itself.

These paradoxes enact the transformation of the craft object into souvenir and, in the context of Kashmir, secure its desirability to the desirability of the place of its making. In Susan Stewart's words, the souvenir's "scandal is its removal from its 'natural' location[,] yet it is only by means of its relation to that material location that it acquires its value."[22] While the tourist's act of purchase perpetuates the scandal of removal, its continuing connection to the place left behind has somehow to be ensured. This duality is most efficiently achieved through the object *handcrafted* in Kashmir (rather than, say, a postcard of the "Half-Inch Himalayas"). Its portability and affordability, as seen in the papier maché object, make it a diminutive, graspable, metaphoric replacement for the experience of Kashmir, and even, when gifted away, for the rumor of that experience. But the possessive force of the phrase, "the arts of Kashmir" endows it with the associative power of metonymy. In its ideal fusion of contraries, compactly crystallized in its simultaneous metaphoric and metonymic relationship to Kashmir, the craft object from the Valley is its perfect souvenir. Like Marx's exemplary commodity, the wooden table, it steps into the world announcing its Kashmiri make;[23] like Freud's exemplary fetish, however, it lets its consumer continue, through its possession, a relationship with an absent Kashmir. The craft object as souvenir generates longing and desire by being tantalizingly suspended between commodity as fetish and the fetish as substitute for loss, inviting our negotiation between Marxian and Freudian theories of fetishism.

The souvenir, like the fetish, embodies displaced longing for that which is sought to be made one's own, but which remains out of one's reach. The significance of this homology for Kashmir emerges through the plastic rose of the enormously popular 1960s Bollywood film, *Jab Jab Phool Khile* (Whenever flowers may bloom) already invoked in my first chapter to suggest the fetish's endless chain of substitutions. That rose is clutched by the doll, an exact replica of the Kashmiri protagonist Raja, gifted by him to Rita at the end of her Kashmiri holiday. Back in Bombay, the doll becomes a substitute for Raja, with Rita repeatedly shown talking to it and caressing it. For Rita, the Raja doll thus functions as a souvenir that "reduces the public, the monumental and the three-dimensional into the miniature, that which can be enveloped by the body, or into the two-dimensional representation, that which can be appropriated within the privatized views of the individual subject."[24] As I have argued, for modern India this "individual subject" has emerged through a discursive relationship with the idea of a pastoral, antique Kashmir. The displacement, on to the Raja doll, of the purity and simplicity of Kashmir that Raja signifies within the film, and the doll's own displacement to urban, ultracapitalist Bombay, fuses that discursive relationship with the tourist's investment in sustaining "the pastoral and the primitive through an illusion of a holistic and integrated cultural other."[25]

The ever-blooming rose recalls, furthermore, that which its industrial plastic-ness camouflages: the floral and garden designs that adorn the surface of Kashmiri craft, from shawls to woodwork to papier maché. It thus converts the Raja doll, already a reduction of the Kashmiri to a souvenir, into a cipher for the more recognizable souvenir from Kashmir, the craft object. Fixed in the Raja doll's hand, the rose draws attention to the hands (and feet, in the case of the weaver) of the artisan as the kernel of the unspoken relationship between the Kashmiri indigene and the Kashmiri craft object. Two photographs from "Kashmir Views," the Delhi exhibition of R. C. Mehta's oeuvre, illustrate this point.[26] In one a Kashmiri man sits on reed matting, kangri at his side, embroidering a carpet. Or, rather, we see him *pause* at embroidering a carpet, while our gaze falls on the central position of his right hand, gesturing toward his half-completed creation. The photograph has caught him out of time, reifying his labor while reinserting it into a "Kashmiri" domestic ensemble through the kangri. In the second photo, the kangri reappears in the company of a samovar and a Kashmiri crewel-embroidered cushion, arranged on the edge of the terraced waterway in Srinagar's Nishat Bagh. While absorbing the foregrounded contiguities between Mughal garden, Kashmiri craft, and domestic objects, we might just glimpse an unshod male foot that the frame has cut off from its owner, and the blurred arms and leg of a boy similarly sliced off by the opposite margin.

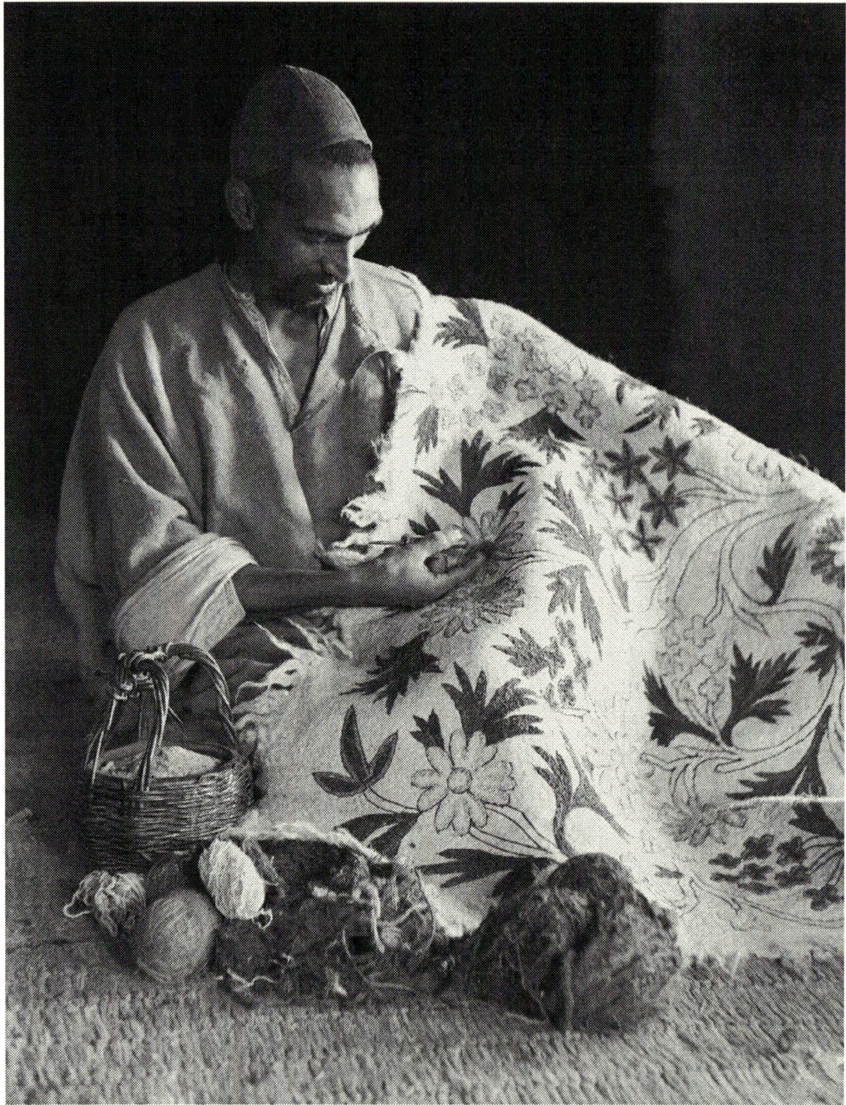

R. C. Mehta, Kashmiri weaver with carpet, mid-twentieth century. Collection of Hemant Mehta and IndiaPicture.com.

The discomfiting proximity of the dislocated yet present limbs of the artisan to the craft object on display iterates the classic fetishistic structure of disavowal—"I know [I'm not interested in its maker], but all the same [I value it as handmade]. . . ."[27] The oscillation between the impulse to cloak the labor behind the making of the craft object, and the impulse to highlight its "made" characteristics arises from the same longing for

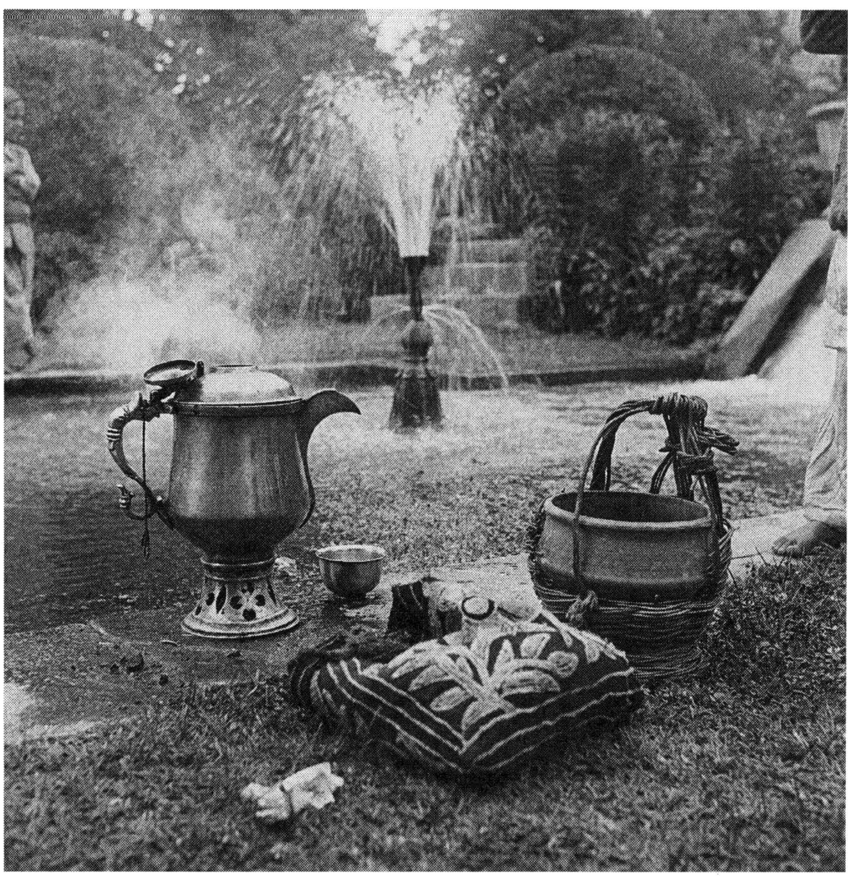

R. C. Mehta, samovar and kangri, mid-twentieth century. Collection of Hemant Mehta and IndiaPicture.com.

authenticity that drove Indologists to render into print the Kashmiri language—although, unlike that disembodied voice, always lost to the printed page, the material or (in Marx's words) the *"stofflich"* quality of the commodity permits the craft object to operate as a more substantial reminder of its place of making.[28] The need for the handicraft souvenir is thus shaped by the same technologies and declarations of modernity that constructed Kashmir as pastoral and nonmodern. Gervis's musings on souvenirs, with which I began this section, are tellingly preceded by a contrast between the road from Kashmir to Jammu, all "blind turnings, steep, short hills, and close, cliff-bound sides," and the "magnificent" new highway connecting Jammu to the plains. "Two cars wide" with "dozens of concreted nullahs," this Nehruvian engineering marvel is nevertheless "not as one wishes to think of Kashmir and Jammu: it is without a soul." Gervis longs for when "the beauty of Kashmir will seep onto the road from the State . . . the glaring concrete will become somber and soft in its colouring; little hamlets, quaint stalls and shops will spring up upon its sides," and the highway will "gain something that will make it live," something organic akin to the "snake-like" Valley road.[29]

Within this intertwined juxtaposition—already encountered in Nehru's writing—of "vitality" with Kashmir, and of "modernity" with India,[30] handicraft, we see now, plays a crucial role. The concrete of dams and highways *must* be encroached upon by continuations of premodern economies: little hamlets, quaint stalls, and the craft object itself, a product not of factories but of what shall emerge, in the following section of this chapter, as an essential cog in the nation's ideological economy: the "cottage industry." Opening a book on Kashmiri handicraft by a veteran bureaucrat and pioneer organizer of the crafts sector in Jammu and Kashmir, we are swept from "the significance of local markets and the many festivals and fairs, where the craftsman himself continues to buy his necessities" to "Vedic and Hindu India [where] all creative expression was believed to be derived from a single inspiration." From here, it is a small step to Kashmir, which lay "directly in the passage of the Vedic peoples to India," its "geographic isolation" ensuring both "closeness to Hindu thinking" and "a strategic position" on "the ancient silk route."[31] Echoing the Valley's usefulness for Indian nationalist thought across the ideological spectrum, these words, written in 1987, confirm the postcolonial naturalization of Kashmiri handicraft within the productive antinomy of modern nation/antique land, already evident four decades earlier in Gervis's account. This naturalization has firmly linked Kashmir's landscape, Kashmir's antiquity and Kashmir's indigenous crafts traditions in the collective Indian imaginary. We need now to ask why, and for whom, it became so necessary both to insist on this linkage and to render it invisible through (to revert to Partha Chatterjee's useful phrase) the forces of "commonsensical obviousness."

Nostalgia

This commonsensical obviousness collaborates with a selective reading of the history of Kashmiri handicraft that parallels the structure of disavowal operating in the fetishization of the Kashmiri craft object as souvenir.

The Valley undeniably has a long tradition of fine handicraft production, exemplified internationally by the cashmere shawl.[32] However, as also exemplified by the shawl's dramatic popularity in Napoleonic France and the sharp decline in demand after the Franco-Prussian war, the political economy of Kashmiri craft right through Mughal and Dogra times was hardly illustrative of "geographic isolation" and "quaint hamlets." "Medieval" Srinagar was a city of karkhanas bustling with the production of woodwork, silverware, copperware, papier maché, and, of course, the shawl in all its different stages (carding, spinning, weaving, embroidery, finishing).[33] Indian merchants traded these luxury items far beyond Kashmir through the old overland routes of the Silk Road.[34] Crafts traditions as well as finished objects circulated through these conduits, Zain-ul-Abedin having famously overseen the arrival of artisans from Central Asia into his domains. Both this precolonial cosmopolitanism and its modern developments are embedded in the very currency of the phrase "papier maché." Imported from Persia, it was initially called *kar-i-qalamdani* (Persian: "the craft of pen-cases"), pointing to its most popular deployment. The prevalence in Kashmir and India today of its French equivalent originates in a new use for the craft during the nineteenth century: the packaging of shawls headed for France in papier maché boxes.[35] British commentators such as Walter Lawrence discussing Kashmiri handicraft traditions further popularized the French rather than the Persian term.[36]

Kashmiri craftwork thus enters the frame of modernity already commodified. But just as the Mughal miniatures of Kashmiri landscape were supplanted by photographic views of Kashmir, the demands of modernity ensured handicraft's transformed interdependence with "the society of the spectacle."[37] By the early twentieth century, shops dedicated to Kashmiri souvenirs opened on The Bund, a prime location in European Srinagar, and a world away from its packed downtown karkhanas. From those very karkhanas had emerged the family of papier maché artisans who, taking advantage of the times, had already moved from pen-cases and packing boxes to making bowls, frames and vases more amenable to Western tastes, and who now also ventured into this novel mode of craft retail.[38] Today, this relatively well-preserved row of European-style half-timbered buildings still stands on the Bund. The café on its corner no longer exists; neither is there evidence of the Parsees who owned the row during the 1900s. But continuing in business are the original crafts shops, the "quaintly"-termed "Suffering Moses" and the more prosaically named "Asia Arts and Crafts," alongside the row's other survivor of a past age: Mahatta's Studio.

During the height of Kashmir's imperial splendor, these shops offered a composite package of the Srinagar experience. Shoppers dropped in to browse through their craft objects on display, visited Mahattas to develop their Kodak rolls and buy postcards (possibly of artisans), and rounded off such expeditions with a visit to the café:[39] a style of commodity consumption well in keeping with the hothouse modernity of early twentieth century Kashmir.

The implications of that modernity, however superficial, were nevertheless perceived with an alarm similar to Younghusband's laments for the lost days of "virgin travel" to the Valley. In 1909, in fact, Younghusband himself decried the declining quality of both the shawl and papier maché;[40] soon thereafter Ananda Coomaraswamy, the prominent Sri Lankan critic and ideologue of South Asian art and craft, observed of papier maché that "very little fine work is still made." Coomaraswamy squarely blamed such degeneration on the growth of tourism in Kashmir: "No work of any importance is done now; in fact no part of India produces more banal and meaningless industry than present-day Kashmir, where the tradesman's chief pride is taken in realistic green chenar leaves executed in floss silk on cotton for sale to tourists."[41] Already, "Kashmir" appears as the limit case for an argument about "India," here buttressing handicraft's emergent usefulness within anticolonial nationalism.[42] Coomaraswamy ardently supported Mahatma Gandhi's praxis of *swadeshi* (self-sufficiency), leading to *swaraj* (sovereignty), and realized through domestic craft, most iconically the *charkha* (the spinning wheel).[43] Specifically a radical response to the importation of colonial raw material to power metropolitan industries, homespun powerfully conveyed anticolonial resistance through an anti-industrial self-sufficiency.[44] The charkha symbolized Gandhi's ideal "village community" that would subsist, spiritually and materially, on its own cottage industries. Ostensibly complicating Nehru's aspirations toward an industrialist, socialist India,[45] it actually drew on the same necessity for the spiritual "vitality" of India that Nehru located in the continuing "enchantment" of Kashmir.

This enchantment gains in significance when placed against the infamous "disenchantment" of industrial modernity, which, as is now commonly acknowledged, was not the sole province of European, post-Enlightenment angst.[46] Rather, as the concepts "village community" and "cottage industry" themselves reveal through their histories, such disenchantment was sharpened through the interchange between the ideas of Enlightenment Europe and the experiences in the increasing outreach of the Empire.[47] The Victorian yearning for the lost world of the medieval artisan, whether of the European guild or the Mughal karkhana, was a complex product of the trauma of industrialization and of exposure to Indian crafts at world fairs and exhibitions, where the colonial mania for collecting combined with the desirability of handmade products.[48] Crystallizing in the philosophies of William Morris and John Ruskin, this nostalgia reverberated through the twentieth century to inform anticolonial nationalism: both Gandhi and Coomaraswamy were avid Ruskin and Morris enthusiasts.[49] The ills of industry now merged with the ills of imperialism. From somewhere between anticolonial insistence on the ethical, redemptive potential of craft, and Marx's nightmarish vision of capitalism as a "monstrous collection of commodities,"[50] arose Coomaraswamy's horror of Kashmiri handicraft's reduction to "banal and meaningless industry."[51] The construction of Kashmir's enchanted antiquity thus interlocked with the nostalgia for the handmade, the pastoral and the rural to pin down Kashmiri handicraft as material remnant of its nonmodern past. The karkhana as factory was pitted against the karkhana as workshop. Ironically, however, this attempted flight from commodity fetishism devolved on an equally powerful fetishism of the handmade.

For Coomaraswamy, Kashmiri handicraft's lamentable "industrialization" was an inevitable consequence of the collusion between tradesman and artisan. Craft had to be protected from the vagaries of the free market to protect the integrity of culture itself: a belief that offered a handy solution to the postcolonial need to forge institutions out of anticolonial utopias. Soon after Independence, Coomaraswamy's views came together with the concept of the cooperative to reconcile Nehruvian five-year plans for steel plants with Gandhian insistence on beekeeping and handmade soap.[52] In 1948, "as a mark of the government's efforts to popularise and market handicrafts," the Ministry of Commerce and Industry joined forces with the Indian Co-Operative Union in "a new experiment." Its result was the birth, in 1952, of the All India Handicrafts Board (also founded in 1952),[53] and its showcase, the Cottage Industries Emporium.[54] Midwifed by Nehru, blessed by Gandhi, and nurtured by its founder president the socialist freedom-fighter Kamaladevi Chattopadhyay,[55] the Cottage (as it is fondly called in India) was on its way to becoming a gigantic one-stop shop for the crafts of the nation, flourishing today in five Indian cities—Delhi, Calcutta, Bombay, Madras, and Bangalore. This formidable combination of wonder-cabinet, panorama, and market-place nevertheless rests on a barely concealable contradiction: is its "monstrous collection" one of mass-marketed commodities or handmade anticommodities? Handicraft, in independent India, began life uneasily stretched between these two poles, even as palpable tensions continued between conceptions of purity and protection. While the artisan's purity lay in the conception of handicraft as existing outside capitalism, protecting him or her meant the State's intervention in easing their products into the market.

The early publications by the All India Handicrafts Board, their prefaces signed by Chattopadhyay, attest to these contradictions. One of its first promotional books declares that "[Handicraft] in India is not an industry as is commonly understood; for the produce is also a creation symbolizing the inner desire and fulfillment of the community."[56] Yet it tantalizes the reader as a potential consumer: "you would no doubt like to acquire a few for your own home, or perhaps to give as gifts to your friends and relations." Domestic shoppers had concerns clearly similar to Pearce Gervis's: they are assured that "these novel and exciting presents" combine "top quality with reasonable prices." The State, via the Board, ensures this economic paradox by "find[ing] out what are the problems of the handicraft industry, how its production can be improved and developed, and its sales promoted at home and abroad." In "promoting major programmes of introducing better techniques of production, prescribing standards of quality, improving designs and creating new patterns" the Board fulfils the State's well-intentioned transformation of craft into a special kind of commodity: "You will get newer, better and cheaper goods all the time through an efficient sales organisation that has your interest at heart, believing that Indian handicrafts will help you in the joyful affirmation of a full life."[57] The postcolonial Sttate generated Indianness by "efficiently" transforming modernity's fixation with the artisan into the spiritual, "joyful" benefits of consuming handicraft. Yet in the materiality of handicraft's production and existence, there remains something stubbornly undigested.

Melancholia

In 1991, a film entitled *The Story of Papier Maché* was produced by the newly set up Audio-Visual Research Centre (AVRC) of Kashmir University and commissioned by the national University Grants Commission (UGC) for Indian national television's afternoon educational programs.[58] Beginning with a series of lingering shots of the Valley's lakes, mountains, and brooks reminiscent of Bollywood's depiction of Kashmir's landscape, it moves to images of "happy peasant" Kashmiris ploughing the fields. Next, we see examples of the fineness of a range of Kashmiri handicraft—woodcarving, shawls, carpets—before the documentary settles down on papier maché itself. A rousing commentary consolidates the linking of Kashmir to concrete deliverables for the nation. Shots of the production process of papier maché—the feet of Kashmiri men pounding gray masses of pulp, brushes held in their hands, etching designs on the molded objects—alternate with images of a typical emporium with rows upon rows of finished products, while a voiceover informs us of the rising exports of papier maché objects, supplemented by tables of figures. This almost surreally cheerful documentary is suffused nonetheless with an eerie melancholia, revealingly generated by its endlessly looped visual repetitions. Melancholia, which seeks but is defeated resolution through infinite repetition of a symptom, is, in its classic Freudian sense, best avoided; far more preferable is mourning loss in a fashion that assimilates it into a fresh narrative.[59] But as Ranjana Khanna has suggestively argued, it is also possible to wrest out of melancholia a critical agency. I locate this critical melancholia in the film's multiply fetishistic use of papier maché.

The Story of Papier Maché bears no indication that it was made during one of the worst years of the Kashmir conflict, when the Indian army and Kashmiri militants had turned the Valley into a battleground; rather, this reality is sought actively to be hidden. The film's scenes of papier maché production were reconstructed in Delhi because of the impossibility of normal life in Kashmir during this period (a move that recalls Mani Ratnam's simulation of Kashmir's landscape in *Roja*).[60] Papier maché is used as a double substitute: for the Valley itself and for the political unrest occurring therein. The film thus offers a textbook illustration of commodity fetishism as "mystification (or levelling out) of historical experience; imagined access to the cultural other through the process of consumption; reification of people and places into exchangeable aesthetic objects."[61] It also submits to a psychoanalytical explication of the fetish as "the simultaneous play between metaphor as substitution (masking absence and difference) and metonymy (which contiguously registers the perceived lack)," giving access thereby to an "identity which is predicated as much on mastery and pleasure as it is on anxiety and defence."[62] But, in summoning these diverse registers of fetishism, it also suggests whose identity this might be. We can uncover this identity by recuperating, as Laura Mulvey does, the fetish as commemorative, flamboyantly marking its own erasure of history.[63] Nevertheless, I depart from Mulvey in seeing this work of commemoration not as an instance of mourning but as a mark of critical melancholia.

The sepulchral quality of the documentary's displayed papier maché objects invites not only interpretations of melancholia as unassimilated remnant of an original trauma; it urges us to use papier maché itself to prise out the undigested kernel that it, as fetish, also masks. This kernel, this phantom secret that haunts *The Story of Papier Maché*, also haunts a larger narrative of the postcolonial State's restoration of handicraft. Attempting to collapse the gaps between marketing and glorifying craft as national heritage that we noted at the close of the previous section, this narrative of postcolonial restoration emerges from successive Handicrafts Board publications.[64] It moves from the Indus Valley civilization, to the Mughals, under whose patronage India's native genius is seen to have combined with Islamist aesthetics to bring forth a full flowering of Indian handicraft, to the much-decried decline of crafts under colonialism, and to the nationalist struggles centered around swadeshi, concluding with craft's triumphant reinstation under the sign of the independent nation. The declared degeneration of Kashmiri craft traditions from the nineteenth century onward, exemplified in Coomaraswamy's comments, fits neatly into this narrative. There is also a sequel: the drive to integrate diverse craft traditions of, and into, the new pluralist, federal India. By 1975, maps of the Indian Union, complete with well-demarcated internal state boundaries, began appearing within the All India Handicrafts Board publications, suggesting the mutual implication of the State's handicraft policies and its evolving federal structure.[65] The incorporation of Kashmiri handicraft within this sequel mimics the nation's desired incorporation of the Valley via the state of Jammu and Kashmir.

The federal politics of power-sharing thus began to coalesce with the State's paternalistic relationship to the artisans it sought simultaneously to shield from and bring into the full glare of capitalism. Government institutions such as the Central Cottage Industries Emporium, with their display and marketing of crafts from across the nation, became a material embodiment of a pluralistic national space that nevertheless regulated the flow of cultural capital from different states. Similar approximations of the nation's spatialized, schematized geo-body emerged through the development of Handicrafts emporia for each state, including Jammu and Kashmir, arranged within prominent shopping precincts in the major Indian cities: each state now has its own craft and textile map. In post-liberalization India, the government's renewed efforts to promote crafts as a lifestyle choice has emerged as a visible contour of a new vernacular postmodernity that actively solicits a premodern vocabulary: hence, the display of the artisan at work at the Crafts Museum in Delhi, where craftspeople from across the nation make and sell their wares to the museum's visitors; and at Dilli Haat, which knowingly mimics the small-scale economies of the rural marketplace.[66] But the simulation penetrates to deeper levels of market control. It is the State that supervises who gets to exhibit their wares at these spaces through complex mechanisms of identity cards for artisans and quotas for each state. For Jammu and Kashmir, this supervisory stance has dovetailed with the special status granted to the state by the Article 370 of the Constitution of India,[67] which, while not explicitly covering craft production, has significantly influenced bureaucratic attitudes to Kashmiri craftspeople.

According to those in charge of State-sponsored crafts efforts, therefore, Kashmiri handicrafts have been given excessive prominence within Dilli Haat, for instance, and Kashmiri artisans overdiligently felicitated on the national stage. These protectionist policies are seen as stultifying Kashmiri craft rather than enabling it to adapt to contemporary market circumstances. Nevertheless, there is a fine line between protectionism per se and perceptions of protectionism. At the annual Republic Day parade in Delhi, which celebrates the birth of the federated Indian Union, the Jammu and Kashmir float regularly portrays "a flower seller and a craftsman, suggesting that Kashmiris are fragile, in need of India's continuing protection."[68] Yet this critique by Jyotindra Jain, founder of the Crafts Museum, must be offset by the fact that, during the past decade, a Kashmiri artist, Veer Munshi, has conceptualized these floats and overseen their construction.[69] Who is the more fragile, the Kashmiri craftsman, the Kashmiri artist, the metropolitan intelligentsia, or the State itself? "You needed me," says Ali in his poem, "Farewell," in an address I interpret as from the Kashmiri to the Indian, "[Y]ou needed to perfect me."[70] Leading us to this question of the necessity of the Kashmiri craft object, itself a cipher for the Kashmiri, is the critical melancholia of *The Story of Papier Maché*. Its Kashmiri makers—both of the film and of papier maché—reappear as the co-opted Indian citizens I theorized earlier through Qazi Touqeer's example: imbricated in webs of production, consumption, and infrastructure, complicating straightforward assumptions of collaboration or resistance, scramblers of codes. The film's disavowal of the political conditions prevalent at the time of its making reveals it as transmitting not normalcy but a desperate hope thereof. It alerts us not to what the State conceals, but the fact that, like the Emperor's new clothes, it might conceal nothing at all.[71]

The stylized floral patterns on the papier maché object certainly reflect "the delicate and hermetically sealed world of the souvenir [as] a world of nature idealized; nature removed from the domain of struggle into the domestic sphere of the individual and the interior."[72] But, far more crucially, this individual is re-interpellated into the collective identity of citizen and consumer by mechanisms such as the government emporium and the documentary's broadcasting on national television. By being coaxed to possess material fragments of "Kashmir" that inhere to a narrative of "Indian handicraft," the citizen-as-consumer participates in a collective process of displacement and mystification. But demystification—defetishization—can also occur. Filmmakers in Kashmir make a film about that which is made in Kashmir by pretending to have made it in Kashmir: this loop of making and unmaking, emplacement, and displacement, takes us to Taussig's deployment of the maleficium to unmask the fetish of the State's power. The word "fetish" originates from *factitius*, past participle of the Latin verb *facere*, "to make [by hand], to fabricate," and, shading into negativity, "to deceive."[73] Following Taussig, we can endow the papier maché object with the quality of the fetish's now-buried counterpart, the maleficium ("the bad-making") "of the medieval sorcerer's tool," deploying it "as a tactic for drawing out the fetish power of the modern state."[74] The papier maché maleficium is a link in a chain of signs pointing toward the absent Other, the Kashmir which is "an integral part of India." But it also discloses the *fantasy* of wholeness—the "fantasy [through which] we learn to desire."[75] The fetish, construct of colonial expansionism and modernity, caves in, leaving the territory of desire as the phantom that points to the unbearable question: might the State itself be a set of symptoms generated by the collective need to cloak the hollowness and violence of "national feeling?"

Making

In downtown Srinagar today, the narrow, unsanitary lanes of Zadibal are packed with houses in turn packed with papier maché objects in various stages of making: basins of paper pulp, moulds of ghostly shapes, lacquered objects that begin to resemble those one sees on emporium shelves, and finished pieces piled high in rooms. The godaam as warehouse collapses into Marx's *Warensammlung* (commodity collection) while doubling as the karkhana, the workshop. My guide is a former fine arts student who, in a tiny front room, makes papier maché souvenirs exported for European tourist consumption in Dubai. His sister and mother mould the basic shapes on which he paints Santas riding camels. Other homes produce objects with the usual Mughal-derived designs for the domestic market. The high turnover demands minimal investment of time and skill: this is mass-produced handicraft made for low prices and quick dispatch. Yet in this neighborhood are also artisans executing delicate objects at slower pace, destined for luxury boutiques in the five-star hotels of metropolitan India, where, typically, someone will have a Kashmiri relative ensconced in the retail end; or commissioned by Asia Crafts and Suffering Moses, the original tradesmen's shops on the Bund where stray foreign tourists, elite Kashmiris and curious researchers still visit, and willingly pay higher prices for the frames, pen knives and letter holders. And, of course, there are master craftsmen such as the one I began this chapter with, who, to sit out the years of conflict, created with no particular consumer in mind the gigantic vase that is now too expensive to keep anywhere permanently but a museum somewhere "abroad."[76]

This network of papier maché artisans exists alongside those producing papier maché for the Cottage Industries and Jammu and Kashmir Handicrafts Emporium. Their rhizomatic existence challenges the State's control over handicraft and the nation's desire for the fetish of paradise, as well as confounds capitalist time.[77] When returned to these conditions of its making, the paradox of the mass–hand-produced papier maché object de-fetishizes the distinctions between the industrial commodity as alienated, the artwork as a luxury good with restricted exchange capacity, a product of solitary genius, and the craftwork as the supposed remnant of an alternative world of paracapitalist exchange.[78] The submissiveness of the souvenir re-emerges as the modus operandi for the chicanery of resistance. To the domestic tourists who are now increasingly returning to Srinagar, their middlemen show only the cheap, mass-handcrafted stuff. Convince them you are willing to pay more, they return the next day bearing material deemed fit for connoisseurs. If you show even further discernment, they might direct you to work declared to be of the standard of Asia Crafts or Suffering Moses. "We want to see first the potential of the customers" is a common explanation. These artisans control the value of what they make, while the itinerant middlemen perform another level of "customer screening." Is it so different when Masood Hussain paints pretty watercolors of "Kashmir Views" for the Jammu and Kashmir Bank's calendar as well as sculpts papier maché into his tortured reliefs? Hidden, cross-cutting levels of value thus further diminish the assumed divergences between the craftwork and the artwork, and between the artisan and the middle-class artist, that have been ensured by contrasting modes of production, consumption, and valuation under modern capitalist conditions.[79]

I want to conjoin Hussain's work to that of the artisan to elaborate on the material alternative to (the nation's) history that Shakeel Bakshi's photographs in the shrine led earlier us to consider. The very materiality of "making" engages a history of the Kashmiri craft object in modernity that rehabilitates the karigar as maker of a community's material heritage. Hussain's most recent papier maché reliefs, exhibited in Delhi in March–April 2005, can be seen as representing the Kashmiri karigar's continuations and interruptions of this heritage. Hence, the centrality, within the exhibition space, of "My Grandfather's Colour Palette," a wooden box sawed into two unequal sections. Its open section displays bowls of paint in disarray and, on the lid, a sepia-tinted photograph of a Kashmiri man; the other section is shut with a wooden latch. Not made of papier maché, this actual paintbox is its marred history—it belonged to Hussain's maternal grandfather, a papier maché artisan, whose work after 1947 was bound up with mourning the departure of his brother for Pakistan. The photograph of that brother radiates the connections between handicraft and family, severed through politics. The irresolution of the latch and the two uneven halves of the broken box together embody the specificity of 1947 for Kashmiris. Inheritor of the box and its imprinted losses, the artist grandson, as contemporary Kashmiri, disfigures the box with the traces of his own, divided self, newly imprinted by the events of the early 1990s. The euphoric street processions, the massive demonstrations, the spontaneous crowds, the relentless reprisals by the Indian State, and the cycle of counterreprisals; the crackdowns, identifications, disappearances, and rapes; uncaptured in official footage, unrepresentable to non-Kashmiris, they are commemorated here.

An emotional vocabulary both allusive and direct returns us to the fetish as commemorative of its own erasure of history. Hussain deploys emblems of conflict through the same logic of metonymy as that operating in the work of fetishism—reduced human heads or stacks of shoes flowing into rivers, envelopes rising in a smoke-like plume from a sagging sack—but the metonymy foregrounds the dismembered human body, as in "River in the River".[80] Multiple condensations and connections emerge in the evocation of latticework, either as fragmentary inserts, or as frames for the pieces, through papier maché: between different registers of craft and the rhythms of domesticity, between the disruptions of those rhythms and the destruction of an entire way of life through bullets, bunkers, and violence. In incorporating objects from daily life into his reliefs—the *traami,* or copper plate, the *samovar* for *kahva* or Kashmiri tea, filigreed holders for tea glasses—Hussain returns craft from the emporium to the Kashmiri home. But while these objects speak to a recognizably Kashmiri lifestyle irradiated by the dignity and aesthetics of tradition, their disfigured presence within the artwork signals the impossibility of not using material traces of that life as carapace for the wounded Kashmiri psyche. Thus the metal glass-holders are "unscrolled" over the surface of the relief, rendering their primary function unreadable. Instead, the disfigured craft object creates its own register of representation, a history in and through distortion that makes sense only because of its erasure through fetishization. Converted into a scroll (that, paradoxically, cannot be read), the glass-holder critiques and escapes the prison-house of written history.

This critique is an all-pervasive element in Hussain's work. Inverting the techniques of the papier maché karigar, who achieves smoothness by stretching muslin cloth over the surface of the object, Hussain

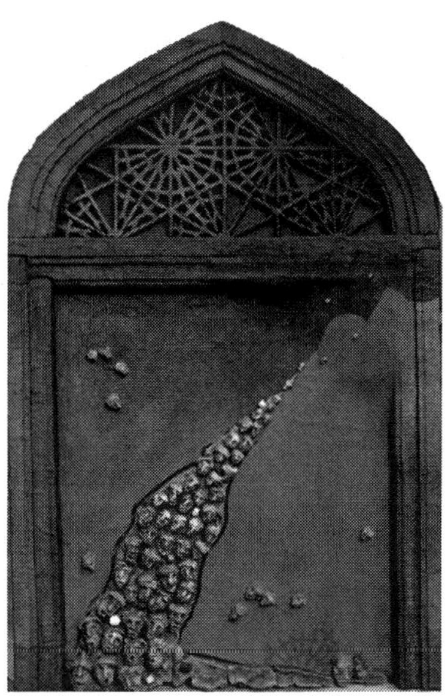

Masood Hussain, *River in the River,* 2004. Relief work in mixed media, including papier maché, 89 × 136.5 × 49 cm. Private collection.

creases cloth of varying thicknesses over his relief, highlighting the resultant textures through an expressionist use of color, as in "Falling of the Black Sky." The puckered folding alludes to but does not quite mimic Islamic calligraphy, suggesting the taint and incompleteness of language, even in its most sacred mode.[81] Instead, texture signifies through elements drawn from a marrying of mysticism to topography, the stiff, exaggerated peaks embodying the tortured consequences of the Valley's prized natural beauty. The pantheism celebrated by Nehru and Foucher is reclaimed through Hussain's evocations of Shaivism, the Valley's topography, its wooden Sufi shrines—and, pertinent to his personal history, Shia Islam.[82] This composite is altogether different from the mainstream Indian conception of a comforting kashmiriyat, refusing, as it does, to forget pain and longing. The primacy of mourning rituals within the Shia collective psyche gains resonance through texture, undercutting assumptions of a homogenous Kashmiri Muslim identity while mediating between divergences. In "Shrouded Lake," rich blue folds recall simultaneously the material gorgeousness of elaborate mourning rituals, the mountains surrounding Srinagar, and the shrouds of not only the original Shia martyrs, Hassan and Hussain, but of countless Kashmiris who have died in the violence over the territory of desire.[83] Even as these deeper levels of signification emerge through

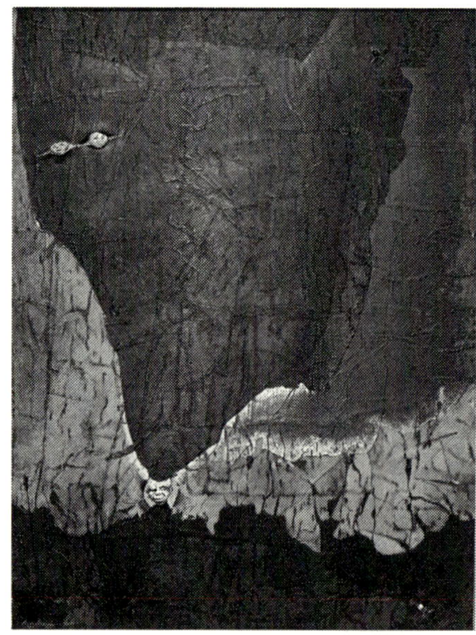

Masood Hussain, *Falling of the Black Sky,* 2004. Relief work in mixed media, including papier maché, 91.5 × 89.5 cm. Private collection.

the attention to texture, texture itself, a deliberate inversion of papier maché's lacquered smoothness, emerges as the metasignifier of political and spiritual meaning.

Hussain's obsessions with texture unmake the fetish's power. His painted reliefs arrest the gaze not through surface sheen, but by encrusting the surface with texture as history. The method of knowing they solicit is an anti-epistemological surrender to that which cannot be known, only recognized. The transparent material, which nevertheless declares its presence through its folds, recalls the veil of Sufi philosophy separating the *zahir* (the obvious) from the *batin* (the esoteric).[84] Through it, we sense pain. For those who have not experienced what Kashmiris have, full understanding is impossible, but might not this humbling recognition itself heal the wounds beneath the carapace? Thus Hussain repeatedly evokes the taveez, or religious amulet, tying the wearer to the Sufi shrine, healing through sympathetic contact, just as Bakshi's photographs in the shrine were believed to be doing.[85] The taveez also returns to the encounter between European expansionism and Muslim and animist West Africans, whose belief in the power of what Portuguese sailors termed the "fetisso," or the amulet as talisman, was later mobilized into Enlightenment modernity's dismissal of the "fetish" as signifier of the credulous pre-modern.[86] This trace of its original enchantment now momentarily suffuses the fetish as object alienated from its making. But Hussain's taveezes have fled the space of representability, leaving behind only their diamond-shaped outlines. The absent taveez becomes a mise-en-abyme for the possible reenchantment of papier maché: in Bakshi's words, a love-longing, a burning desire, a "dash-dash-dash." As the outline of the taveez transforms into a kite whose tail is formed by the melancholy cord of the *dehjor,* or the hanging breast-ornaments of Kashmiri Hindu women—poignantly imaged in his "Exodus," we are reminded, through the widening rift between Kashmiri Pandits and Muslims (an issue we will turn to in chapter 6) of the Kashmiri intellectual's preoccupation with the internal healing of Kashmiri society.

By turning papier maché inside out, Hussain exposes the layered histories of the fetish as both handmade object and "manifestation of desiring machines."[87] While the movement from the karkhana as workshop to the karkhana as factory emerges as the phantom motivating the nation's desire for Kashmir, the Kashmiri artist as aspirant karigar, the artisan as bridge between the artwork and the craftwork, offers himself as a critic

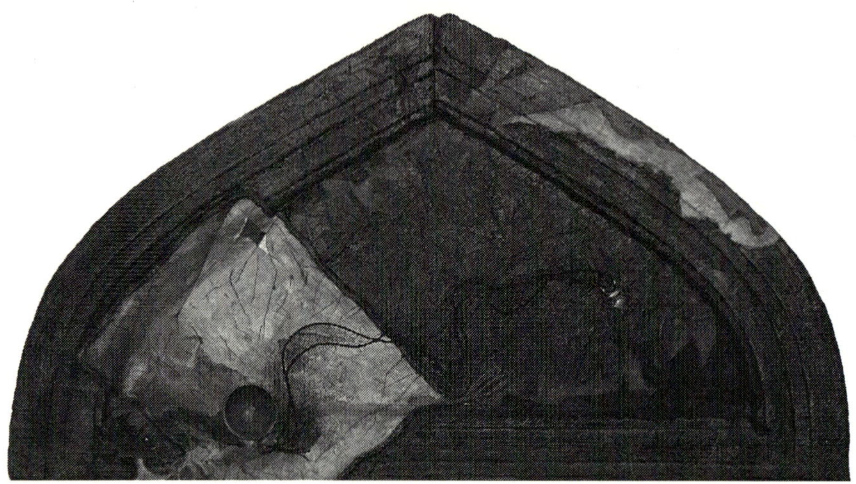

Masood Hussain, *Exodus,* 2004. Relief work in mixed media, including papier maché, 51 × 88.5 × 6.5 cm. Private collection.

of the modern and the healer of its trauma. The creative intellectual as maker interrogates not only the relationship between political and cultural representation but also the relationship between modernity and postcolonial violence. A carping insistence on the class divide between the artist as intellectual, working with ideas, and the artisan, whose condition he aspires to, working with things, misses altogether the finely tuned nature of this attempt toward healing. Through form, content, and philosophy, Hussain's painted reliefs simultaneously retrieve the spiritual connection between craft, everyday life and topography that is his definition of kashmiriyat, while attesting to the destruction of that organic connectivity through the forces of collective desire generated by rival claimants to the Valley's territory. Hussain thus reclaims official South Asian history, which the official discourse of Indian handicraft is subservient to, through a deliberately ruptured and incomplete praxis of papier maché that elucidates the hidden meanings of Kashmiri craft. Into this material counter-history of contemporary Kashmiri subjectivity is inscribed, too, the impossibility of adequately representing the particular violence of the 1990s. Through his artwork, furthermore, signifiers of Sufi and Shia Islam as well as Shaivism converge but do not compete. Is the material object then more able than the written word to move us toward a shared consideration of the possibilities, and impossibilities, of beauty in a tainted world? This is a question that the remaining three chapters shall explore.

Part II

Poetics of Dispossession

Four

Conscripting Silence

Constructing a system of partitions, with their inner and outer surfaces, the cryptic enclave produces a cleft in space, in the assembled system of various places, in the architectonics of the open square within space, itself delimited by a generalized closure, in the forum. Within this forum, a place where the free circulation and exchange of objects can occur, the crypt constructs another, more inward forum like a closed rostrum or speaker's box, a safe: sealed and thus internal to itself, a secret interior within the public square, but by the same token, outside it, external to the interior.

—Jacques Derrida, *"Fors"*

For most of our respondents, it was simply not possible to write a letter in Kashmiri.

—O. N. Koul and R. L. Schmidt,
Kashmiri: A Sociolinguistic Survey

"I wrote you a letter in such ember-hot words . . ." with this line by Rahman Rahi, a Kashmiri poet, writing in Kashmiri, I had opened my first chapter: what, in the light of the sociolinguist's pronouncements on the epistolary unsuitability of Koshur, can we make of this letter-within-a-poem, refashioned into an epigraph? Is this doubly purloined letter hallucination, wish-fulfillment, or, through the magic of the performative speech-act, itself that declaredly elusive object—a "letter in Kashmiri?" Koul and Schmidt's survey, carried out in 1983, reported their sample group of 201 middle-class Kashmiri adults as being overwhelmingly bilingual in Kashmiri and Urdu, and its use of Kashmiri overwhelmingly oral and everyday—a use that, according to subsequent sociolinguistic inquiry, marks Koshur as subordinated "to the status of a domestic vernacular," predicating "a feeling of inferiority and a loss of cultural identity."[1] These negative feelings constellated around Koshur typically configure it as the long-neglected mother tongue.[2] Lurking beneath the class distinctions that adhere to Kashmiri multilingualism are complex affects: of marginalization, dispossession, trauma, shame—but also of love and survival. These affects swirl around language in contemporary Kashmir, and, particularly, around language conceptualized as voice; they seep, too, into the ostensibly dry script of research, especially when the latter is undertaken by a native speaker of Koshur.[3] The ember-hot letter enacted through the Kashmiri poem haunts, but also gives life to, the letter in Kashmiri that the sociolinguistic realm declares a nigh-impossibility. Borrowing the words of my first epigraph, this uncanny doubleness alters the architectonics of the forum as "a place for the free circulation and exchange of objects," and of words-as-objects. The Kashmiri letter-poem is the cryptic enclave that produces the cleft in the forum's open space.

Jacques Derrida uses this image of the crypt underneath the democratic, capitalist, open space of the forum to gloss Abraham and Torok's theory of "encrypting" as a response to trauma.[4] Revisiting the case of the so-called Wolf Man, whose neuroses Freud and his followers famously failed to cure, they use the process of "cryptonymic" substitution to convert his unreadable words into tell-tale clues.[5] Aided by his multilingualism, the Wolf Man is seen to have associated, through sound rather than sense, certain words with an original traumatic event that were consequently buried within "crypts" carved out of his psychic topography. By following their trail, Abraham and Torok offer not merely a revisionist psychoanalysis but "a theory of readability" as a "cure for a particular pathology—the impossibility of trace to speak."[6] In Derrida's visual elaboration of their treatment of "language as a system of expressive traces," there is, moreover, an added memory of the open forum of the late Roman world, and the catacombs and crypts into which early Christian martyrs were driven through persecution by those same Romans.[7] His own association of "crypt" with "forum" thus enables us to move beyond the individual neurosis of the Wolf Man, and his particular pathologies, to the issue of the marginalized group within the supposedly open space of the democratic public sphere. The forum, in this reading, stands for the performative space of the late capitalist postcolony, the clamorous, collective bargaining place where goods, ideologies and interest groups jockey for power.[8] But its surface conceals another enclave-ridden topography, inhabited by the traumatized, the excluded, the censored, and the silenced: in short, the dispossessed.

Of course, the dispossessed are not homogenous in their dispossession. This chapter acknowledges the embourgeoisement of Urdu in contemporary Kashmir, the elite and middle-class positioning of the writers I cite, and the gravitational pull of Kashmiri Muslim elites toward Urdu. Nevertheless, it focuses on a certain language of voicing and silencing through which I unearth the crypt within the forum, the secret other of the nation that deconstructs its territory of desire. It thereby embarks on examining the "poetics of dispossession": Kashmiri counterdiscourse to the "making of Paradise." The relationship between the Valley and the nation is as oppositional, unequal, and intimately interlocked as that of the crypt and the forum. Just as the fetish of handicraft unmasked the State's power, the crypt's angularities traverse the forum's supposed openness. As Derrida reminds us, this openness is paradoxically defined through enclosure; likewise, the nation needs its boundaries to emphasize the freedom of the sovereign subject within. The practice of everyday life in the postcolony blatantly displays *and* anesthetizes us to the founding of sovereignty on the wild zone of the State's absolute power.[9] Kashmir's continual challenge to that power, the response by the machines of the State, and the splintering of resistance through internal power regimes constitute the embrace between anesthesia and egregious display. It is the letter from Kashmir, which cannot but also must exist, that sends coded news of what is happening inside the crypt and, by implication, outside in the forum. For the crypt is the spatial equivalent of censorship. Who speaks in Kashmir, and on whose behalf? When must a theory of readability accommodate an ethics of unreadability? These questions derive from the ways in which language is spoken *of* in Kashmir: from what I term "conscripting voice"—a play between the oral, the written, and the unsaid, between the official and the unofficial, that also hides, in its own sound, the presence of the crypt. Cross-cutting class and religious divisions in contemporary Kashmir, this conscription of voice simultaneously attests to their participation within the deep politics of Kashmiri multilingualism.

My Poem, My Mother (Tongue)

"O my Koshur mother, I swear, you are my vision and you are my cognition." Thus declares Rahman Rahi in his emotionally taut, densely allusive poem, "Jalwa te zubur" (The Epiphany of David). Written in Koshur in 1965, and recently re-anthologized, it is a passionate declaration of love and need for the mother tongue.[10] The poem opens out, accordion-like, an affective history of Koshur and the Koshur speaker. Lal Ded, the poets Rasool Mir and Mahmood Gami, even Sheikh Abdullah, are all evoked to consolidate a "thesaurization" of Koshur: the poem offers an inventory of the language's treasures.[11] Rahi's assertions of personal voice seal within it the entire Koshur-speaking community. From infancy onward, it is the Koshur of his mother's lullabies and spinning songs that structures the poet's expressive self. "Had we not met, I would have suffocated; I could not have constructed any icons; the Moses in me would not have spoken to God." Language empowers the poet with sacral and rapturous epiphanies. And yet, he pleads with the language-as-mother: "Don't slip away—if you do, deserts will be my destiny/storms will have denuded the blooming lotus/words will be orphaned." Rahi, nationally felicitated poet, studied and sung within Kashmir and, on the evidence of this poem alone, fully in command of the language as expressive medium—what precipitates his fear of abandonment by the mother/tongue? Why does language's affective power over its speaker need the metaphor of the mother as capricious beloved? Why is it, to cite another Kashmiri poet, writing a generation later, in English, and also of his mother, that "the loved one always leaves?"[12]

Agha Shahid Ali's final volume of poems, *Rooms Are Never Finished,* to which this latter statement belongs, helps us excavate the problematic linguistic terrain that subtends his poetry of loss as much as Rahi's poem of attempted self-empowerment. While Ali's earlier collection, *The Country without a Post Office,* centered on the devastation of the 1990s, *Rooms Are Never Finished* arose out of his mother's death, after prolonged illness, in a Massachusetts hospital. A prefatory statement nevertheless links the two motivations. "To a home at war, my father, sibling and I brought my mother's body for burial. It was the only thing to do, as she had longed for home throughout her illness." The "ongoing catastrophe," the "focus" of *The Country without a Post Office,* is reiterated as the present volume's "backdrop."[13] The opening poem, "Lenox Hill," enacts these continuities. It draws on the legendary cruelty of the Hun Mihiragula, medieval invader of Kashmir, who took arbitrary delight in hearing the extraordinary cries of elephants driven to their death over the Pir Panjal Range. American windows open on to the blizzard-fall of elephants and fragile wood shrines, Mihiragula's oppression merges with the "punishing khaki" of the Indian army, and sirens segue into elephant cries. "The Hun so loved the cry, one falling elephant's, that he wished to hear it again." Echoing across the centuries, splicing together time and space and entering, via Manhattan's car sirens, his mother's "hospital dream of elephants," the elephant's cry transmits a clear message: "Kashmir/She's dying!" But, is this message really all that clear? Who is the dying "she:" the Kashmiri's mother, or Kashmir itself?

This syntactical blurring is nevertheless disambiguated by another, more direct conflation: "*So, how's the writing*? I answered, *my mother is my poem*."[14] The dying mother, the poem and Kashmir, space of dreams and memories, merge. But the poem of the mother's death works "to save you as you were, young, in song in Kashmir, and I, one festival, crowned Krishna by you, Kashmir, listening to my flute." Not quite life-affirming, then, but life-preserving at least—a slender gain that is compromised further as the poem freezes memories calibrated in sound. The text can only devitalize the voice that possesses the capacity of "singing the world."[15] The mother was young *in song* in Kashmir; "she" (again syntactically conflated with "Kashmir") dressed her son as the Hindu god Krishna, teaser of devotee-lovers through his flute, and celebrated in bhajans, devotional love lyrics from North India. As with the elephant's cry, so with the flute and the song: the poem, in its writtenness, grapples with the paradox of preserving the aural and the oral. These convolutions signpost a deeper "language guilt" that pervaded the earlier *Country without a Post Office*.[16] There, transformative strategies—"half-torn words," the indecipherable "script of storms" and the "torn water" of the god Brahma's voice—relentlessly turn voice into script, and script into fragment. Images of illegibility, destruction, loss and transformation trope language in conflict: lost language, neglected language, dying language, language transformed. "Lenox Hill" recalls these preoccupations. The poem that responds to the mother's death by trying to save her as she was once, in song, and in Kashmir, reminds us how language, the *pharmakon* of Plato's *Phaedrus,* is both poison and cure.[17]

These contradictory functions of language are well known. But drawn forth here, in the specific context of the poet who bears witness to the conflict in Kashmir, they reveal a fundamental presence-in-absence. The ambivalent metonymy between dying mother, formaldehyde poem and the sounds of Kashmir circles around Ali's use of English, *not Koshur,* to voice Kashmir's cultural dispossessions. No mere angst of South Asia's Anglophone postcolonial elite, with its frequent romanticization of "endangered" indigenous languages, but the affective burden of a distinctly Kashmiri multilingualism is what is revealed thereby. As elsewhere in South Asia, this multilingualism is contoured by the pull of the English language in a globalizing world. But beyond that is the infinitely greater seduction of Urdu, the language of North Indian Muslim high culture, revolution, glamour, and romance. First introduced into Kashmir as a link language for the ethnolinguistically diverse Dogra princely state, Urdu was subsequently politicized and romanticized through the exposure of Kashmiri Muslim leaders to anticolonial, Islamist intellectualism of the North Indian plains, in particular that of Aligarh Muslim University. Independent India's pragmatic three-language pedagogic policy could not cope with the layered affects of post-1947 Kashmir, where the long habit of loving Urdu increasingly competed with the need to love Koshur as part of Kashmiri self-assertion.[18] Rather, this already fraught situation was further complicated by Indian secularism's own need to prove to itself its continuing patronage of Urdu, now the official language of Pakistan.[19] These affective complexities of Kashmiri multilingualism had, moreover, special resonance for Ali. His beloved mother Sufia was not Kashmiri, but a native Urdu speaker from Lucknow in North India; furthermore, the Kashmiri poet who moved fluently between *canzones, sestinas,* and *ghazals* had himself little spoken fluency in Koshur.[20]

"Mother" in "Lenox Hill" thus substitutes for a mother-tongue that is *not* Kashmiri. Mourning his mother's death, in English, allows Ali a disguised mourning for Koshur that accepts its unavoidable compromising by Urdu's emotional demands. An earlier poem of Ali's, also textured by this complexly cathected emotional relationship between mother/tongue, takes us deeper into this particular emotional crypt. "I Dream I Am the Only Passenger on Flight 423 to Srinagar" uses an in-flight recording of the diva of Urdu ghazal, Begum Akhtar, Ali's close friend and, seemingly, mother figure, to memorialize their last encounter before her death in 1974.[21] These memories fold into the pilot's announcement of the destruction of the Sufi poet Noor-ud-Din's shrine at Tsrar-e-Sharif even as Ali flies into Srinagar. Burdened by past and present dissolution of culture, "it is to song that one must turn for flight", but, as the poet asks: "with what measure will I shed sunlight/on pain?" Will the "measure" be that of Urdu ghazal, a form which Ali often transposed on to his English poetry, or of Kashmiri lyrics such as the *vakh* of Lal Ded? As in "Jalwa te zubur," the "flight" becomes the repository of the legacies of different Kashmiri folk poets: Lal Ded herself, "robed in the brilliant green/Of Paradise" and "her true heir," Noor-ud-Din, who "still speaks through five centuries of poets." However, "speaking through" leads us to yet another historical burden: could Lal Ded and Noor-ud-Din have "thus foreseen/ the tongue survive its borrowed alphabets?" Pointing, through the current unavailability of an indigenous script for Koshur, its repercussions on collective identity, this question reiterates the compromised conscripting of the Kashmiri voice.

Controversy has long pursued the issue of the most appropriate written form for Koshur. With *Sharada,* the script of pre-Sanskritic manuscripts and rock edicts, now confined to strictly ritualistic uses by Kashmiri Pandits, preference for its modern counterpart has veered between two sets of "borrowed alphabets:" *Devanagari,* the script used for modern Hindi, or *Nastaliq,* the Perso-Arabic script that is also used by Urdu. While the latter has been in official use since 1947, this decision has by no means met with uniform approval or even acceptance among diverse Koshur-speaking constituencies—an issue whose politics will be unraveled further in the next chapter. This fragmentation of consensus has fed directly into the wider ironies attendant on Koshur's disenfranchised status today: a "minority-majority language" that remains unincorporated into primary and secondary pedagogic structures, even as Urdu, claimed by no group in Jammu and Kashmir as its mother tongue, flourishes as the state's official language.[22] The pedagogic invisibility of Koshur, a direct consequence of which is the "impossibility" of writing "a letter in Kashmiri," has led to widespread assumptions in Kashmir of the dying mother tongue, a corollary to Kashmiri self-identification as "a community-in-neglect."[23] The poet writing in English surreptitiously mourns the absence of Koshur through the dying Urdu-speaking mother; the poet writing in Koshur insists, "It is because of your love that I am singing these psalms," but also agonizes: "If you don't talk to me, the inner revelations will turn to stone." If, as one Kashmiri intellectual acknowledges, "Koshur has not been associated with a sense of self," it is in such metause of language—the contemplation, through language, of language's own powers and frailties—that we must begin our search for Kashmiri resistance through self-empowerment.

The Ventriloquized Voice

Silencing, the motivated quelling of voice, is usually the wall that confronts those who want to know more about what is happening inside Kashmir. People talk readily, but about being suffocated, choked, and amputated.

Such silencing is, moreover, often over-determined in its re-narration. Take the dramaturge M. K. Raina's reminiscences of a middle-class life interrupted by conflict: "Srinagar is my birth place, my home town where I grew up, went through school, college, theatre performances, meeting artists, listening to poets and writers, participating in festivals and various activities until I went to the National School of Drama (NSD) in New Delhi. I did come home regularly until militancy took over, and suddenly—life seems to have stopped."[24] Although Raina's subject here is the conflict's repercussions on *bhand pather,* the indigenous folk theatre of Kashmir that combines satire, music, dance, and buffoonery, the autobiographical note is inevitable—not merely because Raina is himself Kashmiri, but because, in his essay's narrative, it is this Kashmiri identity that took him, as theatre professional, toward bhand pather, and that enabled bhand pather in turn to help him overcome his interrupted Kashmiri existence. In the 1990s, "Kashmir had become a distant and estranged land with all its cultural activities buried under the weight of militancy." Cinema theatres and traditional modes of entertainment alike were targeted: "*bhand pather* performances were ordered to cease by warnings and threats, performers beaten up, and often, their musical instruments destroyed in broad daylight." Almost in magic-realist response to these interdictions, the national award-winning bhand pather guru Mohammed Subhan Bhagat "succumbed to a strange illness precipitated by the ban on his performance. A broken heart? Perhaps!"

While militancy is seen as a bodily silencing of indigenous theatre, Raina's response to that silencing also assumes psychosomatic form. It reverberates beyond Kashmir to the Kashmiri intellectual in Delhi, who finds himself unable to sleep until he has written the script of a play about the life and death of bhand pather.[25] Thus the strangling of this form gives vent to a new voice that is further articulated through urban reinterpretations of bhand pather performed in Delhi, Chandigarh, and elsewhere in India. Overt commentary on its contemporary state, including its languishing under the seekers of aazadi, is now interwoven with older stories and mise-en-scenes. So "professional actors trained at the NSD (National School of Drama, Delhi) and the *bhands* of Akhingam village" in Kashmir together created a new play that enacted "the story of the bhands themselves who had lost their *magun* (guru) Mohamed Subhan Bhagat during the militancy in Kashmir. This story of his life, of the restoration of the form, thus became a metaphor."[26] Raina's deep and continuing involvement with Kashmiri folk theatre leads to the imagined resurrection of a collective Kashmiri voice, feared lost to the villain of this particular piece, militancy. Life, voice, and home are entwined: as a Kashmiri Pandit returning to Srinagar (an identity inseparable from his last name), Raina had felt "choked" ("Home? My home was gone, my clan was gone and my friends had vanished.") In the concluding sentiments of his essay, however, the realization that "heritage is, at times, like a cushion offering comfort, unconcerned about caste, creed or colour" returns to him his voice and his place in an altered homeland.[27]

The politics and emotions surrounding the Pandit rendered homeless in Kashmir will become apparent in the following chapter. Here, I want to highlight how bhand pather's silencing is conscripted, indeed, paradoxically ventriloquized, in order to sustain an idyllic Kashmir(iyat) that might yet exist in Kashmir's villages, invested in the theatrical practices of the bhands. This deictic use of the bhand pather, its mobilization to point to something other than itself, has received fresh emphasis in Salman Rushdie's novel, *Shalimar the Clown*.[28] Initiating its typically baroque narrative is the love between the Muslim boy Noman, a.k.a. Shalimar, and the Pandit girl Bhoomi, a.ka. Boonyi, who live in the bhand village of "Pachigam." Their union is blessed by their elders in the name of kashmiriyat. All that subsequently goes wrong with this marriage and the world signifies, in Rushdie's words, Kashmir as a place "of great physical beauty but also a place where the closest thing to a harmonious culture was created and then destroyed."[29] Taking on the persona of an Islamist terrorist, Shalimar ultimately murders Boonyi and her Jewish American lover Max Ophuls; their daughter, India/Kashmira flails under the weight of her multilayered, heavily symbolic name; the novel ends with her about to kill Shalimar. While Rushdie's fictional canvas is infinitely and expectedly larger than Raina's essay, underlying both is the understanding of the bhand's voice as symbolic of "the closest thing to a harmonious culture," kashmiriyat. Its silencing (whether successful or not) becomes ventriloquized for another script—concerning the impact of the conflict on Kashmiri Pandits, or America's role in fostering militant Islam or, indeed, as in a sensitive documentary on the bhands, the State's choking of traditional creativity through excessive subsidy of "folk" artists.[30]

The deictic necessity of the silencing of Kashmir returns us to urban Indian modernity's dependence on Kashmir as its territory of desire—a dependence that shapes, in fact, Rushdie's own imaginative relationship to memories of "the enchanted land" of his childhood summer holidays. Rushdie's dedication of *Shalimar* to "my Kashmiri grandparents" loops back to *Midnight's Children:* here, his alter ego, Saleem Sinai, paradigmatic child of independent India, cannot escape beginning his narrative with his Kashmiri grandfather, Aadam Aziz, relinquishing the paradise on earth for a modern Indian life. In postlapsarian compensation, the narrative heaps love and disgust in equal measure on Tai, boatman of the Dal Lake and putrescent cornucopia of endless tales, ultimately disposing him off through Indo-Pak cross-fire on the LOC.[31] In a later allegorical fable, silenced story-teller Rashid and his concerned son Haroun travel to "the Valley of K" and "the Dull Lake" to seek another phantasmatic cornucopia, the source of all stories that, alarmingly, is itself choking up. Interest in these thinly disguised references to Kashmir in *Haroun and the Sea of Stories* seems to have revived in the wake of *Shalimar*'s overt preoccupations: the latter's almost too-direct critique of the Indian State's role in Kashmir has made it easier to excavate from *Haroun*'s puns and witticisms two monsters of the nation-state—failed democracy and bureaucracy—and situate them alongside the malign forces of Khattam-shud or "silencing" (typically read as a figure of the Ayatollah Khomeini's fatwa).[32] Rushdie's is indeed an bizarrely fabular entanglement of art and life, where each novel reflects, even prophesizes, yet another facet of his complex subjectivity. But what remains constant throughout is Kashmir as territory of desire, the ultimate source of voice, story, and word-power.

Both mirroring and wish-fulfillment mark the relationship between Rushdie the author and Rashid the authored. Rushdie deeply (if perhaps ambivalently) desires his source of storytelling to *be* Kashmir; to that end, in *Haroun,* he creates Rashid in his image, whose narrative inspiration *is* Kashmir. The true nightmare, the "couchemar" of "Kashmir,"[33] is not the choking of the sea of stories but that the silenced storyteller who turns to it for voice should discover it in the process of being choked. Only by saving the sea of stories can Rashid unfreeze the clocks in his own city by the sea and make narrative time flow anew; likewise, only by telling the story of Kashmir's silence, time and again, and in fits and starts can Rushdie find his own voice and narrative. The magical storyteller stepped into international limelight with the removal of one set of (barely fictional) grandparents from Kashmir; his interviews are studded with unelaborated references to Kashmiri ancestry; a children's fable, acrostically dedicated to his son, alludes to a return to the Valley; finally, with *Shalimar,* the Kashmiri grandparents are "outed" and the narrative juggernaut rolls out to lambaste Kashmir's destruction. While the liberal politics of *Shalimar* are impeccable, and the denouncement of statecraft necessary, its corollary invocation of the territory of desire, the idyll of the bhands, slides into a suspiciously familiar position—what I have earlier termed as secular Indian nationalism's endorsement of kashmiriyat as placebo. *Shalimar* certainly strips *Haroun* of its allegorical obfuscations, but only to reveal the acute necessity of that placebo for the secular Indian intellectual and, equally, for the diasporic writer ever more obliquely angled to his past.

Rushdie's authorial dependence on Kashmir exemplifies how, to give urgency and meaning to other crises, including the crisis of narrative itself, the storyteller turns ventriloquist, insisting that the world hear the silencing of Kashmir. His continues to be the classic, Nehruvian, secular Indian position, that built its political and ideological projects on "the wholesale acceptance of *kashmiriyat*,"[34] and for which, therefore, the idea of an untainted Kashmir that existed at least at some mythical point, is crucial. Underlying his carnivalesque but still democratic version of the nation as forum there certainly lurks a crypt—but that crypt is the one we encounter in *Midnight's Children,* within which a failed poet and his dark lover enact in absurd play a once-grand, now-diminished Islamicate high culture.[35] Rushdie has given tragicomic voice par excellence to the bittersweet ironies of a modern, Indian Muslim subjectivity, including its uneasy collusion with nationalist discourses of Kashmir and kashmiriyat. However, notwithstanding all paratextual protestations of ancestral links, it is not a voice that resounds from the crypts of Srinagar, from what Abir Bazaz, co-director of a film we earlier analyzed, calls "the downtown bylanes—the hetacombs of the slaughtered."[36] These voices from the hetacombs, in even being voiced, assert a certain presence in the world, damaged, incomplete and life-endangering though it might be. Decoded through an appropriate hermeneutics, they reverse the assumptions that the ventriloquist's speech implies a body without a voice, a dummy on his knee. Instead, they destabilize the commonly assumed passivity of the ventriloquized, reminding us of ventriloquism's hidden, active dimension that extracts from it the "power to speak through" as much as their "experience of being spoken through by others."[37]

Cryptopolitics: The Living Dead

Can there be an empowering hermeneutics of the hetacombs? "I hope words grow out of Gowkadal, Hawal, Burzalla, Zakura . . ." Bazaz's commentary on "Srinagar-Sarajevo" enables us to pursue further this question.

Originally delivered orally at Delhi, its opening roll-call of those Srinagar *mohallas* (localities) that were the sites of demonstrations and reprisals brings them out of hiding, conjoining them, ultimately, through the internet. Evoking a dilated present of global massacres that is also "an absolute present of freedom," bonding in a fraternity of the oppressed ranging from the Palestinians to the Bosnians and even to Hiroshima, Bazaz sketches Srinagar through other destroyed cities. Not for him the pastoral village-spaces of Akhingam, Dachigam, or even Pachigam, last refuge of endangered species such as the barasingha deer and the bhands—it is the shattered city that makes him speak. The ensuing words are imagined not as liberating, but, in their erratic, overwhelming and uncontrollable multiplication, "cancerous." There is a need "to recover that memory," and yet, the counterquestion intrudes: "Why talk about this revolution?" It, too, resembles a long drawn out burial, with me following the funeral procession." Images of death pervade the prose and Srinagar: "The city *is* the martyrs' graveyard at Eidgah" (emphasis mine). The memory of "ecstatic" hope erupts temporarily: "The city explodes the night of January 20th, 1990." In the months that followed, "Kashmiris turned *aazadi* demonstrations into an *urs* fair." However, the moment was shortlived. His memories tunnel inward: "We dodge grenades for years to meet friends at Hideout Café where I exchange Poetry for coffee and the *aazadi* I carry with myself is the moment when I kicked the barricade outside a military bunker."

We glimpse here a version of the "politics of verticality" that, as Eyal Weizmann has demonstrated, rotates geopolitical two-dimensionality into a three-dimensional struggle over the Occupied Territories.[38] Although the dizzying convolutions of overhead bypasses, viaducts, and tunnels that interconnect Israeli enclaves and isolate Palestinian ones are absent in Srinagar, its urban geography is not dissimilarly layered with "strategic, religious and political strata" that move from "airspace and roads" to "underground sewers and shrines," including those in which militants hide.[39] For the Kashmiri traversing it daily, this multilayered space, "the raw material of sovereignty and the violence it carried with it,"[40] becomes a template for the spatialization of censorship. In turn, censorship no longer predicates merely writing or reading between the lines: it now means the business of dodging bullets, grenades and detention centers, of burrowing beneath the surface of once-familiar territory to seek new modes of contraband existence. Bunkers and sandbags, lookout posts crudely erected in crossroads and squares, gates fortified with metal spikes, military convoys, and the ubiquity of armed troops are its superficial indices. More profoundly, "ground is divided between crust and subterrain."[41] The Hideout Café, that literalizes its once-jocular name, is now the crypt where the pleasures and urgencies of comradeship, of words and of thoughts, may still escape, in Bazaz's words, the radar of "midnight soldiers," a deliberately ambiguous phrase that equally well applies to the soldiers of the Indian army as to those of aazadi. The self-censoring of words melds with the self-censoring of life: the "Kashmiri Palestinian" learns to interiorize, to choose words as well as space carefully, "to maintain and subvert the regime of censorship."[42]

The existentialist dimensions of this condition of existence may be probed through Achille Mbembe's notion of "necropolitics," that connects Foucault's "biopower" (that domain of life over which power has taken control) to the regimes of the plantation, the colony, and the "late colonial occupation" of Palestine by Israel. "Necropolitics and necropower" thereby "account for the various ways in which, in our contemporary world, weapons are deployed in the interest of maximum destruction of persons and creation of death-worlds and new and unique forms of social existence in which vast populations are subjected to conditions of life conferring on them the status of the living dead."[43] Following but also diverging from Mbembe, I coin the term "cryptopolitics" to bring together the crypts of Derrida with the sewers and shrines of Jerusalem/Srinagar, and to differentiate the "living dead" from the "maximum destruction of persons." Cryptopolitics signals an ambiguous existentialist state that recalls "the third zone between subjecthood and objecthood" into which the colonized were relegated.[44] It also takes us to George van den Abbeele's characterization of the fallout of censorship on "the subject as it negotiates the conflicting interests of truth and desire, order and justice, reality and pleasure, life and death."[45] Van den Abeele finds "a double agency" thereby instituted within the subject. I want neither to assume nor to foreclose this possibility of empowerment for the Kashmiri undertaking similar negotiations. But first we need to confront the tremendous sense of inconsequentiality that threatens to overwhelm the search for agency, and that comes through whenever these difficult negotiations are recalled or articulated. To locate agency within subterranean conditions of existence, we have to look to cryptopolitics as guide.

As the Algerian writer Tahar Djaout says of the injunctions imposed on the Algerian intellectual since the 1990s, "If you speak up, you die, if you don't speak up, you die, so speak up and die!"[46] Such radical reclaiming of sovereignty over life—through voicing the death-dealing word—is, however, differently articulated in Kashmir. A Srinagar artist described to me thus his silence during the 1990s: "If I told the truth, I would be killed. If I lied, I would betray future generations. So I hibernated."[47] Neither death nor life, but *hibernation:* the voice that expresses living under fear and uncertainty refers to its own uncertain status as stasis. Some form of living death is, typically, its tropic expression. Srinagar is a graveyard, but, for its denizens, death is too simple a state of non-being. Bazaz castigates not only the revolution as a long drawn-out burial, therefore, but his own ineffectual hovering on the fringes of its death rituals. This double bind consciously echoes Agha Shahid Ali's poem, "I See Kashmir from New Delhi at Midnight."[48] As the "suspended burning tyre" drips on the back of a "naked prisoner," his shadow, dislocated by the pain, "slips out, beckons" to the poet in New Delhi, "*Console me*/And somehow there, across five hundred miles, I'm sheened in moonlight, in emptied Srinagar." Once in Srinagar, he follows from afar Rizwan's funeral procession, a mere reporter of the violence it elicits from the army. The "disappeared," the ghost of a tortured boy, the zombified follower of funeral processions—are these disembodied specters then indices of intellectual paralysis, melancholic and absent "phantom mediators" between the conflict zone and the world?[49]

Yes, but also no. Like melancholia, paralysis too can constitute a critical threshold. These phantom mediators force those who see Kashmir from New Delhi and other privileged viewpoints in India, those whose class positions affords them mobility, to listen to Rizwan. They collaborate with the text as surreal dream-work whose illogical light sources illuminate *(sheen)* Srinagar's cryptopolitical landscape. Interior states are wrenched away from the lakes and gardens, and calqued instead on the urban setting that, like Fanon's colonized town, "hunches like a wild cat: lonely sentries, wretched in bunkers at the city's bridges, far from their homes in the plains, licensed to kill . . . while the Jhelum flows under them, sometimes with a dismembered body."[50] Furthermore, by borrowing the dream's ability to make the inadmissible explicit through condensations and juxtapositions, the dream-text obeys but also evades self-censorship. Using the dream to "reveal most clearly how the subject is itself implicated in the signifying process rather than merely employing or manipulating it from some external standpoint,"[51] Ali's poem becomes the elite Kashmiri's acknowledgment of complicity in the historical processes that have silenced those whom Rizwan represents. Rizwan's ventriloquized injunctions are Ali's attempts to draw poet and victim together in a pact of liminality: "Each night put Kashmir in your dreams," "Don't tell my father I have died." But the very conscripting of his voice stalls the poem's ventriloquism, turning it around into a speaking *through* rather than a speaking *for*. The ventriloquist becomes a channel for the uncanny power of the dislocated voice. When even in *Shalimar the Clown,* Boonyi returns to Pachigam as the living dead, we find cryptopolitics insinuating its disturbing presence into the heart of the ventriloquizing text.[52]

The cryptopolitics of Kashmiri writing can likewise surface in the nation as forum through the contingencies of translation. Thus specters, phantoms, funeral processions, and graveyards spectacularly proliferate in two translated collections of contemporary Kashmiri short stories commissioned by a national publishing house.[53] The title of one of these collections, *Stranger Beside Me,* conveys the splitting of identity enacted through scenarios that are macabre but hardly otherworldly. In fact, the collection demonstrates how, by utilizing the genre's penchant for the unspectacular quality of everyday life and its momentary transformation through its narrative lens, the short story in Koshur emerges the most apt medium for rendering the relentless penetration of Kashmiri life by the State's machines.[54] The book cover depicts the usual shikara on the Dal Lake. But the stories within assemble, through roads, buses, schools, ambulances, and hospitals, an urban landscape both emptied of referentiality and shot through with the sudden specificity of Kashmiri domestic objects, whose daily use, cutting through class barriers, correlates to the vernacular substratum of Koshur: kangris, quilts, and *hak-bhat* (rice and greens). Populating this desert of the real, the living dead are nevertheless *audible.* In one short story, "The Lost Self," a fragmented body and its "strange lingo" is dispersed across Lal Chowk, Srinagar's nerve center, together signaling the lost Kashmiri self.[55] In another, "I Am Still Alive," the narrator stumbles upon an ominously still scene at a crossroads: "everything was dead, nothing moved." These are "the people condemned to live for a thousand years" while vultures pick on them—but, as the narrator admits, "perhaps I too wanted to lie in peace with the vultures picking on me." Piercing the inertia of this concluding statement is, however, the memory of the narrator's earlier scream, "I am lost," whose defeatist meaning is undercut by its indecorous sound.[56]

The State versus the Scream

This scream is the body's response to life suspended in uncertainty. Its deeper meaning emerges in conjunction with the preponderance, in these stories, of hospitals, doctors, nurses, and ambulances. The ubiquity of the medical apparatus projects a matrix of external, inescapable control over the Kashmiri body. As the narrator of "Burnt-Out Sun" states on hearing the ambulance siren that begins the story, "Its call was for me. That is why I came out. Excuses or arguments would serve no purpose. The matter has been settled at the top: I was sick and needed treatment." The description of the ambulance men introduces a mood sinister yet absurd that thickens when the scene shifts to the hospital room: "How long had I been inside? I knew nothing. I had been leading a quiet, harmless enough life. Why then did they put me in a straitjacket?" The combination of disorientation and lucidity deepens as the story moves on to "what happened ultimately": two nameless people enter the room, declare that "one must get acquainted with death before it comes," and proceed to bring "some instruments and cut my face into two. They left one half linked to my skeletal form and severed the other." The severed half was "put in some safe place beyond my gaze." A chain was hung on his neck, bearing a locket with "a number engraved on it," although "the fact was that my eyes had gone with the part of my face which had been removed so how could I read anything?" Nevertheless, the concluding line announces, "Go, you are free now: you will never see an ambulance again, nor will you ever be brought here."[57]

The ambulance siren initiates a chillingly clinical sequence of events whereby the subject is arbitrarily removed from his environment, mutilated, and reidentified through an assigned number. The "systematic application of pain"[58] merges with the systematic withholding of information, including, interestingly, that which might reveal religious affiliation. The absence of contextualizing information and the brevity of the account encourages its conversion into allegorical commentary on the relationship between the self and authority, that overrides, furthermore, any other identity that may define the Kashmiri subject. We gradually realize that the doctor-mutilators, the ambulance and ambulance workers, the straitjacket, and the room with its bed, white walls, and instruments collectively signify the orthopedic regimes of the modern State that progressively diminish the subject's autonomy. As the subject stumbles "free" into the white space beyond the lines on the page, it would seem preferable to have remained within the "clean white sheets of the hospital bed," as the narrator of another hospital story, "The Void" muses.[59] Here, the hospital offers possibility of escape from the "chains that bind people," the daily grind of office, home, "having dinner, listening to the radio, reading the newspaper, keeping an account of daily expenses, paying the insurance premium, provident fund, income tax, house rent, births and deaths, marriages, mourning." But the accident that interrupts this routine is declared by the doctor as inconsequential; the X-rays reveal no bones broken, and the subject, again, undefined by religious or class markers, returns to the void, "the vacuum in my heart and mind" that suspends him in timelessness and concludes the tale: "What a luxury it is to cuddle up in a white quilt! But it is only for those who await the night and then the dawn. But what of him, whom fate denies this wait? Where can he go?"[60]

If *Stranger Beside Me* testifies to a particular Kashmiri state of being by evoking various forms of suspended life, the perpetrator of this condition is seen as the State. As his or her counterpart elsewhere in India, and indeed anywhere in the modern world, the Kashmiri subject becomes defined through the State's myriad juridical and economic registers, to which he or she bears lifelong accountability. Life is measured through endless form-filling (provident fund, income tax, house rent, for example). What further distinguishes the Kashmiri relationship with the State is the constant knowledge that these invisible forms of power can, at any minute, be displaced by the naked display of an ability to exercise sovereignty, not so much by outright execution or death, as necropolitics would declare, but by the promulgation and prolongation of uncertain states of being. The favoring of hospitals by our short story writers foregrounds a widespread interest in revealing the body made vulnerable to the constellations of power that discipline, punish *and* suspend it within regimes beyond both its control and understanding.[61] That schools, too, are summoned to play this role in some stories extends the understanding of the State's work as impacting the mind as well as the body in a long-term program of ensuring the Kashmiri's surrender to its demands. Whether through school or hospital, the State works to stamp the Kashmiri body with indelible traces: the engraved locket, the stamp on the brow, the stamp on the thigh like those on goats led to slaughter.[62] At the same time, the State withholds explanation through a never-ending displacement of meaning and accountability.

These emphases are captured in the story, "The Enemy," which concerns two brothers living on the banks of the Neelum River where it coincides with the LOC.[63] It pivots on the irony that "I lived on the other bank and bore the stamp of India on my brow while he, right across the narrow river, had Pakistan carved on his." Hearing that his brother was calling for him in delirium, the narrator crosses the Athmuqam bridge, only to be "paralysed" by soldiers, who, "on reading the stamp on [his] brow," promptly arrest him. As his protests go in vain—"No, no sir, I am not an Indian. Neither am I a Pakistani. I am only a Kashmiri"—necropower takes its ruthless course, "and then began the torture." On being told to "confess straightaway that I was an Indian spy and an enemy of Pakistan" the narrator asks, "What was I supposed to confess? That I was my brother's enemy?" The pain in this question intensifies the unsparing account of torture that follows, ending the story with the "scream," "it is all over, finished, the human mind, its thinking—which breaks God's kingdom into fragments and calls a brother its brother's enemy." A Foucauldian coda adds that the soldiers who tortured the narrator now weep pointing to his brother's shroud, but prevent him from participating in the burial rites. Pleading helplessness, they declare their officers, and their officers' officers, to be helpless too. "Who is it that can help? Who has the power?" asks the narrator; the reply, "that is something we do not know," concludes this characteristically brief tale. In doing so, it offers a grim reminder of the absolutism underlying any State, including that aspired for by those demanding aazadi. As in the other stories discussed, the absence of detail frees it into a commentary on present conditions as well as prophetic warning against unreasonable hope for a "free" future.

This story's reliance on the topographical convolutions necessitated by the LOC makes it exemplary of the specific repercussions, on the Kashmiri psyche, of prolonged existence in a political no-man's land. It also asks us to make an ethical distinction between the weeping soldiers and the "Indian" brother, even though both are devastated by a system where power is so thoroughly diffused that its source remains mysterious. The soldiers may weep, but the narrator screams. While their guilt may be appreciated, it cannot be equivalent to the Kashmiri's pain. Although the LOC creates two zones that, for all pragmatic purposes, diverge in being subsumed into the separate nation-states of India and Pakistan, the one condition of existence that is shared across the two Kashmirs remains a continually deferred answer to the question, "Why cannot I know who I am meant to be?" The only real equivalence posited in "The Enemy" is located between the brothers on either bank of the Neelum, one muttering in delirium and the other paralyzed. Coursing through this story, then, like the Neelum River, are somatic circuits—paralysis, the mutter of delirium, sobs, and, again, the scream—that increasingly operate in an audible register. At the conclusion of another story, "The Mourners," as all its characters inexplicably "burst into tears," one of them declares to the others (and to the readers): "Let them be. That is what all of us need—a good cry."[64] From sobs to screams, it is the gamut of sounds released by the body in pain through which the body impresses its material presence on the State. This is the auditory arsenal through which the body counters the State's physical violence.

These sounds, moreover, are "pure utterance."[65] Subverbal and prelinguistic, they emerge from a zone beyond the sounds and sense of language. In particular, the scream represents the uncontrollable and the unreasonable dimensions of resistance that can shatter its preliminary articulation through the meaning-making of words. The short stories are, after all, rendered through the orderliness of narrative; they offer an equivalent to the slave's voice and body that resisted the necropower of the plantation through stylized song and dance.[66] But while the plantation desubjectified the slave, the Kashmiri is sought to be hyper-subjectified through the State's bureaucratic machines. It is thus crucial that resistance, via the scream, evacuate language and order altogether. For order, as expressed in language and narrative, represents in the Kashmiri collective imaginary the relentless bureaucracy of the State, whose narratives also subsume "history."[67] In the short story, "The Sunless Tomorrow," a bestialized postman, whose only available modes of communication are either monkey-like screeches or written notes, brings a telegram commanding the narrator to hospital (again). In the operating theatre (again), he faces a paper wall comprising "history." His scream cuts through the passage of narrative temporality, short-circuiting, as we have seen in so many of these stories, the demand for a conclusion. The words that grow from the crypt are cancerous, then, because as words, they inevitably seek out the magnetic pole of narrative causality, the insulating padding of beginning, middle, and end that also characterizes history as narrative.[68] In contrast, it is the scream that, on escaping the crypt, makes itself heard above the forum's normal noise, and like Masood Hussain's papier maché reliefs, enters it as a material alternative to history.

The Blue-Throated One

Steven Connor suggests that "what the scream ties apart, it also holds together. The scream is the guarantee that, after the world has been atomized, it will reassemble and re-resemble itself."[69] The texts from Kashmir I have examined give voice to a world in which the subject's aspirations for sovereignty—the fundamental meaning of aazadi—is forever thwarted by the purveyors of authority. This world is distilled by political indecision and lack of consolidated local resistance, the wanton exercise of violence by those for and against the State, and the petty and not so petty humiliations at the hands of armed men in uniform. The army checkpoints and bunkers crowding the city become nodal points where humiliation and small acts of resistance condense. Here, fathers are abused while their children watch on (but one of them might just kick a bunker one day). Here, a car is stopped and its driver frisked and interrogated because the sari-wearing woman beside him does not look Kashmiri and he, clearly, is.[70] The Indian army *will* protect her, as Indian citizen; indeed, as the film . . . *Yahaan* insists, here *(yahaan)* such protection is solicited by Kashmiris themselves.[71] Bollywood transforms the bunker into the site of romance, while the historical reasons I have outlined earlier in the chapter prevent Kashmiri literature, particularly literature in Koshur, from generating the cultural capital needed robustly to resist Bollywood's fantasy machines in the nation's forum. When cultural and political forces alike ensure a world in perpetual atomization, when, "condemned to multilingualism," as one Kashmiri intellectual puts it,[72] the Kashmiri cannot turn confidently to self-fashioning in the mother-tongue, where then does the reassembling, supposedly guaranteed by the scream, begin?

If there is an answer, it lies in the body. That body, with its arms raised at the soldier's order, submitting itself wordlessly to his probings—on second glance, is it not a shade overly submissive? In this hint of exaggeration, might we not glimpse an alternative mode of resistance, what Achille Mbembe calls the toying with the power that is otherwise inescapable?[73] Body and voice synchronize into almost inscrutable but crucial modes of survival. As Koshur poet Naseem Shifaie writes in a poem translated as "I Failed to Know":[74]

> Were someone to seize my neck
> I would bow my head
> Were someone to question me
> I would be unable to answer
> If any decision emerged in my mind
> I would hide it

The bodily signs of submission shade into the active withholding of information, paralleling the proliferating subjunctives that screen even the decision to be decisive. "Was it that city's custom to weep? Was there an interdiction on laughter? What was the crime that deserved punishment? What was then the truth—that they could, at a whim, inscribe my fate on my forehead?" Instead of answering these questions, the poem repeats, "I failed to know." In posing them, however, and that too in Koshur, it performs a motivated seizing of agency. Its concluding shrug, "when the pen's tongue is cut off, the pen itself is dumb" seems to reverse its initial determination: "I've got to build words, embellish them with pearls, color them with my blood." Yet the pen's subordination to the tongue drags the poem away from what it says (or does not say) toward its function as a vessel for voice, and voice as bodily channel for transformation.

The transformative strategies detectable within the esoteric world of the text thus voice survival strategies in the world outside. The central verse in Shifaie's poem ostensibly moves from references to censorship to quasi-mystical symbolism:

In their jars are contained
Wondrous water
Come, you too drink this
It is nectar
Let no-one say to me
Your throat is blue

These mysterious jars with their precious contents approximate voice to what, in the context of the myths surrounding the Delphic oracle, has been called "a valuable interiority."[75] They represent not the ineffability of voice but a multiply, even dangerously resonant "vocalic body."[76] Language is the jar that contains, through the words "nectar" *(amrit)* and "blue" *(neel),* the myth of Shiva the Blue-Throated One, who drank the poison of the cosmos to save it from destruction. In thus rejecting exclusivist cultural agendas that would see Shaivism as part of Hindu rather than Kashmiri culture—agendas that we have traced to scholarly constructions of Kashmir's Hindu antiquity—Shifaie, a Muslim Kashmiri poet, follows her guru Rahi, who declares in "Jalwa te zubur:" "I drank *amrit* (nectar) and my tongue gave forth to *zamzam* (the sacred spring at Mecca)." Rahi's statement in turn alludes to a *vakh* by Lal Ded herself, whose poetry moved ceaselessly between the poles of Sufism and Shaivism. These transformations from poison to nectar, from amrit to zamzam, from chauvinism to appropriation, occur, moreover, through the throat. The returning of language to the body parallels metaphors commonly used by Kashmiris talking about Koshur: it is "sucked" like the mother's milk; "eaten" like food.[77] Eating, drinking, swallowing, speaking—the throat's multiple functions point to that domain in which Koshur survives despite protestations of its near-death: the word sung and spoken.

It is the valuable interiority of voice that brings together the word and the body. Thus Rahi's "Jalwa te zubur" celebrates Koshur's proximity to the peasant woman's bodily labor, her song and dance, to crystallized instances of nature's fecundity—"language is the touch of the sunbeam that opens the poet's rosebud"—and to the primal substrata of human experience: "Our union is one of body and soul, blood and life." While susceptible to feminist and materialist critique, his recourse to stereotypes of gender and class explicates the modus vivendi of Koshur's survival through orality, here approximated to the body as a sensory, vital and procreational realm, and daringly moving between language as mother and language as beloved. The poem reminds us that, although splintered by script, fragmented by multilingualism, and weighed down by conflict, Koshur's affective energies rejuvenate its oral life. Indeed, new Kashmiri idioms suggestive of subversive humor have transformed even the worst aspects of the political conflict.[78] Moreover, this affective suppleness has survived largely because of Radio Kashmir. Set up in 1947 as part of the autonomy declared by Article 370, this radio station's distinctive name (its counterpart elsewhere in India being All India Radio, or Akashvani) itself offers the hope of voice's resistive and empowering potential.[79] Radio Kashmir continues to privilege Koshur song and drama over Urdu material, and, despite the ubiquity of cable television and Bollywood soundtracks, ensures a distinctive aurality for the Kashmiri public sphere. It enables the sounds of Koshur to circulate through and transform Srinagar's hetacombs, and transform, too, the text that laments linguistic loss: hence the frequent commemoration, in Ali's poetry, of Radio Kashmir in the context of love and song.[80]

It need not be a Koshur song that Ali remembers hearing, moreover. In his poem, "Some Visions of the Word Cashmere," "a song of Mahjoor's in Raj Begum's voice" gives way to a ghazal by celebrated Urdu poet Faiz.[81] If not Radio Kashmir's programming, then at least Ali's memory of it is structured by that old competition between Urdu and Koshur. Mahjoor was an iconic modern(ist) Kashmiri poet, closely associated with the birth of a progressive literary movement in twentieth-century Kashmir, and with the first (and only) Koshur newspaper *Gaash* in 1940.[82] Along with brief attempts to teach Koshur at primary school, *Gaash* fell early victim to the internal politics of the 1950s and the1960s—a period during which the rise and fall of Koshur was closely linked to the fortunes of anti- and pro-India factions within Kashmir.[83] Kashmiri intellectuals today recall those decades in terms of a squandering of a wider opportunity for self-assertion.[84] The ever-present longing for Koshur, sharpened by the love for, and fluency in, other languages such as Urdu or English thus confirms the community-in-neglect and the community's interiorized shame at neglecting the mother-tongue. But it also embodies attempts to rebuild, through and within language and collective memory, a more robust Kashmiri identity. The insistence that "language has never been a problem because our language knows the art of survival" is itself a survival mechanism.[85] Its coexistence alongside lamentations for the dying language is a contradiction leading us deep into an affective history of Koshur and Kashmir that underlies both the official "birth" of the conflict in 1947 and the eruption of armed violence during the 1990s.

This affective history parallels the trauma of modernity that the fetish of handicraft (un)masks. It conscripts modernity's impact on the interior realms of Kashmiri subjectivity—those realms structured by the relationship between language, voice and self, and restructured by the materialist dimensions of class positioning. The same exigencies of the Great Game and indirect rule that had led to the framing of the Valley as a territory of desire had also created the Dogra princely state of Jammu and Kashmir out of a patchwork of ethnolingual groups, and fostered a checkered achievement of rights and capacities across this unwieldy entity. The aspirational multilingualism of Kashmir, the reverse romanticization of Koshur, the "lost" mother-tongue, by the Urdu-literate middle classes, Koshur's restriction as well as survival within a primarily oral sphere, the practical problems of script and pedagogy—all these contemporary issues are their historical consequences. Striating and complicating them is the relationship of crypt and forum that defines the relationship between the Valley and the decolonized nation. The modern nation's attempts to incorporate the fantasy of the Valley resurface in the postcolonial reproduction of the unsatisfactory structure of the princely state within which it was administratively located. Manifesting itself most egregiously in the domain of inadequately thought-through language policies, this failed incorporation is simultaneously given cryptic articulation in the discourses surrounding language that can be heard from Kashmir. This voice from the crypt arises, too, from the gray zone between testifying and making oneself and one's collective identity vulnerable—as powerfully suggested by legendary Kashmiri artist Ghulam Rasool Santosh's quasi-Abrahamic parable, "The Voice."[86] Describing a father, himself a foundling, who kills his foundling son at the behest of a mysterious but commanding Voice, it concludes with the murderer-father in the pose of the ash-smeared, self-abnegating *yogi* (ascetic) that is also an iconic aspect of Shiva.

Can such self-abnegation ever be a successful route to self-regeneration, and, in this particular instance, is it enhanced or problematized by the Shaivite allusion? The answer depends on whether Santosh's reader is in the crypt or the forum, in or outside Kashmir, and, as the next chapter shall argue, what kind of a Kashmiri identity he or she might publicly claim—Pandit, Muslim, or something struggling to live beyond these categories, themselves too born out of modernity. The vectors of modernity that led to the Valley's framing as the territory of desire and the modern nation's antique heart, also led to the uneven and traumatic interpellation of the Kashmiri subject within the apparatus of the decolonized state. In this chapter I have demonstrated that voice offers a potent medium for expressing both this trauma and modes of resilience and survival. The chain of speaking-hearing-testifying adduces censorship on several levels, the weighing up between what can be spoken, what should be heard and what is better not overheard. It is in this spirit that I have refrained from commenting on the religious affiliations of those writers I have examined here. Those in the "know" will recognize from names and surnames what these affiliations might be; those not thus enlightened might offer the others a less over-determined reading practice. Reworking Geeta Kapur's injunction, I have sought to make the critic, that is, myself, "through force of interpretation," the channel that tunnels outward through the subterrain, making silences (including my own) audible, if not comprehensible.[87] For the hope of a transparent, adequate translation is vain in all senses of the term; a methodology that accepts opacity can, perhaps, reveal far more. Critical analysis and academic scholarship cannot pretend to convey fully what the impact of conflict has been on Kashmiri subjectivities. But before the critic comes the artist. It is to the artist as the link between the crypt and the forum, and to the epistemic and reconciliatory possibilities of the artwork as compared to the word, that the final two chapters will accordingly be dedicated.

Five

The Other Possibility

In Srinagar you can still find a small Hindu temple on the banks of the river Jhelum, lost amongst the hundred and one mosques of Srinagar. Its entrance is always heavily guarded by BSF forces and it is protected by sandbags on all sides, as it has been hit a few years ago by a rocket fired by Muslim militants. Inside, a handful of Kashmiri Pandits are still trying to preserve this sacred place, where a natural lingam is said to have emerged 3000 years ago and where their forefathers have worshipped for twenty generations.

—François Gautier, ideologue

I cracked the sun. I took a hammer and a chisel, and I cracked the sun.

—Rajendar Tiku, sculptor

In chapter 4, I examined how contemporary Kashmiris have mobilized voice, both metaphoric and real, within a poetics of dispossession. It concluded with the suggestion that the impact of such mobilization depended on the subjectivity and self-positioning of the voice's bearer: What kind of a Kashmiri was being constructed thereby? I now explore this question further by turning to one of the Kashmir conflict's most discomfiting consequences, the departure of almost Kashmiri Pandits from the Valley during the early 1990s. I do so not in order to take sides or even, as one Kashmiri Pandit author in Jammu demanded of me, to "tell the world the truth";[1] perhaps the only truth under such circumstances is the relativity of "truth" itself. Did the Pandits leave because, being

Hindus, they were collectively threatened and caused bodily harm, by militants aspiring to establish Islamic rule in the Valley? Did they leave because the Indian intelligentsia in the Valley advised them to? Did they flee their homes through "legitimate fear," or even, possibly, through fear, unqualified by any adjective?[2] These are not questions I purport to answer, not least because responses to the Pandits' departure from the Valley have become messily intertwined with other histories, other narratives, and other subjectivities (from which I cannot claim exemption). What remains incontrovertible is, to quote Pandit poet and political activist Agnishekhar, *"Bhagey pandit"* (they fled, the Pandits); that many are still housed in the supposedly temporary, tented camps of Jammu and Udhampur; and, moreover, that this situation has furthered political agendas fanning outward from Kashmir.[3] While cognizant of such appropriation, I do not focus *on* it. Rather, *through* it, I problematize a counterdiscourse of resistance chained to the voicing of the word.

My claim here is simple: any response to Kashmiri Pandit displacement that takes verbal form inevitably succumbs to anterior narratives that have shaped collective emotion within South Asian modernity. Arguably, South Asian modernity is itself shaped by the political mobilization of such emotion, through both the technological dissemination of narratives and the powerful interplay of image, symbol, and story.[4] Thus, my first epigraph illustrates how easily a depiction of the Kashmiri Pandits as a long-beleaguered community enters the Hindutva understanding of the sacred space of the Indian nation pressed upon by the other as Muslim—an understanding propagated through the very technologies of modernity.[5] Gautier's "handful" of Kashmiri Pandits valiantly safeguarding their ancient patrimony against the massed and militant worshippers of Srinagar's "hundred and one mosques" adroitly plays on a deeply demographic imaginary inherited from the colonial use of the census; it simultaneously draws on an affective sacrality spatialized through the strategic intersection of the map of the nation and the autochthonous sign of Shiva, the "lingam."[6] The sacred place of the Srinagar temple aggrandizes into "the sacred soil of Kashyap," so beloved of our Indologists and, through a now-familiar rhetorical move, into the spiritual guarantor of the Indian nation. The Border Security Force (BSF) guarding the temple are incarnated as the nation's saviors, sealing the pact between the army and the nation-state.[7] To this masterful compression of established narratives may be contrasted my second epigraph above, Pandit sculptor Rajendar Tiku's statement concerning his artwork, "Sun Rises Over the Camp."[8]

Although still composed of words, the meaning of the statement remains tightly bound to the stone sculpture it refers to: a deeply cracked disc mounted on a pedestal-like form.

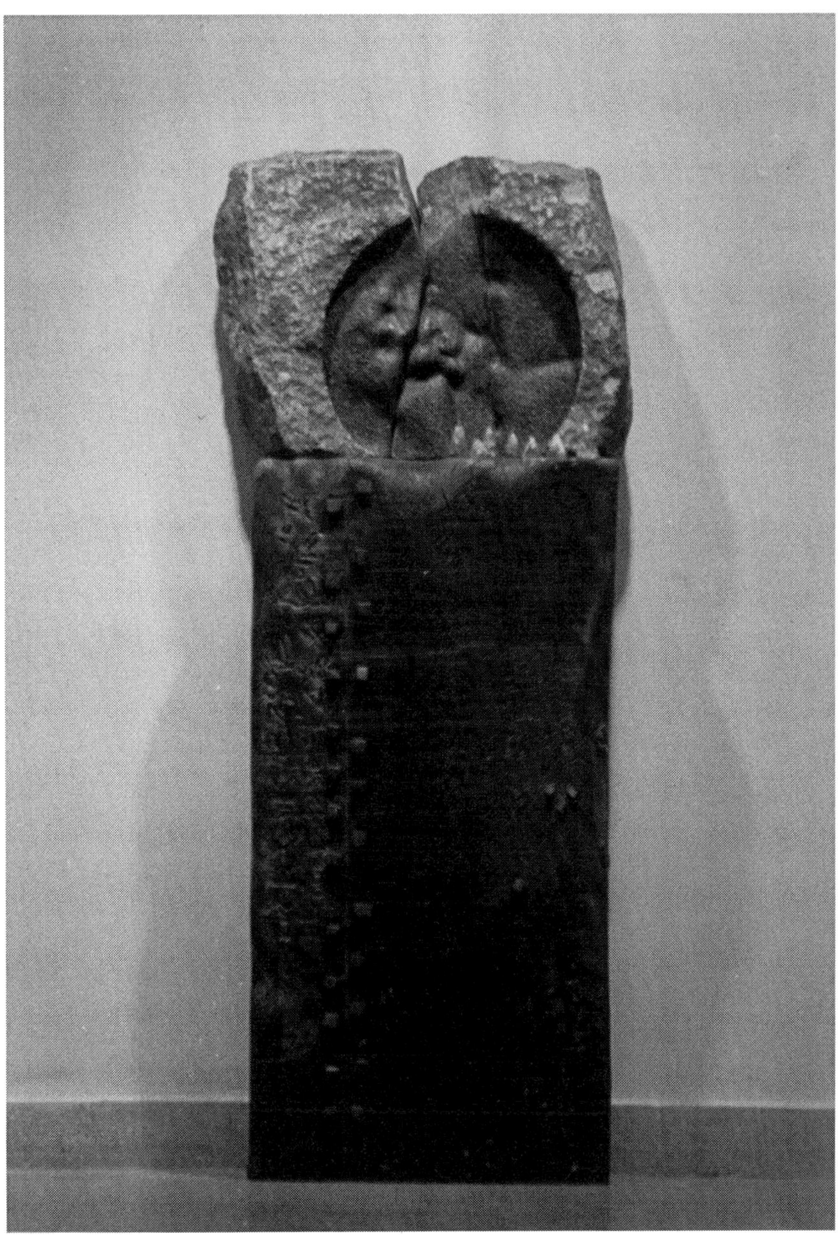

Rajendar Tiku, *Sun Rises on the Camp,* 1993–94. Stained wood, stone, 217 × 78 × 26 cm.

I use Tiku's verbalizing of his artistic decision—to disfigure his created sun—as a "place holder" for the object, whose "thingness" prevents its from entering verbal discussion except through indirect means, or *ekphrasis*.[9] But I also use it to highlight the thing's continuing power over the word.[10] I focus on this power as an antidote to the poison of words, particularly the magnet-like attraction between words and narrative meaning-making. Of course, narrative and nonnarrative forms of representation cannot be too strictly segregated. Gautier's account of Pandit resistance to cultural erosion illustrates not the separateness of but the relationship between narratives of exclusion and belonging and the visual, spatial resources of "the map, the census and the museum."[11] Cultural artifacts and processes generate meaning through a dynamic struggle between what Brunella Antomarini calls the "discursive exigency" of narrative and linear impulses and what we may posit as the "lyric exigency" of their spatialized, nonlinear counterparts.[12] We encounter the word in time and strive to understand temporality as causal sequence. Reading or hearing moves us forward with the thrust of accumulated words that we instantaneously seek to convert into hermeneutic chains. Forms such as the very short story or poem resist this tyranny of temporality, but they are also constantly co-opted by it.[13] In contrast, the nonverbal artifact offers what Tiku calls "the other possibility;"[14] but does its challenge to the word render it too opaque? Taking the Pandit controversy as exemplary of the difficulties of Kashmiri counterresistance to the Valley as the motor of nationalist desire, I use it to probe these political as much as philosophical problems of verbal and nonverbal representation, in particular the latter's "other possibility."

Messages from Displaced Kashmir

April 2004: In Jammu, Pandit Agnishekhar gifts me an anthology of his own poetry. Entitled *Kisi Bhi Samay* (At any moment), it contains forty-nine poems under the heading of "Kram" (Sequence). A second section, entitled "Visthapit Kashmir" (Displaced Kashmir) contains ten poems, each accompanied by a date and place of composition. The dates range from mid 1990 to early 1991; the place is always Jammu. Paradoxically, the poems grouped under "Sequence" are assigned neither dates nor places. The poetic medium is a fairly Sanskritized Hindi. The anthology was published in 1992 by a press based in a small town in North India and typeset in Delhi.[15] My mind focuses on these aspects of the material object in my hand to distract from the increasingly uncomfortable feeling that I am exploring Jammu under false pretences. The Kashmiri Pandit writers I visit never inquire about my religion, but perhaps they assume I am "one of them." How else could they speak so openly about the inherently "communal," "fundamentalist" nature of Kashmiri and even *all* Muslims? One such writer is also a college lecturer in Hindi. Her voice quivering with passion and anger, she punctuates with such remarks a reading list on international terrorism she reels off for my instruction.[16] We converse in candlelight (there is no electricity) in a cramped, hot room where her aged mother lies among stacked trunks and suitcases, and that we have reached after stepping over several gutters and stumbling over several potholes in the gathering dark. Suddenly, she entrusts me with messages to her Muslim friends in Srinagar. "Tell them I miss them very much."

Pandit Agnishekhar, however, is consistent, courteous and in command. In his hardly less unassuming home, he introduces me to a critical vocabulary in Hindi—"the literature of exile," "the literature of displacement"—that supplements the terminology I already know from reading websites and talking to other displaced Kashmiri Pandits: "exodus," "migration," "refugees in one's own country," "camps," "ethnic cleansing," "genocide," even "holocaust."[17] I meet his wife, who writes novels and poems about Kashmiri displacement in Hindi, and their poetically named teenage children, "Thumri" (a genre of North Indian song) and "Himalay." Probably very young when they left Srinagar in 1990, they have grown up "in exile." During the intervening decade and a half, their Kashmiri Muslim counterparts have also grown up without knowing, as one Kashmiri Muslim writer and parent told me in Srinagar, "their amputated other half." Yet in Srinagar I was also told, "We are tired of hearing that the Kashmiri Pandits must return. Let them stay where they are, let them come back to the Valley: we don't care, it isn't our problem."[18] At a "reconciliatory meeting" of women from different parts of Jammu and Kashmir that I attended, such contradictory feelings ran high. Women accused each other's communities of mutual betrayal but also sang together in Koshur and embraced each other, weeping.[19] I found myself witnessing the sad aptness of another terminological distinction I gleaned from the Jammu writers: "this-side Kashmir" and "that-side Kashmir," where the dividing line is the Pir Panjal range, Aurel Stein's "snowy girdle" barricading the Kashmir Valley and its denizens from the Indian plains.[20] Now, however, the Pir Panjal did more than divide Kashmiri from non-Kashmiri; it also underwrote fissures internal to Kashmiri society.

The popular discourse of kashmiriyat is usually deployed to paper over those fissures. Writings from both India and Kashmir frequently assert the primordial amity between Hindus and Muslims that existed under its banner. Kashmir's perceived "enchantment" is associated with this mythic harmony between groups that, particularly during Partition, elsewhere strained for each other's throats. In Gandhi's oft-repeated words, "Kashmir is our only hope."[21] The Pandit exodus in early 1990—and thus the mysterious destruction of this harmony—is neither analytically approached nor historically examined in such writings, but lamented. Again, this tendency is spectacularly exemplified in Rushdie's *Shalimar the Clown*. This novel, as seen in the previous chapter, firmly subscribes to Kashmir as one-time paradise on earth, whose most salient illustration was Pachigam village's sanctioning of the marriage of the Pandit Boonyi and the Muslim Noman in the name of kashmiriyat. It is not surprising, then, that Rushdie prominently laments the Pandit departure from the Valley within one of the novel's two impassioned litanies of unanswered questions. While the failure of Boonyi and Noman's marriage is triggered by the irresistible charms of America's representative, Ambassador Max Ophuls, this temptingly allegorical logic fails to incorporate the real-life departure of the Pandits, even as the laments remain unassimilated within the tenor of Rushdie's prose.[22] The questions regarding this most obvious manifestation of "kashmiriyat's breakdown" are, literally, unanswered. These patterns are replicated in the world outside the text. At the reconciliation meeting described above, an articulate Pandit woman recalled how she used to frequent both the temple of Kheer Bhawani and the shrine of Shah-i-Hamdan. In Jammu, she has "lost [her] address." What happened, she asked the group, in 1990?[23]

This question remained on the rhetorical level, but a stray comment made by the same speaker offered indirect answer. Describing her post-1990 returns to Srinagar in course of reconciliation work, she spoke, with some amazement, at the educational progress of Kashmiri Muslim women in the interim. "You don't seem to need us anymore," seemed the subtext of this digression. An almost imperceptible stir rippled around the room; that I could sense it at all was evidence of my increasing awareness of the Kashmir conflict's complex internal dynamics. At stake was not some romantic notion of kashmiriyat but knotted threads of claim and counterclaim, obligation and self-assertion. Unraveled, these threads led back to the twentieth-century political mobilization of Kashmiri Muslims and the consequent renegotiation of agency through Sheikh Abdullah's socialist program of land reforms and job redistribution. Of a key moment within this mobilization, Chitralekha Zutshi writes: "The tussle between Kashmiri Muslims and Kashmiri Hindus in and around 1931 was more about political and economic representation than religious antagonism."[24] Already at the moment of the first census in Jammu and Kashmir, "Hindus dominated the financial and professional sectors."[25] As made inadvertently clear in a recent, lovingly written memoir of the "vanished" Kashmiri Pandit world, the conspicuous consumption of beautiful objects was a privilege all too often secured through the labor of the Kashmiri Muslim.[26] Sudha Koul's prose in *Tiger Ladies* dwells on the priceless shawls ordered by the women of her family. But, like the blurred bodies sliced off by the margins of the Mahatta photographs, the Kashmiri Muslim artisan waiting for their decisions fits but uneasily into the Kouls' opulent living room and into the remembering text.

Even more tellingly, the artisan's daughter who waits with him returns later to the narrative as the author's classmate at Srinagar's new, egalitarian Government Women's College.[27] Like the bemused speaker at the reconciliation meeting, Koul appears ill-equipped to digest this alteration in circumstances. That education should be the site of such social contestation is fully in keeping with the Pandits' monopoly on linguistic as much as economic capital: they were Kashmiri society's traditional custodians of the word. Sanskrit, Persian, Urdu or English—whatever the socially ascendant language in a given historical epoch, the Pandits' mastery over it inevitably consolidated their social position, particularly with the onset of modernity during Dogra rule.[28] Of course, the same Dogras relentlessly deprived Kashmiri Muslims of the most basic social opportunities. The obvious task of educating the Muslim within an overall project of Kashmiri emancipation, from another perspective, thus, also threatened to destabilize established Pandit ascendancy. Hence, the deep implication of the world of letters within the Kashmiri political arena, an implication that regularly leaves ambiguous traces on cultural productions born out of the post-1990 parting of ways between Pandit and Muslim. A contemporary Kashmiri poet based in Jammu, Bimla Raina, who uses Koshur within a highly esoteric, neomystic poetic mode, opts for parallel pages in two scripts corresponding to the two Kashmirs, the Sanskritic Devanagiri and the Perso-Arabic Nastaliq: Is this compromise writ large, or the indelible trace of a now unbridgeable gap?[29] As this example indicates, furthermore, the controversy over the most appropriate script for Koshur furnishes a visible index to the fissures within contemporary Kashmir.

This issue, briefly touched upon in the previous chapter, once again testifies to the entanglement of Valley and Nation. In echoing the painful politics of script and vocabulary surrounding the ownership of Urdu, it aligns Kashmiri Muslim and Pandit subjectivities to nationalist battles fought over culture and heritage by Muslims and Hindus of the North Indian plains. Nevertheless, I use Kashmiri divergences over script not to reiterate this alignment but to illuminate specific choices made by Kashmiris acting collectively. In other words, rather than subsume uncritically the contestations within Kashmir to narratives of Hindu-Muslim relationships outside of Kashmir, I want to probe when and how convergences of these two histories, such as those suggested by the parallel splintering of script, have occurred. Bimla Raina is one of the few Pandit writers still using Koshur as a creative medium; the majority has increasingly opted to write in Hindi and to print work solely in Devanagiri. The associated decisions to adopt Hindi and espouse Devanagiri are pragmatic choices reflecting new alliances rather than cultural preservation per se.[30] As Henny Sender observes astutely, the twentieth-century history of the Pandits "is not so much the history of a social group left stranded by a commitment to a culture no longer in existence but of a gradual shifting of the centre of gravity within the community."[31] Made prior to the events of 1989 and beyond, Sender's observations are prescient of continued choices made by Kashmiri Pandits in "Displaced Kashmir." Through these choices, furthermore, inherited discourses of what we may term the Valley's geo-spirituality are selectively deployed within a prima facie linguistic cultural politics.

Passions of Adopted Tongues

O vast majority of poets of the Hindi world
My friends!
You were no "Relief Commissioners"
That you now need to send us in your poems
Application forms for the right to some small shelter—
A totally devastated, displaced society's wounds
Simply seek a home somewhere in your sympathy.

These accusations by Agnishekhar appear in his poem "Mahavipada" (Great trouble), written in Jammu in December 1990, and published within the "Displaced Kashmir" section of *Kisi Bhi Samay*.[32] Its references to relief commissioners and application forms give stark testimony to the problems of resettlement encountered by the displaced Pandits at the infamous Jammu camps. The critique of labyrinthine and cumbersome government machinery foreshadows Agnishekhar's political decision to found Panun Kashmir ("Our Kashmir"), a group demanding from the Indian State a separate Pandit homeland within the Valley in order to ensure their cultural rights.[33] But the pointed address to the "the Hindi world" and the allusion to the opinion-shaping power of poems circulating herein suggest political as much as literary alignments sought by the poet-turned-demagogue. In fact, opening images of literary unresponsiveness—"the shutters of multifaceted poems are closed/words enclosed within their pages are silent"—gather explicit political overtones within the concluding query—"where in this heat and moisture can one safeguard/These myriad bundles enclosing the tomes of Abinavagupta, Kalhana/the poems of Lal Ded and [Dina Nath] Nadim?" While the first two names recall the Indologist construction of Kashmir as storehouse of Hindu antiquity, Lal Ded evokes Kashmir's Sufi heritage and Nadim, Koshur's modernist flowering.[34] By binding this select company of to images of displacement and shelter, "Mahavipada" becomes no less than a calling card left by a radicalized poet at the Hindi world's doors.

Who might constitute this Hindi world, and why should Agnishekhar find it necessary to address it in particular? This question returns us to Sender's observation, cited above, concerning the motivated choices made by the Kashmiri Pandit community through the twentieth century. What Agnishekhar defines as the Hindi world is the same "Hindi public sphere" whose cultural politics have been examined recently by Francesca Orsini, and whose ambit of influence has been summarized by Alok Rai as "Hindi nationalism." The near-homology between that latter phrase and "Hindu nationalism" highlights how, to adapt a phrase from a study of Tamil linguistic politics, "passions of the Hindi tongue"[35] have tended to feed into Hindutva nationalist chauvinism. It is beyond the scope of this chapter to dwell on the complex affective politics of those early twentieth-century movements that created the equation in North India between "Hindi," "patriot," and "Hindu," and demonized as their Other the Urdu-speaking, Urdu-loving, Pakistan-loving "Muslim"; suffice it to say that this charged legacy, an aspect of which has already been considered while discussing the hierarchy between Koshur and Urdu, is consciously adopted by Agnishekhar along with the adoption of Hindi as a language of expression. By addressing, in Hindi, contemporary North Indian poets writing for a Hindi audience, and by balancing criticism with a call to friendship, Agnishekhar, a Kashmiri Pandit poet displaced from Kashmir, seeks to consolidate the on-off relationship of two separate constituencies into a legitimate partnership of like-minded bedfellows. All-important in this task is the presentation of the Pandits as rightful custodians of Kashmir's literary heritage, a view that, as we saw earlier, first emerged out of the scholarly labors of the "White Pandits."

In Agnishekhar's poetry, the Pandits leave their homes in ignominious, humiliating haste—a departure brilliantly captured by the staccato rhythm and pungent juxtapositions of his poem "They Fled, the Pandits." But they do not leave behind their books. Books, their readers, and their writers have constituted a very important strategy in show-casing Kashmiri Pandit displacement to the rest of India. Notwithstanding any initial apathy of the sort that kickstarts "Mahavipada," the resources of the Hindi public sphere, a community defined by the oral and print resources of Hindi, have been very successfully mobilized by Kashmiri Pandit spokespeople to present themselves as a community whose protection is tantamount to a responsible attitude toward a heritage not merely regional but *national*. The projection of the Pandit departure as an example of what the Indian press often later termed the "Talibanization of Kashmir" fed right into the revival of the communal question in 1990s India that crested with the demolition of the Babri Mosque in 1992, and ensured the Hindu Right Wing's subsequent ascendancy within the national public sphere. The resurgence of Hindu nationalism during this period coalesced with an emergent vernacular politics to infuse Hindi with renewed power and cultural capital.[36] The sudden proliferation of a Kashmiri Pandit "literature of exile" in Hindi, buttressed by accruing literary criticism in Hindi directed toward exegesis of this literature, thus constituted a pragmatic collective decision to attract the widest possible audience of a particular political predisposition.[37] Indeed, Agnishekhar's dual persona—poet and leader of Panun Kashmir—can be interpreted as a lodestone for the mobilization of the displaced Pandits as a learned community now in exile, and a community, moreover, in shameful neglect.

This self-presentation of the Kashmiri Pandits neatly reverses the respective positions of Pandit and Muslim in modern Kashmir. Apposite here is Mridu Rai's use of the phrase "community-in-neglect" to characterize Kashmiri *Muslim* self-presentation during the Dogra era. It is absolutely necessary both to note the heavy price paid by the secular left in ignoring the humanitarian dimensions of Pandit displacement and to resist, at all costs, airbrushing those dimensions. But let us focus, too, on this little-explored reversal. The pre-1990 poems of *Kisi Bhi Samay* evidence the competing claims on Kashmiri belonging being made on the eve of the dramatic events that culminated in their collective departure from the Valley. Read today, what Agnishekhar calls the "literature of premonition," and illustrates through his own poems "Mihiragula aa raha hai" (Mihiragula is coming) and "Raja teri nagari mein chor" (O King, a thief roams your city) still radiates Kashmiri Pandit disquiet during the overt mobilization of Kashmiri demands for aazadi from 1986 onward.[38] As his other poems, for instance, "Pandrethan ki mandir" (Pandrethan's Temple), "Behti hui Vitasta" (The Flowing Jhelum), and "Shankaracharya parbat" (Shankaracharya Mountain) convey, this disquiet was accompanied by a fervent linking of contemporary Pandit culture to Kashmir's pre-Islamic heritage. The stones of Pandrethan, "the inheritance of a thousand years," permeate the poet's being; his world is defined by the panorama of Srinagar seen from the Shankaracharya peak, and his mother at the kitchen stove. Drawing on sites much favored by both nineteenth-century photographers and Indologists (Pandrethan, in particular, was obsessively photographed by Aurel Stein), these poems domesticate and vernacularize—albeit in Hindi rather than Koshur—the scholarly fascination with pre-Islamic Kashmir.

Such postcolonial transformation of colonial discourse is neither isolated nor new. What distinguishes the Kashmiri Pandit situation is the channeling of this inheritance, in construction considerably more recent than "a thousand years," into overt repudiation of the demands for aazadi voiced by those Kashmiris who, through class-based instrumentalization of religion, were largely Muslim.[39] Even while the latter's demands can be seen as arising from the class-based neglect of non-elite groups within the Dogra period, and their continued disaffection within postcolonial democratic politics, Pandit resistance to the notion of aazadi can be read in terms of their traditionally comfortable relationship with those in power both within and without Kashmir. Here, the iconic power of Jawaharlal Nehru's Pandit heritage cannot be overestimated. The interlocking of "modern nation/antique land" was hardly detrimental to Pandit self-fashioning. Equally, Nehru's presentation of Kashmir's spirituality as essential to India drew on works that had progressively downplayed Muslim claims to the "antique land." The familiar over-determination of religious affiliations in modern South Asia gains here a distinctive spin through alignments with class and power structures within and without the Valley. For Pandits viewing the 1980s, when the political puppeteering between the central and state governments worsened the situation on the ground, the *hangul* deer, native to Kashmir, became an appropriate(d) symbol. As Agnishekhar's poem "Hangul" declares, "No one hears that the hangul is dying/among the snow-clad meadows and sunlit peaks/ . . . through the Vitasta's banks now flows not water a strange melancholy." Unaware of the irony of a postage stamp being issued by the Central Government in its honor, the hangul, prey to "a monstrous conspiracy," moves inexorably toward extinction.[40]

How does "Hangul," which makes no open reference to the Kashmiri Pandits, transform into an allegory of Pandit displacement in particular? What about the interruptive agency of what I earlier termed the lyric, non-narrative form, here exemplified in the poem's close focus on the hangul and its evacuation of human Kashmiri actors? This focus is nevertheless distended by discursive pressure from at least two wider narratives: that of Kashmiri Pandits as a minority within Kashmir, clustering around layered memorializations of their premodern departures from the Valley;[41] and the narrative of the Muslim as the nation's internal Other. In fact, both these narratives shape a screenplay written by Agnishekhar himself for the Bollywood-style film *Sheen,* that promised to show national and international audiences how the Pandit became "a refugee in [his] own country."[42] Also directed by a Pandit, it narrates the love story of Pandit youngsters Sheen (Koshur: "snow") and Manu, against the backdrop of their community's displacement. Sheen, symbolizing Kashmir the mother/daughter/beloved, lies in coma as the story unfolds in flashback. Unlike Agnishekhar's poems of displaced Kashmir, *Sheen* explicitly narrates, and thereby interprets, events centering on muhajideen threats to Pandits on 19 January 1990, and the latter's departure the following day. It ends with violence: the Kashmiri Muslim militant, one-time friend of Manu, is brutally killed and his sister raped by his Afghan mujahideen mentors. This conclusion unleashes, through the immense ideological power of "the end," altogether disturbing fantasies of extermination through revenge. It also suggests how narratives that formally exist outside the margins of a poem such as "Hangul" have the power retrospectively to shape it into a self-fulfilling prophecy of the Pandits' fate under militancy.

The Prison-House of Narrative

While "Hangul" encrypts, through lyric compression, an intra-Kashmiri history of community competition, interdependence, and self-fashioning, *Sheen* unfurls that same history through narrative dilation. Together, they suggest how "the content of form" impacts the terrain of South Asian collective memory.[43] To unpack fully these connections, however, we need first to complicate some commonly held arguments about the epistemology and phenomenology of narrative. From Aristotle onward, Western thought has recognized the importance of the beginning, middle, and end that converts a linear sequence into a causal one.[44] It is a peculiar and universal aspect of human experience, it is argued, that we can "grasp together" and extract from a sequence, the logic of cause and effect.[45] However, if "narrative" signifies the telling of a story which is bound together with a certain experience of linear temporality, how does it differ from other modes of representing experience, such as lyric poetry, which are by no means necessarily nonlinear? Given the role played by "the end" in converting a linear series into a causal sequence, how does our experience of narrative differ from our response to a painting, a sculpture, or even a poem, that we grasp together in ways other than sequential reading?[46] I have found it useful, therefore, to posit, within different modes of telling, a dialectic relationship between the "narrative" and "lyric" impulses. The former moves forward discursively in time; the latter, what I also refer to above as "lyric compression," lingers over moments and demands we linger too. The intertextuality between *Sheen* and "Hangul" encapsulates how this dialectic has collapsed within the memorializing of Pandit displacement: the narrative impulse now *contaminates* the lyric.

The unwelcome consequences suggested by the word "contamination" are fully intended, and their source may be traced to what I shall call "narrative superimposition." The moral of *Sheen*'s story is that, for the Kashmiri Pandits to pull together as a collective, the memory of fear and the utterly destabilizing experience of displacement must be controlled through another metanarrative—that of the Muslim as Other. This metanarrative has haunted the Indian nation since the ur-trauma of Partition, whose primal position in the Indian collective psyche is both predicated upon and complicated by its temporal contiguity with decolonization and the achievement of independence. Under the phantasmatic sign of Partition as original trauma, sites of violence—"communal" violence as well as wars and confrontations between India and Pakistan over Kashmir—proliferate with frightening predictability. This proliferation is tied to the compulsive narrating of the memory of Partition, and the inability of melancholia to cross that threshold between unproductive iteration and critical self-searching. It is not (as Freudian psychoanalysis would suggest) the failure of narrative that causes this "uncritical" melancholia. Rather, the problem is the opposite one: the proliferation, lamination, and superimposition of narratives, and their empowerment through mutual self-confirmation. Narrative superimposition constantly seeks to restore order to the traumatized self by remaking it as part of a community; yet, in the context of South Asia, interlocked subjectivities and histories all too often mean that this re-affirmation of one community is conducted at the expense of designating an "other." This interlocking is most acutely manifested in Kashmir, where the demographic relationship of "Hindu majority" and "Muslim minority" within postcolonial India stands reversed.

Sheen stokes subliminal fears associated with this reversal, fears that are no longer containable within anodyne discourses of kashmiriyat. By miming narratives of Partition, its teleological drive inevitably replicates the separating out of shared cultural resources into antagonistic, "[Kashmiri] Hindu" and "[Kashmiri] Muslim" subjectivities. In being compelled to record that very separation, such narratives of Pandit displacement from Kashmir replicate and compound the conflicts within Kashmiri society. It is particularly necessary to emphasize this point since, following Benedict Anderson's *Imagined Communities,* and the elaboration of its thesis by Homi Bhabha, the mutual implication of "nation" and "narration" has become almost a truism in scholarship that may be termed "postcolonial."[47] Furthermore, narrative and acts of narration, including the juridical procedures of witnessing and testimony, have played a key role in analyses of Partition and its repercussions that draw inspiration from broadly psychoanalytical examinations of trauma, collective identity, and memory.[48] In the context of South Asia, narrative in one guise or another—whether in discussions of the State's deployment and propagation of nationalist narrative, or the adoption of their own narratives by anti-State movements—has been granted the role of prime mover as well as prime vehicle of identity formation.[49] Such narratocentric readings may help us grapple with complicated relationships between discourse, power, and identity-formation, especially in light of the combination of categories, "Hindu," "Muslim," "Brahmin/Pandit," themselves in a state of stasis, and political situations that are constantly in flux. Yet, as the example of *Sheen* reminds us, they bring with them inevitable problems. Narrative has reified as primordial the materialist workings of Kashmiri history, and has spawned further competing narratives of authenticity and indigeneity.

The most vocal Kashmiri Pandit alignments with the identity politics of India have not merely addressed the Hindi-speaking world; they have tended to adopt the narratives of Hindutva exclusionism. Unfortunately, the sympathy that has been sought thereby from a pan-Indian audience has stymied reconciliatory possibilities within Kashmir. The word and even its most immediate contexts of utterance have become hypersensitized to narrative contamination. Thus while the tight formal control of a poem such as "Hangul" can potentially offer an effective medium for the generation of empathy between polarized Kashmiri groups, its being written in Hindi contaminates it with the wider narrative of the Hindi-Urdu divide. A pertinent and philosophical response to this impasse is a poster by Inder Tikku alias Indersalim, a displaced Pandit and a performance artist now living in Delhi. It comprises a large double photograph of himself as "Hindu" (identified by a caste mark) and "Muslim" (identified by a beard and cap) respectively. Inscribed under each photograph is the word "Indersalim," which Tikku calls his "conceptual name," and which is itself a hybrid comprised of "Hindu" and "Muslim" elements ("Inder" and "Salim" respectively). Each photograph bears the signature in the "appropriate" script: Nastaliq for the "Muslim" image and Devanagari for the "Hindu" one. This doubling proclaims the self-as-other while splitting the image, and psyche, in two near-identical halves. The repetition of the artist's name through different scripts ironizes, explicates, *and* laments this simultaneous splitting/doubling. Within the gallery spaces it has been exhibited in, the poster, typically arranged in repeating rows to cover the wall and the floor of its assigned space, relentlessly and endlessly reiterates this split without any hope of formal closure.[50]

Indersalim is also a self-abnegating artwork. During my first viewing of it, I was encouraged by the artist to "step on the image" in order to read, literally, the writing on the wall—a declaration offering his "ass" to all those desirous of annihilating the "other."[51] The simultaneous relinquishing of narrative, closure and of the controlling, authorial "I" coalesces into a powerful ethical alternative to the divisiveness of narrative. If, as Rama Mani has suggested, societies traumatized by group violence need to move beyond assigning victimhood and blame toward perspectives of shared survival,[52] Indersalim confirms that no "truth and reconciliation" exercise reliant on narrative forms—including those of witnessing and testimonial—can accomplish this task. A similar conclusion may be drawn from the essays and excerpts collected in *Speaking Peace: Women's Voices from Kashmir,* an Oxfam-sponsored project entitled VMAP (Violence Mitigation and Prevention). The pieces, written by Pandit, Muslim, and Kashmiri women of Punjabi ethnicity, as well as Indian activists and artists, concur on the conflict's heavy emotional toll; they diverge considerably, however, in their political perspectives. There are broader ideological divergences: a narrative relentlessly recounting the rape of one community's women rubs shoulders with the observation that "the image of the raped woman is a key ideological tool used by both the militants and the Pandits to justify their political positions."[53] There is no editorial attempt to pull threads together. Ironically, the resultant polyphony makes "speaking peace" seem a chimera. Violence leaves a void that the word cannot replenish. Memory can become "a repository of the sublime"[54] only by escaping the imprisonment of narrative.

This example only confirms that the moment of a possible South Asian "narrative literacy" is now past, leaving us to work responsibly with fragments of collective memory.[55] From defending the fragment, moreover, we need to move toward analyzing its antinarrative possibilities. This aesthetics of the fragment, and its deployment within both the poetics of dispossession and the hope of reconciliation, is embodied in "Farewell," Agha Shahid Ali's celebrated poem that offers "on one level—but on one level only—a plaintive love letter from a Kashmiri Muslim to a Kashmiri Pandit."[56] Opening by taking responsibility for the Pandit's departure ("At a certain point I lost track of you"), Ali hints later at a darker history of inequalities, one where the Pandit has both "history" and "memory," but the Muslim only the latter.[57] However, rather than replicate the Pandit control of language and therefore of history and narrative, Ali inserts formal antidotes to narrative contamination within his own poem. Incantatory, lyrical repetitions alternate with powerful dream-like images that enact a haiku-like stripping of narrative context; temporal sharpness is blunted through sensuous memory. "In the smoking oil of headlights—time dissolved—all winter, crushed fennel."[58] But the taint of language also emerges dialectically through deep investment in artifactuality: Kashmiri shawls, gemstone manufacture, and the organic connection between nature and cultural heritage. Through images of delicately worked, all-too-fragile artifacts—the porcelain waves broken by the lotus paddle that itself withers in the soft breeze—Ali turns words toward a celebration of the cultural artifact, but also warns of its all-too-easy destruction. This fragility itself makes the object trump the word as a material witness and indeed alternative to history.

Dip Your Fingers Gently in the Lake . . .

The alignment of history with language renders it too contested a site for reconciliation, and even the task of remembering can provoke further controversy: "my memory," as Ali reminds his Kashmiri Pandit addressee, gets in the way of both "your history" and "your memory." Hence, through poetry Ali gestures instead toward collective remembrances of the sensuous, material world. This world comprises things as artifacts that, in their very presentness, bear the impress of the past. Its nodes—the seashell from the Indus River, the bronze statue at a museum—gather the counterhistory of things with the counterhistory of nature.[59] These fragile objects are also durable in their ability to trigger nonverbal, noncerebral memory that escapes the annals of history. This philosophy of the object-as-artifact, a nodal point for the forces of nature and traditional creativity, animates Ali's quest for a record of Kashmiri cultural history that can exist outside of language. Thus the air, that "chainstitched itself till the sky hung its bluest tapestry" and the Kashmiri "shawls bound for Egypt" are both united by the paisley shape, and both kinds of paisleys are united by the Hindu myth of Shiva and Parvati that Ali cites as epigraph to this characteristic counterhistory of the paisley motif: "Their footsteps formed the paisley when Parvati, angry after a quarrel, ran away from Shiva. He eventually caught up with her. To commemorate their union, he carved the Jhelum River, as it moves through the Vale of Kashmir, in the shape of a paisley."[60] Myth, nature, and craft—weaving, embroidery—fuse into a fluid memorial for Kashmir that attempts to transcend language's joint servitude to history and chronology.

Ali's "History of Paisley" does not point accusing fingers at the forces of colonial trade that appropriated the paisley from Kashmir's artisans to Scotland's mechanized looms; his poem subsumes that history into vignettes of trade as cultural encounter from precolonial times onwards. Likewise, in reuniting Srinagar's landscape—the Zabarvan mountains, the river and its banks—with pre-Islamic myths of its creation, the poem performs an act of simultaneous reconciliation and reclaiming. Kashmiri Muslim Ali might have been, but as Kashmiri, he proclaimed his entitlement to those very cultural resources that, particularly since the Pandit exodus from Kashmir, continue to be mined to declare either the validity or illegitimacy of competing claims to Kashmiriness. Beyond Pandit and Muslim, elite and subaltern, his poems seem to say, there remains the landscape. This is the message too of Indersalim, who, estranged from the Valley since 1990, could still write in response to another's visit to Srinagar, "Let us look at the clear blue sky upon the vibrant lake below and imagine it as a human being. . . . I insist on the inclusion of this blue sky as a citizen of Kashmir." The pantheism of Foucher and Nehru returns, but transformed into a newly poignant plea for reconciliation: "let us be together, smell and see, and be silent." The trauma of displacement crowds his psyche: a stream-of-consciousness exercise produces himself as a smiling, two-headed entity (one "Inder," the other, "Salim") that other Kashmiris flee from. Interpreted as a monstrous, inexplicable creature, he is drowned in the lake of his memory. Through this imagined destruction, however, he renews his belonging: "Please dip your fingers gently in the lake, I am there, touch me."[61]

The sensuous connection of the water and the fingers sparks what another writer, concluding a novel about ethnic conflict and cultural sedimentation in Sri Lanka, calls "this sweet touch of the world."[62] And yet, as with Ali's poems, these yearnings toward a time and space anterior to the word are expressed and communicated through the word. Ultimately, the word is restricted by its verbal nature—this is why Ali so admired Masood Hussain's artwork, that offered him an image for the cover of *The Country without a Post Office*. Words, furthermore, are the nuts and bolts of discourse—the very discourse that, in tandem with the photographic image, has constructed the Valley as a territory of desire. Thus the impossible attempt to leave language through language is no poetic conceit, and neither is the poem pitted against the artifact while aspiring toward artifactuality, mere literary paradox. Through these conundrums, we are led to ask: how does one revive "this sweet touch of the world" when that world seems always already given in discourse? The fantasy of the territory of desire has so stamped the modes of representing the Valley that any counter-representation seems only able to pull the subject into a mimetic quagmire.[63] And it is not only words that bear the corrosive freight of narratives. As chapters 1 and 2 of this book demonstrated, mechanically reproduced images of the Valley's landscape are as deeply implicated in creating this fantasy. Even artifacts, for all Ali's espousal of artifactuality, are tainted, as I argued in my discussion of Kashmiri handicrafts as the fetish of colonial and postcolonial nationalism: hence Hussain's distortion of papier maché to extract its embedded counterhistory of the artisan's trauma.

These philosophical problems lead us to consider on both cognitive and ethical levels the significance of contemporary activism from within and outside Kashmir. How may we interpret, for instance, the signature campaign of the JKLF (Jammu and Kashmir Liberation Front) that, in March 2005, culminated in their bringing to Delhi several hundred chests full of collected signatures from Kashmiris in Kashmir, demanding from the Indian government the right to decide their own political fate?[64] This "exhibition" was held with deliberate symbolic intent in the public space of the nation's memorial to Gandhi. Within that space, each signature gained significance far in excess of its basic status as "written words," and in excess, too, of its normal performative capacity as representative of the absent person. For these people, whose signatures were brought to the nation's capital, were not absent because of some routine inconvenience. They had been absented from the performance of democracy. The scandal of their "reappearance" within a monument memorializing the nation's founding father was conducted through the material traces of their signatures—a prosthetic function rendered even more transparent in the several cases where thumbprints were produced. The word here gains the materiality of the thing and the mystery of the talisman. These "signatures of the impossible" were subsequently scanned into thirty CDs, creating a portable counterarchive whose infinitely repetitive and static character defies analysis: what do you *do* with them?[65] Nevertheless, their uncanny power seems diminished by the first CD that frames the signatures with an introduction to the JKLF and their aims; the accompanying images are a series of panned shots of Valley's natural beauty, including Bollywood-style mountain panoramas and close-ups of nodding flowers.

On viewing those images, I felt some exasperation and dismay: did resistance *have* to hug so closely the contours of fetishization? Of course, my response may itself be a product of "hyper-analysis." It is possible that, for other viewers, the word-as-thing reverses the narrative contamination of the visual images by their intertextuality with Bollywood Kashmir films. After all, Kashmiri responses to Bollywood's use of Kashmir, film, and allusions to film, can produce unpredictable trajectories of pleasure and power. Yet the talismanic mystery of the accumulated signatures, palpable even through their digitalization, throws into relief what is problematic about the accompanying images of the Valley: these are still within the framework of broadly realist representation. In mimetically echoing the photographic capture of Kashmir, they inadvertently consolidate the discursive construction of the territory of desire. "Images are part of the arsenal," Indian activist-artist Sheba Chachchi declares, albeit in the ostensibly different context of images of the Kashmir conflict circulating within the Indian print media: photographs of "sets of men with guns," "dead men that occupy the space left over by armed men,""the burka clad woman" and "traces [of] childhood memories of summer holidays [and] film memories of the 50s and 60s," including the "quintessential tourist postcard image of the shikara on the Dal Lake" periodically announcing "the return to 'normalcy.'"[66] The genealogy of the shikara image aligns these post-1989 photographs, otherwise divergent in content and intent, to their cinematic and photographic predecessors. Uniting them is the camera's realism, as ideologically potent as Renaissance perspectivism, and linked, via the rise of the European realist novel during the nineteenth century, to the hegemony of linear narration.[67]

When the Gun Is Raised, Dialogue Stops, an evolving photo-installation on the Kashmir conflict by Chachhi and her artistic collaborator Sonia Jabbar, wrestles with precisely these realist and linear obstacles to counter-representation. Exhibited several times since 1995, it comprises two rows of earth and rice, each punctuated by twelve low brick platforms, some smaller platforms at each end closing the rows into a loop. A wooden *rihal* (bookstand for sacred texts) on each platform carries rusted sheets mounted with a black-and-white photograph of a Kashmiri woman and a typed page of (English) text quotes from testimonies "culled from interviews with Kashmir women over six years [from] a wide range of subjective positions." Sometimes, the rows are covered with barbed wire, and the installation separated from the main space through a Kashmiri walnut-wood screen. The assemblage reflects the desire to reverse standard expectations. The photographs and text snap the collusion between image and narrative within media reportage by "not necessarily bear[ing] a literal one-to-one relation." The materials used are domestic (earth, bricks, rice), sacral (rihals) and brutal (iron, barbed wire). "As the viewer is invited to step behind the screen of the dominant media and enter the private space of war," space is transformed. Through "the solemn rows," "the viewer is slowed down and the usual mode of viewing photographs altered as she/he is drawn into intimate contact with each image/text."[68] Freed from the ekphrastic constraints of the purely written text, the installation allows materiality to seep into the image and the word, restoring an intimate relationship between signification and sacrality. Not through realism, but through meditative contact with the object-as-artifact, the viewer's relation to the Valley is respiritualized.

Iris, Inside

Chachhi and Jabbar's installation invites a consideration of the artwork's ability to reclaim the now clichéd reduction of Kashmir as a spiritual place, whose "mountain ramparts" enclose the heart of Shaivism, Sufism and, needless to say, kashmiriyat. The artwork that critiques narrative and the realist image also takes us into "a third space beyond polarization"[69]—the space where the spirituality of Kashmir is revived as a dynamic guide to interpersonal relations within Kashmir, and between Kashmir and India. This task involves returning to the term kashmiriyat in order to work through nostalgia, bitterness, and pain, including anger at the term's appropriation. For the Kashmiri artist in particular, it also involves the reconnection to the landscape as a source of spiritual succor. I want to demonstrate this work of reconnection by returning to the Kashmiri sculptor Rajendar Tiku. A small plaque displayed in his Jammu home reads: "On behalf of the Kashmiri Pandit community (in exile), Panun Kashmir felicitates Pandit Rajendar Tiku on his being awarded the prestigious 8th Triennial India Award. Jammu, 6th April." The year is not mentioned.[70] This omission suggests an experience of being blasted out of history. Tiku's life, Pandit estranged from Kashmir, parallels his chosen medium of artistic expression. If, as I have argued, narrative offers a phenomenological experience of temporality, sculpture, "the transformation of sequence into form," congeals and arrests time.[71] This dovetailing of art, life and personal philosophy embodies, in Tiku's words, the artwork's power to express "the other possibility." Beyond the word, beyond the image, to the thing itself, and bypassing the gap between signified and signifier highlighted through the concepts of "metaphor" and "metonym," we arrive at sculpture as the manifestation of its creator's relationship to the Valley's materiality.

A discernible repertoire of semiotic and symbolic elements marks Tiku's sculptures. Orientation—whether a ground-hugging horizontality or a vertical sweep—offers overall formal definition. The typical placement of a small piece on a tall pedestal characterizes the monumentalization of the everyday. While natural materials such as wood, stone and terracotta signal connectivity with the land, the processes of rupturing and suturing are suggested through leather knots, threads and nails. Vermilion streaks, purple seepages and gold leaf daubs convey "something rich and strange." Such vestigial, attenuated signifiers invite interpretation even while flaunting elusiveness. The absence of narrative sequentiality suspends the viewer in interpretative uncertainty. Is the splinter in the wood caused by the driven nail, or does the nail hold together two fragmented halves? The sculptures seem silent, yet radiate semiotic promise and sacral aura. Tiku seems unconcerned about this opacity. Reluctant to pin his work down to any local referent, he prefers its universal interpretation either through the appreciation of its form, or the extrapolation of general sentiments. This message is reiterated through another ubiquitous formal element—indecipherable, would-be graffiti scratched on surfaces. These quasi-linguistic marks illuminate the reasons behind Tiku's penchant for obfuscation: the history of the Kashmir conflict demands, we have seen, a motivated departure from language. At the same time, the distortion and mutilation of script taps into an intuitive understanding of how trauma configures the artwork. It is not "reading" that these sculptures demand of us. Their formal semiotics take us beyond language, moving us from the very specific pain of being Kashmiri, and being Kashmiri Pandit, to what Tiku calls "the erosion of those human values that makes even those in place dispossessed."

Within individual pieces, signifiers of unreadability strategically interact with spatial orientation to augment meaning through material presence. In *Fragments of a White River* a long, low open chest contains slices of white marble interspersed with twigs that jut out as loops and pegs, and as three-dimensional rendering of would-be graffiti. The ensemble is reflected in a mirror that forms the base of the chest. This exemplary transformation of sequence into form and of flowing water into stone signals other conceptual and emotional transformations—of nature into art(ifact), of separation into possession, of a particular nostalgia into universal longing. "Like a child who would keep hidden and secure otherwise meaningless objects" the chest of memory protectively encloses the village river. In contrast, the vertically-oriented *Legend Flowers* suggests that nostalgia can become productive only when the enclosed is set free: golden flowers blossom out of branches covered with the now defunct Sharada script, used by Kashmiri Pandits only for ritualistic, astrological

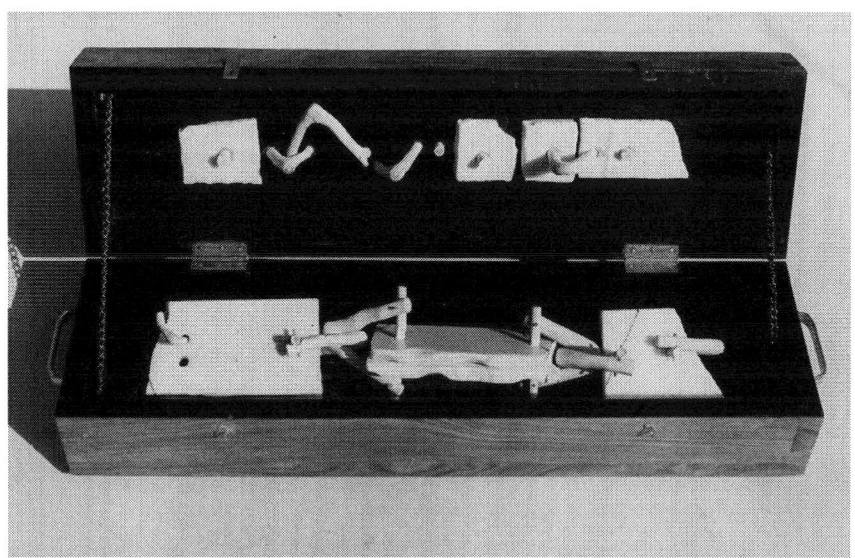

Rajendar Tiku, *Fragments of the White River,* 2002. Wood, marble, mirror, 104 × 42 × 40 cm.

purposes. Horizontality indicates nostalgia as the inability to let go, whereas verticality indicates looking upward, the ability to set free. A dialectical relationship thereby emerges between the forces of nostalgia, yearning, memory, and forgiving, made visible through the play with orientation, as in *Blue Rosary*, where the circular, vertical drop of the tasbih is stylized into a horizontal sequence of lapis and gold beads. Signs of the sacred for Kashmiri Hindus and Muslims are fused with celebrating the tactile and the natural, with the same ceremonial gold flecking pieces referring to the union of nature and home, such as *Fish Tackle,* where a gold trout, typical Kashmiri fish, is placed within a green, half-open box.

The sacred transforms, too, Tiku's *Sun Rises on the Camp,* that I referred to in introducing this chapter. The disk on a pedestal dwarfs conical shapes suggestive of tents. These tents and the "camp" undoubtedly refer to the cramped refugee camps of Jammu, where displaced Pandit families continue to live today. Yet when pressed to clarify, Tiku insisted on the universality of the refugee camp all over the world—pointing to Bosnia and Palestine as two other instances of displaced peoples for who the transience of camp life has become a permanent condition. The black sun, too, speaks locally and universally. The sun that dawns over a refugee camp is perforce black, its natural functions of sustenance and warmth inevitably perverted. Even a casual conversation with a displaced Pandit will bring home the particular misery of being ejected from the valley to the hot and dusty plains of Jammu, of experiencing for the first time temperatures of forty-five degrees centigrade. The cracked sun inscribes the fragmented exhausted subjectivity that is crippled further by the knowledge of impossible return. To return to the statement that gave me an epigraph, it is the sculptor himself who "cracked the sun." Not merely the despoliation of the artwork but the physicality of the act communicates the necessity of rupture for the artwork that bears witness to trauma. But the sun also bears a streak of vermilion powder, sacred to Hinduism. Both color and charged substance, it becomes here the very residue of sacrality.

The vermilion that anoints the camp is also a material signifier of an earlier phase in Tiku's personal history—his first (voluntary) departure from the Valley, where he had grown up, to the Jammu Institute of Fine Arts, in 1979. Leaving behind what he describes as the implied, esoteric culture of the Valley (and unsurprisingly attributes to an amalgam of Shaivite Tantrism, Sufism, and Central Asian influences), the shock of encounter with the expressive culture of Jammu with its myriad local Hindu deities and vernacular religious practices exploded in the threads, knots and vermilion of his semiotics. Today his work fuses those earlier influences with formal manifestations of his yearning for another Kashmir—flowers, especially irises, gold daubs (a reference to papier maché techniques), fragmentation, and suturing. This fusion of elements from different moments of his life is not, Tiku insists, to be approximated to kashmiriyat—a term whose current usage he scathingly dismisses as anaesthesia for the guilt of those in power: "kashmiriyat is a geographic, cultural and spiritual entity: it is not about *goshtaba* [a Kashmiri dish] and ethnic dress."[72] Rather than a passive embodiment of kashmiriyat, then, his work enacts a composite sacrality that draws out optimism and hope. This sacrality is the aura of the artwork, the affective equivalent of its conversion of sequence to form. It lifts the sculpture out of a narrative of displacement that would declare, "I left Kashmir then, and now I can't go back." The vermilion connects the viewer to the temples of Jammu, including the Dogra cosmic pole and original storehouse for the early Indologists, the Raghunathji Temple, freeing them, momentarily, from Hindutva narratives of cultural exclusionism.

The hope born out of a resilient sacrality is the persistence of the spiritual. It underscores the recurrence, within Tiku's evolving series entitled "Iris Inside," of the purple iris flower, figured as a petal-shaped stain on the horizontal blocks of wood. At Tiku's Delhi exhibition in December 2002,

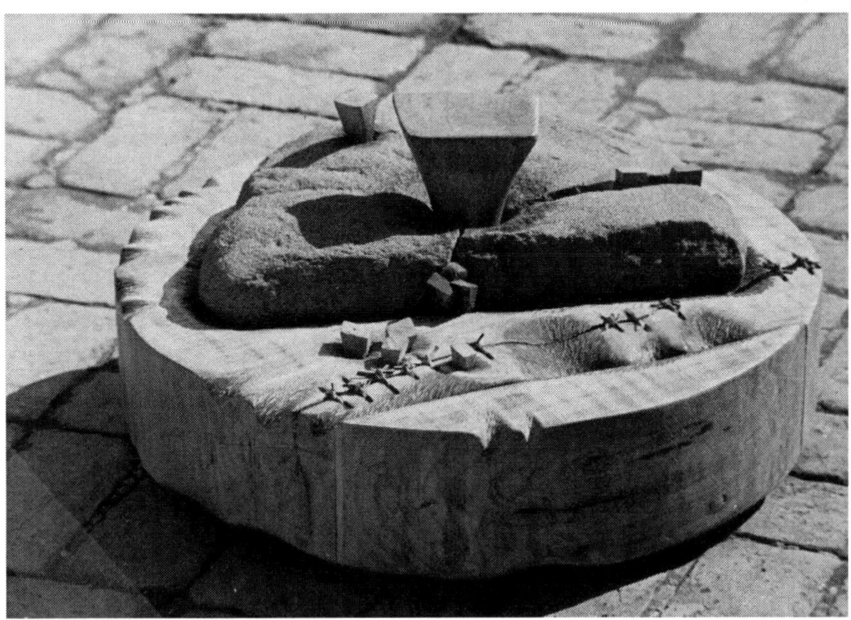

Rajendar Tiku, *Iris Inside,* 1997. Wood, sandstone, paints, leather string, 55 × 55 × 35 cm.

I read one of its component pieces, *Illustration for the Hanging of an Iris,* as suggestive of despair.[73] I did not know then that the iris grows profusely in Kashmiri graveyards. What I *had* grasped, however, from the impression of bleeding purple petals wedged between the tall green gallows was the fragility of beauty in the face of oppression. Attesting again "the other possibility," Tiku explicated this fragility as resilience: "lying between two segments, the iris is in safe custody." If, as Kashmiri Pandit, he carries his iris inside himself, in *Illustration,* the crushed flower seeps into the instrument of its own hanging, transforming the brutalization of truth into the survival of beauty. The vertical thrust of the piece lifts it, and the viewer, away from debilitating lamentation. Tiku's most recent work, however, responds to the continuing complications of Kashmir through a retreat into the small scale and domestic. Small objects are rendered life-size *(Snowflowers),* or immeasurably reduced *(My House in the Snow).* In white marble and wood, these recent pieces offer, like *Fragments of a White River,* the memory of a child's perspective, where the peak of the house rising above the snow is the sole point of security. This interiorization of trauma explores nostalgia through an element of play, of doodling. The necessity to return while letting go is communicated through yet another set of artistic transformations.

Rajendar Tiku's sculptures enable, to cite Sheba Chachhi's comments on her own artwork, "a stepping aside from history."[74] Their eloquent silences teach viewers to unlearn through leaving behind the word. The sheer materiality and abstractions of his sculpture present, rather than re-present, fragments of the Valley. Eschewing the constraints of mimetic referentiality, his work transcends the egotism of desire for the Valley through reconnecting with the land rather than the landscape. Nevertheless, its impeccable three-dimensionality also exemplifies how the artwork, whose physical presence is so crucial to its impact, is restricted by its very materiality. It cannot be disseminated like the written word, and, when placed in front of a viewer, demands a commitment that must break the shackles of readability that is the first and instinctive mode of response. And yet, as Chacchi also remarks, "art is a privileged space. It can say things that other spaces cannot, and yet it can say them only because it reaches out to a few."[75] It is these ironies of the artwork that the next and final chapter of this book shall engage. Its focus is the artistic dialogue between the poem and the painting conducted through the evolving Kashmir series of Indian artist Nilima Sheikh, that responds to the poetry of Agha Shahid Ali. If Tiku offered us a route beyond religious compartmentalization through extracting the spiritual from the sacred, Sheikh offers similar routes beyond nationalist desire. Through her work, we will retrace our steps on this journey through the construction of the territory of desire, and look toward its possible unmaking.

Six

New Maps of Longing

My whole understanding of spatiality in art stems from travels in Kashmir; my notion of yearning comes from there.

—Nilima Sheikh, artist, on her Kashmir paintings

This is an archive. I've found the remains
Of his voice, that map of longings without limits.

—Agha Shahid Ali, "Pastoral"

In April 2002, one of India's leading artists began executing a series of miniature paintings on the subject of Kashmir. These paintings were the first realizations of a long-term wish to, in Nilima Sheikh's own words, "rework my fairly confused or at least mixed feelings on Kashmir." Although Sheikh had "planned a bigger, more ambitious take, wanting to read and refer to various accounts of Kashmir historical and contemporary," it was the "incredibly moving and also extremely visual" poetry of Agha Shahid Ali that galvanized her into beginning this "formidable" project.[1] Sheikh's Kashmir paintings have continued to evolve beyond that first set created in 2002. Thus far, they have been completed and exhibited in four successive phases: in Manchester, within an exhibition entitled "New Indian Art" in April 2002, at Bombay's Chemould Art Gallery in March 2003, at Berlin's Alexander Ochs Gallery in 2004, and, most recently, within another exhibition of contemporary Indian art, "Edge of Desire," that has traveled from Perth to New York, to Mexico City, and to Delhi. At the moment of writing, Sheikh is working on two new paintings for the fourth phase. The thematic and formal coherence of each phase enables a retrospective understanding of the project as a whole. No mere painterly dialogue with Ali's poetry—the poet and artist themselves never met as she encountered his work only after his death—this unfolding, agonistic collaboration between the verbal and the visual encompasses a multitude of other conversations—between the Indian and the Kashmiri, between the self and the collective, between longing and belonging. The philosophical enacts the political. Unexpected pathways open up through the phanstasmatic yet persistent entanglement of nation with its territory of desire.

The continuing dialogue between Sheikh's paintings and Ali's poetry shapes this, my final chapter. In fact, it has shaped the conceptualization of the entire book. If the discovery of Ali's poetry enabled Sheikh to realize her wish to work with "Kashmir," it was the almost simultaneous discovery of Sheikh's paintings and *The Country without a Post Office* that enabled me to envision my own Kashmir project. Thus what now occupies the concluding position in this book's argument is actually its moment of genesis. This duality has helped me pull inside out the analytical burden of my writing to develop a methodology for confronting, among other things, my own early encounters with Kashmir, encounters that I now recognize as moments when the child was acculturated to the conditions of citizenship. The family and subsequently the school became spaces for the child's performative and pedagogic internalization of specific cartographies of collective desire. This is the same yearning for Kashmir that Sheikh admits her creative debt to. And yet, as Ali's words from his astonishingly complex "Pastoral" reminds us—and as I have demonstrated through this book—such yearning is intertwined with yearnings from within Kashmir. Fragmentary and ephemeral, these latter are nevertheless bestowed legitimacy by Ali's performative articulations. This is an archive, albeit one comprised of remains; the Kashmiri's voice is a map of longing, but a map without limits. Through these transformative paradoxes, Ali highlights the *arcana imperii,* the mystery of the State, as the mesmerizing power of its institutions (maps, archives). This is a mystery that Sheikh too confronts, as epitomized in the painting, "Map of Longing," which has provided this book a cover, and inspired this chapter's title.

Taking a cue from Sheikh's as-yet-unfinished Kashmir series, I outline here "new maps of longing" for the Indian citizen. The central challenge emerges as the subject's wrestling with internalized tools of intellection, naturalized modes of interpellation, and complicit surrender of autonomy.

The emotional sign of "nation" conjoined to the bureaucratic sign of "State" subsumes the individual into orchestrated pageants of belonging and identity, but at the expense of the designated scapegoat-fetish burnished with declarations of "beauty." How does one emerge out of the archive, how does one leave the map, when on the other side seems only yet another map of longing? Is there any force to the adjective "new?" In answer, I turn to the magnetic insistence of Sheikh's Kashmir paintings that helped me conceptualize spaces and modes of exchanging new maps for old. By following these paintings, and by supplementing my analysis with recollections of that path, I reinsert within the realm of the political and the activist the therapeutic, epistemic resources of visual art. If the artist is the most effective vigilante of national desire, it is the artwork that can compel viewers to revisit traumas, realize silences, and empathize with suffering. Sheikh's response to Ali's poetry initiates one such chain of recognition, mourning, remembrance and reconciliation. To absorb the political significance of her Kashmir paintings we must unpack her work's "medieval/oriental sensibility" that, by drawing the Indo-Persian miniature tradition into an "elliptical feminine space," forges a "radical compound of formalism and history."[2] Representation, that constructs the territory of desire, is reworked as the only means of freeing Kashmir from "Kashmir."

Pluck the Blood

"A terrible beauty is born." This quote from W. B. Yeats's poem, "Easter 1916," furnishes the epigraph to "I See Kashmir from New Delhi at Midnight," a poem by Ali that has appeared several times in this book. The poem is also pivotal to Sheikh's first phase of Kashmir paintings, entitled *Reading Agha Shahid Ali*. Two of these paintings bear titles that quote directly from it: "Don't Tell My Father I Have Died" and "The City from Which No News Can Come." The titles of two others cite the statement "I Broadcast the Crimson" from Ali's poem "The Last Saffron." The fifth painting borrows the hope, "We Shall Meet Again, in Srinagar" from the poem "A Pastoral." All three poems are from *The Country without a Post Office,* an anthology that Sheikh keeps returning to in her Kashmir paintings, although two poems from *Rooms Are Never Finished,* "Lenox Hill" and "I Dream I am at the Ghat of the Only World" are also used from their second phase onward. We shall consider later this iterative, additive quality of Sheikh's "illustration" of Ali's poetry. First, I want to probe, through the poems cited in *Reading Agha Shahid Ali,* the initial layer of response they elicited from Sheikh as artist. If *Country without a Post Office* presents Ali's most delicately worked elegies for Kashmir, these poems in particular showcase the collection's lyric grammar that converts political conflict into cultural loss as personal tragedy. This grammar is picked up by Sheikh and, in this first attempt to "embark on an alternative way of reading signs," converted into her equally delicate style, described by Geeta Kapur as "the coded inflection of a carefully crafted visual language."[3]

In "I See Kashmir," emblematic figures caught in the Kashmir conflict—the boy tortured by soldiers, the poet rendered helpless by distance, women waiting for missing menfolk, Pandits forced out of the Valley—alternate with images whose jewel-like clarity illuminates condensed pain: the rubies of blood on snow, the green thread of hope tied at the Shah-i-Hamdan shrine. Such surreal dreamscapes recur in "The Last Saffron." Here, the boatman who no longer rows tourists in shikaras, Srinagar's floating gardens, and saffron, expensive and all-too-fragile, join audacious departures from grammatical rules tying memory to the grid of past, present, and future tenses:

> Yes, I remember it,
> the day I'll die, I broadcast the crimson,
> so long ago of that sky, its spread air,
> its rushing dyes, and a piece of earth
> bleeding, apart from the shore, as we went
> on the day I'll die, past the guards, and he,
> keeper of the world's last saffron, rowed me
> on an island the size of a grave.

These temporal irregularities are a distorting yet heightening lens that projects the already faintly unbelievable image of the floating garden on to the imprecise ontological realm of the strange meeting between Rizwan and the poet.[4] "A Pastoral," likewise, is entirely cast in the future tense. The combination of a grammatical convention for the expression of that which is as yet unknown with details of fabular precision (the horned lark that draws two dispersed Kashmiris into deserted graveyards and dusty rooms, the glass map of their country that will tear them into lace) engenders a compulsive urgency simultaneously prophetic, inevitable, and mysterious, that spills out of these poems into the entire collection.

"Pluck the blood," orders "A Pastoral," turning wounds into flowers. Sheikh's paintings obey and echo this order. The *Reading Agha Shahid Ali* series engages primarily with Kashmir as a space of desire, invoked inevitably through the hindsight of unbearable loss. The most poignant images of *The Country without a Post Office* reappear here: women crouched over fires, boys glancing backward in reluctant departure, a trail of shoes left by mourners dispersed through police firing, houses consumed by sooty, sword-like flames; temples and mosques reflected in lakes; recumbent bodies in island-graves ferried by hunched oarsmen. Etched in charcoal, these images iterated within the paintings stall the potential for narrative elaboration offered by their narrow horizontal extent, repeating the same "story" across different frames. These abject figures move across a lost utopia of cultural synthesis that is graphically represented by the artist's use of *vasli,* the laminated handmade paper that serves as the traditional surface for Indian miniatures. On this laminate comprising three sheets of handmade paper, her deployment of highly saturated tones of saffron, red, and turquoise, liberally stippled with gold pigmentation, recall the colors of Indo-Persian miniature painting. The lapidary colors visualize the brilliance of Ali's images, as seen, for instance, in "The Last Saffron." Through the interaction of richly colored surface and fraily outlined images, Sheikh develops a vocabulary for the "terrible beauty" that Yeats refers to. This ability to enter unflinchingly the twin worlds of beauty and pain constitutes what she calls "a meticulous drowning of the soul," and that she finds in common with Ali and the refined, yet highly sensuous aesthetics of the Indo-Persian, Mughal miniature tradition.[5]

This common ground is the desire to arrest the passage of time through freezing the moment within the hyperstylized image.[6] The composite Indian miniature tradition that developed through the Mughal courts certainly drew on parallel traditions of story telling and showing: "sacred texts, . . . quasi- religious narratives, . . . secular literatures," and "scrolls, banners and murals, made for miscellaneous ritual, festive, seasonal and performative purposes."[7] Yet, miniature painting's sheer concentration of meaning frees the image from the constraints of the forward-moving story. Its flat-planed picture surface invites a vivid yet subtle chromatic language that returns representation from mimesis to the affect of things: "the shared translucences of sherbets, liquors, sliced fruits like melons, the shimmers of coloured glass, veils of transparent muslin, the sheens of pearls and precious stones, ceramic and porcelain, the milky coolness of marbles and flowing waters, the rust of metals, red or brown or corrosive, poisonous, acidic greens."[8] These are aesthetic and philosophical challenges that Ali, too, repeatedly undertook in his poetry, and Sheikh's use of the miniature tradition to articulate similar projects is no serendipity. Miniature painting is currently experiencing a renaissance, with artists from India, Pakistan and their diasporas expressing, through its precolonial courtly aesthetic, cultural losses, displacements and social critique. Sheikh herself has worked on such "postcolonial miniature" before starting her Kashmir series, dialoguing, for instance, with the pioneering Pakistani miniaturist Shazia Sikandar.[9] In contrast to Pakistani women artists, who stretch form and technique to protest (Pakistani) nationalist appropriation of miniature painting, Sheikh has tapped into the spirit of miniature to contest Hindutva-style nationalism, recuperate disappearing cultural possibilities, and excavate formative layers of her subjectivity.[10]

In her first Kashmir phase, accordingly, delicate washes of color strategically interact with the layered *vasli* to signify erasure and lamination, and with stylized landscape forms, particularly mountains bearing multiple resonances. The geological folding of the Himalayas, abstracted as cross-sectional stratification, doubles back into a vaginal form that echoes the island-grave's marble-white hues, and encloses the same sleeping figure that lies in that grave. The vagina-womb-mountain-grave, source of pleasure, pain, life, and orgasmic oblivion, illustrates Kashmir's role in Sheikh's personal mythmaking. Not herself Kashmiri, she bears an emotional, even spiritual relationship to the region, forged through difficult treks across "impossible terrain" undertaken along with her parents during childhood and adolescence. Kashmir thus represents an awakening of sensuous response to nature as well as to the female body: "A whole landscape was out there to be desired."[11] Yet, as we now know, this desire far exceeds the individual subject's innocent reveling in nature. The child's response to the beauty of Kashmir is overlaid by the discourse of, in Nehru's phrase, Kashmir's "long-memoried loveliness."[12] Sheikh recognizes this education when she notes how select aspects of Kashmiri culture, expressed in the texts of Hindu aestheticians and the Sufi songs of Habba Khatoon and Lal Ded have granted Kashmir a depth of "civilizational layering," an "imaginative status" far in excess of any other South Asian region. Kashmir has thereby become the "complete symbol of a syncretism that one has wanted to believe is all pervasive."[13] However, the verb "to want" locates Sheikh's self-awareness at a significant remove from similar beliefs expressed (for example) by Rushdie's recollections of Kashmir as an "enchanted land."[14]

The *Reading Agha Shahid Ali* paintings thus begin interrogating Sheikh's personal memories of Kashmir in order to clarify her intuitive grasp of the libidinal economies of the nation. Again, Sheikh's mountains play a crucial role in initiating this task. Their form returns Indo-Persian miniature to its Chinese influences, reviving premodern cultural and economic routes across the plateaus of Ladakh and Tibet. The trail of the shawl goat was also the trail of Buddhism—connections that, in the popular imagination today, are as half-forgotten as the almond-eyed Buddhas languishing in the dusty gallery of Srinagar's Pratap Singh Museum.[15] For Sheikh, restoring this Buddhist past of Kashmir is an aesthetic impulse charged with political urgency. Significant here is her long-standing interest in the format of the *thangka,* or Buddhist scroll, typically mounted on brocade from Benaras. Sheikh finds in the thangka the possibility of taking the debate about Kashmir beyond the impasse represented by Hindu and Muslim, Indian and Pakistani, to a South Asian civilizational layer that preceded those distinctions. Buddhism too has its multiple valences: as the religion of nonviolence, but almost erased from contemporary India, "its capacity to be brutalized is less." Like the stylized mountains, the thangka relocates Kashmir within a wider Himalayan cultural zone, making visible its situation on a particular intersection of the personal and the political: "the thangka and its associations with the hills has to do with remembering a land—a certain potency."[16] Nevertheless, it is only as the four phases unfold that the iconic meaning of the thangka increasingly manifests itself. In these first five paintings, it is glimpsed only in the faint echo of their broad brocade mounts.

Blood on the Road

This brocade is a vestige of Sheikh's original conception of the *Reading Agha Shahid Ali* miniatures as eight-foot-high thangkas. Mounted on them would have been texts on Kashmir, past and present: quotations from Ali as well as reportage and statistics pertaining to the State's handling of the situation in Kashmir. Together these would have made "notes on Kashmir," that the painted image would have, in a sense, framed. Embroidered on a narrow border for each thangka would have been that well-known Mughal aphorism of Kashmir, also cited by Ali in "The Last Saffron:" "If there is a paradise on earth, it is this, it is this, it is this." But these banner-like thangkas could not be executed. Through April 2002,

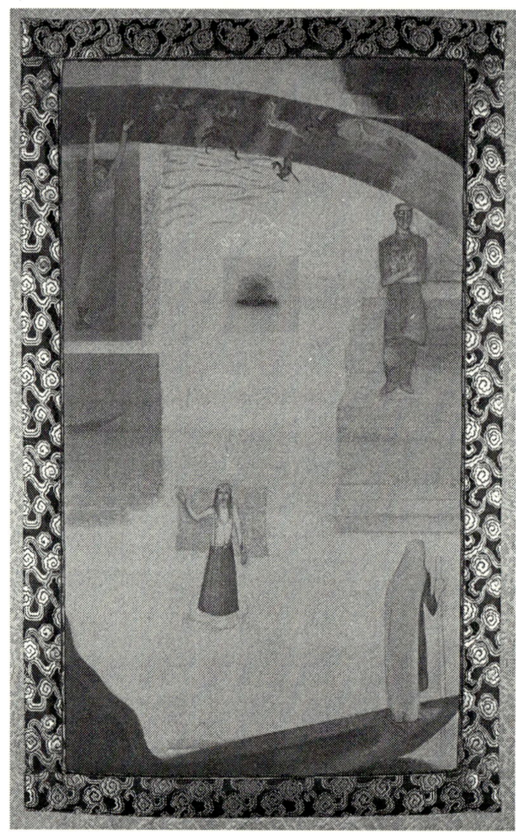

Nilima Sheikh, *Island of Burnt Chinars,* 2003. Tempera on Sanganeri paper, mounted on silk brocade, 28 × 16 inches. Collection of Cawas Bharucha.

rioting Hindu mobs unleashed carnage on Gujarat's Muslims. In a terrible replay of the violence of Partition, homes were ransacked, women raped, and even children not spared. This orgy of public violence was sanctioned and abetted by the BJP government then in ascendancy. Sheikh herself had to flee her home and studio in Baroda, Gujarat, to the relative safety of her Delhi home. Her flight was profoundly representative of the destruction of pluralism and the peaking of a nationwide politics of polarization. Thus circumstance turned her creative plans for Kashmir into a palimpsest of a more immediate loss, following which "doing small paintings and reading Agha Shahid Ali became hugely therapeutic."[17] This painful conflation of life and art, and their coming into being in the shadow of a more personal and immediate tragedy, explicates the introspective and tentative mood of these paintings.

This mood deepened in the work Sheikh executed immediately after the first phase was exhibited in Manchester. In her Delhi home in December 2002, she showed me two halves of a new painting, entitled "Papier Maché Inlaid with Gold, then Ash." Like the sentiment of that quote from Ali, this diptych moves toward mourning rather than any hopeful recreation through art of destroyed beauty. The narrow horizontality of the first phase has been stretched to twice that length; images of humans and houses have shrunk dramatically; the striated mountains and chalky-white vaginal forms take center stage. Most importantly, the colors have changed to muted maroons and ash. An overwhelming sense of what Sheikh calls a "crumbling of beauty" radiates the painting's complete power to transform nature into artifact[18]—not just through mimetic representation but in the creation of an alternative reality. Rajendar Tiku's "other possibility," again?[19] I find "Papier Maché Inlaid with Gold" too sorrowful and brooding for that interpretation. Rather, its exaggerated orientation formally proclaims its status as a punctuation-mark—an interregnum between the first phase and that which was to follow, facilitating our appraisal of an evolving artistic exploration of violence, nationalism, and collective desire. The vulnerability of a particular subject position within the nation and the psychic hurt caused thereby draws the artist deeper into communion with the poet whose own psyche has been "torn" by the shards of his nonnation's glass map. Sheikh's second phase of paintings, completed by early 2003, is a visual equivalent of that shredded psyche that can transcend brutalization by being beautified as lace.

I call this second phase *Each Night Put Kashmir in Your Dreams*. The boy Rizwan's injunction to the poet in New Delhi is already familiar to us. This same injunction lends a title to one of the paintings in the second phase, a depiction of two figures facing each other, one kneeling, the other bent but standing. The painting's midnight blue backdrop lucidly crystallizes the poem's semantic burden. Its visual rendering of a hallucinatory dreamscape is representative of this phase's overall affective impact. The crayon-like outlines have disappeared, as have the seeping pastels. Now, luminous colors and sharper chromatic contrast couple with a new vertical orientation. The overall size of each painting increases somewhat from those of the first phase, but we face a completely new format: the paintings are stitched on to, not mounted, on a brocade margin that emphasizes the image's verticality by being broader on the top and bottom than on each side. This formatting follows the thangka's spatial distribution of brocade and image. After the sorrowful pause of "Papier

Maché Inlaid with Gold," Sheikh clearly felt empowered enough to return to the original intention of marrying the aesthetic languages of miniature painting and Buddhist scroll. This increased confidence enables the awkward yet necessary embrace of self and other enacted through "Each Night Put Kashmir in Your Dreams." The picture planes open up spaces within the individual psyche that can accommodate the pressures of the other's presence. This process is aided by supplementing the poems "A Pastoral," "I See Kashmir," and "The Country without a Post Office" with "Lenox Hill" and "I Dream I Am at the Ghat of the Only World," two poems from Ali's subsequent anthology, *Rooms are Never Finished.*[20]

The former poems offer the titles "Each Night Put Kashmir in Your Dreams," "Map of Longings, and "Each Post Office Is Boarded Up" to three of the phase 2 paintings. The latter poems provide titles for three further paintings: "Hospital Dream of Elephants," "Island of Burnt Chinars" and "The Loved One Always Leaves." Ali's poems "Lenox Hill" and "I Dream" are virtuoso performances, marrying his characteristic dexterity with rhyme and cadence with hauntingly sharp images to offer an almost somatic experience of that "meticulous drowning of the soul." We are submerged in a Kashmir where nightmare, dream, and reality merge in vivid confusion. This controlled efflorescence of splicing and montage is reflected in Sheikh's artistic technique within this phase. Evocative figures—woman on shikara, departing boy, old man digging a grave—frequently imaged as quotations from Persian miniatures, are interspersed among topographic markers of Kashmir: mountains, lakes, river, *chinar* (Kashmiri Poplar) trees. Sharply delineated, they float on the picture space divided into units expressing an affective chromatic logic. In phase 1, these divisions were repeatedly breached by figures traversing two or more units. In phase 2, such breaching gains oppositional significance by the containment of motifs within units, often centrally placed: the cobalt-blue square enclosing an ash-green tree (the "Char [four] Chinars" motif) suspended within the flaming reds of "The Loved One Always Leaves;" the silvery hexagon signifying the Dal Lake similarly suspended within the midnight blue of "Each Night." The mountain thrusting through the picture plane in "Map of Longing," its surface divided into parallel bands of color that seeps through while demarcating boundaries, lays bare the lamination of desire, landscape, and territoriality.

"And I Followed Him through Blood on the Road," quotes Sheikh from Ali's "I See Kashmir" articulating her increasing depiction of love and desire as the hard path, so as to work through such attachments with a patience bordering on self-abnegation. The eleven paintings within her third phase unfold the congruence of such recognitions with Sufi modes for intuiting the world. "It was but now I saw the river inside me and now there's no bridge nor ferry/It was but now I saw a bush in bloom and now there's no flower nor thorn"; "Be ready to endure lightning or cloudbursts or a sudden pall of darkness at noon/Or the body crushed between the two grindstones. Accept it all with patience and content will come"; "With thread untwisted I tow my boat would the Lord help and ferry me? Water seeps through my pots of unbaked clay oh my heart longs to go back home." These aphorisms from Kashmiri Sufi poet Lal Ded transmit a mystic potency that evades narrative. Ali is now read obliquely. One of his couplets, cited in a phase 3 painting, makes explicit his own interest in the Sufi search for the transcendent, expressed as a longing for the beloved: "I must go down to a place I have loved/To tell those you will efface I have loved."[21] No naïve assertion of Kashmir as source of idealized syncretism, Sheikh's juxtaposition of Lal Ded and Ali interrogates Indian nationalist appropriations of Kashmiri Sufism, illuminating her meditations on love and longing for an othered yet desired space. In Lal Ded's words, also quoted by Sheikh, "You have still time, go look for the friend."

Thus what I call the *Blood on the Road* phase signals new entanglements of the visual and the verbal while returning to the introspectiveness of phase 1. This affinity is proclaimed through a return to horizontal format miniatures with brocade mounting—albeit reshaped into less radically narrow rectangles tending toward the square. There are other continuities and changes. While in the first phase, quotes from Ali's poetry were handwritten along a distinct margin between the picture space and the mount, in the *Blood on the Road* paintings handwritten words enter the picture space, climbing up, creeper-like, around their four edges. Repetition of motifs gains meaning through experimentation with scale. Some details are blown up: the shoes and snow/soot flakes that constitute one element of the composition in the phase 1 "I See Kashmir," are zoomed into and, together with a fallen figure, made to cover the entire picture plane in the phase 3 "Blood on the Road." With its companion painting, "Majnun in the Wilderness," the violence earlier implied becomes explicit. The *Blood on the Road* phase reveals how the exposure of the self's inner recesses also exposes the fetishization of Kashmir within the national imaginary. This lifting of the carapace, the glittering exterior that conceals/reveals the wounded psyche, unmasks, too, its formation through the simultaneity of attraction and confrontation shaping the perception of "self" and "other."

The grappling with size, color, and textuality now evident through the phases visualizes a constant questioning of the most appropriate format for such explorations—an acceptance that to work through the layered accretions of memory and desire in her subjectivity, the paintings have to pass through different stages.

Inside the Fire

These realizations blossom into the fourth and latest phase of Sheikh's Kashmir paintings, that she calls her *Firdaus* (Persian, Urdu: "Paradise") series. Four *Firdaus* works have been exhibited already; a fifth has been very recently completed; and a sixth is under way at the time of writing.[22] As with the earlier phases, *Firdaus* is marked by consistency of size and format: in this case, vast, banner-like painted scrolls that are suspended from the ceiling to graze the floor. We face the fruition of Sheikh's initial desire to recreate the thangka. Yet the *Firdaus* scrolls do more than come full circle. They reveal a trajectory shaped not by abstract, predetermined conceptualization but the evolving logic of the artwork as it comes to exist in the world. The scrolls display established topographical motifs and human figures, executed in her recognizable visual register that draws on Persian and Central Asian elements. As usual, these both define and transgress the grid-like distribution of "color units" that, in each scroll, play with a single chromatic theme. But the familiarity of vocabulary established through the repetition of details and technique across the phases is now also relocated from the small scale of the miniature and the thangka to the larger-than-life scroll. This effect is replicated in the relationship between the verbal and the visual, most strikingly illustrated by "Firdaus II: Each Night Put Kashmir in your Dreams." Its title announces yet another return to a poem frequently cited through the series. In the first and third phases, Ali's "I See Kashmir" offered Sheikh different perspectives on Kashmiri trauma; in the second phase, it took us into the arena of the artist's psyche. Now the poem is "read" by "Firdaus II" to offer a panoramic view of what the artist, as citizen, might "see" anew.

The correspondence between progression in size and the movement from the individual to the citizen is representative of the *Firdaus* phase as a whole. Although historically indebted to inherited formats such as miniature, thangka and scroll, the divergences in size across the phases gains specific meaning for the artist's struggle with an ethical representation of Kashmir: for Sheikh, "reducing size signals an intimacy, blowing up a theatrical projection,"[23] but "the intimate gives context to the theatrical." Giganticism offers a visual correlative to Freudian "ingestion" or swallowing of trauma—in other words, melancholia—but, in keeping with our recuperation of this psychoanalytical term, can also be seen as a critical alternative (to) mourning.[24] The movement from miniature to the gigantic also privileges size as a means to work against the drive to reduce reality to a consumed souvenir, and to interrogate the relationship between the subject (artist) and its subject (Kashmir). These changes in size further ensure that, far from diluting meaning, repetition re-emerges as another privileged signifier, the refrain, whereby "meaning is gained through minimizing or increasing size."[25] As with the rhythm-cycles *(taal)* of traditional Indian music, where changes of tempo announce new stages in the unfolding experience within a cyclical framework, the result is a deeply satisfying interplay of completion and anticipation. This stabilizing disorientation is the most striking feature of the scrolls. Gigantic and encyclopedic, they proclaim the artwork as counter-archive that combats amnesia through a considered reworking of Ali's poetry. Their greatly increased surface area also renders inescapable the viewer's engagement with detail, making clear, in particular, the intricacy of layered ornamentalism that now covers the picture plane in a literalizing of vasli, the laminate of handmade paper that was the medium for the first three phases.

Stenciled patterning, visually echoing the geometric *khatamband* parquetry covering ceilings and walls of Kashmiri Sufi shrines, was already present in some phase 2 paintings, albeit restricted therein within specific color units.[26] In the *Firdaus* scrolls, in contrast, khatamband patterns, executed with variegated pressure on the stencils, have spread over the entire picture space. The proliferating presence of this visual quotation moves Sheikh's emotive but still metaphoric references to Kashmiri craft in "Papier Mache Inlaid with Gold," to another realm of meaning-making altogether. Neither metaphorical nor allegorical, the relationship of the scroll to khatamband, and via it, to Kashmiri craft in general, follows a hermeneutic code akin to the Sufi concept of the *silsila* (chain), that does not distinguish between signifier and signified, but enables the artwork to oscillate endlessly between loss, guilt, and gnosis. The increased presence of khatamband patterns in *Firdaus* illustrates Sheikh's interest in defetishizing and reenchanting both Kashmiri handicraft and Kashmiri Sufism by drawing them into dynamic interaction within the artwork—as did Hussain's papier maché reliefs. A metacomment on this process is offered

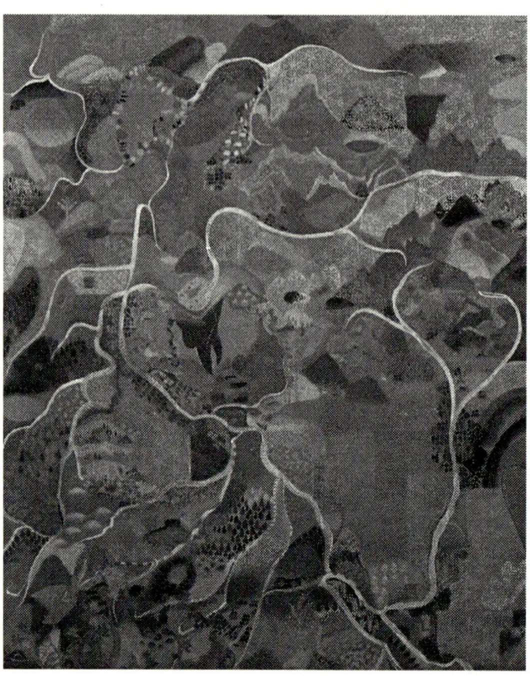

Nilima Sheikh, *Firdaus 1: Valley*, 2004. Casein tempera on canvas scroll, 10 × 6 feet. Artist's collection.

by "Firdaus III: Gathering Threads." Here, the autochthonous yet ephemeral materiality of the much-traded, much-degraded Kashmiri shawl is insisted on through quotes from Ali's "A History of Paisley" and "Country without a Post Office:" the title of the scroll itself, and the statements stenciled on it: "dark fossils of paisley"; "The air chainstitched itself till the sky hung its bluest tapestry"; "I throw paisleys to clouds."[27] Images of domesticity, intertwined with dissonant snatches of violence, enact a fragile but determined return of indigenous history to the fetishized object that stands in metonymic relationship to the territory of desire.

On another level, and also reminiscent of Hussain's play with texture to recall the veil separating the esoteric *(batin)* from the exoteric *(zahir)*, Sheikh emulates through khatamband the Sufi understanding of how knowledge is to be gained. Although referencing parquetry, she refashions khatamband to bestow a filigree effect on her paintings. We are reminded both of Kashmiri latticework, and of the *jaali*, or filigreed screens, in South Asian Sufi shrines that physically separate devotees from the sanctum sanctorum but also enhance the emotion of longing through the partial glimpses it enables. Longing here is not a negative, disabling emotion but a means to attain benison and self-knowledge.[28] "Firdaus IV: Farewell," in particular, highlights this effect by stenciling khatamband patterns over fragments of Ali's most impassioned poems. From "Farewell," Sheikh cites the cynical observation "They make a desolation and call it peace," those searing admissions of discordance, "My memory is again in the way of your history," "Your history gets in the way of my memory, and "Your memory gets in the way of my memory," the question, "If only somehow you could have been mine/What would have not been possible in the world?" and the single word, "Farewell." From "Country without a Post Office," she borrows the statement, "We're inside the fire, looking for the dark," repeats thrice its epiphanic successor, "I'm inside the fire, I have found the dark," and the refrain, "Inlaid with gold, then ash."[29] Etched in flame-like red, glimpsed through the ashen filigree, the quotes predicate a shimmering dialectic between reading and seeing that, like the saint's grave beyond the jaali, holds out a possibility of transcendence through the transformation of longing.

This transformation is also visualized through the central image in "Firdaus IV," a figure that bares his breast to reveal the peninsular shape of India imprinted within, and reminding the viewer of the Hindu monkey-god Hanuman within whose bared breast is imprinted the beloved images of the god Rama and his wife Sita. The "geo-piety" inspired by the map is also assimilated to the dangerous love inspired by the militaristic cults of Hanuman and Rama in contemporary India.[30] Behind the map-baring citizen, furthermore, and partially obscured by him, we see another, female figure. This deliberate turn to gender foregrounds an unequal power-relation that takes us back to Mbembe's formulations, cited in the introductory chapter, of the unequal spaces within the postcolony.[31] We realize the potential of Shahid's note to "Farewell": "this poem is on one level, but one level only, a plaintive love letter from a Kashmiri Muslim to a Kashmiri Pandit."[32] Sheikh's interpretation of "Farewell" reveals what its other level might be: a plaintive love letter from an Indian, imprinted with the image of the nation, to a Kashmiri with whom he is coupled. It also conveys graphically the citizen's internalization of the map as archive, institution but also instrument of othering and marginalizing. But the somatic branding of the citizen by the nation's map also recalls the stigmata borne by medieval Christian saints, evoking yet another semiotics of love as self-abnegation rather than possessive desire.[33] This assertion of a counter-archive of affect reinforces the impact of "Firdaus I: Valley." Its luminous green hues present a stylized relief map, whose meandering, fish-filled rivers, undulating mountains and lush meadows echo the famous Dogra "shawl maps" of Srinagar.[34]

Is "Firdaus I" a nostalgic yet messianic new map for the Valley, invoking diverse artifacts (shawls, miniature paintings, scrolls) that offer modes of representation alternative to the technologies of modernity? Running down its right-hand margin is a sequence of blurred color units that certainly recalls, in its chromatics, the phase 2 "Map of Longings." Looming behind maps old and new, however, is the shadow presence of the nation's institutions: post offices, armies, and histories, the last conveyed through the Persian form of the Mughal couplet, "If there is a heaven on earth, it is this, it is this, it is this," that is calligraphed throughout *Firdaus* with escalating urgency. If Ali transforms these institutions to reveal the cost they have exacted on Kashmir and Kashmiris, Sheikh acknowledges her own complicity as Indian citizen through repetitions, condensations, and juxtapositions of text, shadow-text, and image. Her relentless questioning of the limits of textuality breaks the sequential relationship between representation and narration, foregrounding instead the spatial dynamics of the image. Readability is dismantled and reconstituted as the image prises open the interstices of discourse. Thus Sheikh's most recent *Firdaus* scroll mobilizes her repertoire of affective chromatics, topographical motifs and human figures to cite those poems by Ali referencing pre-modern layers in Kashmir's construction: the Mughals terracing the slopes into landscaped submission, Parvati hurling a mountain at the demon Jalodbhava, to prevent him stalling the emergence of habitable land from the lake waters, the Hun Mihiragula who pushed elephants off cliffs for entertainment.[35] Myth, history, and poetry are equated within the bold yet delicate collage. Across the filigreed canvas hurtles the startling image of a falling elephant, frozen forever across the centuries as archetypal victim of the avarice of desire.

The Time for Being Covetous Is Over

On the white refrigerator stands a framed black-and-white photograph. It shows a child, looking up but away from the camera, wearing a sleeveless, hand-knitted vest over a frock, sprawling in a deckchair on a lawn. One can see a house with a sloping roof and open windows, the outline of a mountain slope and cloudless sky. Sharp short shadows proclaim noon. A breeze seems to ruffle a tree caught between the house and the

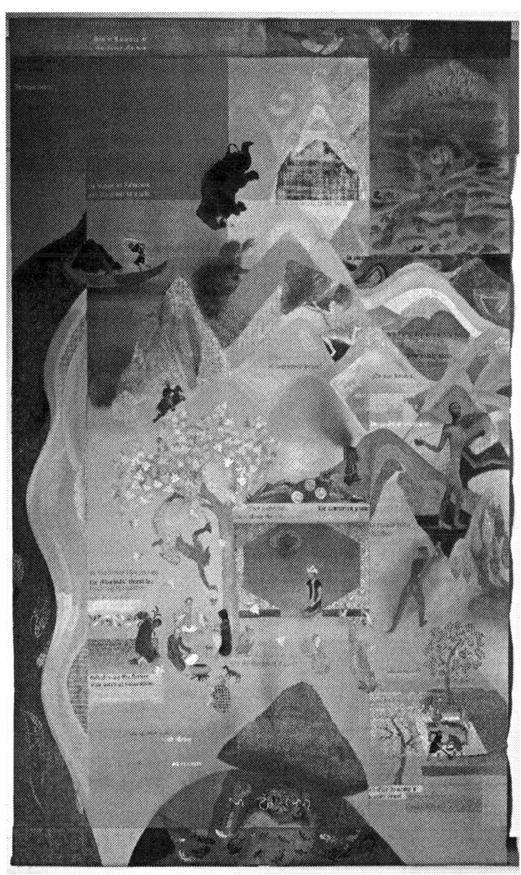

Nilima Sheikh, *Firdaus 5,* 2006. Casein tempera on canvas scroll, 10 × 6 feet. Artist's collection.

mountain. In the white space below, a neat hand notes in black ink: "Pahalgam, Oct, 1973." The writing is my father's; that girl is me, age three. The girl who looks up at that photograph everyday is not much older. I remember myself seeing myself daily, in that photograph, on that fridge, in a house that I lived in from 1974 to 1977. Today, as I write this chapter in my parents' home in Calcutta, I rummage within old albums and triumphantly fish it out, stripped of its frame. Behind, my father's hand, in that same black pen, repeats: "Oct, 1973, Fishing Lodge, Pahalgam, Kashmir." Another message written in pencil, in a sloping hand that I recognize as my aunt's, declares: "This negative wasn't good, so I couldn't get a better photo. I've developed another photo and it is much better than this one." I do not know whether the framed photograph was the photograph I now hold, or that "even better" copy promised by my father's sister, who, in the early 1970s, would have been learning how to develop photographs as a student at the Government Art College in Calcutta.

The photograph disappeared at some point from overt display, but never from our family's collective memory. For my parents, aunts and uncles, it was a shorthand mode of recollecting a time when they were young adults, and in particular, their long holiday in Kashmir in autumn 1973. Stories about the Kashmir holiday, precious reminders of a carefree past, continue to be told at family gatherings. "What was so special about that trout you caught at Pahalgam?" I asked one of my uncles recently at one such gathering. "Of course it was special: it was *Kashmiri* trout," he replied, tongue-in-cheek.[36] That "special" aura has passed into the common sense of the Indian middle classes, old and new. It was the reason why, in 1986, when my school decided to take sixty-odd teenage schoolgirls, five nuns, five class teachers, and two cooks on an ambitious excursion, the destination was, naturally enough, Kashmir. I remember the sense of exhilaration as, leaving behind the hot and dusty plains after a long train journey from Calcutta to Jammu, we climbed the mountain roads in a bus, entered the Banihal Tunnel, and emerged to be bedazzled by the brilliance of Haroun's "Valley of K."[37] In my memory, the Valley's green beauty, the crisp air and the feel of snow are fused with the excitement of being away from home unsupervised (albeit under the eagle eye of convent school guardians). We bought handicraft souvenirs, flirted with handsome Kashmiri boys, rode shikaras while singing Shammi Kapoor songs, and took photographs in the Mughal Gardens wearing Kashmiri "ethnic dress." When I left for Oxford in 1992, my "ethnic Kashmiri" photograph went with me.

These encounters with Kashmir do not mark my family, or my school, or even my developing subjectivity, as unique. Rather, they locate them within a horizon of urban, middle-class, Indian sensibility. The photograph in Pahalgam that was the mirror for the child, distilling her sense of individuality and her place in a family history, also made Kashmir the "enchanted land," whose desirability was confirmed, not questioned, by the adolescent's experiences on her school excursion. Neither geography nor history nor political science opened up the disputed status of Kashmir for pedagogic discussion; rather, mysterious stamps over the map of South Asia reproduced in foreign books declared the inaccuracy of those borders and the subject beyond questioning. When, from 1989 onward, television screens depicted violence in Kashmir, the JKLF's kidnapping of the then Home Minister's daughter, and young militants barely older than me being escorted to the nation's most notorious prisons, I was attending college parties, writing essays on medieval English literature, and planning to study in England. The yawning gap between my metropolitan life and that of my Kashmiri peers is now obvious to me years after those events have left their mark as the impossible necessity of yearning for aazadi. If I have wanted to scrutinize the collective processes that subsumed me within the secret politics of the nation's desires, and that naturalized Kashmir as a backdrop for my formative experiences, this counterdesire was catalyzed by the estranging experiences of 1990s India, when Hindutva chauvinism targeted the Indian Muslim as the Nation's internal other. But it was Sheikh's Kashmir paintings that finally led me "inside the fire" to "look for the dark."

A series of coincidences and connections took me to Manchester Art Gallery in June 2002, to view Sheikh's *Reading Agha Shahid Ali* paintings in the stimulating context of the exhibition "New Indian Art: Home-Street-Shrine-Bazaar-Museum" at the Manchester Art Gallery. Commissioned by Shisha, a Manchester-based agency for the promotion of South Asian Arts and Crafts, it brought together folk and urban artists from contemporary India.[38] This juxtaposition of widely different Indias within the postimperial museum showcased multiple negotiations of neotraditionalism, modernity, and the violence of nationalism—a fecund milieu, indeed, for my introduction to Sheikh's work. In November 2005, at the Museo Rufino Tamayo in Mexico City I stood facing the *Firdaus* scrolls within "Edge of Desire," another impressive exhibition of contemporary Indian art.[39] Those paintings I could not see exhibited in Bombay and Berlin I followed instead to the homes of art collectors and enthusiasts in Bombay, and to a Bombay gallery, Sakshi, where some phase 3 pieces were being stored. These opened up further learning opportunities, such as the unforgettable experience of viewing "The Loved One Always Leaves" in an apartment within a Bombay Parsee Colony. The rich brocade surrounding its intense, flame-red hues led the eye to a keening female figure of Central Asian vintage, surrounded by other women acolytes, and the tree signifying the holocaust of desire: the Island of Burnt Chinars. Within that room, filled with domestic furniture in use and examples of Bazaar art collected by a Parsee couple—she, an artist, he, the director of India's MTV style music video channel, Channel V—I took in the radiance of the artwork truly at home.[40]

This space was paradigmatic "of the luxuriance of objects and of their comfortable place in the order of things" that mark, in India, the synergies of (to return to Shisha's exhibition title) home, street, bazaar, museum, and shrine.[41] Indeed, it is such multivalent spaces and even the simulation thereof that provide the most meaningful viewing context for the Indian artwork, best at home in a postcolonial world that is governed by rules orthogonal to those imposed on it by Eurocentric separations of the "aesthetic," "economic," and "political" realms. This is a world where, in spite of Kant and Marx, images can still live as things, where things are not totally stripped of enchantment, where the profusion of things and people enact the paradoxical mingling of globalization, transnational capitalism and the legacies of Nehruvian socialism, and where "the materiality of objects is not yet completely penetrated by the logic of the market."[42] As Appadurai points out, such formulations do not necessarily return to neo-Orientalist characterizations of India as a "bazar of thingness, as a civilization enamoured of the Borgesian endlessness of its own object world"; rather, "this tension between the rule of the commodity and the unruliness of the thing in itself marks the space where Indian art and its makers can find a possible space of redemption, in which abstraction can become the servant of materiality rather than its master."[43] Such redemption capitalizes on the postcolonial postmodernity of the object that retains the possibility of an aesthetics founded on the participation between audience and practitioner/performer, and on the artwork as processual rather than a framed and completed event.[44]

This processual understanding is embodied in the long journey with Sheikh's paintings that has challenged me to shed inherited analytical biases and respond instead to the postcolonial artwork's capacity to transmit aesthetic and political messages. Sheikh's dialogue with Ali's lyrical fragments have been facilitated by their similar interest in exposing the conjunction of narrative and the word, the word's co-opting of the image within discourse, and discourse's attrition of materiality through visual and verbal modes of representation. But Ali's rebellion against discourse is constrained by his own, ultimate dependence on the printed word. Sheikh, in contrast, uses Ali, Lal Ded and the Firdaus couplet to reveal the collusions of modernity, whereby text, camera and technologies of mechanical reproduction together shield truths about Kashmir from the Indian citizen. Moving from the straightforward referencing of Ali's poems within the phase 1 paintings, to an increasingly allusive, meditative relationship between word and text in the subsequent phase, her paintings critique these symptoms of modernity in order to critique the nation's need to desire

Kashmir. Thus her paintings have enabled me analyze and contextualize the discursive pressures that distilled my yearnings for Kashmir. By moving from the individual to the encyclopedic, and through a meta-aesthetic critique of modernity, Sheikh's work insists on the intimacy between such personal yearnings and the collective desire for Kashmir that underwrites its position within the national imaginary. As she declared of what became the first phase of her Kashmir paintings: "The time for being covetous is over: it is now time to undo in oneself the greed for Kashmir."[45]

Poetics of Dispossession

How might the artwork's capacity to undo greed contribute to wider practices of healing and reconciliation within Kashmir, and between Kashmir and India? Here, I offer some observations on the pressing need to mobilize the artistic dimension of human experience within State and civil society practices. As Ronald Bleiker asserts in the context of International Relations, "it is crucial to legitimise insights derived from other knowledge practices, be they of a philosophical, historic, poetic, visual, acoustic or any other nature. Indeed, many of these aesthetic practices can give us insight into politics that the more mimetic social scientific methods may miss, for the latter often fail to deal with the inevitable but inherently problematic dimension of representation."[46] Our responsibility, "both as numbed spectators of televised realities and as scholars wedded to social scientific conventions" (and, I would add, Humanities-trained scholars possibly too immersed in the text), "is to reclaim the political value of the aesthetic, because the modern triumph of technological reason has eclipsed creative expression from our political purview. The dilemmas that currently haunt world politics, from terrorism to raising inequalities, are far too serious not to employ the full register of human intelligence to understand and deal with them."[47] If "solutions to entrenched political problems can by definition not be found through the thinking patterns that have created them in the first place," the poetics of dispossession, that illuminates the artists I have discussed, offer direct aesthetic encounters with the political that "challenge our very notion of common sense by allowing us to see what may be obvious but has not been noted before."[48]

Sheikh's dialogue with the written word, moreover, enables her Kashmir series to demonstrate as well as embody the artwork's destabilizing of "the symbolic maintenance of the nation-state [through the] contentious management of historical narratives as well as territorial space."[49] Particularly relevant for a divided South Asia is her progressive transformation of margins, frames and borders. Meaning flows between the image and the brocade borders, aided by textual citations placed on the margins. By becoming the conduit for the relationship between word and image, the margin becomes a privileged space where the artwork engages the most philosophically acute questions of identity formation and meaning-making. The absence of the brocade surround in the *Firdaus* phase heralds not marginality's disappearance but its epiphany. The sharpened, recuperative focus on the border in "Firdaus I: Valley," as discussed earlier, is followed by the implosion of margins in the subsequent scrolls, announced by the scattering of textual citations across the picture space. The scrolls are flooded by significant marginality that cascades across the picture space through its traversal by rivers. The river motif, in this case the Jhelum/Vyeth/Vitasta, in an earlier scroll on the Partition of India, the Chenab of the Punjab, points up the porosity of political borders through an excavation of memory and suffering buried under post-1947 national self-assertion.[50] The color units that divide her picture space, but are themselves blurred and breached, re-iterate this more productive response to boundaries. Inasmuch such self-assertion energizes itself through possessiveness toward the territory of desire, this riverine fluidity makes the Kashmir paintings the continuation of an artistic commitment to interrogate the unfinished business of 1947 and beyond.

Interrogate, not complete: in this project Sheikh joins those women writers, activists and other artists who have been at the vanguard of questioning the masculinist politics of military aggression, exclusionary identities and closed minds/borders/bodies that dominate the public spheres of postcolonial South Asia.[51] The openness of an evolutionary process in art becomes the antidote to the phallic thrust of adversarial nationalisms. The play with intimacy and theatricality suggests multiple ways of expressing libidinal economies of self and other, not merely one where the gaze conflates with the logic of penetration suggested by the post-Enlightenment format of viewing the painting on the wall. Sheikh's alternative modes of viewing the artwork—the scroll, the miniature that is ideally viewed close-up, like a book—recuperate the pre-modern as the feminine without reifying either through nostalgic nativism.[52] Instead, as for other women artists questioning India's relationship with Kashmir, repetition, circularity and the rejection of closure lead to self-critique. Yet Sheikh pushes these boundaries furthest through her multifaceted critique of the self caught in collective desire.

In this she rejects aesthetic minimalism and austerity for a lush and delicate idiom. Feminist because of its politics, it is feminine by dint of its fruitful interaction with craft practices (that in India belong to a predominantly male domain feminized through colonialist ideologies),[53] and also by dint of ornament and detail being associated with the feminine. Hers, therefore, is a historicist feminist idiom that embraces the saliency of these feminine markers by accepting the persistence of psychosocial and historical processes, but which moves beyond sterile binaries and the anxieties they perpetuate.

It may seem appropriate to fit this feminine-feminist aesthetics of significant marginality into Homi Bhabha's influential "interstitial third space" of postcolonial hybridity.[54] However, I prefer to understand it through Deleuze and Guattari's counterintuitive call for a minoritarian aesthetics and politics: "How many styles or genres or literary movements, even very small ones, have only one single dream: to assume a major function in language, to offer themselves as a sort of state language, an official language. Create the opposite dream: know how to create a becoming-minor."[55] This dream of a radical minoritarianism can encompass, far more impassionedly than the too-theoretical "third space," the materialist spiritualities and feminine resistive force of Sheikh's Kashmir paintings. The alternative phenomenology of the border they communicate recalls too the borderland of Gloria Anzaldúa, the gaping wound where divergent worlds meet and grate against each other.[56] Nevertheless, even Alzaldúa's borderland cannot accommodate Sheikh's art that is feminist because it is feminine, modernist because it reaches back to the premodern, and that shatters the limits of representation only to reassemble the unboundedness of desire. That very unboundedness is thereby diverted into new, more productive channels of circulation. To understand fully this ornamental, resistive, "meticulous drowning of the soul," that repudiates boundaries through visual reminders of pre-national cultural flows, I turn to yet another imaginative boundary-crossing enacted by Sheikh's paintings: from the artwork to the devotional practices of the *dargah,* or the South Asian Sufi shrine, that, in the sacred geographies it plots, emotions it commands, and collective identities it generates, offers vernacular alternatives to "the wide popular appeal and deep-rooted attachments evoked by nationalism."[57] This move should not blind us to the politics of identity and jockeying for power that historical dargahs have been central to in regions across South Asia, including Kashmir;[58] however, taking cues from not only Sheikh but also Hussain and Tiku, I wish to extract certain *spiritual* possibilities from the dargah's material, and materialist, history.

The South Asian dargah exemplifies how the abstract and philosophical Sufism of the early medieval Islamic heartlands was transformed into performative, embodied, expressive, Sufisms wherever Islam took local roots. [59] In South Asia, this Islamicisation of the indigenous[60] most commonly manifested itself in regionally inflected rhythmic music expressive of the bodily abjection, submission, longing and separation that animate the central Sufi concept of attaining transcendence through surrender to divine love.[61] The strongly iterative quality of such music and its lyrics, as most clearly demonstrated in *qawwali,* its best known example,[62] binds performers and listeners into an organic whole, charging the performance space with a sacred aura and encouraging members of this new collective to lose themselves through trance-like states. Despite the onslaught of Enlightenment discourses on rationality and superstition, colonial programs of modernization and the corresponding drive toward Weberian disenchantment, and pan-Islamic reformist traditions, all of which strive to reduce, in Appadurai's earlier-cited description of a related context, "materiality to the servant of abstraction," these embodied, localized Sufisms live and thrive across South Asia, offering communities and individuals viable, participatory modes of sacrality.[63] Yet contemporary, dargah-centric Sufism remains, in public perception, a marginalized "little tradition" that fits at best uneasily within both orthoprax Islam and chauvinistic nationalism. Not coincidentally, such lack of fit is propagated through the adoption of bodily and performative markers of the feminine at dargahs and within the music of the dargahs.[64] Signifying an excess of reverence, love and longing toward the sacred in order to aim for the transcendental, this performative femininity is not gender-constrictive, but is available to anyone who may be so predisposed toward the sacred.

Of course, the politicisation of religion in South Asia may not make such ecumenism always possible in praxis. Yet dargahs and their associated practices remain spaces of refuge and resistance, and have been responded to as such by South Asian musicians and activists. Pushing forward such intuitions, I see the dargah's feminized marginality as homologous to Sheikh's aesthetic praxis for dismantling the territory of desire. Her new map transmits the same ceaselessness of longing as does the dargah, whose force projects its effulgence across distances and separations. The embodied space of liminality and ambivalence created by the dargah, the saint, and the devotee/worshipper/pilgrim generates amity, egalitarianism, ecumenism—an alternative ethical order that expresses the inexpressible under conditions of ecstasy. It is this inexpressible that makes of dargah and artwork alike "alternative texts—utopian experiential imaginaries of other, possible world orders."[65] We are invited to defy the quotidian constrictions of gender, nation, geography, history, and identity itself, releasing our universal potential to become something other than ourselves. The "other possibility" then re-emerges as the possibility of the artwork on Kashmir being able to summon its viewers into contemplating and even participating in such transformations. If "the sanitized discourse of defense policy is a form of rationalized fear," then the aesthetic, in turn can be seen "as offering an alternative response, a creative enchantment."[66] Unifying materiality, enchantment and resistance, the artwork moves beyond being mere "representation." Aided by the critic as translator between the artist and civil society, its rejuvenated mode can create a new community that, through empathy, eschews condoning and perpetuating violence by questioning the citizen's role within the majoritarianism always lurking within democracy.

To summarize this book's arguments, then, and point forward: representation in modernity constructed Kashmir as the territory of desire. Fetishized and commoditized as "the work of art," modes of representation stripped the Valley and its inhabitants of materiality through the ostensibly disinterested promotion of its beauty. Attendant claims for the Valley's "spirituality" rendered this very spirituality meaningless through positing it as a disenchanted modernity's conveniently imagined other. It is not paradoxical that to learn to restore materiality to this undeniably beautiful space and to reinsert it into history, we must rescue the artwork from its own fetishization through the conditions of modernity. After all, the arts are essential to a full human life. They enable us to enter and understand the human psyche in ways that other discourses cannot; they allow individuals and communities therapeutic expression and modes of mourning and reconciliation. The artistic dimension of human existence offers us ways of being, ways of knowing as well as ways of consoling.

In this book I have hoped to demonstrate that the artwork, in the hands of the creative intellectual, has a unique role to play within the proper functioning of a democracy, and within strategies for both "negative" and "positive" peace: that is, in maintaining the absence of conflict in a given society, as well as in restoring justice within conflicted areas and preventing the eruption of future conflict therein.[67] If "the roots of the Kashmir problem lie in processes internal to Indian federalism and democracy,"[68] I have aimed to show how the artist's "capacity to make us look at the world in a new way" can effect a metamorphosis of democratic decision-making from static consensus toward dynamic political compromise.[69] I have also tried to reconceptualize, through a spiritual Sufi performativity and through the necessary irrationality of the talisman, the artwork that confronts the Kashmir conflict and its discursive history. The shared conditions of significant marginality that I have foregrounded through this affective analysis can also reposition, I believe, the Valley of Kashmir from being the passive subject of desire. Even if cartography cannot transform its position as "the just beyond," through a new map of longing the majority can discover its own potential for becoming-minor. For, "on the path which leads to that which is to be thought all begins with sensibility."[70]

Notes

Introduction: The Valley and the Nation

1. See Ashutosh Varshney, "Three Compromised Nationalisms: Or Why Kashmir Has Been a Problem," in Thomas, ed., *Perspectives on Kashmir;* for an older but necessary perspective, see Abdullah, "Kashmir, India and Pakistan," 528–35.

2. The poem by Rahman Rahi, *Watsun,* is in Koshur (Kashmiri). I overheard it sung at a reconciliation meeting of women from Jammu and Kashmir, held in Srinagar in August 2004. I am grateful to Jyoti Singh for enabling me to be present at that historic occasion. Later that month at the Department of Kashmiri, Kashmir University, Srinagar, I was privileged to translate it into English with the help of Professor Rahman Rahi himself, together with Professor Majrooh Rashid and Ifat Hamid. The quotation from Agha Shahid Ali is from the poem, "I See Kashmir from New Delhi at Midnight," in Ali, *The Country without a Post Office,* 25. The line is addressed to the poet by the ghost of Rizwan, a Kashmiri boy killed in custody by the Indian Army. Both Rahi and Ali will be discussed in detail in chapter 6, and Ali's poetry is invoked through this book. For Ali's life and career, see Amitav Ghosh, "The Ghat of the Only World: Agha Shahid Ali in Brooklyn," in Ghosh, *The Imam and the Indian,* 1–12.

3. Ellias, *Gallerie International.*

4. Bina Sarkar Ellias, private communication, April 2005. For the evaluation of contemporary Indian art, see Shahane, "The Cult of Rejection," 32–34, and Graham, Mishra, Sagar, and Vazirani, "Painting a Happy Picture," 38–42.

5. See Ellias, *Identity, Alienation, Amity.* The Kashmiri artists here were Masood Hussain, Harsh Vardhan Sharma, Rajendar Tiku, Shabir Mirza, Shafi Chaman, Shuja Sultan, Veer Munshi; the photographers from Kashmir were Altaf Qadri and Rafiq Maqbool. The non-Kashmiri artists represented included Nilima Sheikh, Gulammohammed Sheikh, Arpana Caur, M. F. Husain, Sheba Chacchi, and Sonia Jabbar.

6. I discuss Lal Ded and her legacy in chapters 3 and 5. For historical approaches to Sufism in Kashmir, see Mohammad Ishaq Khan, *Kashmir's Transition to Islam,* Bamzai, *Cultural and Political History of Kashmir,* vol. 2, and Yoginder Sikand, *The Role of Kashmiri Sufis;* for a literary evaluation, see Raina, *A History of Kashmiri Literature,* 13–35; and for a revisionist discussion, see Zutshi, *Languages of Belonging,* 18–28.

7. The exhibition opened on the 22 August 2005. The Jammu and Kashmir Academy of Art, Culture, and Languages is the cultural research and publication wing of the state government of Jammu and Kashmir.

8. Appadurai, "Disjuncture and Difference," 1–24.

9. See Mehta, *Maximum City.*

10. Mbembe, *On the Postcolony,* 104.

11. Ibid., 104.

12. Ibid., chap. 1.

13. Ibid., 89; for the general point, see Kohli et al., eds., *The Success of India's Democracy.*

14. See James Manor, "Centre-State Relations," in Kohli et al., eds., *The Success of India's Democracy,* 95; Bose, *The Challenge in Kashmir;* Chandhoke, *Of Broken Social Contracts and Ethnic Violence.*

15. For the links between political and aesthetic representation, see Ankersmit, *Political Representation,* 91–132.

16. Gelvin, *The Israel-Palestine Conflict;* the phrase is the title of his first chapter.

17. Jahangir (r. 1605–27 CE) visited Kashmir regularly and described its beauty in his memoir, *Tuzuk-i-jahangiri;* he also constructed the Shalimar Garden in Srinagar in 1619 for his Empress, Nur Jahan; her brother Asaf Jah in turn constructed the Nishat Garden in 1633–34; the third Mughal Garden in Srinagar, Chashme Shahi, was built for Jahangir's son and successor, Shah Jahan, in 1632. However, the association between his love of Kashmir and the Persian couplet, *agar firdaus bar roo-e zameen ast/hameen ast-o hameen ast-o hameen ast* (if there be paradise on earth, it is this, it is this, it is this), appears to be an urban legend of sorts. The couplet is by the Sufi poet of Delhi, Amir Khusrau Dehlavi (1253–1325 CE), who used it in praise of India: see http://www.alif-india.com/shayr.html (I am grateful to Samira Sheikh for these clarifications). Its popular ascription to Jahangir seems to have been aided by Thomas Moore's poem *Lalla Rookh: An Orientalist Romance,* on which more below, in chapters 2 and 3.

18. This brief account summarizes, as "neutrally" as possible, arguments from a range of commentators, particularly Bose, *Kashmir,* Hewitt, *Reclaiming the Past,* and Lamb, *Crisis in Kashmir.*

19. Landmarks in Partition scholarship are: Bhasin and Menon, *Borders and Boundaries;* Butalia, ed., *The Other Side of Silence;* Kaul, ed., *The Partitions of Memory;* and the historiographic work of Joya Chatterji, Mushirul Hasan, Ayesha Jalal, and Gyanendra Pandey.

20. See Chatterji, "The Fashioning of a Frontier."

21. The issue of princely states, and particularly Dogra-ruled Jammu and Kashmir, is discussed in detail in chapter 3.

22. The key date here is 13 July 1931, when a group of Kashmiri Muslim men gathered to present their grievances to the Maharaja was fired on by the Maharaja's police; see Bose, *Kashmir,* 19. For these politics of pre-1947 Jammu and Kashmir, see Mridu Rai, *Hindu Rulers, Muslim Subjects,* and Zutshi, *Languages of Belonging.*

23. These wars are: 1947–48 over Kashmir; 1965 also over Kashmir; 1971 over the creation of Bangladesh, but with repercussions over the Ceasefire Line in Kashmir; and 1999 in Kargil, Jammu, and Kashmir.

24. Aggarwal, *Beyond Lines of Control,* 1.

25. For the "grey zone," see Agamben, *Remnants of Auschwitz.*

26. The phrase is from Taussig, *Colonialism, Shamanism and the Wild Man,* 120 and passim.

27. Winichakul, *Siam Mapped;* his arguments have been elaborated for India by Sumathi Ramaswamy, "Visualising India's Geo-body: Globes, Maps, Bodyscapes," in Ramaswamy, ed., *Beyond Appearances?,* 151–91.

28. Winichakul, *Siam Mapped,* 56.

29. The phrases are from Hasan, ed., *Inventing Boundaries,* and Anderson, *Imagined Communities,* respectively.

30. Homi K. Bhabha, "Dissemination: Time, Narrative and the Margins of the Modern Nation," in Bhabha, *Location of Culture,* 139–70.

31. As indeed that between India and Bangladesh; for reasons of space, I bypass completely this equally fraught emotional issue.

32. See *Atlas of Pakistan,* published under the direction of Major General Anis Ali Syed, Surveyor General of Pakistan (Rawalpindi: Survey of Pakistan, 1985).

33. For China's involvement in the dispute, see Samina Yasmeen, "The China Factor in the Kashmir issue" in Thomas, ed., *Perspectives,* 319–40. Aggarwal, *Beyond Lines of Control,* discusses the LOC's impact on self-fashioning in Ladakh.

34. See, for instance, the *Nelles Map of Pakistan*; for a more "scholarly" example, see Schwartzberg et al., eds., *A Historical Atlas of South Asia,* 87–88.

35. Aggarwal, *Beyond Lines of Control,* 1.

36. Bose, *Kashmir,* 295: "At its northern end, the LOC terminates at a point called NJ 9842 in the high Himalayas, beyond which lies a glacial region, Siachen, contested between Indian and Pakistani forces and then Chinese territory."

37. For the Great Game, see chapter 2.

38. Rose, *The Question of Zion,* 69, and Aggarwal, *Beyond Lines of Control,* 1.

39. See Derrida, *Archive Fever,* 7; for citizenship as "pact," see Brantlinger, in the introduction to his *Fictions of State.* For forgetting and national feeling, see Renan, "What is a Nation?," 11–19.

40. Derrida, *Archive Fever,* 3.

41. Anzaldúa, *Borderlands/La Frontera,* 25.

42. Yi-Fu Tuan, "Geo-Piety: A Theme in Man's Attachment to Nature and to Place," in Lowenthal and Bowden, eds., *Geographies of the Mind,* 11–39.

43. "Crackdown": this dreaded word has come to signify in Kashmir the worst horrors and humiliations of the Indian army's presence. A crackdown involves the rounding up of Kashmiri men and boys from homes in both Kashmir and India by the army, usually at dawn, in order to identify active participants in the "Movement," called "militants" (and in Indian cinema and the press, also called "terrorists"). The tip-offs for these crackdowns usually come from "surrendered militants." Army "bunkers," guarded by sandbags, are ubiquitous in Kashmir. These terms are now of ordinary currency in the languages spoken in Kashmir. On this issue, I have learned much from Basharat Peer's unpublished paper, "Militarising the Narrative in Kashmir," delivered at the "Language, Culture, and Urban Publics Workshop," April 2004, Sarai (see http://www.sarai.net [last accessed 24 October 2008]), Delhi.

44. *Mujahideen* is the Arabic noun for "fighters" (sing.: *mujahid*), specifically of the *jihad;* on this over-determined term, see Devji, *Landscapes of the Jihad.* In contemporary India, however, it is more common to call anyone perceived to be an agent of *jihad,* a *jihadi* rather *mujahid* (the morphologically correct Arabic word); when *mujahid or mujahideen* is used it often is specifically used by Kashmiris to describe the non-Kashmiri presence in Jammu and Kashmir; this specialized use is also apparent sometimes in the Indian print media.

45. Taussig, *Terror and Healing,* 128.

46. See the account of the JKLF leadership in Qureshi, *Kashmir.*

47. Note here the changed emphases of Bose's first and second Kashmir books. In the first, *The Challenge in Kashmir,* he vehemently denies that Islam could have had any formative influence on the movement for *aazadi;* but in the second, *Kashmir,* he is more willing to acknowledge the role of global and local Islamic identities.

48. This issue is the focus of chapter 6.

49. These shifting meanings are discernible in the responses of a wide range of Kashmiri youth, available in the privately circulated report written for Oxfam (India) Trust by Fazili, Kanth, and Kashani, *The Impact of Violence.*

50. http://meaindia.nic.in/interview/2001/07/12i01.htm [last accessed 24 October 2008].

51. "Gurukul" is the Sanskrit word for "academy."

52. "Boys to Men" (interview with Qazi Touqeer), *Filmfare,* January 2006, 109: "My one and only ambition was to be a [film] star. I used to pose in the Mughal Gardens of

Srinagar and get my younger brother to shoot my moves and moods. Inshallah [God willing] I'll face the arclights myself one day soon."

53. For the influence of cable television in South Asia, see Page and Crawley, *Satellites over South Asia.*

54. Qazi Touqeer, "Hero," in the music album *Qazi Ruprekha Jodi no. 1* (Sony India, 2005). It should be added that Qazi's partner in his dizzy rise to fame was a Bengali woman, Ruprekha, of stronger vocal talent but far less charisma.

55. On 7 October 2005, this comment was widely reported in the Indian press.

56. Bose, *Kashmir,* 103–63.

57. See Dhiraj Nayyar, "The Importance of Being Qazi," *Indian Express,* 27 October 2005. The Kashmiri reaction is captured in *Greater Kashmir's* letters to the editor through October 2005. I am grateful to Mr Fayaz Kaloo, editor, *Greater Kashmir,* Srinagar, for letting me go through their archives at short notice, and to Gowhar Fazili (private communication, January 2006) for details on the Kashmiri reaction to Qazi's success.

58. Mbembe, *On the Postcolony,* 129. Two years on, Qazi seems far less sanguine about the prospect of succeeding in Bollywood; see http://in.rediff.com/movies/2007/jun/28qazi.htm. [last accessed 24 October 2008].

59. Here, the role of the Bradford-born Kashmiri, Maqbool Butt, first imprisoned by the Indian State and then hanged within Delhi's notorious Tihar Jail on 11 February 1984, has been all-important; see http://www.geocities.com/jklf-kashmir/tribute.html [last accessed 24 October 2008].

60. Ramaswamy, "India's Geo-Body," has traced this anthropomorphizing.

61. Mamdani, *When Victims Become Killers,* 19.

62. Benjamin, "The Work of Art in the Age of Mechanical Reproduction," in his *Illuminations,* 211–44.

63. See Karlekar, *Re-Visioning the Past.*

64. Thakurta, *Monuments, Objects, Histories.*

65. Arjun Appadurai and Carol Breckenridge, "Museums are Good to Think: Heritage on View in India," in Karp, Levine, and Kraemer, eds., *Museums and Communities* (Washington D.C.: Smithsonian Institute Publications, 1992), 34–55; and Philip Lutgendorf, "Evolving a Monkey: Hanuman, Poster Art, and Postcolonial Anxiety," in Ramaswamy, ed., *Beyond Appearances,* 71 and 11, respectively.

66. Taussig, *Mimesis and Alterity,* 24, alluding to Walter Benjamin here; see Benjamin, *Selected Writings,* 4:266.

67. Mamdani, *When Victims Become Killers,* 8, 18.

68. For imperial cartographic ventures, see Keay, *The Great Arc;* for the Valley and Srinagar, see Mohammad Ishaq Khan. The adventure of early photography in the Himalayas is discussed in chapter 3.

69. I discuss Kashmir in Indian popular cinema in chapter 1.

70. Amit Rai, "Patriotism and the Muslim Citizen in Hindi Films."

71. Žižek, *The Sublime Object of Ideology,* 119 (emphasis in original).

72. Mridu Rai, *Hindu Rulers,* 3.

73. A similar point is made, in the related context of early photographs of the Indian "Mutiny," by Chaudhary, "Phantasmagoric Aesthetics," 63–119.

74. Chaudhary, "Phantasmagoric Aesthetics," 71; Sontag, *On Photography;* see also Prosser, *Light in the Dark Room.*

75. I explain my use of fetishism in chapter 4.

76. Taussig, "Maleficium: State Fetishism," in his *Nervous System,* 111–40.

77. Khanna, *Dark Continents,* 23.

78. Ibid., 24. Khanna's approach to melancholia attempts to re-articulate for collective identities the psychoanalytical revisionism of Abraham and Torok, *The Shell and the Kernel* and *The Wolf Man's Magic Word.*

79. Khanna, *Dark Continents,* 25; Said, *Orientalism,* on which see n. 89 below.

80. Khanna, *Dark Continents,* 15.

81. Debord, *Comments on the Society of the Spectacle.*

82. This formulation is not a homogenizing one; rather, the phrase should be read to suggest that "the Kashmiri as co-opted Indian citizen" is only one kind of Kashmiri subjectivity thrown up by the long-standing complexities of this conflict zone.

83. Michel Foucault, "Introduction," in Deleuze and Guattari, *Anti-Oedipus,* xxi.

84. M. A. Mahboob, *Documentary 2000,* oil painting exhibited at Jammu and Kashmir Academy, August 2005. I thank Masood Hussain for taking me to the Mahboob Retrospective in Srinagar.

85. See chapters 1 and 2.

86. Greenblatt, *Marvelous Possessions,* 6; I discuss this concept fully in chapter 2. For the continuum of different kinds of capital, see Mbembe, *On the Postcolony,* 77.

87. On "quilting," see Žižek, *The Sublime Object,* 111.

88. Monk, *An Aesthetic Occupation.* The influence of the "picturesque" on nineteenth-century fantasies of the Valley is discussed in chapter 2.

89. Said, *Orientalism;* for Foucault, see, most obviously, his *Discipline and Punish* and *The Order of Things;* see also his *Languages Counter-Memory, Practice* and *Power/Knowledge.*

90. See Foucault, *Language, Counter-Memory, Practice.*

91. Geeta Kapur, "subTerrain: Indian Artists Dig the Contemporary," in Kapur, *Body. City,* 47.

92. Taussig, *Terror and Healing,* 128.

93. See Copjec, *Read My Desire,* 1–14, and Stoler, *Race and the Education of Desire.*

94. Nelson, *A Finger in the Wound.*

95. Mbembe, *On the Postcolony,* 5.

96. Ibid., 103 and 128, respectively.

97. Ibid., 103.

98. Ibid., 103.

99. Taussig, *Mimesis and Alterity,* 31, and *Terror and Healing,* 4.

100. Taussig, *Mimesis and Alterity,* 21.

101. The dilated witchhunt over S. A. R. Geelani and Afzal Guru, the two Kashmiri men accused (differently) of involvement in a terrorist plot to blow up the Indian Parliament indicates the viciousness with which the Indian public has pursued these scapegoats; see *13 Dec: A Reader. The Strange Case of the Attack on the Indian Parliament,* introduced by Arundhati Roy, and Vajpeyi, "The Bare Life of S.A.R. Geelani, Ph.D."

102. Taussig, *Terror and Healing,* 120.

103. Ibid., 128.

104. Mridu Rai, *Hindu Rulers,* 185.

105. Sufism, a conglomeration of mystic, ascetic, and individualistic movements within Islamic societies and cultures, emerged along the nonmetropolitan frontiers of early Islam and has historically offered alternative, para-orthodox spaces for working out syncretic Islamic identities by merging with "popular" Islam at local levels. This propensity toward syncretism has also made Sufi practices ripe for appropriation and collusion with dominant ideologies. For the cultural politics surrounding Sufism in India, see Stewart, "In Search of Equivalence," 261–88; Muzaffar Alam, "Assimilation from a Distance: Confrontation and

Sufi Accommodation in Awadh Society," in Champakalakshmi and S. Gopal, eds., *Tradition, Dissent, Ideology,* and Dominique-Sila Khan, *Crossing the Threshold,* 8–29.

106. Agha Shahid Ali, "I See Kashmir from New Delhi at Midnight," *The Country without a Post Office,* 26.

107. Khanna, *Dark Continents,* 108.

108. Taussig, *Terror and Healing,* 53.

109. Mbembe, *On the Postcolony,* 25.

110. Khanna, *Dark Continents.*

111. Seminal examples being the work of Caruth, ed., *Trauma,* and her *Unclaimed Experience;* also Bal et al., eds., *Acts of Memory.* Pierre Janet's arguments for the necessity of mourning to convert "traumatic memory" into "narrative memory" are summarized by Bessel A.Van der Kolk and Onno van der Hart, "The Intrusive Past: The Flexibility of Memory and the Engraving of Trauma," in Caruth, ed., *Trauma,* 160. The text that began it all is Sigmund Freud, "Mourning and Melancholia," in Freud, *The Standard Edition,* 14:239–58.

112. See Kabir, "Beyond Narrative," 28–42.

113. Pandey, "In Defence of the Fragment," 27–55.

114. For a methodological defense of the anecdote, see Gallagher and Greenblatt, "Counterhistory and the Anecdote," 49–74.

115. Adorno, *Aesthetic Theory,* 229.

116. Van Alphen, *Caught by History;* Agha Shahid Ali, "The Blessed Word," in Ali, *The Country without a Post Office,* 15–17.

1. Masks of Desire

1. Žižek, *The Plague of Fantasies,* 29–30.

2. Žižek, *Sublime Object,* 65.

3. In this context, see Sandria Freitag, "Visions of the Nation: Theorising the Nexus between Creation, Consumption and Participation in the Public Sphere," in Dwyer and Pinney, eds., *Pleasure and the Nation,* 35–75; Chakravarty, *National Identity;* and Ashish Rajadhyaksha, "Viewership and Democracy in Indian Cinema," in Vasudevan, ed., *Making Meaning in Indian Cinema,* 267–96. Useful analogies are to be found in the aesthetics of totalitarianism, as described by Todorov, *Red Square Black Square,* and Groys, *The Total Art of Stalinism.*

4. Renan, "What Is a Nation?"

5. Nelson, *A Finger in the Wound,* 75.

6. Witness the first epigraph, from Žižek, *Sublime Object,* 28. For the mask of the state, see Philip Abrams, "Notes on the Difficulty of Studying the State," 58–89.

7. All translations from Hindi are mine.

8. As in the Introduction, I use the term "melancholia" in a specific way, distinguishing it from "mourning," or the resolution of trauma through successful assimilation through narrative.

9. The term "fatwa" signals Bollywood's increasing interest in depicting South Asian Muslims through the vocabulary of pan-Islamism; for an in-depth discussion, see Kabir, "The Kashmiri as Muslim in Recent Bollywood Films."

10. See Guha, *A Corner of a Foreign Field,* and Majumdar, *Lost Histories of Indian Cricket.*

11. For good (and bad) Muslims in Indian cinema, see Preckel and Kumar, eds., *Muslims in Bollywood;* on Indian secularism, see Sunderrajan and Needham, eds., *The Crisis of Secularism in India.*

12. Christopher Pinney, "A Secret of Their Own Country: Or How Indian Nationalism Made Itself Irrefutable," in Ramaswamy, ed., *Beyond Appearances?* 113–50. On Indian Bazaar art, see Kajri Jain, *Gods in the Bazaar.*

13. Both of these songs draw on popular Koshur lyrics but in different ways. *Bhumbro* was written in the 1950s by Kashmiri poet Dina Nath Nadim as part of his opera *Bombur o Yamberzal* (Bumblebee and Narcissus), a thinly disguised political allegory on Sheikh Abdullah's imprisonment and his replacement by Ghulam Mohammad Bakshi. I discuss these events later in this chapter (Nadim was a Bakshi supporter). While the song's words are very loosely translated by *Mission Kashmir*'s lyrics writer, the original melody has been retained. *Hrind Poshmal* was written by Kashmiri romantic poet Rasul Mir (d. 1870 CE). *Mission Kashmir*'s version retains as its chorus its first couplet: *"Hrind Poshmal gindne drai lo lo/oobi shaabaash chani potshayi lo lo"* (O Intoxicated ones, Poshmal, drunk [on spring] has come out to play/even your shadow deserves our offerings of praise); "lo lo" is a typical refrain in Koshur folk lyrics. However, this couplet remains untranslated even in the DVD's subtitling, and is simply offered as a snatch of "Kashmiri exotica." I am grateful to Professor Shafi Shauq, Department of Kashmiri, University of Kashmir, Srinagar, for these insights (April 2006).

14. Doordarshan (Sanskrit: "distance-vision") is the brand name of Indian national television, paralleling Aakashvani ("sky-voice") for All India Radio; the latter is also known by its acronym AIR. While the term "Doordarshan Srinagar" is a fiction, "Doordarshan Kashir" ("Kashir" being the indigenous name for Kashmir) does exist, as does Radio Kashmir; for the latter, see chapter 5.

15. On the relationship between apertures and fantasy, see Žižek, *The Plague of Fantasies,* 29–30.

16. Chakravarty, *National Identity,* 209.

17. See "Shammi Kapoor," http://www.upperstall.com/people/shammi-kapoor [last accessed 24 October 2008].

18. This section condenses arguments made in Kabir, "Nipped in the Bud," 83–101.

19. See Amit Rai, "An American Raj in Filmistan," 51–77.

20. Nehru, *Discovery,* 619. For a discussion of this quote and its ramifications, see chapter 3.

21. On melodrama, see Vasudevan, "Addressing the Spectator of a Third World National Cinema," 305–24.

22. By "pastoral" I mean a deliberate, imaginative evocation of rural life as simple and unspoiled, in order to make a political statement about the urban. Pastoral has had a long life in Western thought, starting from Greek antiquity onward. For a classic study, see Empson, *Some Versions of Pastoral.*

23. This issue returns in chapter 4.

24. Anderson, *Imagined Communities.*

25. See, in this context, Kabir, "Allegories of Alienation and Politics of Bargaining," 141–60; also, in general, see Kohli et al., eds. *The Success of India's Democracy.*

26. See Chibber, *Locked in Place.*

27. On Article 370 (full text at http://www.constitution.org/cons/india/p21370.html [last accessed 24 October 2008]), see Bose, *Kashmir,* 68–84.

28. Bazaz, *Kashmir in Crucible,* 71.

29. Lamb, *Crisis in Kashmir,* 77.

30. Hewitt, *Reclaiming the Past,* 144.

31. Bazaz, *Kashmir in Crucible,* 191.

32. Bose, *Kashmir,* 78–80; for the Hazratbal mosque's political significance, see Mohammad Ishaq Khan, "The Significance of the Dargah of Hazratbal," in Troll, ed., *Muslim Shrines in India,* 188.

33. Mridu Rai, *Hindu Rulers,* 185.

34. Abdullah, "Kashmir, India and Pakistan," 534.

35. Lamb, *Crisis in Kashmir,* 113.

36. Bazaz, *Kashmir in Crucible,* 85.

37. Abdullah, "Kashmir, India and Pakistan," 533.

38. Niranjana, "Integrating Whose Nation?" 80.

39. Nandy, *The Secret Politics of Our Desires.* Hindutva is the political mobilization of Hindu nationalism, the benign façade of which barely conceals an aggressive equation of Hinduism with Indianness. During the 1990s, under the umbrella of the Sangh Parivar (the Hindutva "family"), the BJP government ensured a fascist, exultant dimension to Hindutva's penetration of the public sphere. See Sarkar and Sarkar et al., *Khaki Shorts and Saffron Flags.*

40. This debate took place in the pages of *Economic and Political Weekly;* triggered by Niranjana's "Integrating Whose Nation?" it was followed by, among others, Srinivas, "*Roja* in Law and Order State," 1225–26, and Bharucha, "On the Border of Fascism," 1389–95. For a slightly apologetic take on *Roja,* see Dirks, "The Home and the Nation," in Dwyer and Pinney, eds., *Pleasure and the Nation,* 161–85.

41. For a detailed discussion of this issue, see Kabir, "Allegories of Alienation and Politics of Bargaining."

42. See Rai, "Patriotism and the Muslim Citizen."

43. Dwyer and Pinney, eds., *Pleasure and the Nation.*

44. I return to this film and its significance for the souvenir from Kashmir, in chapter 4.

45. On the counterfetish, see the Introduction and chapter 5.

46. See Abraham and Torok, *The Wolf Man's Magic Word.*

47. See Kabir, "Allegories of Alienation and Politics of Bargaining."

48. This complaint is Niranjana's, as understood by Dirks, "Home and the Nation," 163.

49. *Paradise on a River of Hell* (dir. Bazaz and Gaur, 2002). Of the codirectors, the conceptualization and detail was largely Bazaz's, while Gaur provided the technical input. I am grateful to Meenu Gaur for confirming this detail, and to Abir Bazaz for several illuminating discussions about his films, his politics, and Kashmir between December 2003 and April 2005 in Srinagar, Delhi, and Leeds. Interestingly, a nurturing relationship has evolved between Jamia Millia Islamia (National Islamic University) and Kashmiri Muslims students fleeing academic and political uncertainty in Jammu and Kashmir to the hardly welcoming environs of the nearest metropolis, Delhi. Jamia Millia Islamia was founded in 1920 in Aligarh and moved to its present location in Delhi in 1936 as a testament to the scholarly ecumenism of Indian Islam. Following Bazaz, one other Jamia student from Kashmir, Shabnam Ara, has taken up the documentary medium to report on Kashmir; her work is discussed in chapter 2.

50. Ali, "I See Kashmir from New Delhi at Midnight," in *Country without a Post Office,* 24.

51. The film was commissioned for broadcast over PBST (Public Broadcasting Service Trust) and, according to Bazaz (private communication, Leeds, January 2005), escaped the censor's scissors because of its allusive and lyrical nature. That an arm of the State should sponsor a film critiquing the State might appear confusing but is actually typical of the feigning of normalcy that is the State's usual take on Kashmir. Throughout the 2000s, the

film has been screened at American and British university campuses, as well as various civil society meetings in South Asia. It won a Special Recognition award at the Karachi Film Festival, 2003.

52. See, for instance, the discussion of Daniel Libeskind's Jewish Museum in Berlin, in Huyssen, *Present Pasts,* 48–84.

53. *Kun'ear* (dir. Bazaz and Gaur, 1999).

54. Lawrence, *The Valley of Kashmir,* 255; Agha Shahid Ali, "Farewell," in Ali, *The Country without a Post Office,* 22: "I am being rowed to paradise on a river of hell/exquisite ghost, it is night."

55. Thus, bookshops in Srinagar stock cheap reprints of all the nineteenth- and early twentieth-century British commentators on Kashmir, which I discuss in chapter 3.

56. See Fazili, "The Rebuilding of Chrar-e-Sharif."

57. Agha Shahid Ali, "I Dream I Am the Only Passenger on Flight 423 to Srinagar," in Ali, *The Country without a Post Office,* 34.

58. See the compassionate account by Sonia Jabbar, "Blood Soil: Chittisinghpora and After," in Butalia, ed., *Speaking Peace,* 226–40.

59. See the Introduction.

60. Kunanposhpora village was the site for an infamous mass rape of Kashmiri women by Indian Army soldiers in early 1990. For details, see *The State of Human Rights in Kashmir.*

61. An ironic play on saffron here brings together its traditional cultivation in Kashmir with saffron as Hindutva's signature color.

62. Metz, "Photography and Fetish," 81.

2. Framing Fantasy

1. I refer to the phenomenon of the Kashmiri "half-widow," whose husbands have "gone missing" after being taken in custody, but who cannot re-marry, according to Shariat law, unless there is definite proof of widowhood. It is in the Indian State's interest to deny even the fact of enforced disappearances. See Butalia, ed., *Speaking Peace,* for a range of female responses to these and other human rights abuses in Kashmir.

2. "With its largely female membership, the APDP has a single point agenda: tracking down the hundreds, indeed thousands of missing persons, so that families can either regain their loved ones, or put a closure on their lives" (Butalia, "Introduction," in *Speaking Peace,* xiii). The APDP, an association of the relatives of those wronged by the state and its agents, was formed in 1994 by Parveena Ahangar, mother of a disappeared Kashmiri youth. Since then it has worked against enforced disappearances in Jammu and Kashmir. Technically not a non-governmental organization (NGO), it is registered as a trust. In 2000, along with other similar civil society initiatives, it entered a new umbrella organization termed Jammu and Coalition of Civil Society; see http://www.jkccs.org/ [last accessed 24 October 2008]. In 2007, however, the APDP and CCS split. Shabnam Ara, a Kashmiri student of Mass Communications at Delhi's Jamia Millia Islamia, now lives in Srinagar and volunteers with the APDP. For some controversy regarding the authorship of her documentary, see http://www.greaterkashmir.com/full_story.asp?Date=12_2_2006&ItemID=23&cat=1, [last accessed 24 October 2008].

3. Catherine Grant, "Still Moving Images: Photographs of the Disappeared in Films about the Dirty War in Argentina," in Hughes and Noble, eds., *Phototextualities,* 64.

4. Metz, "Photography and Fetish," 81, 87.

5. Grant, "Still Moving Images," 79.

6. Agha Shahid Ali, "Postcard from Kashmir," in Ali, *The Half-Inch Himalayas,* 1.

7. Of course, Bourne and Burke were not the only photographers operating in Kashmir during this early period of photography. William Baker, the partner of Burke, Edward Saché, and George and James Craddock were among the others that operated around their time or shortly thereafter. For reasons of space, but, more importantly, for reasons of emphasis, I focus on Bourne and Burke here, arguing for the particular impact of their growing reputations and their efficient commercial operations on the reception of Kashmir.

8. As Mridu Rai, *Hindu Rulers,* comments in a note to her citation of *Lalla Rookh:* "The poem was first published in 1817 and Thomas Moore was offered the princely sum of £3150 as an advance for it. Moore read up on the region availing himself of detailed descriptions from colonial historians such as Alexander Dow and travel writers such as François Bernier and George Forster" (1, n.1). This quintessentially Romantic Orientalist text remains, however, understudied, and its impact on European fantasies of Kashmir awaits detailed examination. I thank John Whale for confirming the existence of this desideratum.

9. See http://www.majlisbombay.org/ [last accessed 24 October 2008].

10. The photographer is Syed Muzaffar, and the Kashmiri newspaper in question, *The Daily Afaq*. I am deeply indebted to Hansa Thapliyal and Kavita Rao, the original receivers of the photographs, and to Majlis for facilitating my access to them.

11. *Kangri,* Kashmiri fire-pot; *pheran,* Kashmiri woolen smock worn by both sexes.

12. Metz, "Photograph and Fetish," 81, and Price, *The Photograph*. However, the theoretical preoccupations of both critics seem strangely too aesthetic compared to the horrifyingly political realities captured in these photographs. I thank Jay Prosser for this insight.

13. The classic texts here are Barthes, *Camera Lucida,* and Sontag, *On Photography.* Prosser, *Light in A Dark Room,* provides useful commentary on both. The photograph's relationship to loss and memorializing plays an important role in Holocaust studies; see, for example, Hirsch, *Family Frames,* and Huyssen, *Present Pasts.*

14. Silverman, *The Threshold.*

15. See *Godaam: Disseminating the Political,* http://www.majlisbombay.org/godaam.htm [last accessed 2008]; this project has since evolved into an archive of images from a range of conflict zones. South Asian activism displays a penchant for the postmodern juxtaposition of vernacular words with rich affective connotations to contemporary civil society agendas; hence, Majlis itself (Urdu: "meeting," but also "Shia Muslim gatherings"), and *godaam*. This latter word will recur through the chapter.

16. "Ekphrasis," the prose description of a picture, is a suggestive cross-cultural literary device. For ekphrasis and photography, see Mitchell, *Picture Theory,* chap. 5. An earlier copyright statement from Majlis did not refer to these photographs but it did insist that "footage will not leave the library premises except for noncommercial viewing—and not even for that, if the author/producer so wishes. Footage shall be kept for viewing only, within the library premises on dvd/vcd format (unless the author/producer allows otherwise)." http://www.majlisbombay.org/culture-video-pkf.htm [site no longer accessible]. The statement has since evolved to "material . . . specially on Kashmir can be viewed at Majlis only on Fridays and by prior appointment." http://www.majlisbombay.org/godaam.htm [last accessed 2008].

17. And even books on India in general—see Tully and Wright's *India in Slow Motion*.

18. Ami Vitale, "The World Outside is Yet Not Mine" (photo: 20 × 16 inches), and, in Ellias, *Gallerie International,* 74–75 (spread over two A4 pages).

19. See Introduction.

20. Pinney, *Camera Indica,* 15.

21. Ibid., 197.

22. Ibid., 15.

23. Samuel Bourne, "On Some of the Requisites Necessary for the Production of a Good Photograph" (31 January 1860), reprinted in Rayner, ed., *Photographic Journeys in the Himalayas,* 182.

24. Ibid., 180–81.

25. Ollman, "Samuel Bourne," 1123, and Sampson, "The Success of Samuel Bourne," 337.

26. Samuel Bourne, "Narrative of a Photographic Trip," 4. For the imperial picturesque, see Leask, *Curiosity.*

27. Bourne, "Photography in the East," 268.

28. Pinney, *Camera Indica,* 17–20.

29. Ibid., 21.

30. See, here, the burgeoning work in colonial visualities, for instance: Pinney, *Camera Indica;* Ramaswamy, ed. *Beyond Appearances;* Jain, *Gods in the Bazaar;* and Karlekar, *Re-Visioning the Past.* See also Thomas, "The First Four Decades of Photography," 215–26; Falconer, "India," 45–48; and, for an interesting comparative perspective, Onta, "A Suggestive History," 181–212.

31. On Hodges, see Quilley and Bonehill, eds., *William Hodges.*

32. Sampson, "Success," 337, and Ollman, "Samuel Bourne."

33. Sampson, "Success," 336, and Ollman, 1124–25.

34. Sampson, "Success," 336.

35. Bourne, "Narrative," 4.

36. Sampson, "Success,"336.

37. Sprague, "Samuel Bourne," 28. On Simla, see Kanwar, *Imperial Simla.*

38. Bourne, "Photography in the East," 345.

39. Ibid., 345–46.

40. See n. 45 below.

41. Bourne, "Ten Weeks with the Camera," 50.

42. Bourne, "Narrative," 560.

43. Ibid., 619.

44. Bourne, "Photography in the East," 268.

45. My analysis of Bourne's Kashmir photographs, as well as those taken by Burke, to be discussed below, are based on my examination of nineteenth-century albums and loose-mounted photographs in the Alkazi Collection of Photography, Delhi and London. Whenever possible, I cite catalogue numbers in parenthesis. I am extremely grateful to Rahaab Allana and Stéphanie Roy for facilitating my access to these photographs, and for initiating me into the delicate process of examining them close-up. I have also used the extensive Bourne, Burke, and later Kashmir photographs held at the Prints, Photographs, and Drawings Collection (India Office) of the British Library, London. I thank Ainslee Cameron for her help in viewing this material. The material experience of photographs as archival material is incorporated into the theorizing on value that is part of this chapter's aim.

46. Ollman, "Samuel Bourne," 1122.

47. As, for example, when, having run out of distilled water in the mountains, he had to use spring water but found the results "remarkable," with "a peculiar aptitude for rendering clouds" (Bourne, "Ten Weeks With the Camera," 51.

48. Some typical Bourne views of Srinagar are "The Third Bridge (742)," "View on Dhul Canal (741)," "View across the Lake (764)," "Sunset on the Lake (765)," "Lake View (769)," "On the Lake (771)." For the more "dramatic" mountain views, see, particularly, his "Head of Scinde Valley (989)" and "View in Zojji-la Pass (990)."

49. Particularly apparent in the series of Lake photographs in the impressive Bourne album monogrammed "A.C.A." in the Alkazi Collection, Delhi (photograph numbers 76, 77, 79, 80, 81, 82, and 85).

50. Sampson, "Success," 345.

51. As evident from the accounts of British travelers to Kashmir during the Sikh period, such as Clarke, *From Simla,* and Egerton, *Journal of a Tour.*

52. Ollman, *Samuel Bourne,* 8.

53. Omar Khan, *From Kashmir to Kabul,* 12; see also Huttenback, *Kashmir and the British Raj,* 33–58, and Hopkirk, *The Great Game.*

54. See Huttenback, *Kashmir and the British Raj,* 1–32, and Rai, *Hindu Rulers,* 18–60. For the connections with photography, and Burke and Baker as pioneering "war photographers," see Omar Khan, *From Kashmir to Kabul,* 11–14.

55. Sampson, "Success," 337; Omar Khan, *From Kashmir to Kabul,* 15; and Chaudhary, "Phantasmagoric Aesthetics."

56. Omar Khan, *From Kashmir to Kabul,* 19, 100.

57. Exemplified in Burke's "Bridge on the Mar Canal (686)," "Houses on the Mar Canal (688)," and "City Below the Third Bridge (694)."

58. Bourne, "Narrative," 39. For some of Burke's ethnographic photographs, such as those of Kashmiri "nautch girls," see Omar Khan, *From Kashmir to Kabul,* 60 (Baker and Burke 413) and 74 (Baker and Burke 1229).

59. See Edney, *Mapping an Empire.*

60. Cole, *Illustrations of Ancient Buildings,* i.

61. Particularly apparent in Burke's photographs of Martand; for Cole's commentary, see *Illustrations of Ancient Buildings,* 19.

62. See Rosaldo, "Imperialist Nostalgia," 107–22.

63. Omar Khan, *From Kashmir to Kabul,* 61.

64. Ollman, *Samuel Bourne,* 8.

65. Bourne, "Narrative," 4–5.

66. Omar Khan, *From Kashmir to Kabul,* 62. Omar Khan, "John Burke," 236–43.

67. Omar Khan, *From Kashmir to Kabul,* 61.

68. Ibid., 61.

69. For a succinct compilation of early European writer-travelers, see Shauq et al., *Europeans on Kashmir.*

70. See Greenblatt, *Marvelous Possessions.*

71. See Benjamin, "The Work of Art," in his *Illuminations.*

72. See here Bourdieu and Boltansky, *Photography.* The commodification of the photograph amplifies and complicates Chaudhary's suggestive, but ultimately merely analogical, relationship postulated in his "Phantasmagoric Aesthetics," between the commodity and the photography in modernity.

73. The catalogues are "Photographic Views in India, by Baker and Burke, Punjab," "Photographic Views in India, by Bourne and Shepherd, Simla," and "Photographic Views in India by Bourne and Shepherd, Calcutta and Simla," dating c. 1866–72. I thank John

Falconer at the British Library for making available to me these catalogues, on which the description and discussion in this paragraph is based.

74. See Omar Khan, *From Kashmir to Kabul,* 89.

75. The catalogues of both the firms state the availability, for customers of their photographs, "photographic scrap-books," and "albums," in "various sizes and styles." This entanglement of the photograph album with imperial commerce casts a different light on to current scholarly preoccupations with nineteenth-century metropolitan albums as evidence for the consolidation of the bourgeois family, e.g., Kuhn, *Family Secrets.*

76. Thus see, for instance, the albums belonging to "old India hands," such as L.W. Dane, the Marquess of Zetland, H. S. Barnes, J. H. Reid, and Randolph Bezzant Holmes in the British Library. The Alkazi Collection has, on the whole, more anonymous albums the original owners of which are announced often through initials monogrammed on the covers, such as "E.C.A." and "E.A.L," but these are no less handsome in their make and preservation.

77. This is particularly true of albums from the nineteenth century; see, for instance, the albums entitled "Himalayas and Cashmere," "Kashmir 1876," "Views in India," and "The John J. Hort Album," all in the Alkazi Collection, London. However, even when the albums begin including more social subjects, as described in n. 81 below, they do not lose interest in these older views. This increasing uniformity of the "Kashmir view" makes somewhat inappropriate, for my usage, Chaudhary's characterization of colonial photography as "phantasmagoric," which reaches back to the kaleidoscopic implications of the "phantasmagoria" (Chaudhary, "Phantasmagoric Aesthetics"). In contrast, I find in early photographs of Kashmir a relentless stabilizing through repetition—characteristics to which I find the word "phantasmatic" better suited.

78. On colonial postcards, see Pinney, *Camera Indica,* 19, and Alloula, *The Colonial Harem,* 4. The British Library has at least one handsome orange album from the 1900s with "Postcard Album" emblazoned diagonally across its front cover, including five postcards of Kashmir views, captioned "Baramulla," "Boat Girl," "The Mar Canal," "Sind Valley," and "Gulmarg from Bazaar."

79. David Harvey, "Colonial Nostalgia and Cultures of Travel," in AlSayyad, ed., *Consuming Tradition, Manufacturing Heritage,* 138: "The 'kodak' was the apotheosis of the appropriation of Egypt as a late Victorian and Edwardian exhibition in which scopic pleasure was not compromised by physical vulnerability."

80. These developments culminate in the imperial retinues and lifestyles captured, for instance, in the Dane, Zetland, and Barnes albums in the British Library.

81. The growth of tourism is discussed further in the following chapter.

82. Huttenback, *Kashmir and the British Raj,* 49, 61; Rai, *Hindu Rulers,* 133–36.

83. I am grateful to Mr. Salim Beg, Director, Jammu and Kashmir State Tourism, for sharing with me his vast knowledge about early tourism in Jammu and Kashmir (interview, Srinagar, August 2005).

84. See "The Kashmir-Dharampur Wedding Album (1923)," and "The Visit of Lord and Lady Ampthill and Suite to Kashmir (1904)," both at The Alkazi Collection, Delhi.

85. Photograph 58 in the Ampthill Visit Album. The garden, according to the caption, is that of Raja Amar Singh, Prime Minister of the state of Jammu and Kashmir, and brother of the Maharaja Pratap Singh. It is taken by Alim Chand, the state photographer; note the passing of the camera into indigenous hands here, but without, seemingly, a change in vision—or can we detect here a note of irony?

86. "They Call it Paradise, I Call it Home!," http://www.Kashmir.wordpress.com/2006/05/10: "numero uno." Also relevant is the entry for 5 May 2006: "Which Kashmir Do You Know?" [last accessed 24 October 2008].

87. 2–8 June 2006. I am grateful to Jagdish and Hemant Mehta, to Sanjeev Saith, and also to Inder Salim, Gowhar Fazili and Satish Sharma for teaching me to view the images from multiply critical perspectives.

88. See http://www.indiapicture.com [last accessed 24 October 2008].

89. As stated in their press release, 1 June 2006.

90. Press release, 1 June 2006, and the exhibition catalogue, Hemant Mehta, *Kashmir Views 1934–1965* (Delhi: IndiaPicture.com, 2006), 1.

91. A report of a conversation between said printer and Inder Salim, New Delhi, June 2006.

92. Jag Mohan's time in Jammu and Kashmir ended with the exodus of the Pandits in early 1990, and many in Srinagar today claim that he played some role in this debacle. For his own account of the events, see Jag Mohan, *My Frozen Turbulence.*

93. Press release, "IndiaPicture.com showcases 'Kashmir Views.'"

94. On which see Zutshi, *Languages of Belonging,* 286–99.

95. Pinney, "The Secret of His Own Country," 147–48, also Partha Chatterjee, in "The Sacred Circulation of National Images," in Pelizzari, ed., *Traces of India,* 276–92, 283, comments on the "economy of [national] iconicity that requires that the image be cleansed of all traces of a self-conscious artistic aesthetic."

96. Shown to me from R. C. Mehta's original albums by the curators (Delhi, April 2006).

97. I thank Khurram Parvez for arranging this meeting.

98. Here, Foucault's comments on the contrast between the museum and the fair are suggestive: "Opposite these heterotopias that are linked to the accumulation of time [such as the museum and the library], there are those linked, on the contrary, to time in its most fleeting, transitory, precarious aspect, to time in the mode of the festival" (Foucault, "Of Other Spaces," 26).

99. The photograph as amulet is fleetingly considered by Metz, "Photograph as Fetish."

100. Mahjoor is discussed further in chapter 5.

101. Partha Chatterjee, "Sacred Circulation," 289.

102. Adorno, *Aesthetic Theory,* 229. Ironically, the very elision of Kashmiri bodies from the frame necessitates this caveat; contrast the easier linking of violence and photography within the images examined by Chaudhary in "Phantasmagoric Aesthetics."

103. See, here, Derrida, *Archive Fever.*

3. Modern Nation, Antique Land

1. Nehru, *The Discovery of India,* 56. This classic work was written during Nehru's nine year long imprisonment at the hands of the colonial authorities, and was published in 1946.

2. Timothy Mitchell, "Making the Nation: The Politics of Heritage in Egypt," in AlSayyad, ed., *Consuming Tradition, Manufacturing Heritage,* 212.

3. Daud Ali, "Introduction," in Daud Ali, ed., *Invoking the Past,* 1.

4. Mitchell, "Making the Nation," 212.

5. Nehru, *Discovery,* 619. It should be clarified that Nehru's vision of India at this historical moment rests on its pre-Partition geographic unity; nevertheless, the full

incorporation of the Kashmir Valley into post-1947 (and post-1948) India made Nehru's claims to its emotional and spiritual primacy persistently relevant to post-Partition India.

6. Genette, "Introduction to the Paratext," 261; all quotes in this paragraph are from this source. See also Genette, *Paratexts.*

7. See Taylor, *A Dream of England*, 20.

8. All biographical details for Stein are taken from Walker, *Aurel Stein.*

9. These photographs and albums are available within the Stein Collection in the India Office Prints, Photographs and Drawings Collection of the British Library; see below for further commentary.

10. Van der Veer, "Monumental Texts," 134–55.

11. Stein, trans. and ed., *Kalhaṇa's Rajataraṅgiṇi,* 1: vi.

12. Stein, *Catalogue,* ix.

13. See Sheldon Pollock, "Deep Orientalism: Notes on Sanskrit and Power beyond the Raj," in Breckenridge and Van der Veer, eds. *Orientalism and the Postcolonial Predicament,* 76–133.

14. Stein, *Catalogue,* xiii.

15. For which see Mridu Rai, *Hindu Rulers,* 119–21.

16. Bühler, *Detailed Report.*

17. Bühler, *Detailed Report,* 17.

18. See Wilson, "An Essay," 1–119, and Moorcroft and Trebeck, *Travels in the Himalayan Provinces.* The comment about Moorcroft is by Younghusband, *Kashmir,* 48.

19. Cunningham, *Description of the Temples of Kashmir.* For Cole, see chapter 2.

20. I paraphrase Lieut.-Col. Henry Torrens, *Travels in Ladâk, Tartary, and Kashmir,* 297: "[H]ere all are officials, either of the sword or pen." For missionaries, Empire, and language, see Viswanathan, *Masks of Conquest,* 45–67, and Van der Veer, *Imperial Encounters.*

21. Elmslie, *A Vocabulary of the Kashmiri Language.*

22. Wade, *A Grammar of the Kashmiri Language,* v.

23. Knowles, *Folktales of Kashmir,* v, and *Dictionary of Kashmiri Proverbs and Sayings,* iii, respectively.

24. See Viswanathan, *Masks of Conquest.*

25. A tendency already glimpsed in Wilson's "Essay."

26. Grierson and Barnett, *Lalla-Vakyani.*

27. Grierson, *Essays on Kāçmīrī Grammar,* ix, and *Dictionary of the Kashmiri Language.*

28. Stein, *Rajatarangini* I, xxiv.

29. Stein, *Rajatarangini* I, xxi, and Grierson, *Essays,* xi.

30. Knowles, *Dictionary,* iv.

31. I echo William Dalrymple, *White Mughals,* though this work concerns an earlier generation of India enthusiasts.

32. Arthur Neve, *Thirty Years in Kashmir;* his brother Ernest F. Neve, *Beyond the Pir Panjal;* Tyndale-Biscoe, *Kashmir in Sunlight and Shade;* Lawrence, *The Valley of Kashmír;* and Younghusband, *Kashmir.*

33. See Huttenback, *Kashmir and the British Raj,* 63, 5, and Mridu Rai, *Hindu Rulers,* 28–35, 44–60.

34. Younghusband, *Kashmir,* 87.

35. Battye, *The Kashmir Residency,* 47.

36. M. A. Stein, *Rajatarangini* I, xxiii; *Catalogue,* xii.

37. M. A. Stein, *Catalogue,* ix.

38. M. A. Stein, *Rajatarangini* I, xxiii.

39. Mridu Rai, *Hindu Rulers,* Index, 299.

40. Cannadine, *Ornamentalism.*

41. Ibid., 109. For Durbars in general, see Bernard Cohn, "Representing Authority in Victorian India," in Cohn, *An Anthropologist among The Historians,* 632–82.

42. Wakefield, *The Happy Valley,* 11.

43. As Mridu Rai, in *Hindu Rulers,* has persuasively demonstrated.

44. See Ibid., 184–92.

45. For this paratextual information, see the early volumes of The Kashmir Series of Texts and Studies.

46. As declared in a handsome copperplate hand in the inside jacket of the Cambridge University Library's copy of the *Catalogue.*

47. Knowles, *Folk-Tales,* 9, and Grierson, *Essays,* x.

48. For Indology and Brahminism, see Pollock, "Deep Orientalism." Shaivism is the cult of Shiva, often associated with the esoteric practices of Tantric Hinduism; Vaishnavism, that of Vishnu, including the cults of Krishna and Rama. See, in this context, Flood, *Body and Cosmology.* For the political relationship between Dogra Vaishnavite practice and Dogra Shaivite patronage, see Mridu Rai, *Hindu Rulers,* 121–26.

49. J. C. Chatterji, ed., *Shiva Sutra Vimarshini,* Kashmir Series of Texts and Studies I (Bombay: Nirnaya-Sagar Press, 1911), i–ii.

50. Chatterji, ed., *A Prospectus.*

51. Shastri, *The Para-Trimshikha,* 1, 3.

52. Lawrence, *Valley of Kashmir,* 161.

53. For Lawrence's mixed results in obtaining a fair settlement, see Mridu Rai, *Hindu Rulers,* 148–49.

54. See note 28 above.

55. See frontispiece, Chatterji, ed., *Shiva Sutra Vimarshini.* For the geological angle, see, for instance, Diener, *Triassic Faunae of Kashmir;* Lawrence, *Valley of Kashmir,* cites extensively from Lydekker, *The Geology of the Kashmir and Chamba Territories.*

56. See Stein, *Rajatarangini* I, 5 (I.26–38). The *Nilmatha Purana* is discussed in chapter 6.

57. Stein, *Rajatarangini* II, 353–54, though note his own skepticism about this derivation.

58. Madhusudan Koul, Superintendent, Research Department, Jammu and Kashmir State, "Preface," in Shastri, ed., *The Ishvara-Pratyabhijna Vimarshini of Utapaladeva,* i.

59. Ibid., ii.

60. Alfred Foucher, "Introduction," in Kak, *Ancient Monuments,* xii–xiii.

61. Kak, *Ancient Monuments,* xv.

62. Ibid., xv.

63. Francis Younghusband, "Foreword," in Kak, *Ancient Monuments,* i.

64. Foucher, "Introduction," ix.

65. Younghusband, *Kashmir,* 47.

66. As Culler, "The Semiotics of Tourism," in his *Framing the Sign,* 153–68, has demonstrated through a critique of the position advanced by Boorstin, *The Image,* and Fussell, *Abroad.*

67. These distinctions are accepted and explored by Fussell, *Abroad,* and Buzard, *The Beaten Track.*

68. For the concept of the "marker," see Culler, "Semiotics," and for the tourist gaze in general, MacCannell, *The Tourist,* and Urry, *The Tourist Gaze.*

69. The souvenir is discussed thoroughly in chapter 4.

70. Younghusband, *Kashmir,* 48.

71. For papier maché and Kashmir, see chapter 4.

72. Testimonial from the private collection of Mr. Abdul Rahman Ratta, H.B. Holiday Inn, Dal Lake, Srinagar, Kashmir.

73. *Rajatarangini* I, xiv.

74. For parallel examples, see, for instance, Alarcón, *Aztec Palimpsest,* and the essays in AlSayyad, ed., *Consuming Heritage.*

75. Spurr, *The Rhetoric of Empire,* cited as frontispiece to Alarcón, *Aztec Palimpsest.*

76. See Introduction.

77. Mridu Rai, *Hindu Rulers,* 18–65.

78. Torrens, *Travels,* 2.

79. Aysnley, *Our Visit,* 75.

80. Wakefield, *Happy Valley,* Appendix I, "Routes to the Valley," 273–81, Appendix II, "Treaty of Amritsar," 282–84, Appendix III, "Rules for the Guidance of Officers and Other Travellers visiting the Dominions of HH Runbeer Singh," 285–58, Appendix IV, "Local Rules for the Guidance of Visitors in Kashmir, Published Under the Sanction of the Punjab Government," 289–91, Appendix V, "Tariff of Boat Hire," 292, and Appendix VI, "Kashmir Postal Rules," 293–94.

81. Vigne, *Travels in Kashmir,* ii.

82. See the memoirs of Younghusband, Lawrence, and the Neves.

83. This discussion is condensed from the testimonials and assorted documents, including telegrams, grocery lists and letters in the private collection of Mr. Abdul Rahman Ratta and also from those in a similar collection owned by his cousin Mr. Rashid Dongola, owner, *H.B. Golden Fleece,* Nageen Lake, Srinagar.

84. For Nedou's Hotel in Srinagar, see Younghusband, *Kashmir,* 70. The Gulmarg Nedou's is still in business, but the Srinagar counterpart is now used as an Indian Army Barracks, as is the Srinagar Club. Michael Nedou, born in Ragusa, was a subject of the Austro-Hungarian Empire who came to Lahore in the 1820s, opened his first hotel there, and subsequently managed to obtain the "rights, privileges and capabilities of a naturalized British subject"—as declared by a certificate signed by W. W. Aitcheson, Lieut.-Governor of the Punjab and its Dependencies, in 1859. This certificate, framed, is still on display in Nedou's Hotel, Gulmarg.

85. Compare Murray Aynslee's account, *Our Visit,* 75–80, with Younghusband, *Kashmir,* 42–67, and Ernest Neve, *Beyond the Pir Panjal,* 21–22.

86. Undated pamphlet in the collection of Mr. Abdul Rehman Ratta.

87. The collection of Mr. Abdul Rahman Ratta contains a typed testimonial from Thomas Cook, dated 1930. On Cook's pioneering travel agency, see Williamson, *The Golden Age of Travel;* for details on his early years, see Boorstin, *Image,* 87–89. No substantial work has been done on Thomas Cook's penetration of India.

88. Kaye, *Golden Afternoon,* 179.

89. Ibid., 117.

90. Ibid., 179.

91. Most recently, on 11 July 2006.

92. For such émigré Pandit families, see Sender, *The Kashmiri Pandits.*

93. See the discussion of *The Discovery of India* in Chakravarty, *National Identity,* 1–18.

94. Nehru, *Discovery,* 633–34.

95. Nehru, *Discovery,* 40–41.

96. Ibid., 42. For these Chinese witnesses, see now Amartya Sen, "China and India," in Sen, *The Argumentative Indian,* 161–90.

97. Nehru, *Discovery,* 46–47.

98. Ibid., 49.

99. Ramaswamy, "Geo-bodies."

100. Nehru, *Discovery,* 619.

101. Ibid., 619–20.

102. Ibid., 619, 628.

103. Ibid., 620–21.

104. K. N. Panikkar, "Foreword," in Ray, *Early History of Kashmir,* vii.

105. *A Descriptive Analysis of the Kashmir Series of Texts and Studies,* Kashmir Series of Texts and Studies 80, 1.

106. *Descriptive Analysis,* 9, 12, 19, 25, 44, 46. Three "non-Hindu" photographs—the Shalimar Garden (27), Dal Lake (36) and Nishat Bagh (34)—now stand reintegrated into this new visual ensemble. The term "tantra" encapsulates the modern retrieval of Hindu esotericism, including that which overlaps with esoteric strands of Buddhism, in order to empower the self. That such empowering often takes the form of the jettisoning of all taboos, including sexual, has undoubtedly contributed to its peculiar attractions. For the often strange links between colonial modernity, anticolonial nationalism, and the occult, see Sumathi Ramaswamy, *Fabulous Geographies,* 53–96.

107. Chatterjee, "Sacred Circulation," 281, 284–85.

108. For the implications of this conflation, see Sarkar, *Beyond Nationalist Frames.*

109. *Descriptive Analysis,* 47.

110. For a detailed discussion of these sociopolitical changes, see Zutshi, *Languages of Belonging,* 259–322.

111. See Ananya Jahanara Kabir, "Border Crossings," *The Hindu,* 24 April 2005.

Hinge

1. Masood Hussain (b. 1953, Srinagar) graduated in commercial art from Sir J.J. Institute of Applied Art, Bombay, in 1977; currently he heads the Department of Applied Arts at the state government-run Institute of Music and Fine Arts, Srinagar. His "painted reliefs" are large, averaging 3 × 4 feet; some are freestanding and fully three-dimensional, while others are in the nature of bas-reliefs.

2. Syed Hasan, felicitated by the Indian Government with a National Award for handicraft in 2003, started this vase in 2000. It took him two years to finish, and he declared it to be "unique" and a means of bringing people "happiness." Both he and Khazir Hasan Qasba, maker of the crab-apple tree, deploy hereditary skills which they have tried to pass on to their own children. My conversation with them took place in August 2005, Rajbagh, Srinagar, at the home of Agha Ashraf Ali, father of Agha Shahid Ali, and Qasba's comment, cited above, was made during that conversation; they were "summoned" here once it was learnt that I had an interest in their work. I wish to both emphasize these class differences evident here but also note that the "extraordinary" time of conflict had momentarily rendered them irrelevant by bringing us all together to discuss the making of Kashmiri handicraft.

3. Taussig, "Maleficium," in his *Nervous System,* 140.

4. Tirthankar Roy, *Traditional Industry;* see also Dipesh Chakrabarty, "The Time of History and the Times of the Gods," in Lowe and Lloyd, eds., *Politics of Culture in the Shadow of Capital,* 35–60.

5. Pietz, "The Problem of the Fetish I," 5–17, "The Problem of the Fetish II," 23–45, and "The Problem of the Fetish IIIa," 105–23.

6. "Carapace" is the hard exoskeleton covering the crustacean's vulnerable body. In using it to illuminate the work of the fetish, I follow Mulvey, *Fetishism and Curiosity,* 121 and passim.

7. Taussig, "Maleficium," 129.

8. Agha Shahid Ali, "A Poetic Response," *Indian Design and Interiors Magazine,* February–March 1999, 23–24.

9. Ali, "A Poetic Response," 23.

10. This is a Koshur word, as are all other words for craft and domestic objects referred to in this article, unless otherwise specified. For *panr* windows, see Khan, *Srinagar,* 26.

11. Ali, "A Poetic Response," 23.

12. See P. N. Kachru, "Papier maché," in Jaitly, ed., *Crafts,* 121–39.

13. Agha Shahid Ali, *The Country without a Post Office,* 48. The reference to the fleeing refugees is to the Kashmiri Pandit exodus in the early 1990s, a much-contested issue that I examine in chapter 6.

14. The relationship between metaphor (substitution) and metonym (contiguity, association) was originally set out by Roman Jakobson; see his celebrated "Two Aspects of Language and Two Types of Aphasic Disturbances," in his *On Language,* 115–33.

15. For its further transformation into another visual medium, see chapter 6.

16. MacCannell, *Tourist,* 91–104.

17. The exhibition took place at the Art Heritage Gallery of the Triveni Kala Sangam, New Delhi, during March–April 2005. I am grateful to the Mellon Foundation and the Foundations of Democracy Program at the Centre for History and Economics, King's College, Cambridge, for making possible my viewing of this exhibition. The works, which I discuss in detail in the final section, were all executed during 2003–5.

18. See Deleuze and Guattari, *Kafka,* 16.

19. Mulvey, *Fetishism and Curiosity,* 6.

20. Gervis, *This Is Kashmir,* 329–30.

21. See chapter 3, n. 60.

22. Stewart, *On Longing,* 135.

23. See the brilliant explication of "Marx's table" by Thomas Keenan, "The Point Is to (Ex)Change It: Reading Capital, Rhetorically," in Apter and Pietz, eds., *Fetishism as Cultural Discourse,* 182–85.

24. Stewart, *On Longing,* 135–36.

25. Stewart, *On Longing,* 149.

26. "Chain-Stitch Rug, Srinagar, c. 1940" and "Samovar, and a Kangri, Nishat Bagh, Srinagar, c. 1939, in Hemant Mehta, *Kashmir Views 1934–1965* (Delhi: IndiaPicture.com, 2006), 11, 15. See chapter 2, for details.

27. The phrasing is from Octave Mannoni, "*Je sais bien, mais quand-même . . .*," in Mannoni, *Clefs pour l'imaginaire,* 9–33.

28. Marx, *Capital,* 126; for a subtle reading of Marx's use of the German word *stofflich,* see Keenan, "The Point," in Apter and Pietz, eds., *Fetishism,* 161.

29. Gervis, *Kashmir,* 229.

30. See chapter 3.

31. Saraf, *Arts and Crafts,* 9.

32. See Zutshi, *Languages of Belonging,* 57–117.

33. Khan, *Srinagar,* 43–84.

34. Markovitz, *The Global World of Indian Merchants.*

35. Khan, *Srinagar,* 52.

36. Lawrence, *Valley of Kashmir,* 373, 378.

37. Debord, *Society of the Spectacle Comments.*

38. Interview with Afzal Abdullah, proprietor, Asia Arts and Crafts, Srinagar, August 2005; I am grateful to him for these insights into his family history and the history of The Bund.

39. Battye, *Kashmir Residency,* 57–59, and 64. The photographs she uses to illustrate her book, although unacknowledged, are mostly from Mahatta's Studio.

40. See Younghusband, *Kashmir,* 214, and also Lawrence, *Valley of Kashmir,* 378.

41. Coomaraswamy, *Arts and Crafts,* 251.

42. See Guha-Thakurta, *The Making of a New "Indian" Art,* and her magisterial *Monuments, Objects, Histories;* and Mitter, *Art and Nationalism.*

43. See, for instance, the essays collected in Coomaraswamy, *Art and Swadeshi.* For Coomaraswamy's seminal influence on Indian art and art history, see Guha-Thakurta, *Monuments, Objects, Histories,* 154–55, 254–55 and *passim.*

44. For the importance of cloth within swadeshi, see C. A. Bayly, "The Origins of Swadeshi," in Appadurai, ed., *The Social Life of Things,* 285–321.

45. For Nehruvian socialism, see Sunil Khilnani, "Temples of the Future," in Khilnani, *The Idea of India,* 61–106; on Gandhian thought, see Ashis Nandy, "From Outside the Imperium: Gandhi's Cultural Critique of the West," in his *Traditions, Tyrannies and Utopias,* 127–61.

46. See Dipesh Chakrabarty, *Provincializing Europe.*

47. See, for instance, Gandhi's comments on the importance of the village community in Fischer, ed., *The Essential Gandhi,* 291: "I would say if the village perishes India will perish too. . . . Industrialization on a mass scale will necessarily lead to passive or active exploitation of the villages as the problems of competition and marketing come in. Therefore, we have to concentrate on the village being self-contained, manufacturing mainly for use." For his description of handspinning as "an ancient cottage industry," see ibid., 288; and, for his ideal village as comprised of cottages, as well as cottage industries, see ibid., 395.

48. See Breckenridge, "Aesthetics and Politics," 195–216; suggestive, also, is the analysis of the Gothic revival by Biddick, *The Shock of Medievalism,* though this is a problematic work on the whole, as demonstrated within its review by Lee Patterson, http://www.historycooperative.org/journals/ahr/104.4/br_1.html [last accessed 26 October 2008].

49. Brantlinger, "A Postindustrial Prelude," 466–85.

50. Marx, *Capital,* 49, that however translates his German phrase, "ungeheuere Warensammlung" as "immense collection of commodities;" for the replacement of "immense" by "monstrous," see Keenan, "The Point," 157.

51. Coomaraswamy, *Arts and Crafts,* 251.

52. Fischer, ed., *The Essential Gandhi,* 299: "Village economy cannot be complete without the essential village industries such as hand-grinding, hand-pounding, soap-making, paper-making, match-making, tanning, oil-pressing, etc."

53. Shanker, *Crafts of India,* 56.

54. Ibid., 44.

55. See Ibid., 44–46.

56. All India Handicrafts Board Ministry of Production, *Handicrafts of India,* 1.

57. Ibid., 87.

58. *The Story of Papier Maché* (Srinagar: AVRC, 1991); available for viewing at *Majlis,* Bombay.

59. See my discussions in the Introduction and chapter 1.

60. For this information, I thank Hansa Thapliyal (Bombay, April 2004).

61. Huggan, *The Postcolonial Exotic,* 19.

62. Bhabha, *The Location of Culture,* 74–75.

63. Mulvey, *Fetishism as Curiosity,* 5.

64. See the evolving contents of the first *Handicrafts of India* to Kamaladevi Chattopadhyay, *Indian Handicrafts* (Allied Publishers, 1963), and Kamaladevi Chattopadhyay, *Handicrafts of India* (New Delhi: ICCR, 1975).

65. See frontispiece, Chattopadhyay, *Handicrafts of India*. The logical extension of this move is Jaya Jaitly's production, in recent years, of beautifully detailed craft maps for each state of India, available at Dilli Haat.

66. See the official promotional websites, http://www.indiasite.com/delhi/museums/craft.html and www.delhitourism.com/dttdc/dilli-haat.html [both sites last accessed 22 October 2008]. The complex semiotics of a space such as Dilli Haat, particularly, whose postmodernity is precisely its aspiration to premodernity, needs separate explication; the comments by Appiah, "Is the Post- in Postmodernism the Post- in Postcolonial?" 336–57, made in the context of neotraditional Yoruba art, offer a helpful conceptual plumbline. Appadurai and Breckenridge, "Museums Are Good to Think," provide provocative conceptualization of the postcolonial "exhibition complex" of Indian public culture, "a gray zone where display, retailing and festivity shade into each other," 39. While they do not refer to Dilli Haat, and in fact declare they will not deal with "handicraft" but focus instead on "heritage," their comments are useful in thinking through the relationship between craft marketing and the museum proper, and for "a generalized, mass-media-provoked preoccupation with heritage and with a richly visual approach to spectacle," 42.

67. For the ramifications of Article 370 for Jammu and Kashmir, see Bose, *Kashmir*, 67–70.

68. Jyotindra Jain, private communication, May 2005.

69. Veer Munshi, private communication, August 2005.

70. Shahid, "Farewell," 22. I return to this interpretation in chapter 6.

71. Abrams, "Notes."

72. Stewart, *On Longing*, 141.

73. "Via the late medieval Portuguese feitiço, to the sixteenth-century pidgin fetisso on the African coast," an etymological history that demonstrates "that the fetish could originate only in conjunction with the emergent articulation of the ideology of the commodity form that defined itself within and against . . . two radically different types of non-capitalist societies [Christian feudal and African lineage], as they encountered each other in an ongoing cross-cultural situation." (Pietz, "Problem, I," 7). This "situation" was that of the emergence of merchant capital social systems through European expansionism radiating outward from the Iberian Peninsula to the West African coasts and beyond. In "Problem, II," Pietz elaborates the semantic range of Latin *factititus*, including the connections with witchcraft and magic through *maleficium*.

74. Taussig, "Maleficium," 129.

75. Žižek, *Sublime Object*, 118.

76. This is the opinion of both the creator of the vase and its current guardian, Agha Ashraf Ali. For organizing my "tour" of Zadibal, I thank Qalab Hussain and Masood Hussain.

77. On the rhizome, see Deleuze and Guattari, *Anti-Oedipus*.

78. See Arjun Appadurai, "Introduction" and Igor Kopytoff, ed., "The Cultural Biography of Things: Commoditization as Process," in Appadurail, ed., *The Social Life of Things*, 64–92. On the contemporary persistence of Romantic ideas of art and the artist, see Carroll, "Art, Practice, Narrative," 115–36, and Shusterman, *Pragmatic Aesthetics*.

79. See Keith Hart, "On Commoditization," in Goody, ed., *From Craft to Industry*, 40–41. The complication of these categories under globalization has been interestingly discussed by Appiah, "Is the Post- in Postmodernism."

80. Also particularly apparent in his works "The Procession" and "Stampede."

81. These issues are fully discussed in the next chapter.

82. For the much-discussed topic of Kashmiri Sufism, see the Introduction. The schism between Shia and Sunni took place during the eighth century CE, as a consequence of

protracted doctrinal and political controversies that culminated in the deaths of the Prophet Muhammad's grandsons, Hasan and Hussain, at the battle of Karbala (680 CE). While far from monolithic, Shia identity is distinguished by persistent dissatisfaction with the ruling house, divergent understanding of the legal tool of interpretation *(ijtehad),* intense emotional investment in the memory of the martyrdom of Hasan and Hussain, and the practice of dissimulation *(takiyya).* In its overt interest in the expressive, the emotive, the charismatic and the esoteric, Shia Islam overlaps substantially with the conglomeration of mystic, ascetic, and individualistic movements within Islam gathered under the umbrella of Sufism. See Ananya Jahanara Kabir, "Islam," in Poddar and David Johnson, eds., *A Historical Companion to Postcolonial Literatures,* 247–52; for Shia mourning rituals, see, for instance, Hussain, "The Mourning of History," 78–88.

83. For the overlap between Sufism and Shia Islam, particularly in the South Asian context, see Hyder, *Reliving Karbala,* 105–36.

84. See the work of the classic scholars of Sufism, Annemarie Schimmel, Henry Corbin, and Louis Massignon. See also Netton, *Muslim Neoplatonists;* and Basu and Werbner, ed., *Embodying Charisma.*

85. See chapter 2.

86. Pietz, "Problem, I."

87. Deleuze and Guattari, *Anti-Oedipus,* 183.

4. Conscripting Silence

1. Koul and Schmidt, *Kashmiri,* especially their conclusion, 66–67: "To be Kashmiri means to be bilingual." The second remark is from Tickoo, "Kashmiri," in Skutnab-Kangas and Phillipson, eds., *Linguistic Human Rights,* 317–33, at 326. See also Tickoo, "When Is a Native Language Worth Teaching? Native Languages and English in India," in Khoo, Kreher, and Wong, eds., *Towards Global Multilingualism,* 29–44.

2. Note here my use of the verb "configure," which points away from reified assumptions of Koshur's neglected condition toward attempts to deconstruct why Kashmiris insist on this neglect.

3. Both Koul (also spelled "Kaul") and Tickoo (also spelled "Tiku," "Tikku," or "Tikkoo") are Kashmiri Pandit surnames.

4. Derrida, *"Fors,"* in Abraham and Torok, *Wolf Man's Magic Word,* xi–xlviii.

5. Ibid.

6. Nicholas Rand, "Translator's Introduction," in Abraham and Torok, *Wolf Man's Magic Word,* il and lxix.

7. For a detailed examination of the crypt in Derrida's writing, including *"Fors,"* see Laurent Milesi, "Jacques Derrida in Secret(s)," in Evans, Hughes, and Letissier, eds., *Secrets, Mysteries, Silences,* 113–24.

8. Recall here Mbembe's formulation of the postcolony, cited in the Introduction.

9. On the State as wild zone, see Buck-Morss, *Dreamworld and Catastrophe,* 2–11.

10. I am grateful to Professors Rahman Rahi and Majrooh Rashid for helping me translate this poem on three separate occasions, August 2004, April 2005, and August 2006, at the Department of Kashmiri, Kashmir University, Srinagar.

11. For Rasul Mir and Mahmood Gami, see Braj Kachru, "The Middle Period (1750–1900)," in his *Kashmiri Literature,* 34–43; and Trilokinath Raina, "Longer Narrative

Poetry," in Kachru, *Kashmiri Literature,* 65–77. For processes of thesaurization, see Dubois, *Sowing the Body,* 107–8; see also Connor, *Dumbstruck,* 53.

12. Agha Shahid Ali, "I Dream I Am At the Ghat of the Only World," in his *Rooms Are Never Finished,* 97–104, at 104. Rahi received a Sahitya Akademi Award in 1961 and a Sahitya Akademi Fellowship in 1999.

13. Agha Shahid Ali, Preface to "Lenox Hill," *Rooms,* 15. The subsequent quotes in this paragraph are from "Lenox Hill," *Rooms,* 17–19.

14. Ibid., 17; emphasis in the original.

15. Merleau-Ponty, *Phenomenology of Perception,* 187.

16. I have developed this point further in my "Language in Conflict in the Poetry of Agha Shahid Ali," in Huggan and Klasen, eds., *Perspectives on Endangerment,* 199–208.

17. On the *pharmakon,* see Derrida, "Plato's Pharmacy," in his *Dissemination,* 65–117.

18. For Koshur in the context of the three-language policy in India, see Tickoo, "Native Language"; see also my larger argument for the affective politics of Urdu versus Koshur in "Koshur Today: Death, Survival or Revival?," in Anchimbe, ed., *Linguistic Identity,* 182–200.

19. For these politics of Hindi/Urdu, see Orsini, and Alok Rai, *Hindi Nationalism.*

10. I thank Irfan Hassan for this information.

21. Agha Shahid Ali, *Country,* 30–34.

22. See Tickoo, "Kashmiri."

23. Mridu Rai, *Hindu Rulers,* 87.

24. M. K. Raina, "Bhand Pather," 30–43.

25. For this information, I thank M. K. Raina, whom I was fortunate enough to observe in rehearsal at Srinagar, August 2005.

26. M. K. Raina, "Bhand Pather," 42. This Hindi play "Bhand Duhaayee," by Moti Lal Kemmu, led to the playwright composing several similar contemporary *Bhand Pather* in Koshur; for details, see Trilokinath Raina, *History of Kashmiri Literature,* 184–85.

27. M. K.Raina, "Bhand Pather," 43.

28. Rushdie, *Shalimar the Clown.*

29. Blog article at http://www.nouse.co.uk/2005/11/30/arguing-with-the-world/ [last accessed 24 October 2008].

30. *The Play Is On* (dir. Pankaj Rishi Kumar, 2000): this sensitive documentary on the bhands layers the filmmaker's visits to the Bhand community of Wathora village onto footage of the Bhands performing in India in order to dissect the relationship between State patronage of "folk art" and his own subjectivity as Indian citizen.

31. See the first frontispiece to Rushdie, *Shalimar.*

32. See, for instance, Segal, "Salman Rushdie," 611–18; Teverson, "Fairy Tale Politics," 444–66, and Mukherjee, "Politics and Children's Literature," 163–77.

33. Agha Shahid Ali, "The Blessèd Word," in his *Country without a Post Office,* 15; compare Rushdie, *Haroun,* 40.

34. Zutshi, *Languages of Belonging,* 3.

35. I have argued this point in my "Subjectivities, Memories, Loss," 245–64.

36. Abir Bazaz, "Srinagar-Sarajevo.".

37. Connor, *Dumbstruck,* 14–20.

38. See Eyal Weizman, "The Politics of Verticality," www.opendemocracy.net/conflict-politicsverticality/issue.jsp [last accessed 24 October 2008].

39. There is, in fact, considerable similarity between some of the terminology used to describe the urban conflict zone by Weizmann and that by Bazaz in his "Srinagar-Sarajevo" essay.

40. Mbembe, "Necropolitics," 26.

41. Van den Abbeele, "The Persecution of Writing," 3.

42. Ibid., 12.

43. Mbembe, "Necropolitics," 40; Mbembe cites here the notion of biopower elaborated in Michel Foucault, *Il faut défendre la société: Cours au Collège de France, 1975–1976* (Paris: Seuil, 1997).

44. Ibid., 26.

45. Van den Abbele, "The Persecution of Writing," 12.

46. Cited in ibid., 12.

47. Cited in Kabir, "Kashmir: Rebuilding an Identity."

48. Agha Shahid Ali, *Country without a Post Office,* 24–26.

49. Bensmaia and Melehy, "The Phantom Mediators," 85–97.

50. Agha Shahid Ali, "The Blessed Word," 17; compare Fanon, *The Wretched of the Earth,* 39: "The native town is a crouching village, a town on its knees."

51. Van den Abbeele, "The Persecution of Writing," 12.

52. See Rushdie, "Boonyi," in his *Shalimar,* 217–41.

53. Mattoo, trans. and ed., *The Stranger Beside Me* and *Contemporary Kashmiri Short Stories.* Neither collection provides details of when these stories were written and where they were first published. Nevertheless, most of the writers cited here, as discussed by Trilokinath Raina, *A History of Kashmiri Literature,* 190–205, flourished between the late 1950s and the 1980s, that is, before the events of 1989 and beyond. I am grateful to Dr Neerja Mattoo for this information.

54. The genesis of the Koshur short story in the early 1950s is linked with the birth of the Kashmiri Progressive Writers Group that, like its northern Indian counterpart, was strongly influenced by socialist views of art. See Trilokinath Raina, *A History of Kashmiri Literature,* 190–91, and 192–205, for later phases in the Koshur short story's development.

55. Sohan Lal Kaul, "The Lost Self," from Mattoo, *Contemporary Kashmiri Short Stories,* 79–82.

56. Nayeema Ahmad, "I Am Still Alive," in Mattoo, *Stranger Beside Me,* 71–76, 76 and 75.

57. Anees Hamadani, "The Burnt Out Sun," in Mattoo, *Stranger Beside Me,* 133–37.

58. Mbembe, see the Introduction.

59. Ali Muhammad Lone, "The Void," Mattoo, *Stranger Beside Me,* 123–26.

60. Ibid., 126.

61. Cf. the discussion of the surgeon as clinical re-assembler of the body shattered through the shock of modernity, in Buck-Morss, "Aesthetics and Anasethetics," 27–33.

62. See Hamadani, "Burnt-Out Sun," and A. G. Athar, "My Brother's Enemy," in Mattoo, *Stranger Beside Me,* 29–32, and Hari Kishan Koul, "Tomorrow," *Stranger Beside Me,* 15–26, respectively.

63. Athar, "The Enemy," in Mattoo, *Stranger Beside Me.*

64. Hari Kishan Koul, "The Mourners," in Mattoo, *Stranger Beside Me,* 14–25, at 25.

65. Connor, *Dumbstruck,* 32.

66. Mbembe, "Necropolitics," 22.

67. As I have argued in the context of Ali's poetry; see Kabir, "Language in Conflict."

68. Hriday Kaul Bharati, "The Sunless Tomorrow," in Mattoo, *Contemporary Kashmiri Short Stories,* 106-10. For the conceptualization of the beginning, middle, and end of a text, see *Aristotle's Poetics,* trans. Malcolm Heath (London; New York, N.Y.: Penguin Books, 1996). A critique is offered by Landow, *Hypertext 3.0.n.*

69. Connor, *Dumbstruck,* 34.

70. This happened to me in Srinagar, December 2003, when I was being driven to the airport by two Kashmiri friends.

71. See my discussion of . . . *Yahaan* in chapter 1.

72. Interview with Professor Shafi "Shauq," Srinagar, April 2004.

73. Mbembe, in the Introduction.

74. This poem, written in the 1990s, was made available to me in its Hindi translation by Dr Naseem Shifai, Srinagar, August 2003. Its Kashmiri original appeared in her collection *Darichi Mastrith* [Open Window] (Srinagar: Kashmir Publications, 1999). The English translation is mine.

75. See Connor, *Dumbstruck,* 53; Dubois, *Sowing the Body,* 28.

76. Connor, *Dumbstruck,* 35–37.

77. These observations depend on various conversations with Kashmiris on the topic of "mother tongue" that I conducted during April 2004, August 2004, and August 2005.

78. Basharat Peer, "Militarising the Narrative in Kashmir," unpublished paper, April 2004.

79. On Radio Kashmir's role in promoting Koshur, see Kachru, *Kashmiri Literature,* 89–99, and Raina, *Kashmiri Literature,* 182–83.

80. See Kabir, "Language in Conflict."

81. On Ghulam Ahmad Mahjoor (1885–1952) as a pioneer of modern Koshur poetry, see Kachru, *Kashmiri Literature,* 45–62, and Trilokinath Raina, *A History of Kashmiri Literature,* 102–11. I am also deeply indebted to the Mahjoor family of Srinagar and London for several valuable discussions from August 2004 onward concerning Kashmiri cultural politics.

82. On *Gaash,* published by Majhoor's son Mohammed Amin, see Kachru, *Kashmiri Literature,* 93, and Trilokinath Raina, *A History of Kashmiri Literature,* 166; both are taciturn about the reasons for its demise.

83. Interview with Abdal Mahjoor and Nayeema Ahmad, Srinagar, August 2004; for literature and politics in Kashmir during the 1950s and 1960s, see Kachru, *Kashmiri Literature,* 63–83.

84. See the documentary on Koshur cultural politics by Abir Bazaz and Meenu Gaur, dir., *Kun'ear* (1999).

85. Interview with Farooq Nazki, Srinagar, April 2004.

86. Ghulam Rasool Santosh, "The Voice," in Mattoo, *Stranger Beside Me,* 92–99.

87. See Kapur, "SubTerrain," in Kapur, *Body. City,* 47, cited in the Introduction.

5. The Other Possibility

1. Interview with Kshama Kaul, Jammu, April 2004.

2. For "legitimate fear," see Evans, "A Departure from History," 22; for "fear," see Bazaz and Gaur, *Paradise on a River of Hell.* More generally, see Madan, *Family and Kinship.*

3. Agnishekhar, *Kisi Bhi Samay.*

4. As increasingly explicated by the "visual turn" in South Asian studies, for example, within the work of Arjun Appadurai, Rachel Dwyer, Kajri Jain, Christopher Pinney, and Sumathi Ramaswamy, that should be read alongside Geeta Kapur's art-critical examination of Indian modernity.

5. One of the newest technologies congenial to Hindutva othering of the Muslim is the World Wide Web, the most prolific medium for the circulation of the words of

Hindutva ideologues such as François Gautier, from whose *Rewriting Indian History,* 62, I take my first epigraph; see also http://www.francoisgautier.com/Written%20Material/KP%20IN%20LONDON.doc [last accessed on 24 October 2008]. These issues are well explicated by Will J. Grant, "The Space of the Nation," 321–47.

6. On maps, see Ramaswami, "Geo-Body"; for the colonial census, see Bernard Cohn, "The Census, Social Structure and Objectification in South Asia," in his *An Anthropologist Among the Historians,* 224–54. For the significance of the lingam within Shaivism, see Richard H. Davis, *Lives of Indian Images* (Princeton, N.J.: Princeton University Press, 1997), 23, 30, 33, and passim.

7. Note here the critique of the Indian army's role in Kashmir by P. R. Chari, "Protecting Human Rights," 224.

8. Interview with Rajendar Tiku, Jammu, August 2003.

9. On the "place holder," see Brown, "Thing Theory," 4. On ekphrasis, see chapter 2.

10. See Schwenger, "Words and the Murder of the Thing," 99–113.

11. See Anderson, *Imagined Communities,* 163–85, and Grant, "Space of the Nation."

12. See Antomarini, "The Acoustic Prehistory of Poetry," 368; I have theorized and contrasted narrative and lyric impulses in Kabir, "Beyond Narrative."

13. See Paul Ricoeur, *Time and Narrative,* 3 vols. (Chicago: University of Chicago Press, 1984–88). See also Susan Lohafer and Jo Ellyn Clarey, ed., *Short Story Theory at a Crossroads,* co-edited with Jo Ellyn Clarey (Baton Rouge: Louisiana State University Press, 1989).

14. Interview with Rajendar Tiku, Jammu, August 2003.

15. These details are taken from the book's front and back matter.

16. The interviewee's list included Salman Khurshid, *Beyond Terrorism: A New Hope for Kashmir* (Delhi: UBS, 1995); Benjamin Netanyahu, *Fighting Terrorism* (London: Allen and Busby, 1996); Rafiq Zakaria, *Communal Rage in Secular India* (Mumbai: Popular Prakashan, 2003), and *The Man Who Divided India* (Delhi: Sangam Books, 2002); and Kuldeep Singh Bajwa, *Jammu and Kashmir War 1947–48* (Delhi: Har-Anand Publications, 2003).

17. See http://www.hindujagruti.org/activities/campaigns/national/hindu-gencide/; http://ia.rediff.com/cms/print.jsp?docpath=//news/2007/feb/16francois.htm; http://in.rediff.com/news/2004/jul/30franc.htm;http://www.tribuneindia.com/2003/20030913/nation.htm#2; http://www.rediff.com/news/2003/oct/21franc.htm [all sites last accessed 24 October 2008].

18. These comments, that I keep anonymous, were made by Kashmiris I met during April 2004, August 2004, and August 2005.

19. See the Introduction.

20. Interview with Rajendar Tiku, Jammu, April 2004; for Aurel Stein's comment, see chapter 3.

21. As cited, for instance, by Mridu Rai, *Hindu Rulers,* 43.

22. Rushdie, *Shalimar,* 296–97 and 308–9.

23. Peace and Reconciliation Meeting, Badami Villa, Srinagar, August 2004. See also the Introduction.

24. Zutshi, *Languages of Belonging,* 254.

25. Evans, "Kashmiri Pandits," 29.

26. Koul, *The Tiger Ladies,* 12.

27. Ibid., 104.

28. Evans, "Kashmiri Pandits," 27: "Drew [a nineteenth-century colonial commentator] describes their chief occupation as writing."

29. Interview with Bimla Raina, Jammu, April 2004; see Bimla Raina, *Reshy Maalyon Myon.*

30. Krishna Kumar, *Political Agenda of Education,* 17: "The manner in which collective self-identity came to be defined in the Hindi belt from the 20s onwards was a new and uniquely northern phenomenon. Language and education became the means to evolve a Hindu identity in which the rejection of English was but one layer sitting above a painstakingly assembled mass of anti-Muslim consciousness." See also his comments on the Sanskritisation of Hindi (126–29), on Hindustani as the "mixed code of Hindi and Urdu" (144–45), and his [translated] quote from Purushottam Tandon, *Shashan Path Nidarshan* (Delhi: Atmaram, 1959): "The basis of our culture is our country's language and our country's script; to be fond of Persian is one thing, and what language the country should have is another" (115).

31. Henny Sender, *Kashmiri Pandits,* 301.

32. Translations from the Hindi are mine. See "Bhagey Pandit" (dated 12/6/90), "Kisi Bhi Samay," 117, and "Mahavipada" (dated 17/11/90); ibid., 111–13.

33. See Evans, "Kashmiri Pandits," 30–31, for a summary of Panun Kashmir's development, including the eventual split between "Panun Kashmir" and the "Panun Kashmir Movement."

34. On Nadim, see Kachru, *Kashmiri Literature,* 64–71.

35. See Orsini, *Hindi Public Sphere;* Rai, *Hindi Nationalism;* and Ramaswamy, *Passions of the Tongue.* Evans, "Kashmiri Pandits," 31, sees the Pandits as a marginalized group, a conclusion that differs from mine somewhat.

36. See Rai, *Hindi Nationalism.*

37. As explained to me by Agnishekhar, Jammu, April 2004. For some instances of this literature of exile and its criticism, see Sanjana Koul's novel *Pashanyug* (Age of Stone) (Chandigarh: Haryana Aadhar Prakashan, 2000), Kshama Koul's poetry anthology *Baadalon Mein Aag* (Clouds on Fire), her memoir *Samay Ke Baad* (After Time), and novel *Dardpur* (Unhappy Town), Agnishekhar, *Kalpvriksh Ke Chhaya Mein* (In the Shade of the Tree of Time) (Delhi: Saaransh Prakashan, 2003), and Bhushanlal Koul, *Sahitya aur Visthapan: Sandharb Kashmir* (Literature and Displacement: Exiled Kashmir) (Jammu: Sanmukh Prakashan, 2003); the latter has a preface by the sociolinguist Omkar Koul, cited in the first epigraph of chapter 5.

38. See the following in *Kisi Bhi Samay:* "Raja Teri Nagari Mein Chor," 15–18; "Mihiragula Aa Raha Hai," 19–21 (this poem refers to the same Hun king cited by Agha Shahid Ali in "Lenox Hill"); "Pandrethan Ki Mandir," 78; "Behti Hui Vitasta," 55–56, "Shankaracharya Parbat," 81–82.

39. A position carefully explicated by Bose, *Kashmir.*

40. "Hangul," *Kisi Bhi Samay,* 57–58.

41. See Sender, *Kashmiri Pandits,* 47–91. For the collective memorialization of these departures, see also Koul, *Tiger Ladies.*

42. *Sheen* ("Snow," dir. Ashok Pandit, 2004).

43. White, *The Content of the Form.*

44. For the relationship of sequentiality and "the end," see Barbara Herrnstein Smith, *Poetic Closure: A Study of How Poems End* (Chicago: University of Chicago Press, 1968).

45. For "grasping together," see Louis O. Mink, *Historical Understanding,* ed. Brian Fay et al. (Ithaca: Cornell University Press, 1987), 49.

46. On narrative and closure, see Kermode, *The Sense of an Ending,* and D. A. Miller, *Narrative and Its Discontents: Problems of Closure in the Traditional Novel* (Princeton, N.J.: Princeton University Press, 1981).

47. Anderson, *Imagined Communities,* and Bhabha, "DissemiNation," in his *The Location of Culture,* 139–70. For a critique of Anderson, see Chatterjee, *The Nation and its Fragments.*

48. Seminal examples being the work of Caruth, ed., *Trauma,* and her *Unclaimed Experience;* also Bal, et al., ed., *Acts of Memory.*

49. Note the analytical reliance on narrative in Amena Mohsin, *The Politics of Nationalism: The Case of the Chittagong Hill Tracts Bangladesh* (Dhaka, The University Press, 1998); Varshney, *Ethnic Conflict and Civic Life,* and Chaddha, *Ethnicity, Security and Separatism in India.*

50. See http://indersalim.livejournal.com/ [last accessed on 24 October 2008].

51. For the text full text, see ibid., 23 July 2006. My reluctance to walk over the image probably arose from internalizations of South Asian cultural habits concerning the "animate" quality of images, for which see Davis, *Indian Images.*

52. Rama Mani, *Beyond Retribution: Seeking Justice in the Shadows of War* (Cambridge: Polity Press, 2002).

53. Compare the essay by Kshama Kaul, "A Pandit Story," in Butalia, ed., *Speaking Peace,* 185–88, with the caveats by Sheba Chachhi, "Finding Face: Images of Women from the Kashmir Valley," ibid., 189–226, at 191: "The image of the raped woman is a key ideological tool used by both the militants and the Pandits to justify their political positions." See also her critique of the collaged photograph, as discussed in my chapter 2: "Unwittingly, these photographs—of armed men, dead men, leaders, faceless victims—repeat current tropes of Kashmir in the mainstream media." Chachhi also critiques "the displaced Kashmiri Pandit community [that] has its own version, equally morbid. Sadly rather than bringing home the extent of suffering more forcefully, the repeated showcasing of wounds defeats its own purpose."

54. Van Alphen, *Caught by History,* 195.

55. As I have elaborated in Kabir, "Gender, Memory, Trauma."

56. Agha Shahid Ali, "Farewell," *Country without a Post Office,* 21–23 and 93.

57. Ibid., 21–23: "My memory is again in the way of your history," "Your history gets in the way of my memory," "Your memory gets in the way of my memory," "My memory keeps getting in the way of your history."

58. Ibid., 21.

59. I have elaborated this point in Kabir, "Language in Conflict."

60. Ali, *Country without a Post Office,* 66.

61. http://indersalim.livejournal.com/, 23 July 2006 [last accessed on 24 October 2008].

62. Michael Ondaatje, *Anil's Ghost* (London: Bloomsbury, 2000), 307.

63. On the practical and political problems of mimesis, see Bleiker, "The Aesthetic Turn," 551–28.

64. I thank Yasin Malik for making available to me details of this event (private communication, April 2005).

65. Ranjana Khanna, "Signatures of the Impossible," in http://www.law.duke.edu/shell/cite.pl?11+Duke+J.+Gender+L.+&+Pol'y+69 [last accessed on 24 October 2008].

66. Chacchi, "Finding Face," 191.

67. For the convergence of realist narrative and visual perspectivism, see Ermarth, *Realism and Consensus: Time, Space and Narrative,* for a South Asian(ist) view, see Christopher Pinney on "the fiction of the unseeing "I" in his "Piercing the Skin of the Idol," in Pinney and Thomas, eds., *Beyond Aesthetics,* 157–80.

68. Chachhi, "Finding Face," 193. The installation has been exhibited at The Women's Conference in Beijing, 2000; soon thereafter in Delhi, and most recently at the Gallerie-sponsored exhibition, "Identity, Alienation, Amity" in Bombay, August 2005.

69. Interview with Sheba Chachhi, Delhi, December 2002. I return to the "third space" in the chapter 6.

70. Interviews with Rajendar Tiku, August 2003 and April 2004; see also Ananya Jahanara Kabir, "The Other Possibility," *ArtIndia* 9, no. 1 (2004): 30.

71. Interview with Rajendar Tiku, Jammu, August 2003.

72. Ibid.

73. This exhibition took place at the Art Heritage Gallery, Delhi, through December 2002.

74. Interview with Sheba Chachhi, Delhi, December 2002.

75. Ibid.

6. New Maps of Longing

1. Nilima Sheikh, quoted in http://www.saffronart.com/artist/artistprofile.aspx?artistid=104&a=Nilima%20%20Sheikh [last accessed 24 October 2008].

2. Kapur, "Dismantled Norms: Apropos an Indian/Asian Avantgarde," in Kapur, *When Was Modernism,* 336 and 411.

3. Interview with Nilima Sheikh, Manchester, August 2002; Kapur, "Dismantled Norms," 396.

4. Ali, *Country without a Post Office,* 27. For Ali's play with tenses, see Kabir, "Language in Conflict."

5. Interview with Nilima Sheikh, Manchester, August 2002.

6. For a philosophical exposition on this dimension of the miniature, see Pamuk, *My Name is Red,* trans. Erdag Göknar.

7. Sheikh, "Making of a Visual Language: Thoughts on Mughal Painting," 7.

8. Ibid., 23.

9. See Desai, *Conversations with Traditions.*

10. On Pakistani miniature artists, see Dalmia and Hashmi, *Memory, Metaphor, Mutations,* 9–68.

11. Interview with Sheikh, Manchester, August 2002.

12. See chapter 4.

13. Interview with Sheikh, Manchester, August 2002.

14. See chapter 5.

15. See chapter 2.

16. Interview with Sheikh, Manchester, August 2002.

17. Interview with Sheikh, Manchester, August 2002. On the events in Gujarat in 2002, see Varadarajan, ed., *Gujarat,* and Dionne Bunsha, *Scarred: Experiments with Violence in Gujarat* (Delhi: Penguin India, 2006).

18. Interview with Nilima Sheikh, Delhi, December 2002.

19. See chapter 6.

20. I acknowledge most gratefully here all those in Bombay who allowed me to view these paintings in their homes and galleries: Cawas Bharucha, Shireen Gandhi, Usha Gowde, and Simeen Oshidar.

21. Agha Shahid Ali, "I Have Loved," in his *The Final Collections,* 1. I thank Sakshi Gallery, Bombay, for enabling me to view these paintings.

22. I thank Tatiana Cuevas, Chaitanya Sambrani, and Gulammohammed Sheikh for enabling me to view the Firdaus scrolls at the Museo Rufino Tamayo, Mexico City, and Nilima Sheikh for showing me the two latest, yet incomplete scrolls in Delhi, November 2006.

23. Telephone communication with Nilima Sheikh, March 2004.

24. Khanna, "Post-palliative."

25. Telephone communication with Nilima Sheikh, March 2004.

26. Telephone communication with Nilima Sheikh, December 2005. The stencils she uses are made by Sanjay Soni of the family of Vishnu Prasad Jadiya. Based in Mathura, North India, this family keeps alive the craft tradition of *sanjhi,* or paper-cutting for ritualistic purposes, and who now create plastic stencils for a variety of new purposes, including the requirements of studio-based artists such as Sheikh; this collaboration illustrates both the fruitful relationships between "art" and "craft" in contemporary India and the flexibility of living craft practices across South Asia.

27. Ali, *Country without a Post Office,* 66 and 51.

28. See Ananya Jahanara Kabir, "The Sacred, the Feminine and the Ecumenical," in Pollock, ed., *The Sacred and the Feminine,* 75–87.

29. Ali *Country without a Post Office,* 21–23, 48–51.

30. For "geo-piety," see the Introduction. For Hanuman and his relationship to Rama and Sita, see Lutgendorf, *Hanuman's Tale.*

31. See the Introduction.

32. See Ali, *Country without a Post Office,* 93.

33. E-mail conversation with Nilima Sheikh, September 2005.

34. On shawl maps, see Zutshi, *Languages of Belonging,* 80–105.

35. See chapters 5 and 6.

36. Calcutta, December 2007.

37. See chapter 5.

38. See Rangaswamy et al., ed., *ArtSouthAsia.* Multiply curated, the exhibitions ran concurrently from July to September 2002 at Manchester Art Gallery (art from India), Oldham Art Gallery (art from Bangladesh), the University Art Gallery Liverpool (art from Sri Lanka) and the Harris Museum & Art Gallery Preston (art from Pakistan).

39. "Edge of Desire," curated by Chaitanya Sambrani; see Sambrani et al., ed. *Edge of Desire.*

40. Again, I thank Simeen Oshidar for so graciously enabling me to experience this artwork.

41. Arjun Appadurai, "The Thing Itself," in *ArtIndia,* 40–46, 42.

42. Ibid., 44.

43. Ibid., 46.

44. I take these ideas from Shusterman, *Pragmatist Aesthetics.*

45. Interview with Sheikh, Manchester, August 2002.

46. Bleiker, "Learning from Art," 418.

47. Bleiker, "The Aesthetic Turn," 529.

48. Ibid., 529.

49. Shapiro, "Sounds of Nationhood," 583.

50. See Sheikh's scroll on the Partition of India, "River: Carrying Across, Leaving Behind" (40 ft. × 6 ft.), exhibited at Bombay's Sakshi Gallery in June 2004, and the review by Jain, "Vision by Night."

51. Neloufer De Mel, *Women and the Nation's Narrative: Gender and Nationalism in Twentieth Century Sri Lanka* (New Delhi: Kali for Women, 2001), 1–56.

52. The display format in Berlin enabled this alternative viewing experience, although Sheikh had wanted this format at the Manchester exhibition itself (interview with Nilima Sheikh, Manchester, August 2002, and Delhi, April 2004.)

53. On South Asian craft and femininity, see Nita Kumar, *The Artisans of Banaras.*

54. Bhabha, "Introduction: Locations of Culture," in his *Location of Culture,* 1–18.

55. Deleuze and Guattari, *Kafka,* 27.

56. See the Introduction.

57. Smith, "Will and Sacrifice," 572.

58. See here Zutshi, *Languages,* 118–68.

59. Basu and Werbner, "The Embodiment of Charisma," in their *Embodying Charisma,* 3–30, 3. See also Katherine Pratt Ewing, *Arguing Sainthood: Islam, Modernity and Psychoanalysis* (Durham, N.C.: Duke University Press, 1997).

60. I refer here to the debate surrounding the exact nature of South Asian "syncretism." It is now acknowledged that the labeling of popular South Asian Islam as "syncretic" participates within a complex discursive tradition of subordinating it to Hinduism while cloaking, too, the myriad Hinduisms that exist across South Asia. Rather than read the relationship between the two religions as syncretic, glossed as the indigenization of Islam, revisionist scholars are now calling for a model that re-reads that relationship as the Islamicisation of the indigenous. The debate is usefully summarized by Basu and Werbner, "Embodiment of Charisma," 19; see also Eaton, *Essays on Islam and Indian History.*

61. See Basu and Werbner, "The Embodiment of Charisma," 8.

62. For *qawwali* see Qureshi, *Sufi Music From India and Pakistan*; Omar Khalidi, "Qawwali and Mahfil-i-sama," in Troll, ed., *Muslim Shrines in India,* 257–61; and S. B. Abbas, *Female Voice in Sufi Ritual: Devotional Practices of Pakistan and India.*

63. Mark R. Woodward, "Modernity and the Disenchantment of Life: A Muslim-Christian Contrast," and Lukas Werth, "Pakistan: A Critique of the Concept of Modernity," both in *Islam in the Era of Globalization: Muslim Attitudes towards Modernity and Identity,* ed. Meuleman, 111–42 and 143–70, respectively.

64. Ananya Jahanara Kabir, "The Sacred, the Feminine and the Ecumenical."

65. Basu and Werbner, "Embodiment of Charisma," 8.

66. Bleiker, "Art after 9/11," 87 and 90.

67. See Mani, "Beyond Retribution," 12–15.

68. Chandhoke, "Broken Social Contracts," 2.

69. Ankersmit, *Political Representation,* 196; see also ibid. 193–213, where he discusses the creative dynamism of compromise over the static nature of consensus.

70. Deleuze, *Difference and Repetition,* 144.

Bibliography

Abdullah, Sheikh Mohammad. "Kashmir, India and Pakistan." *Foreign Affairs* 43, no. 3 (1965): 528–53.

Abraham, Nicholas, and Maria Torok. *The Shell and the Kernel: Renewals of Psychoanalysis, I.* Edited, translated, and with an introduction by Nicholas T. Rand. Chicago: University of Chicago Press, 1994.

———. *The Wolf Man's Magic Word: A Cryptonymy*. Translated by Nicholas Rand, foreword by Jacques Derrida. Minneapolis: University of Minnesota Press, 1986.

Abrams, Philip. "Notes on the Difficulty of Studying the State." *Journal of Historical Sociology* 1, no. 1 (1988): 58–89.

Adorno, Theodor. *Aesthetic Theory*. Edited by Gretel Adorno and Rolf Tiedermann, translated by C. Lenhardt. London: Routledge and Kegan Paul, 1984.

Agamben, Giorgio. *Remnants of Auschwitz: The Witness and the Archive*. Translated by Daniel Heller-Roazen. New York: Zone Books, 1999.

Aggarwal, Ravina. *Beyond Lines of Control: Performance and Politics on the Disputed Borders of Ladakh, India*. Durham, N.C.: Duke University Press, 2004.

Agnishekhar. *Kisi Bhi Samay*. Hapud: Sambhavana Prakashan, 1992.

Alarcón, Daniel Cooper. *The Aztec Palimpsest: Mexico in The Modern Imagination*. Tucson: University of Arizona Press, 1997.

Ali, Agha Shahid. *The Country without a Post Office*. New York: Norton, 1998.

———. *The Half Inch Himalayas*. Middletown, Conn.: Wesleyan University Press, 1987.

———. "A Poetic Response." *Indian Design and Interiors Magazine* (1999): 23–24.

———. *Rooms Are Never Finished*. New York and London: W. W. Norton and Co., 2002.

———. *The Final Collections: Call Me Ishmael Tonight*. Delhi: Permanent Black, 2004.

Ali, Daud, ed. *Invoking the Past: The Uses of History in South Asia*. Oxford: Oxford University Press, 1999.

All India Handicrafts Board Ministry of Production. *Handicrafts of India*. New Delhi: Government of India, 1955.

Alloula, Malek. *The Colonial Harem*. Minneapolis: University of Minnesota Press, 1986.

AlSayyad, Nezar, ed. *Consuming Tradition, Manufacturing Heritage: Global Norms and Urban Forms in the Age of Tourism*. London: Routledge, 2001.

Anderson, Benedict. *Imagined Communities: Reflections on the Origin and Spread of Nationalism*. Revised edition. London: Verso, 1991.

Ankersmit, F. R. *Political Representation*. Stanford: Stanford University Press, 2002.

Antomarini, Brunella. "The Acoustic Prehistory of Poetry." Translated by Susan Stewart. *New Literary History* 35 (2004): 355–72.

Anzaldúa, Gloria. *Borderlands/La Frontera: The New Mestiza*. San Francisco: Aunt Lute, 1987.

Appadurai, Arjun. "Disjuncture and Difference in the Global Cultural Economy." *Public Culture* 2, no. 2 (1990): 1–24.

———, ed. *The Social Life of Things: Commodities in Cultural Perspective*. Cambridge: Cambridge University Press, 1986.

———. "The Thing Itself." *ArtIndia: The Art News Magazine of India* 9, no. 4 (2005): 40–46.

Appiah, Kwame Anthony. "Is the Post- in Postmodernism the Post- in Postcolonial?" *Critical Inquiry* 17 (1991): 336–57.

Apter, Emily, and William Pietz, eds. *Fetishism as Cultural Discourse.* Ithaca: Cornell University Press, 1993.

Atlas of Pakistan. Published under the direction of Major General Anis Ali Syed, Surveyor General of Pakistan. Rawalpindi: Survey of Pakistan, 1985.

Aysnley, Harriet Murray. *Our Visit to Hindostán, Kashmir, and Ladakh.* London: W. H. Allen and Co., 1879.

Bal, Mieke, et al., eds. *Acts of Memory: Cultural Recall in the Present.* Hanover, N.H., and London: University Press of New England, 1999.

Bamzai, P. M. K. *Cultural and Political History of Kashmir,* vol. 2. New Delhi: M.D. Publications, 1994.

Barthes, Roland. *Camera Lucida: Reflections on Photography.* Translated by Richard Howard. London: Jonathan Cape, 1982.

Basu, Helene, and Pnina Werbner, eds. *Embodying Charisma: Modernity, Locality and the Performance of Emotion in Sufi Cults.* London and New York: Routledge, 1998.

Battye, Evelyn Desirée. *The Kashmir Residency: Memories of 1939 and 1940.* Putney: BACSA, 1997.

Bazaz, Abir. "Srinagar-Sarajevo," in *Sarai Reader 1002: The Cities of Everyday Life,* http://www.sarai.net/publications/readers/02-the-cities-of-everyday-life/06srinagar.pdf [last accessed 24 October 2008].

Bazaz, Prem Nath. *Kashmir in Crucible.* New Delhi: Pamposh Publications, 1967.

Benjamin, Walter. *Illuminations.* Translated by Harry Zohn. London: Pimlico, 1999.

———. *Selected Writings,* vol. 4: 1938–40. Cambridge, Mass.: Bellknapp Press, 2003.

Bensmaia, Reda, and Hasan Melehy. "The Phantom Mediators: Reflections on the Nature of the Violence in Algeria." *Diacritics* 27, no. 2 (1997): 85–97.

Bhabha, Homi K. *The Location of Culture.* London: Routledge, 1994.

———, ed. *Nation and Narration.* New York: Routledge, 1990.

Bharucha, Rustam. "On the Border of Fascism: Manufacturing Consent in *Roja.*" *Economic and Political Weekly* 29, no. 3 (1994): 1389–95.

Bhasin, Kamla, and Ritu Menon. *Borders and Boundaries: Women in India's Partition.* New Delhi: Kali for Women, 1998.

Biddick, Kathleen. *The Shock of Medievalism.* Durham, N.C.: Duke University Press, 1998.

Bleiker, Ronald. "The Aesthetic Turn in International Political Theory." *Millennium: Journal of International Studies* 30, no. 3 (2001): 551–28.

———. "Art after 9/11." *Alternatives* 31 (2006): 77–90.

———. "Learning from Art: A Reply to Holden's Literature and World Politics." *Global Society* 17, no. 4 (2003): 415–28.

Boorstin, Daniel. *The Image: A Guide to Pseudo-Events in America.* New York: Atheneum, 1973.

Bose, Sumantra. *Kashmir: Roots of Conflict, Paths to Peace.* New Delhi: Sage, 2003.

———. *The Challenge in Kashmir: Democracy, Self-Determination, and a Just Peace.* New Delhi; and London: Sage, in association with the Book Review Literary Trust, 1997.

Bourdieu, Pierre, and Luc Boltansky. *Photography: A Middle-Brow Art.* Translated by Shaun Whiteside. Cambridge: Polity, in association with Blackwell, 1990.

Bourne, Samuel. "Narrative of a Photographic Trip in the Higher Himalayas (dated January 4th, 1867)." *British Journal of Photography* 14 (1867): 4–5, 38–39, 63–64.

———. "Narrative of a Photographic Trip to Kashmir (Cashmere) and Adjacent Districts." *British Journal of Photography* 13 (1866): 474–95, 524–25, 617–19.

———. "Photography in the East (1st September 1863)." *British Journal of Photography* 10 (1863): 268–70, 345–47.
———. "Ten Weeks with the Camera in the Himalayas (7th November, 1863)." *British Journal of Photography* 11 (1864): 50–51, 69–70.
"Boys to Men." Interview with Qazi Touqeer. *Filmfare,* January 2006.
Brantlinger, Patrick. "A Postindustrial Prelude to Postcolonialism: John Ruskin, Morris, and Gandhism." *Critical Inquiry* 22, no. 3 (1996): 466–85.
———. *Fictions of State: Culture and Credit in Britain, 1694–1994.* Ithaca, N.Y.: Cornell University Press, 1996.
Breckenridge, Carol A. "The Aesthetics and Politics of Colonial Collecting: India at World Fairs." *Comparative Studies in Society and History* 31, no. 2 (1989): 195–216.
Breckenridge, Carol A., and Peter Van der Veer, eds. *Orientalism and the Postcolonial Predicament: Perspectives on South Asia.* Philadelphia: University of Pennsylvania Press, 1993.
Brown, Bill. "Thing Theory." *Critical Inquiry* 28, no. 1 (2001): 1–22.
Bühler, G. H. *Detailed Report of a Tour in Search of Sanskrit Manuscripts: Made in Kaśmîr, Rajputana, and Central India.* Bombay: India Society's Library, 1877.
Buck-Morss, Susan. *Dreamworld and Catastrophe: The Passing of Mass Utopia in East and West.* Cambridge: The Massachusetts Institute of Technology Press, 2000.
Burckhardt Qureshi, Regula. *Sufi Music From India and Pakistan.* Cambridge: Cambridge University Press, 1986.
Butalia, Urvashi, ed. *Speaking Peace: Women's Voices from Kashmir.* New Delhi: Kali for Women, 2002.
Buzard, James. *The Beaten Track: European Tourism, Literature, and The Ways to Culture, 1800–1918.* Oxford: Clarendon Press, 1993.
Cannadine, David. *Ornamentalism: How the British Saw their Empire.* Harmondsworth: Penguin, 2001.
Carroll, Noel. "Art, Practice, Narrative." *The Monist* 71 (1988): 115–36.
Caruth, Cathy, ed. *Trauma: Explorations in Memory.* Baltimore: Johns Hopkins University Press, 1995.
———. *Unclaimed Experience: Trauma, Narrative and History.* Baltimore: Johns Hopkins University Press, 1996.
Chaddha, Maya. *Ethnicity, Security and Separatism in India.* New York: Columbia University Press, 1997.
Chakrabarty, Dipesh. *Provincializing Europe.* Princeton, N.J.: Princeton University Press, 2000.
Chakravarty, Sumita S. *National Identity in Indian Popular Cinema 1947–1987.* Austin: University of Texas Press, 1993.
Champakalakshmi, R., and S. Gopal, eds. *Tradition, Dissent, Ideology: Essays in Honour of Romila Thapar.* Delhi: Oxford University Press, 2001.
Chandhoke, Neera. *Of Broken Social Contracts and Ethnic Violence: The Case of Kashmir,* Working Paper no. 75. London School of Economics: Crisis States Research Centre, 2005.
Chari, P. R. "Protecting Human Rights in Times of Conflict: An Indian Perspective." *Terrorism and Political Violence* 17 (2005).
Chatterjee, Partha. *The Nation and its Fragments.* Princeton, N.J.: Princeton University Press, 1992.
Chatterjee, Partha. "The Sacred Circulation of National Images," in Pelizzari, ed., *Traces of India.*

Chatterji, J. C., ed. *A Prospectus of the Publications of the Archaeological and Research Department of the Jammu and Kashmir State.* Kashmir Series of Texts and Studies II. Bombay: Nirnaya Sagar Press, 1912.

———, ed. *Shiva Sutra Vimarshini.* Kashmir Series of Texts and Studies I. Bombay: Nirnaya-Sagar Press, 1911.

Chatterji, Joya. "The Fashioning of a Frontier: The Radcliffe Line and Bengal's Border Landscape, 1947–1952." Modern Asian Studies 33, part I, no. 1/1-A (1999): 185–242.

Chaudhary, Zahid. "Phantasmagoric Aesthetics: Colonial Violence and the Management of Perception." *Cultural Critique* 59 (2005): 63–119.

Chibber, Vivek. *Locked in Place: State-Building and Late Industrialization in India.* Princeton, N.J.: Princeton University Press, 2003.

Clarke, Melville. *From Simla through Ladac and Cashmere, 1861.* Calcutta: Saville and Cranenburgh, 1862.

Cohn, Bernard. *An Anthropologist Among the Historians and Other Essays.* Delhi: Oxford University Press, 1987.

Cole, Henry Hardy. *Illustrations of Ancient Buildings in Kashmir, Prepared . . . From Photographs, Plans, and Drawings Taken by Order of the Government of India.* London: Archaeological Survey of India, 1869–70.

Connor, Steven. *Dumbstruck: A Cultural History of Ventriloquism.* Oxford: Oxford University Press, 2000.

Coomaraswamy, Ananda K. *Art and Swadeshi.* Madras: Ganesh and Co., 1912.

———. *The Arts and Crafts of India and Ceylon.* London and Edinburgh: T. N. Foulis, 1913.

Copjec, Joan. *Read My Desire: Lacan Against the Historicists.* Cambridge, Mass.: MIT Press, 1994.

Culler, Jonathan. *Framing the Sign: Criticism and its Institutions.* Oxford: Basil Blackwell, 1988.

Cunningham, Alexander. *Description of the Temples of Kashmir.* Calcutta, 1848.

Dalmia, Yashodhara, and Salima Hashmi. *Memory, Metaphor, Mutations: Contemporary Art of India and Pakistan.* Delhi: Oxford University Press, 2007.

Davis, Richard H. *Lives of Indian Images.* Princeton, N.J.: Princeton University Press, 1997.

Debord, Guy. *Comments on the Society of the Spectacle.* Translated by Malcolm Imrie. London: Verso, 1998.

Deleuze, Gilles, and Félix Guattari. *Anti-Oedipus: Capitalism and Schizophrenia.* Translated by Robert Hurley et al. Minneapolis: University of Minnesota Press, 1983.

———. *Kafka: Toward a Minor Literature.* Translated by Dana Polan. Minneapolis: University of Minnesota Press, 1986.

Derrida, Jacques. *Archive Fever: A Freudian Impression.* Translated by Eric Prenowitz. Chicago: University of Chicago Press, 1995.

———. "*Fors*: The Anglish Words of Nicolas Abraham and Maria Torok," in Abraham and Torok, *The Shell and the Kerne.*

———. "Plato's Pharmacy." In his *Dissemination,* trans. Barbara Johnson. Chicago: University of Chicago Press, 1983.

Desai, Vishakha. *Conversations with Traditions: Nilima Sheikh, Shazia Sikander.* New York: Asia Society, 2001.

A Descriptive Analysis of the Kashmir Series of Texts and Studies. Kashmir Series of Texts and Studies 80. Srinagar: Research and Publications Department, Jammu and Kashmir Government, 1953.

Devji, Faisal. *Landscapes of the Jihad: Militancy, Morality, Modernity*. London: Hurst, 2006.

Diener, C. *Triassic Faunae of Kashmir*. Calcutta: Office of the Geological Survey, 1913.

Dirks, Nicholas B. "The Home and the Nation: Consuming Culture and Politics in *Roja*," in Dwyer and Pinney, eds., *Pleasure and the Nation*.

Dubois, Page. *Sowing the Body: Psychoanalysis and Ancient Representation of Women*. Chicago: University of Chicago Press, 1988.

Dwyer, Rachel, and Christopher Pinney, eds. *Pleasure and the Nation: The History, Politics and Consumption of Public Culture in India*. Delhi: Oxford University Press, 2000.

Eaton, Richard. *Essays on Islam and Indian History*. Oxford: Oxford University Press, 2000.

Edney, Matthew. *Mapping an Empire: The Geographical Construction of British India, 1765–1843*. Chicago: University of Chicago Press, 1997.

Egerton, Philip Henry. *Journal of a Tour through Spiti, to the Frontier of Chinese Thibet, with Photographic Illustrations*. London: L Cundall, Downes and Co., 1864.

Ellias, Bina Sarkar, ed. *Gallerie International: A Journal of Ideas* 6, no. 2 (2003).

———. *Identity, Alienation, Amity: Twenty Five Artists, Four Photographers Together for Kashmir*. Mumbai: Privately Published, 2005.

Elmslie, W. J. *A Vocabulary of the Kashmiri Language in Two Parts: Kashmiri-English, and English-Kashmiri*. London: Church Missionary House, 1872.

Empson, William. *Some Versions of Pastoral: A Study of Pastoral Form in Literature*. Harmondsworth: Penguin, 1966.

Evans, Alexander. "A Departure from History: Kashmir Pandits, 1990–2001." *Contemporary South Asia* 11, no. 1 (2002): 19–37.

Falconer, John. "India: Pioneering Photographers 1850–1900." *Orientations* 32, no. 9 (2001): 45–48.

Fanon, Frantz. *The Wretched of the Earth*. Translated by Constance Farrington. New York: Grove Weidenfeld, 1991.

Fazili, Ehsan. "The Rebuilding of Chrar-e- Sharif." http://www.tribuneindia.com/2000/20001021/windows/main3.htm [last accessed 24 October 2008].

Fazili, Gowhar, Idrees Kanth, and Sarwar Kashani. *The Impact of Violence on the Student Community in Kashmir*. Privately circulated report written for Oxfam (India) Trust. 2003.

Fischer, Louis, ed. *The Essential Gandhi: An Anthology*. London: George Allen and Unwin, Ltd., 1963.

Flood, Gavin D. *Body and Cosmology in Kashmir Śaivism*. San Francisco: Mellen Research University Press, 1993.

Foucault, Michel. *Discipline and Punish: The Birth of The Prison*. Translated by Alan Sheridan. Harmondsworth: Penguin Books, 1979.

———. *Language, Counter-Memory, Practice: Selected Essays and Interviews*. Edited and introduction by Donald F. Bouchard, translated by Donald F. Bouchard and Sherry Simon. Oxford: Blackwell, 1977.

———. "Of Other Spaces." *Diacritics* 16, no. 3 (1986): 22–27.

———. *Power/Knowledge: Selected Interviews and Other Writings, 1972–1977*. Edited and translated by Colin Gordon. Brighton: Harvester Press, 1980.

———. *The Order of Things: An Archaeology of the Human Sciences*. London: Routledge, 1974.

Freud, Sigmund. *The Standard Edition of the Complete Psychological Works of Sigmund Freud*, 24 vols. Translated and edited by James Strachey. London: Hogarth Press and the Institute of Psychoanalysis, 1953–74.

Fussell, Paul. *Abroad: British Literary Travelling Between The Wars*. Oxford: Oxford University Press, 1982.

Gallagher, Catherine, and Stephen Greenblatt. "Counterhistory and the Anecdote." In their *Practicing New Historicism,* 49–74. Chicago: University of Chicago Press, 2000.

Gautier, François. *Rewriting Indian History.* New Delhi: India Research Press, 2003.

Gelvin, James L. *The Israel-Palestine Conflict: One Hundred Years of War.* Cambridge: Cambridge University Press, 2005.

Genette, Gérard. "Introduction to the Paratext." *New Literary History* 22, no. 3 (1991): 261–72.

———. *Paratexts: Thresholds of Interpretation.* Translated by Jane E. Lewin, foreword by Richard Macksey. Cambridge: Cambridge University Press, 1997.

Gervis, Pearce. *This Is Kashmir.* London: Cassell, 1954.

Ghosh, Amitav. *The Imam and the Indian: Prose Pieces.* Delhi: Ravi Dayal, 2002.

Goody, Esther, ed. *From Craft to Industry: The Ethnography of Proto-Industrial Cloth Production.* Cambridge: Cambridge University Press, 1982.

Graham, Martin, Geetha Mishra, Mallika Sagar, and Minal Vazirani. "Painting a Happy Picture," *ArtIndia* 8, no. 1 (2003): 38–42.

Grant, Will J. "The Space of the Nation: An Examination of the Spatial Productions of Hindu Nationalism." *Nationalism and Ethnic Politics* 11 (2005): 321–47.

Greenblatt, Stephen. *Marvelous Possessions: The Wonder of the New World.* Oxford: Clarendon Press, 1992.

Grierson, George. *Dictionary of the Kashmiri Language, Compiled Partly from Materials Left by the Late Pandita Isvara Kaula.* Calcutta: Asiatic Society of Bengal, 1932.

———. *Essays on Kāçmīrī Grammar.* London: Luzac & Co., 1899.

Grierson, George, and Lionel Barnett. *Lalla-Vakyani, or the Wise Sayings of Lal Ded, a Mystic Poetess of Ancient Kashmir.* London: Royal Asiatic Society, 1920.

Groys, Boris. *The Total Art of Stalinism: Avant-garde, Aesthetic Dictatorship, and Beyond.* Translated by Charles Rougle. Princeton, N.J.: Princeton University Press, 1992.

Guha, Ramachandra. *A Corner of a Foreign Field: The Indian History of a British Sport.* London: Picador, 2003.

Guha-Thakurta, Tapati. *The Making of a New "Indian" Art: Artists, Aesthetics, and Nationalism in Bengal, c. 1850–1920.* Cambridge: Cambridge University Press, 1992.

———. *Monuments, Objects, Histories: Institutions of Art in Colonial and Postcolonial India.* Columbia University Press, New York, 2004.

Guha Thakwita, Tapah. *Monuments, Objects, Histories: Institutions of Art in Colonial and Postcolonial India.* New York: Columbia University Press, 2004.

Hasan, Mushirul, ed. *Inventing Boundaries: Gender, Politics and the Partition of India.* Oxford: Oxford University Press, 2000.

Hewitt, Vernon. *Reclaiming the Past: The Search for Political and Cultural Unity in Contemporary Jammu and Kashmir.* London: Portland Press, 1995.

Hirsch, Marianne. *Family Frames: Photography Narrative and Postmemory.* Cambridge, Mass.: Harvard University Press, 1997.

Hopkirk, Peter. *The Great Game: On Secret Service in High Asia.* Oxford: Oxford University Press, 2001.

Huggan, Graham. *The Postcolonial Exotic: Marketing the Margins.* London: Routledge, 2001.

Hughes, Alex, and Andrea Noble, eds. *Phototextualities: Intersections of Photography and Narrative.* Albuquerque: University of New Mexico Press, 2003.

Hussain, Ali J. "The Mourning of History and The History of Mourning: The Evolution of Ritual Commemoration of the Battle of Karbala." *CSSAAME* 25, no. 1 (2005): 78–88.

Huttenback, Robert A. *Kashmir and the British Raj, 1847–1947.* Oxford : Oxford University Press, 2004.

Huyssen, Andreas. *Present Pasts: Urban Palimpsests and the Politics of Memory.* Stanford, Calif.: Stanford University Press, 2003.

Hyder, Syed Akbar. *Reliving Karbala: Martyrdom in South Asian Memory.* Oxford: Oxford University Press, 2006.

Jain, Kajri. *Gods in the Bazaar: The Economies of Indian "Calendar Art."* Durham, N.C.: Duke University Press, 2007.

Jain, Madhu. "Vision by Night." *The Hindu.* http://www.hindu.com/mag/2004/06/06/stories/2004060600560700.htm [last accessed 22 October 2008].

Jaitly, Jaya, ed. *Crafts of Jammu, Kashmir and Ladakh.* Ahmedabad: Mapin Publishing, Ltd., 1990.

Jakobson, Roman. "Two Aspects of Language and Two Types of Aphasic Disturbances." In his *On Language.* Cambridge, Mass.: Harvard University Press, 1990.

Kabir, Ananya Jahanara. "Allegories of Alienation and Politics of Bargaining: Minority Subjectivities in Mani Ratnam's *Dil Se.*" *South Asian Popular Culture* 1, no. 2 (2003): 141–60.

———. "Beyond Narrative: Song and Story in South Asia." *Moving Worlds: A Journal of Transcultural Writings* 5, no. 2 (2005): 28–42.

———. "Kashmir: Rebuilding an Identity," *The Hindu,* 14 September 2003.

———. "The Kashmiri as Muslim in Recent Bollywood Films," in Preckel and Kumar, *Bollywood and Muslims.*

———. "Koshur Today: Death, Survival or Revival?," In *Linguistic Identity in Postcolonial Multilingual Spaces,* ed. Eric A. Anchimbe. Newcastle: Cambridge Scholars Publishing. 2008.

———. "Language in Conflict in the Poetry of Agha Shahid Ali." In *Perspectives on Endangerment,* ed. Graham Huggan and Stephan Klasen. Hildesheim, 199–208. Zurich and New York: Georg Olms Verlag, 2005.

———. "Nipped in the Bud: Pleasure and Politics in the 1960s Kashmir Films." *South Asian Popular Culture* 4, no. 1 (2005): 83–101.

———. "The Sacred, the Feminine and the Ecumenical." In *The Sacred and the Feminine,* ed. Griselda Pollock. London: I. B. Tauris, 2008.

———. "Subjectivities, Memories, Loss: Of Pigskin Bags, Silver Spittoons, and the Partition of India." *Interventions* 4, no. 2 (2000): 245–64.

Kachru, Braj. *Kashmiri Literature.* Wiesbaden: Harrasowitz, 1981.

Kak, Ram Chandra. *Ancient Monuments of Kashmir.* London: The India Society, 1933.

Kalhaṇas, Rājataraṅgiṇí a Chronicle of the Kings of Kaśmīr [With maps.], 3 vols. Edited and translated by M. A. Stein. Westminster: Constable and Co., 1900; repr. Delhi: Motilal Banarsidass, 1989.

Kanwar, Pamela. *Imperial Simla: The Political Culture of the Raj.* Delhi: Oxford University Press, 1990.

Kapur, Geeta, ed. *Body. City: Siting Contemporary Culture in India.* New Delhi: Tulika, 2003.

———. *When Was Modernism? Essays on Contemporary Cultural Practice in India.* Delhi: Tulika Press, 2000.

Karlekar, Malavika. *Re-Visioning the Past: Early Photography in Bengal, 1875–1915.* New Delhi: Oxford University Press, 2005.

Karp, I., S. Levine, and C. M. Kraemer, eds. *Museums and Communities.* Washington D.C.: Smithsonian Institute Publications, 1992.

Kaul, Suvir, ed. *The Partitions of Memory: The Afterlife of the Division of India.* Delhi: Permanent Black, 2001.

Kaye, M. M. *Golden Afternoon.* Harmondsworth: Penguin, 1997.

Keay, John. *The Great Arc: The Dramatic Tale of How India Was Mapped and Everest Was Named.* London: HarperCollins, 2001.

Kermode, Frank. *The Sense of an Ending.* New York: Columbia University Press, 1967.

Khalidi, Omar. "Qawwali and Mahfil-i-sama." In Troll, ed. *Muslim Shrines in India.*

Khan, Dominique-Sila. *Crossing the Threshold: Understanding Religious Identities in South Asia.* London: I. B. Tauris, 2004.

Khan, Mohammad Ishaq. *History of Srinagar, 1846–1947: A Study in Socio-Cultural Change.* Srinagar: Cosmos Publications, 1999.

———. *Kashmir's Transition to Islam.* New Delhi: Manohar, 2002.

———. "The Significance of the Dargah of Hazratbal in the Socio-Religious and Political Life of Kashmiri Muslims," in Troll. ed., *Muslim Shrines in India.*

Khan, Omar. *From Kashmir to Kabul: Photography 1860–1900.* Munich and Berlin: Prestel, 2002.

———. "John Burke, Photo-Artist of the Raj." *History of Photography* 21, no. 3 (1997): 236–43.

Khanna, Ranjana. *Dark Continents: Psychoanalysis and Colonialism.* Durham, N.C.: Duke University Press, 2003.

———. "Post-palliative: Coloniality's Affective Dissonance." *Postcolonial Text* 2, no. 1 (2006). http://postcolonial.org/index.php/pct/article/view/385 [last accessed 24 October 2008].

Khilnani, Sunil. *The Idea of India.* New York: Farrar Straus Giroux, 1997.

Knowles, J. Hinton. *Folktales of Kashmir.* London: Trübner and Co., 1888.

———. *Dictionary of Kashmiri Proverbs and Sayings.* Bombay: Education Society's Press, Calcutta: Thacker, Spink and Co., London: Trübner and Co., 1885.

Kohli, Atul, et al., eds. *The Success of India's Democracy.* Cambridge: Cambridge University Press, 2001.

Koul, Omkar N., and R. L. Schmidt. *Kashmiri: A Socio-Linguistic Survey.* Patiala: Indian Institute of Language Studies, 1982.

Koul, Sudha. *The Tiger Ladies: A Memoir of Kashmir.* London: Review, 2002.

Kuhn, Annette. *Family Secrets: Acts of Memory and Imagination.* London: Verso, 1995.

Kumar, Krishna. *Political Agenda of Education: a Study of Colonialist and Nationalist Ideas.* New Delhi: Sage Publications, 2005.

Kumar, Nita. *The Artisans of Banaras: Popular Culture and Identity, 1880–1986.* Princeton, N.J.: Princeton University Press. 1988.

Lamb, Alastair. *Crisis in Kashmir: 1947 to 1966.* London: Routledge and Kegan Paul, 1966.

Landow, George P. *Hypertext 3.0: New Media and Critical Theory in an Era of Globalization.* Baltimore: Johns Hopkins University Press, 2006.

Lawrence, Walter R. *The Valley of Kashmir.* London: H. Frowde, 1895; repr. Srinagar: Gulshan Publishers, 2002.

Leask, Nigel. *Curiosity and the Aesthetics of Travel Writing, 1770–1840.* Oxford: Oxford University Press, 2002.

Lowe, Lisa, and David Lloyd, eds. *Politics of Culture in the Shadow of Capital.* Durham, N.C.: Duke University Press, 1997.

Lowenthal, D., and M. Bowden, eds. *Geographies of the Mind.* New York: Oxford University Press.

Lutgendorf, Philip. *Hanuman's Tale: Messages of a Divine Monkey*. New York: Oxford University Press, 2004.

Lydekker, Richard. *The Geology of the Kashmir and Chamba Territories and the British District of Khagan*. Calcutta: Geological Survey of India, N.D.

MacCannell, Dean. *The Tourist: A New Theory of The Leisure Class*. New York: Schocken Books, 1976.

Madan, T. N. *Family and Kinship: A Study of the Pandits of Rural Kashmir*. New York: Asia Publishing House, 1966.

Majumdar, Boria. *Lost Histories of Indian Cricket: Battles off the Pitch*. New York: Routledge, 2006.

Mamdani, Mahmood. *When Victims Become Killers: Colonialism, Nativism, and the Genocide in Rwanda*. Oxford: J. Currey, 2001.

Mannoni, Octave. *Clefs pour l'imaginaire ou l'autre scène*. Paris: Editions du Seuil, 1969.

Markovitz, Claude. *The Global World of Indian Merchants: Traders of Sind from Bukhara to Panama*. Cambridge: Cambridge University Press, 2000.

Marx, Karl. *Capital: A Critique of Political Economy I*. Translated by Ben Fowkes. New York: Vintage, 1977.

Mattoo, Neerja, trans. and ed. *The Stranger Beside Me: Short Stories from Kashmir*. New Delhi: UBSPD, 1994.

———, trans. and ed. *Contemporary Kashmiri Short Stories, Compiled by Hriday Kaul Bharti*. New Delhi: Sahitya Akademi, 1999.

Mbembe, Achille. *On the Postcolony*. Berkeley and Los Angeles: University of California Press, 2001.

———. "Necropolitics." *Public Culture* 15, no. 1 (2003): 11–40.

Mehta, Hemant. *Kashmir Views, 1934–1965*. Delhi: IndiaPicture.com, 2006.

Mehta, Suketu. *Maximum City: Bombay Lost and Found*. London: Review, 2004.

Merleau-Ponty, Maurice. *Phenomenology of Perception*. Translated by rans. Colin Smith. New York and London: Routledge, 1996.

Metz, Christian. "Photography and Fetish." *October* 34 (1985): 81–90.

Milesi, Laurent. "Jacques Derrida in Secret(s)." In *Secrets, Mysteries, Silences*, ed. Ruth Evans, Terence Hughes, and Georges Letissier. Nantes: Université de Nantes, 2005.

Mitchell, W. J. T. *Picture Theory: Essays on Verbal and Visual Representation*. Chicago: University of Chicago Press, 1994.

Mitter, Partha. *Art and Nationalism in Colonial India, 1850–1920*. Cambridge: Cambridge University Press, 1994.

Mohan, Jag. *My Frozen Turbulence in Kashmir*. Cavendish, Suffolk; New Delhi: Cambridge Book Company, in association with Allied Publishers Limited, 1991.

Monk, Daniel Bertrand. *An Aesthetic Occupation: The Immediacy of Architecture and the Palestine Conflict*. Durham, N.C.: Duke University Press, 2002.

Moorcroft, William, and George Trebeck. *Travels in the Himalayan Provinces of Hindustan and the Panjab: in Ladakh and Kashmir; in Peshawar, Kabul, Kunduz, and Bokhara: from 1819 to 1825; Prepared for the Press by Horace Hayman Wilson*. London: J. Murray, 1841.

Mukherjee, Meenakshi. "Politics and Children's Literature: A Reading of *Haroun and the Sea of Stories*." *Ariel* 29, no. 1: 163–77.

Mulvey, Laura. *Fetishism and Curiosity*. Bloomington: Indiana University Press; London: British Film Institute, 1996.

Nandy, Ashis. *The Secret Politics of Our Desires: Innocence, Culpability and Popular Indian Cinema*. New Delhi: Oxford University Press, 2002.

———. *Traditions, Tyrannies and Utopias: Essays on the Politics of Awareness.* Delhi: Oxford University Press, 1987.

Nehru, Jawaharlal. *The Discovery of India.* Delhi: Penguin India, 2004.

Nelson, Diane M. *A Finger in the Wound: Body Politics in Quincentennial Guatemala.* Berkeley and Los Angeles; London: University of California Press, 1999.

Netton, I. R. *Muslim Neoplatonists.* Edinburgh: Edinburgh University Press, 1991.

Neve, Arthur. *Thirty Years in Kashmir.* London: E. Arnold, 1913.

Neve, Ernest F. *Beyond the Pir Panjal: Life Among the Mountains and Valleys of Kashmir.* London; Leipzig: T. F. Unwin, 1912.

Niranjana, Tejaswini. "Integrating Whose Nation? Tourists and Terrorists in *Roja*." *Economic and Political Weekly* 29, no. 3 (1994): 79–82.

Ollman, Arthur. "'Samuel Bourne: The Himalayan Images." *Creative Camera Magazine* 226 (1983): 1122–29.

———. *Samuel Bourne, Images of India.* Carmel, Calif.: Friends of Photography, 1983.

Onta, Pratyush. "A Suggestive History of the First Century of Photographic Consumption in Kathmandu." *Studies in Nepali History and Society* 3, no. 1 (1998): 181–212.

Orsini, Francesca. *The Hindi Public Sphere 1920–1940: Language and Literature in the Age of Nationalism.* New York: Oxford University Press, 2002.

Page, David, and William Crawley. *Satellites over South Asia: Broadcasting, Culture and the Public Interest.* New Delhi: Sage, 2001.

Pandey, Gyanendra. "In Defence of the Fragment: Writing about Hindu-Muslim Riots in India today." *Representations* 37, no. 4 (1992): 27–55.

Pandit Mukunda Shastri, ed. *The Ishvara-Pratyabhijna Vimarshini of Utapaladeva, with Commentary by Abhinava Gupta, Kashmir Series of Texts and Studies XXII.* Bombay: Nirnaya-Sagar Press, 1918.

Pandit Mukunda Rama Shastri. *The Para-Trimshikha, With Commentary, the latter by Ahinava Gupta, Kashmir Series of Texts and Studies XVIII.* Bombay: The Tatva-Vivechaka Press, 1918.

Peer, Basharat, "Militarising the Narrative in Kashmir." Unpublished paper delivered at the "Language, Culture and Urban Publics Workshop," April 2004, Sarai (http://www.sarai.net), Delhi.

Pelizzari, Antonella Maria, ed. *Traces of India: Photography, Architecture, and the Politics of Representation, 1850–1900.* New Haven, Conn.: Yale University Press, 2003.

Pietz, William. "The Problem of the Fetish I." *RES: Anthropology and Aesthetics* 9 (1985): 5–17.

———. "The Problem of the Fetish II: The Origin of the Fetish." *RES: Anthropology and Aesthetics* 13 (1987): 23–45.

———. "The Problem of the Fetish IIIa: Bosman's Guinea and the Enlightenment Theory of Fetishism." *RES: Anthropology and Aesthetics* 16 (1988): 105–23.

Pinney, Christopher, and Nicholas Thomas, ed. *Beyond Aesthetics: Art and the Technologies of Enchantment.* Oxford: Berg, 2001.

Pinney, Christopher. *Camera Indica: The Social Life of Indian Photographs.* London: Reaktion Books, 1997.

Poddar, Prem Kumar, and David Johnson. *A Historical Companion to Postcolonial Literatures in English.* Edinburgh: Edinburgh University Press, New York: Columbia University Press, 2005.

Pratt Ewing, Katherine. *Arguing Sainthood: Islam, Modernity and Psychoanalysis.* Durham, N.C.: Duke University Press, 1997.

Preckel, Claudia, and Nirmal Kumar, eds. *Bollywood and Muslims.* Delhi: Manohar Publications, forthcoming.

Price, Mary. *The Photograph: A Strange, Confined Space.* Stanford, Calif.: Stanford University Press, 1994.
Prosser, Jay. *Light in the Dark Room: Photography as Loss.* Minneapolis: University of Minnesota Press, 2004.
Quilley, Geoff, and John Bonehill, eds. *William Hodges 1744–1797: The Art of Exploration.* New Haven, Conn.: Yale University Press, 2004.
Qureshi, Humra. *Kashmir: The Untold Story.* Delhi: Penguin India, 2004.
Rai, Alok. *Hindi Nationalism.* Delhi: Orient Longman, 2001.
Rai, Amit. "An American Raj in Filmistan: Images of Elvis in Indian Films." *Screen* 35, no. 1 (1994): 55–77.
———. "Patriotism and the Muslim Citizen in Hindi Films." *Harvard Asia Quarterly* 7, no. 3 (2003). http://www.fas.harvard.edu/~asiactr/haq/200303/0303a001.htm [last accessed 22 July 2007 (site now unavailable)].
Rai, Mridu. *Hindu Rulers, Muslim Subjects: Islam, Rights and the History of Kashmir.* New Delhi: Permanent Black, 2004.
Raina, Bimla. *Reshy Maalyon Myon.* Srinagar: Funkaar Cultural Organisation, 1998.
Raina, M. K. "Bhand Pather: The Theatre of the Not So Absurd." *Gallerie* 6, no. 2 (2005): 30–43.
Raina, Trilokinath. *A History of Kashmiri Literature.* Delhi: Sahitya Akademi, 2002.
Ramaswamy, Sumathi, ed. *Beyond Appearances? Visual Practices and Ideologies in Modern India.* New Delhi: Sage, 2003.
Ramaswamy, Sumathi. *Passions of the Tongue: Language Devotion in Tamil India, 1891–1970.* Berkeley and Los Angeles: University of California Press, 1997.
Rangaswamy, Jacques, et al., ed. *ArtSouthAsia: The First International Programme of Visual Culture From Bangladesh, India, Pakistan and Sri Lanka.* Manchester: Shisha, 2004.
Ray, S. C. *Early History of Kashmir.* Calcutta, Publishers N.A., 1957.
Rayner, Hugh Ashley, ed. *Photographic Journeys in the Himalayas.* Bath: Pagoda Tree Press, 2000.
Renan, Ernest. "What Is a Nation?" [1882], trans. Martin Thom, in Bhanha, ed., *Nation and Narration.*
Research and Publications Department, Jammu and Kashmir Government. *A Descriptive Analysis of the Kashmir Series of Texts and Studies.* Kashmir Series of Texts and Studies 80. Srinagar: Research and Publications Department, Jammu and Kashmir Government, 1953.
Rosaldo, Renato. "Imperialist Nostalgia." *Representations* 26 (1989): 107–22.
Rose, Jacqueline. *The Question of Zion.* Princeton, N.J.: Princeton University Press, 2005.
Roy, Tirthankar. *Traditional Industry in the Economy of Colonial India.* Cambridge: Cambridge University Press, 1999.
Rushdie, Salman. *Shalimar the Clown: A Novel.* London: Jonathan Cape, 2005.
———. *Haroun and the Sea of Stories.* London: Granta, 1991.
Said, Edward. *Orientalism.* Reprinted with new afterword. Harmondsworth: Penguin, 1995.
Sambrani, Chaitanya, et al., eds. *Edge of Desire: Recent Art in India.* New York: Philip Wilson Publishers, 2005.
Sampson, Gary D. "The Success of Samuel Bourne in India." *History of Photography* 16, no. 4 (1992): 336–47.
Saraf, D. N. *Arts and Crafts Jammu and Kashmir: Land, People, Culture.* Delhi: Abhinav Publications, 1987.
Sarkar, Sumit. *Beyond Nationalist Frames: Relocating Postmodernism, Hindutva, History.* Delhi: Permanent Black, 2002.

Sarkar, Sumit, Tanika Sarkar, et al. *Khaki Shorts and Saffron Flags: A Critique of Hindutva.* Delhi: Orient Longman, 1993.

Schwartzberg, Joseph E., et al., eds. *A Historical Atlas of South Asia.* New York: Oxford University Press, 1992.

Schwenger, Peter. "Words and the Murder of the Thing." *Critical Inquiry* 28, no. 1 (2001): 99–113.

Segal, Hanna. "Salman Rushdie and the Sea of Stories: A Not-So-Simple Fable about Creativity." *International Journal of Psycho-Analysis* 75 (1994): 611–18.

Sen, Amartya. "China and India." In *The Argumentative Indian.* London: Allen Lane, 2005.

Sender, Henny. *The Kashmiri Pandits: A Study of Cultural Choice in North India.* Oxford: Oxford University Press, 1988.

Shahane, Girish. "The Cult of Rejection." *ArtIndia* 8, no. 1 (2003): 32–34.

Shanker, Durgesh. *Crafts of India and Cottage Industries.* New Delhi: UBSPD, 2003.

Shapiro, Michael. "Sounds of Nationhood." *Millennium: Journal of International Studies* 30, no. 3 (2001): 583–601.

Shastri, Pandit Mukunda Rama, ed. *The Ishvara-Pratyabhijna Vimarshini of Utapaladeva, with Commentary by Abhinava Gupta.* Kashmir Series of Texts and Studies XXII. Bombay: Nirnaya-Sagar Press, 1918.

———. *The Para-Trimshikha, With Commentary, the latter by Ahinava Gupta.* Kashmir Series of Texts and Studies XVIII. Bombay: The Tatva-Vivechaka Press, 1918.

Shauq, Shafi, et al. *Europeans on Kashmir.* Srinagar: Summit, 1997 .

Sheikh, Gulammohammed. "Making of a Visual Language: Thoughts on Mughal Painting." *Journal of Arts and Ideas* 30–31 (1997): 7–32.

Shifaie, Naseem. *Darichi Mastrith.* Srinagar: Kashmir Publications, 1999.

Shusterman, Richard. *Pragmatist Aesthetics: Living Beauty, Rethinking Art.* Oxford: Rowman and Littlefield, 2000.

Sikand, Yoginder. *The Role of Kashmiri Sufis in the Promotion of Social Reform and Communal Harmony [14th-16th Century].* Mumbai: Centre for Study of Society and Secularism, 2000.

Silverman, Kaja. *The Threshold of the Visible World.* New York; London: Routledge, 1999.

Smith, Anthony D. "Will and Sacrifice: Images of National Identity." *Millennium: Journal of International Studies* 30, no. 3 (2001): 571–84.

Sontag, Susan. *On Photography.* Harmondsworth: Penguin, 1979.

Sprague, Sean F. "Samuel Bourne, Photographer of India in the 1860s." *The British Journal of Photography* 124, no. 2 (1977): 28–32.

Spurr, David. *The Rhetoric of Empire: Colonial Discourse in Journalism, Travel Writing, and Imperial Administration.* Durham, N.C.: Duke University Press, 1993.

Srinivas, S. C. "*Roja* in Law and Order State." *Economic and Political Weekly* 29, no. 3 (1994): 1225–26.

The State of Human Rights in Kashmir: 1990–2005. Srinagar: APDP, 2006.

Stein, M. A. *Catalogue of the Sanskrit Manuscripts in the Raghunatha Temple Library of His Highness the Maharaja of Jammu and Kashmir.* Bombay and London: Nirnaya-sagara Press, Luzac & Co., 1894.

———, trans. and ed. *Kalhaṇa's Rajataraṅgiṇi, a Chronicle of the Kings of Kashmir* [With maps.], 3 vols. Westminster: Constable and Co., 1900; repr. Delhi: Motilal Banarsidass, 1989.

Stewart, Susan. *On Longing: Narratives of the Miniature, the Gigantic, the Souvenir, the Collection.* Durham, N.C.: Duke University Press, 1993.

Stewart, Tony. "In Search of Equivalence: Conceiving Muslim-Hindu Encounter through Translation Theory." *History of Religions* 40, no. 3 (2001): 261–88.

Stoler, Laura Ann. *Race and the Education of Desire: Foucault's History of Sexuality and the Colonial Order of Things*. Durham, N.C.: Duke University Press, 1995.

Sunderrajan, Rajeswari, and Anuradha Needham, eds. *The Crisis of Secularism in India*. Durham, N.C.: Duke University Press, and New Delhi: Permanent Black, 2006.

Schwartzberg, Joseph E., et al., ed., *A Historical Atlas of South Asia*. New York: Oxford University Press, 1992.

Taussig, Michael. *Colonialism, Shamanism and the Wild Man: A Study in Terror and Healing*. Chicago: University of Chicago Press, 1987.

———. *Mimesis and Alterity: A Particular History of the Senses*. New York: Routledge, 1993.

———. *Nervous System*. London and New York: Routledge, 1992.

Taylor, John. *A Dream of England: Landscape, Photography and the Tourist's Imagination*. Manchester: Manchester University Press, 1994.

Teverson, Andrew S. "Fairy Tale Politics: Free Speech and Multiculturalism in *Haroun and the Sea of Stories*." *Twentieth-Century Literature* 47, no. 4 (2001): 444–66.

13 Dec: A Reader. The Strange Case of the Attack on the Indian Parliament, introduced by Arundhati Roy. New Delhi: Penguin, 2006.

Thomas, G. "The First Four Decades of Photography in India." *History of Photography* 3, no. 3 (1979): 215–26.

Thomas, Raju, ed. *Perspectives on Kashmir*. Boulder, Colo.: Westview Press, 1992.

Tickoo, Makhan K. "Kashmiri: A Majority-Minority Language: An Exploratory Essay." In *Linguistic Human Rights: Overcoming Linguistic Discrimination*, ed. Tove Skutnab-Kangas and Robert Phillipson. Berlin and New York: Mouton de Gruyter, 1995.

———. "When Is a Native Language worth Teaching? Native Languages and English in India." In *Towards Global Multilingualism: European Models and Asian Realities*, ed. Rosemary Khoo, Ursula Kreher, and Ruth Wong. Clevedon, U.K.: Multilingual Matters Ltd, 1994.

Todorov, Vladislav. *Red Square Black Square: Organon for Revolutionary Imagination*. Binghampton: State University of New York Press, 1994.

Torrens, Henry. *Travels in Ladâk, Tartary, and Kashmir*. London: Saunders, Otley, 1862.

Troll, Christian, ed. *Muslim Shrines in India*. New Delhi: Oxford University Press, 1989.

Tully, Mark, and Gillian Wright. *India in Slow Motion*. London: Viking, 2002.

Tyndale-Biscoe, Canon. *Kashmir in Sunlight and Shade*. London, Seeley, Service & Co., 1922.

Urry, John. *The Tourist Gaze*. 2nd edition. London: SAGE, 2002.

Vajpeyi, Ananya. "The Bare Life of S.A.R. Geelani, Ph.D.," at http://www.sacw.net/hrights/GEELANI.pdf [last accessed 24 October 2008].

Van Alphen, Ernst. *Caught by History: Holocaust Effects in Contemporary Art, Literature, and Theory*. Stanford, Calif.: Stanford University Press, 1997.

Van den Abbeele, George. "The Persecution of Writing: Revisiting Strauss and Censorship." *Diacritics* 27, no. 2 (1997): 2–17.

Van der Veer, Peter. *Imperial Encounters: Religion and Modernity in India*. Princeton, N.J.: Princeton University Press, 2001.

———. "Monumental Texts: The Critical Edition of India's National Heritage," in Ali, ed., *Invoking the Past*, 134–55.

Varadarajan, Siddhartha, ed. *Gujarat: The Making of a Tragedy*. Delhi: Penguin India, 2002.

Varshney, Ashutosh. *Ethnic Conflict and Civic Life: Hindus and Muslims in India*. New Haven, Conn.: Yale University Press, 2002.

Vasudevan, Ravi. "Addressing the Spectator of a Third World National Cinema: The Bombay 'Social' Films of the 1940s and 1950s." *Screen* 36, no. 4 (1995): 305–24.

———, ed. *Making Meaning in Indian Cinema*. Delhi: Oxford University Press, 2000.

Vigne, G.T. *Travels in Kashmir, Ladak, Iskardo, the Countries Adjoining the Mountain-Course of the Indus, and the Himalaya, North of the Punjab.* London: H. Colburn, 1842.

Viswanathan, Gauri. *Masks of Conquest: Literary Studies and British Rule in India.* London: Faber, 1990.

Wade, T. R. *A Grammar of the Kashmiri Language as Spoken in the Valley of Kashmir, North India.* London: Society for the Promotion of Christian Knowledge, 1888.

Walker, Annabel. *Aurel Stein: Pioneer of the Silk Road.* London: John Murray, 1995.

Wakefield, W. *The Happy Valley: Sketches of Kashmir and the Kashmiris.* London: Sampson Low, Marston, Searle and Rivington, 1879.

Weizman, Eyal. "The Politics of Verticality." www.opendemocracy.net/conflict-politicsverticality/issue.jsp [last accessed 24 October 2008].

Werth, Lukas. "Pakistan: A Critique of the Concept of Modernity." In *Islam in the Era of Globalization: Muslim Attitudes Towards Modernity and Identity,* ed. Johan Meuleman. New York and London: Routledge Curzon, 2002.

White, Hayden. *The Content of the Form.* Baltimore: Johns Hopkins University, 1987.

Williamson, Andrew. *The Golden Age of Travel: The Romantic Years of Tourism in Images from the Thomas Cook Archives.* Peterborough: Thomas Cook Publishing, 1998.

Wilson, H. H. "An Essay on the Hindu History of Cashmir." *Asiatic Researches, or Transactions of the Society Instituted in Bengal* 15 (1825): 1–119.

Winichakul, Thongchai. *Siam Mapped: A History of the Geo-Body of a Nation.* Honolulu: University of Hawai'i Press, 1994.

Woodward, Mark R. "Modernity and the Disenchantment of Life: A Muslim-Christian Contrast." In *Islam in the Era of Globalization: Muslim Attitudes Towards Modernity and Identity,* ed. Johan Meuleman. New York and London: Routledge Curzon, 2002.

Younghusband, Francis. *Kashmir.* London: Adam and Charles Black, 1909.

Žižek, Slavoj. *The Plague of Fantasies.* London: Verso, 1997.

———. *The Sublime Object of Ideology.* London: Verso, 1989.

Zutshi, Chitralekha. *Languages of Belonging: Islam, Regional Identity, and the Making of Kashmir.* New Delhi: Permanent Black, 2003.

Filmography

Ara, Shabnam, and Atul Gupta, dir. *Waiting.* 2005.

Bazaz, Abir, and Meenu Gaur, dir. *Kun'ear.* 1999.

Bazaz, Abir, and Meenu Gaur, dir. *Paradise on a River of Hell.* 2002.

Chopra, Vidhu Vinod, dir. *Mission Kashmir.* 2001.

Kumar, Pankaj Rishi, dir. *The Play Is On.* 2000.

Mukherji, Subodh, dir. *Junglee.* 1961.

Prakash, Suraj, dir. *Jab Jab Phool Khile.* 1965.

Sagar, Ramanand, dir. *Aarzoo.* 1965.

Samanta, Shakti, dir. *Kashmir Ki Kali.* 1964.

Sircar, Shoojit, dir. *. . . Yahaan.* 2004.

The Story of Papier maché. Srinagar: AVRC, 1991.

Index

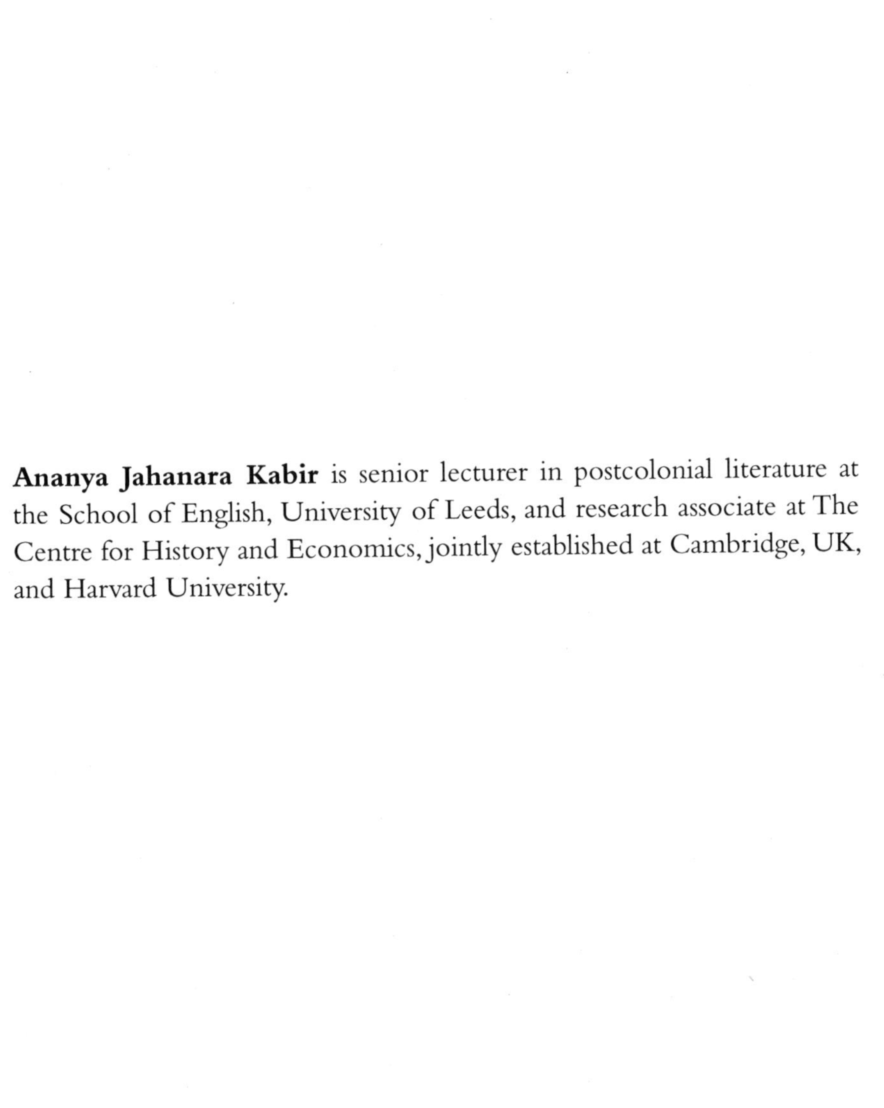

Ananya Jahanara Kabir is senior lecturer in postcolonial literature at the School of English, University of Leeds, and research associate at The Centre for History and Economics, jointly established at Cambridge, UK, and Harvard University.